STUDENT'S SOLUTIONS MANUAL FOR

Intermediate Algebra
FIFTH EDITION
Keedy/Bittinger

STUDENT'S SOLUTIONS MANUAL FOR

Intermediate Algebra
FIFTH EDITION
Keedy/Bittinger

Judith A. Beecher
Indiana University-
Purdue University at Indianapolis

ADDISON-WESLEY PUBLISHING COMPANY
Reading, Massachusetts • Menlo Park, California • Don Mills, Ontario
Wokingham, England • Amsterdam • Sydney • Singapore • Tokyo
Madrid • Bogotá • Santiago • San Juan

ISBN 0-201-15381-5
ABCDEFGHIJ-AL-8987

TABLE OF CONTENTS

Special thanks are extended to Julie Stephenson for her excellent typing. The combination of her mathematical knowledge and her exceptional typing skills made the author's work much easier. Her dedication to perfection is greatly appreciated.

Exercise Set 1.1

<u>1</u>. Substitute 5 for w.

w + 8 = 5 + 8 = 13

The length is 13 yd when the width is 5 yd.

Substitute 14 for w.

w + 8 = 14 + 8 = 22

The length is 22 yd when the width is 14 yd.

Substitute 52 for w.

w + 8 = 52 + 8 = 60

The length is 60 yd when the width is 52 yd.

<u>3</u>. Substitute 16 for ℓ and 9 for w.

$\ell w = 16 \times 9 = 144$

The area is 144 square centimeters when the length is 16 cm and the width is 9 cm.

<u>5</u>. Substitute 3 for y and multiply.

$97y = 97 \cdot 3 = 291$

<u>7</u>. Substitute 15 for x and 3 for y and divide.

$\frac{x}{y} = \frac{15}{3} = 5$

<u>9</u>. Substitute 36 for m and 4 for n and carry out the calculations.

$\frac{m - n}{8} = \frac{36 - 4}{8} = \frac{32}{8} = 4$

<u>11</u>. Subustitute 9 for z and 2 for y and carry out the calculations.

$\frac{5z}{y} = \frac{5 \cdot 9}{2} = \frac{45}{2}$, or $22\frac{1}{2}$, or 22.5.

<u>13</u>. Phrase: 7 more than m

Algebraic expression: 7 + m, or m + 7

<u>15</u>. Phrase: 11 less than c

Algebraic expression: c - 11

<u>17</u>. Phrase: 26 greater than q

Algebraic expression: 26 + q, or q + 26

<u>19</u>. Phrase: b more than a

Algebraic expression: b + a, or a + b

<u>21</u>. Phrase: x less than y

Algebraic expression: y - x

<u>23</u>. Phrase: 28% of x

Algebraic expression: 28%x, or 0.28x

<u>25</u>. Phrase: the sum of a and b

Algebraic expression: a + b, or b + a

<u>27</u>. Phrase: twice x

Algebraic expression: 2x

<u>29</u>. Phrase: seven times t

Algebraic expression: 7t

<u>31</u>. Phrase: the difference of 17 and b

Algebraic expression: 17 - b

or

b - 17

<u>33</u>. Phrase: 8 more than some number

Let y represent the number.

Algebraic expression: 8 + y, or y + 8

<u>35</u>. Phrase: 54 less than some number

Let x represent the number.

Algebraic expression: x - 54

<u>37</u>. Phrase: a number x plus three times y

Algebraic expression: x + 3y, or 3y + x

<u>39</u>. We first draw a picture.

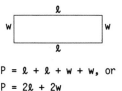

P = ℓ + ℓ + w + w, or

P = 2ℓ + 2w

<u>41</u>. Substitute 3 for y and 4 for x and carry out the calculations.

$\frac{256y}{32x} = \frac{256 \times 3}{32 \times 4} = \frac{768}{128} = 6$

Exercise Set 1.2

<u>1</u>. Given numbers:

$-5, \ 0, \ 2, \ -\frac{1}{2}, \ -3, \ \frac{7}{8}, \ 14, \ -\frac{8}{3}, \ 2.43, \ 7\frac{1}{2}$

The natural numbers in the list are 2 and 14.

<u>3</u>. Given numbers:

$-5, \ 0, \ 2, \ -\frac{1}{2}, \ -3, \ \frac{7}{8}, \ 14, \ -\frac{8}{3}, \ 2.43, \ 7\frac{1}{2}$

<u>All</u> numbers in the list are rational. Each one can be named by fractional symbols with integers for numerator and denominator.

5. $\frac{3}{16}$ means $3 \div 16$, so we divide.

```
        0.1 8 7 5
16 ⟌3.0 0 0 0
     1 6
     1 4 0
     1 2 8
       1 2 0
       1 1 2
           8 0
           8 0
             0
```

Decimal notation for $\frac{3}{16}$ is 0.1875.

7. $\frac{5}{3}$ means $5 \div 3$, so we divide.

```
      1.6 6 6...
3 ⟌5.0 0 0
   3
   2 0
   1 8
     2 0
     1 8
       2 0
       1 8
         2
```

Decimal notation for $\frac{5}{3}$ is 1.666..., or $1.\overline{6}$.

9. The last decimal place is tenths so the denominator is 10.

$2.\underline{7} = \frac{27}{10}$

11. The last decimal place is thousandths so the denominator is 1000.

$0.14\underline{5} = \frac{145}{1000}$

13. $\frac{4}{5} = \frac{4}{5} \times (100 \times \frac{1}{100})$

$= (\frac{4}{5} \times 100) \times \frac{1}{100}$

$= 80 \times \frac{1}{100}$

$= 80\%$

We can also work this problem another way.

$\frac{4}{5} = 0.8$ (Dividing 4 by 5)

$= 0.8(100 \times 0.01)$

$= (0.8 \times 100) \times 0.01$

$= 80 \times 0.01$

$= 80\%$

15. We first divide 3 by 8.

```
      0.3 7 5
8 ⟌3.0 0 0
   2 4
     6 0
     5 6
       4 0
```

$\frac{3}{8} = 0.375$ (Decimal notation)

$= 0.375 \times (100 \times 0.01)$

$= (0.375 \times 100) \times 0.01$

$= 37.5 \times 0.01$

$= 37.5\%$

17. $\frac{12}{5} = \frac{12}{5} \times (100 \times \frac{1}{100})$

$= (\frac{12}{5} \times 100) \times \frac{1}{100}$

$= 240 \times \frac{1}{100}$

$= 240\%$

19. We first divide 3 by 80.

```
       0.0 3 7 5
80 ⟌3.0 0 0 0
     2 4 0
       6 0 0
       5 6 0
         4 0 0
         4 0 0
             0
```

$\frac{3}{80} = 0.0375$ (Decimal notation)

$= 0.0375 \times (100 \times 0.01)$

$= (0.0375 \times 100) \times 0.01$

$= 3.75 \times 0.01$

$= 3.75\%$

21. $0.412 = 0.412 \times (100 \times 0.01)$

$= (0.412 \times 100) \times 0.01$

$= 41.2 \times 0.01$

$= 41.2\%$

23. $0.001 = 0.001 \times (100 \times 0.01)$

$= (0.001 \times 100) \times 0.01$

$= 0.1 \times 0.01$

$= 0.1\%$

25. $1.25 = 1.25 \times (100 \times 0.01)$

$= (1.25 \times 100) \times 0.01$

$= 125 \times 0.01$

$= 125\%$

27. 4.9 = 4.9 × (100 × 0.01)
      = (4.9 × 100) × 0.01
      = 490 × 0.01
      = 490%

29. 56.7% = 56.7 × 0.01
             = 0.567   (Decimal notation)

The last decimal place is <u>thousandths</u> so the denominator is 1000.

$0.567 = \frac{567}{1000}$ (Fractional notation)

31. 6.85% = 6.85 × 0.01
             = 0.0685   (Decimal notation)

The last decimal place is <u>ten-thousandths</u> so the denominator is 10,000.

$0.0685 = \frac{685}{10,000}$, or $\frac{137}{2000}$ (Fractional notation)

33. 120% = 120 × 0.01
            = 1.2   (Decimal notation)

The last decimal place is <u>tenths</u> so the denominator is 10.

$1.2 = \frac{12}{10}$, or $\frac{6}{5}$ (Fractional notation)

35. 0.5% = 0.5 × 0.01
            = 0.005   (Decimal notation)

The last decimal place is <u>thousandths</u> so the denominator is 1000.

$0.005 = \frac{5}{1000}$, or $\frac{1}{200}$ (Fractional notation)

37.
```
<———+———————+———+———————>
    0       40  55
```
Since 55 is to the right of 40 on the number line, 55 is greater than 40.

55 > 40

39.
```
<———+———+———+—+———+—+———>
    0   1   2 2.3 3 3.2
```
Since 2.3 is to the left of 3.2 on the number line, 2.3 is less than 3.2.

2.3 < 3.2

41.
```
<———+———————+———+———————>
   -10      -4   0
```
Since -10 is to the left of -4 on the number line, -10 is less than -4.

-10 < -4

43.
```
<——+—+————+—+————+————+———>
  -3.2 -3 -2.3 -2  -1   0
```
Since -2.3 is to the right of -3.2 on the number line, -2.3 is greater than -3.2.

-2.3 > -3.2

45. The distance of 16 from 0 is 16, so |16| = 16.

47. The distance of -32 from 0 is 32, so |-32| = 32.

49. The distance of 0 from 0 is 0, so |0| = 0.

51. The distance of 3.8 from 0 is 3.8, so |3.8| = 3.8.

53. We replace x by 8 and y by 20.
     8 × y = 8·8·20 = 1280

55. For comparison, we first write each number in decimal notation.

1.1% = 0.011

$\frac{1}{11}$ = 0.090909...

$\frac{2}{7}$ = 0.285714285714...

0.3% = 0.003

0.11 = 0.11

$\frac{1}{8}$ % = 0.00125 $(\frac{1}{8} = 0.125)$

0.009 = 0.009

$\frac{99}{1000}$ = 0.099

0.286 = 0.286

$\frac{1}{8}$ = 0.125

$\frac{9}{100}$ = 0.09

1% = 0.01

55. (continued)

The rational numbers from least to greatest are as follows.

$\frac{1}{8}$ % = 0.00125   (Least)

0.3% = 0.003

0.009 = 0.009

1% = 0.01

1.1% = 0.011

$\frac{9}{100}$ = 0.09

$\frac{1}{11}$ = 0.090909...

$\frac{99}{1000}$ = 0.099

0.11 = 0.11

$\frac{1}{8}$ = 0.125

$\frac{2}{7}$ = 0.285714285714...

0.286 = 0.286   (Greatest)

57. $-\frac{29}{5} = -5\frac{4}{5}$

a) The largest integer less than $-\frac{29}{5}$ is -6.

b) The smallest integer greater than $-\frac{29}{5}$ is -5.

c) The integer closest to $-\frac{29}{5}$ is -6.

Exercise Set 1.3

1. -12 + (-16)

The sum of two negative numbers is negative. We add their absolute values, 12 + 16 = 28, and make the answer negative.

-12 + (-16) = -28

3. 8 + (-3)

We find the difference of their absolute values, 8 - 3 = 5. Since the positive number has the greater absolute value, the answer is positive.

8 + (-3) = 5

5. -8 + (-8)

The sum of two negative numbers is negative. We add the absolute values, 8 + 8 = 16, and make the answer negative.

-8 + (-8) = -16

7. 7 + (-11)

We find the difference of their absolute values, 11 - 7 = 4. Since the negative number has the greater absolute value, the answer is negative.

7 + (-11) = -4

9. -16 + 9

We find the difference of their absolute values, 16 - 9 = 7. Since the negative number has the greater absolute value, the answer is negative.

-16 + 9 = -7

11. -24 + 0

For any real number a, a + 0 = a.

-24 + 0 = -24

13. -8.4 + 9.6

We find the difference of their absolute values, 9.6 - 8.4 = 1.2. Since the positive number has the greater absolute value, the answer is positive.

-8.4 + 9.6 = 1.2

15. -2.62 + (-6.24)

The sum of two negative numbers is negative. We add the absolute values, 2.62 + 6.24 = 8.86, and make the answer negative.

-2.62 + (-6.24) = -8.86

17. $-\frac{2}{7} + \frac{3}{7}$

We find the difference of their absolute values, $\frac{3}{7} - \frac{2}{7} = \frac{1}{7}$. Since the positive number has the greater absolute value, the answer is positive.

$-\frac{2}{7} + \frac{3}{7} = \frac{1}{7}$

19. $-\frac{11}{12} + (-\frac{5}{12})$

The sum of two negative numbers is negative. We add their absolute values, $\frac{11}{12} + \frac{5}{12} = \frac{16}{12}$, or $\frac{4}{3}$, and make the answer negative.

$-\frac{11}{12} + (-\frac{5}{12}) = -\frac{4}{3}$

21. $\frac{2}{5} + (-\frac{3}{10})$

We find the difference of their absolute values.

$\frac{2}{5} - \frac{3}{10} = \frac{2}{5} \cdot \frac{2}{2} - \frac{3}{10} = \frac{4}{10} - \frac{3}{10} = \frac{1}{10}$.

Since the positive number has the greater absolute value, the answer is positive.

$\frac{2}{5} + (-\frac{3}{10}) = \frac{1}{10}$

23. $-\frac{2}{5} + \frac{3}{4}$

   We find the difference of their absolute values.

   $$\frac{3}{4} - \frac{2}{5} = \frac{3}{4} \cdot \frac{5}{5} - \frac{2}{5} \cdot \frac{4}{4} = \frac{15}{20} - \frac{8}{20} = \frac{7}{20}$$

   Since the positive number has the greater absolute value, the answer is positive.

   $$-\frac{2}{5} + \frac{3}{4} = \frac{7}{20}$$

25. When $a = 7$,

   $-a = -(7)$

   $= -7$ (The additive inverse of a positive number is negative.)

27. When $a = -2.8$,

   $-a = -(-2.8)$

   $= 2.8$ (The additive inverse of a negative number is positive.)

29. Replacing a number by its additive inverse is sometimes called changing the sign.

   The additive inverse of 10 is $\underline{-10}$. We changed the sign from positive to negative.

31. The additive inverse of 0 is $\underline{0}$.

33. $5 - 7 = 5 + (-7) = -2$

35. $-5 - 7 = -5 + (-7) = -12$

37. $23 - 23 = 23 + (-23) = 0$

39. $-23 - 23 = -23 + (-23) = -46$

41. $-6 - (-11) = -6 + 11 = 5$

43. $10 - (-5) = 10 + 5 = 15$

45. $15.8 - 27.4 = 15.8 + (-27.4) = -11.6$

47. $-18.01 - 11.24 = -18.01 + (-11.24) = -29.25$

49. $-\frac{21}{4} - (-\frac{7}{4}) = -\frac{21}{4} + \frac{7}{4} = -\frac{14}{4} = -\frac{7}{2}$

51. $-\frac{1}{2} - (-\frac{1}{12}) = -\frac{1}{2} + \frac{1}{12} = -\frac{6}{12} + \frac{1}{12} = -\frac{5}{12}$

53. $-\frac{7}{8} - \frac{5}{6} = -\frac{7}{8} + (-\frac{5}{6}) = -\frac{21}{24} + (-\frac{20}{24}) = -\frac{41}{24}$

55. $\frac{1}{3} - \frac{4}{5} = \frac{1}{3} + (-\frac{4}{5}) = \frac{5}{15} + (-\frac{12}{15}) = -\frac{7}{15}$

57. $1.23 + 3.21 = 3.21 + 1.23$

   The order has been changed. This sentence illustrates the commutative law of addition.

59. $(2.6 + 5.2) + 3.4 = 2.6 + (5.2 + 3.4)$

   The grouping has been changed. This sentence illustrates the associative law of addition.

61. $8 + (-2.3) = -2.3 + 8$

   The order has been changed. This sentence illustrates the commutative law of addition.

63. $0.567 = 0.567 \times (100 \times 0.01)$

   $= (0.567 \times 100) \times 0.01$

   $= 56.7 \times 0.01$

   $= 56.7\%$

65. $(8 - 10) - (-6 + 2)$

   $= (-2) - (-4)$

   $= -2 + 4$

   $= 2$

67. $475.362 + (-123.814) + 30.105 + (-649.914)$

   $= 505.467 + (-773.728)$

   $= -268.261$

69. $\frac{1}{r_1} + \frac{1}{r_2}$

   $= \frac{1}{10} + \frac{1}{5}$ (Substituting 10 for r_1 and 5 for r_2)

   $= \frac{1}{10} + \frac{1}{5} \cdot \frac{2}{2}$

   $= \frac{1}{10} + \frac{2}{10}$

   $= \frac{3}{10}$

   The conductance is $\frac{3}{10}$.

Exercise Set 1.4

1. $3(-7)$

   The product of a positive number and a negative number is negative. We multiply their absolute values, $3 \cdot 7 = 21$, and make the answer negative.

   $3(-7) = -21$

3. $-2 \cdot 4$

   The product of a negative number and a positive number is negative. We multiply their absolute values, $2 \cdot 4 = 8$, and make the answer negative.

   $-2 \cdot 4 = -8$

5. $-8(-2)$

The product of two negative numbers is positive. We multiply their absolute values, $8 \cdot 2 = 16$, and make the answer positive.

$-8(-2) = 16$

7. $-9 \cdot 14$

The product of a negative number and a positive number is negative. We multiply their absolute values, $9 \cdot 14 = 126$, and make the answer negative.

$-9 \cdot 14 = -126$

9. $-6(-5.7)$

The product of two negative numbers is positive. We multiply their absolute values, $6(5.7) = 34.2$, and make the answer positive.

$-6(-5.7) = 34.2$

11. $-\frac{3}{5} \cdot \frac{4}{7}$

The product of a negative number and a positive number is negative. We multiply their absolute values, $\frac{3}{5} \cdot \frac{4}{7} = \frac{12}{35}$, and make the answer negative.

$-\frac{3}{5} \cdot \frac{4}{7} = -\frac{12}{35}$

13. $-3(-\frac{2}{3})$

The product of two negative numbers is positive. We multiply their absolute values, $3 \cdot \frac{2}{3} = \frac{6}{3} = 2$, and make the answer positive.

$-3(-\frac{2}{3}) = 2$

15. $\quad -3(-4)(5)$

$= 12(5)$ (The product of two negative numbers is positive.)

$= 60$ (The product of two positive numbers is positive.)

17. $-4.2(-6.3)$

The product of two negative numbers is positive. We multiply the absolute values, $4.2(6.3) = 26.46$, and make the answer positive.

$-4.2(-6.3) = 26.46$

19. $-\frac{9}{11} \cdot (-\frac{11}{9})$

The product of two negative numbers is positive. We multiply their absolute values, $\frac{9}{11} \cdot \frac{11}{9} = \frac{99}{99} = 1$, and make the answer positive.

$-\frac{9}{11} \cdot (-\frac{11}{9}) = 1$

21. $\quad -\frac{2}{3} \cdot (-\frac{2}{3}) \cdot (-\frac{2}{3})$

$= \frac{4}{9} \cdot (-\frac{2}{3})$ (The product of two negative numbers is positive.)

$= -\frac{8}{27}$ (The product of a positive number and a negative number is negative.)

23. When a negative number is divided by a positive number, the answer is negative.

$\frac{-8}{4} = -2$

25. When a positive number is divided by a negative number, the answer is negative.

$\frac{56}{-8} = -7$

27. When a negative number is divided by a negative number, the answer is positive.

$-77 \div (-11) = \frac{-77}{-11} = 7$

29. When a negative number is divided by a negative number, the answer is positive.

$\frac{-5.4}{-18} = \frac{5.4}{18} = 0.3$

31. $\frac{9}{0}$ is not possible because division by 0 is undefined and not possible.

33. $\frac{0}{16}$ is possible.

$\frac{0}{16} = 0$ because $0 \cdot 16 = 0$

35. $\frac{9}{y - y}$ is not possible because $y - y = 0$ for any y and division by 0 is undefined and not possible.

37. The reciprocal of $\frac{3}{4}$ is $\frac{4}{3}$ because $\frac{3}{4} \cdot \frac{4}{3} = 1$.

39. The reciprocal of $-\frac{7}{8}$ is $-\frac{8}{7}$ because $-\frac{7}{8} \cdot (-\frac{8}{7}) = 1$.

41. The reciprocal of 15 is $\frac{1}{15}$ because $15 \cdot \frac{1}{15} = 1$.

43. The reciprocal of 4.4 is $\frac{1}{4.4}$ because $4.4 \times \frac{1}{4.4} = 1$.

45. $\frac{2}{7} \div (-\frac{11}{3}) = \frac{2}{7} \cdot (-\frac{3}{11}) = -\frac{6}{77}$

47. $-\frac{10}{3} \div -\frac{2}{15} = -\frac{10}{3} \cdot (-\frac{15}{2}) = \frac{150}{6}$, or 25

49. $18.6 \div (-3.1) = \dfrac{18.6}{-3.1} = -\dfrac{18.6}{3.1} = -6$

51. $(-75.5) \div (-15.1) = \dfrac{-75.5}{-15.1} = \dfrac{75.5}{15.1} = 5$

53. $-48 \div 0.4 = \dfrac{-48}{0.4} = -\dfrac{48}{0.4} = -120$

55. Phrase: The sum of p and q.

    Algebraic expression: p + q, or q + p

57. $-5.6 + (-7.8)$

    The sum of two negative numbers is negative. We add their absolute values, 5.6 + 7.8 = 13.4, and make the answer negative.

    $-5.6 + (-7.8) = -13.4$

59. $\dfrac{(-7 - 3) \div (-5)}{(4 - 8)(-2 + 5)}$

    $= \dfrac{-10 \div (-5)}{(-4)(3)}$

    $= \dfrac{2}{-12}$

    $= -\dfrac{1}{6}$

61. $-80,397 \times (-583) = 46,871,451$

    The product of two negative numbers is positive.

63. $7(6 - 1) + 4(3 - 12)$

    $= 7(5) + 4(-9)$

    $= 35 - 36$

    $= -1$

Exercise Set 1.5

---

1. Substitute -2 for x and 3 for y.

   $xy + x = -2 \cdot 3 + (-2) = -6 + (-2) = -8$

3. Substitute -2 for x, 3 for y, and -4 for z.

   $(x + y)z = (-2 + 3)(-4) = 1(-4) = -4$

5. Substitute -2 for x, 3 for y, and -4 for z.

   $xy - xz = -2 \cdot 3 - (-2)(-4) = -6 - 8 = -14$

7. Substitute -2 for x.

   $3x + 7 = 3(-2) + 7 = -6 + 7 = 1$

9. Substitute 120 for P, 6% for r, and 1 for t.

   $P(1 + rt) = 120(1 + 6\% \cdot 1)$

   $\qquad\qquad = 120(1 + 0.06)$

   $\qquad\qquad = 120(1.06)$

   $\qquad\qquad = 127.2$

   The value of the account is $127.20.

11. $3(a + 1)$

    $= 3 \cdot a + 3 \cdot 1$

    $= 3a + 3$

13. $4(x - y)$

    $= 4 \cdot x - 4 \cdot y$

    $= 4x - 4y$

15. $-5(2a + 3b)$

    $= -5 \cdot 2a + (-5) \cdot 3b$

    $= -10a - 15b$

17. $2a(b - c + d)$

    $= 2a \cdot b - 2a \cdot c + 2a \cdot d$

    $= 2ab - 2ac + 2ad$

19. $2\pi r(h + 1)$

    $= 2\pi r \cdot h + 2\pi r \cdot 1$

    $= 2\pi rh + 2\pi r$

21. $\dfrac{1}{2} h(a + b)$

    $= \dfrac{1}{2} h \cdot a + \dfrac{1}{2} h \cdot b$

    $= \dfrac{1}{2} ha + \dfrac{1}{2} hb$

23. $4a - 5b + 6 = 4a + (-5b) + 6$

    The terms are 4a, -5b, and 6.

25. $2x - 3y - 2z = 2x + (-3y) + (-2z)$

    The terms are 2x, -3y, and -2z.

27. $18x + 18y$

    $= 18 \cdot x + 18 \cdot y$

    $= 18(x + y)$

29. $9p - 9$

    $= 9 \cdot p - 9 \cdot 1$

    $= 9(p - 1)$

31. $7x - 21$

    $= 7 \cdot x - 7 \cdot 3$

    $= 7(x - 3)$

33. $xy + x$

    $= x \cdot y + x \cdot 1$

    $= x(y + 1)$

35. $2x - 2y + 2z$

    $= 2 \cdot x - 2 \cdot y + 2 \cdot z$

    $= 2(x - y - z)$

37. $3x + 6y - 3$

    $= 3 \cdot x + 3 \cdot 2y - 3 \cdot 1$

    $= 3(x + 2y - 1)$

39.   ab + ac - ad

    = a·b + a·c - a·d

    = a(b + c - d)

41. $\frac{1}{4}$ πrr + $\frac{1}{4}$ πrs

    = $\frac{1}{4}$ πr·r + $\frac{1}{4}$ πr·s

    = $\frac{1}{4}$ πr(r + s)

43.   4a + 5a

    = (4 + 5)a

    = 9a

45.   8b - 11b

    = (8 - 11)b

    = -3b

47.   14y + y

    = 14y + 1y

    = (14 + 1)y

    = 15y

49.   12a - a

    = 12a - 1a

    = (12 - 1)a

    = 11a

51.   t - 9t

    = 1t - 9t

    = (1 - 9)t

    = -8t

53.   5x - 3x + 8x

    = (5 - 3 + 8)x

    = 10x

55.   5x - 8y + 3x

    = (5 + 3)x - 8y

    = 8x - 8y

57.   7c + 8d - 5c + 2d

    = (7 - 5)c + (8 + 2)d

    = 2c + 10d

59.   4x - 7 + 18x + 25

    = (4 + 18)x + (-7 + 25)

    = 22x + 18

61.   1.3x + 1.4y - 0.11x - 0.47y

    = (1.3 - 0.11)x + (1.4 - 0.47)y

    = 1.19x + 0.93y

63. $\frac{2}{3}$ a + $\frac{5}{6}$ b - 27 - $\frac{4}{5}$ a - $\frac{7}{6}$ b

    = ($\frac{2}{3}$ - $\frac{4}{5}$)a + ($\frac{5}{6}$ - $\frac{7}{6}$)b - 27

    = ($\frac{10}{15}$ - $\frac{12}{15}$)a + (- $\frac{2}{6}$)b - 27

    = - $\frac{2}{15}$ a - $\frac{1}{3}$ b - 27

65.   2ℓ + 2w

    = 2·ℓ + 2·w

    = 2(ℓ + w)

67.   - $\frac{1}{4}$(- $\frac{1}{2}$) = $\frac{1}{8}$

The product of two negative numbers is positive.

69.   0.23(-200) = -46

The product of a positive number and a negative number is negative.

71.   Substitute -1 for a, 7 for b, -6 for c, and $\frac{1}{2}$ for d.

$$\frac{d(ab - c)}{2a} = \frac{\frac{1}{2}[-1·7 - (-6)]}{2(-1)}$$

$$= \frac{\frac{1}{2}[-7 + 6]}{-2}$$

$$= \frac{\frac{1}{2}(-1)}{-2}$$

$$= \frac{-\frac{1}{2}}{-2}$$

$$= \frac{\frac{1}{2}}{2}$$

$$= \frac{1}{2} · \frac{1}{2}$$

$$= \frac{1}{4}$$

Exercise Set 1.6

1.   -(-4b) = -1·(-4b)

        = [-1·(-4)]b

        = 4b

3.   -(a + 2) = -1(a + 2)

         = -1·a + (-1)·2

         = -a + (-2)

         = -a - 2

5. $-(b - 3) = -1(b - 3)$
    $= -1 \cdot b - (-1) \cdot 3$
    $= -b + [-(-1)3]$
    $= -b + 3$, or $3 - b$

7. $-(t - y) = -1(t - y)$
    $= -1 \cdot t - (-1) \cdot y$
    $= -t + [-(-1)y]$
    $= -t + y$, or $y - t$

9. $-(a + b + c)$
    $= -a - b - c$ (Changing the sign of every term inside parentheses)

11. $-(8x - 6y + 13)$
    $= -8x + 6y - 13$ (Changing the sign of every term inside parentheses)

13. $-(-2c + 5d - 3e + 4f)$
    $= 2c - 5d + 3e - 4f$ (Changing the sign of every term inside parentheses)

15. $-(-1.2x + 56.7y - 34z - \frac{1}{4})$
    $= 1.2x - 56.7y + 34z + \frac{1}{4}$ (Changing the sign of every term inside parentheses)

17. $a + (2a + 5)$
    $= a + 2a + 5$
    $= 3a + 5$

19. $4m - (3m - 1)$
    $= 4m - 3m + 1$
    $= m + 1$

21. $3d - 7 - (5 - 2d)$
    $= 3d - 7 - 5 + 2d$
    $= 5d - 12$

23. $-2(x + 3) - 5(x - 4)$
    $= -2(x + 3) + [-5(x - 4)]$
    $= -2x - 6 + [-5x + 20]$
    $= -2x - 6 - 5x + 20$
    $= -7x + 14$

25. $5x - 7(2x - 3) - 4$
    $= 5x + [-7(2x - 3)] - 4$
    $= 5x + [-14x + 21] - 4$
    $= 5x - 14x + 21 - 4$
    $= -9x + 17$

27. $8x - (-3y + 7) + (9x - 11)$
    $= 8x + 3y - 7 + 9x - 11$
    $= 17x + 3y - 18$

29. $\frac{1}{4}(24x - 8) - \frac{1}{2}(-8x + 6) - 14$
    $= \frac{1}{4}(24x - 8) + [-\frac{1}{2}(-8x + 6)] - 14$
    $= 6x - 2 + [4x - 3] - 14$
    $= 6x - 2 + 4x - 3 - 14$
    $= 10x - 19$

31. $9a - [7 - 5(7a - 3)]$
    $= 9a - [7 - 35a + 15]$
    $= 9a - [22 - 35a]$
    $= 9a - 22 + 35a$
    $= 44a - 22$

33. $5\{-2 + 3[4 - 2(3 + 5)]\}$
    $= 5\{-2 + 3[4 - 2(8)]\}$
    $= 5\{-2 + 3[4 - 16]\}$
    $= 5\{-2 + 3[-12]\}$
    $= 5\{-2 - 36\}$
    $= 5\{-38\}$
    $= -190$

35. $2y + \{8[3(2y - 5) - (8y + 9)] + 6\}$
    $= 2y + \{8[6y - 15 - 8y - 9] + 6\}$
    $= 2y + \{8[-2y - 24] + 6\}$
    $= 2y + \{-16y - 192 + 6\}$
    $= 2y - 16y - 192 + 6$
    $= -14y - 186$

37. $[8(x - 2) + 9x] - \{7[3(2y - 5) - (8y + 7)] + 9\}$
    $= [8x - 16 + 9x] - \{7[6y - 15 - 8y - 7] + 9\}$
    $= [17x - 16] - \{7[-2y - 22] + 9\}$
    $= 17x - 16 - \{-14y - 154 + 9\}$
    $= 17x - 16 - \{-14y - 145\}$
    $= 17x - 16 + 14y + 145$
    $= 17x + 14y + 129$

39. $-3[9(x - 4) + 5x] - 8\{3[5(3y + 4)] - 12\}$
    $= -3[9x - 36 + 5x] - 8\{3[15y + 20] - 12\}$
    $= -3[14x - 36] - 8\{45y + 60 - 12\}$
    $= -42x + 108 - 8\{45y + 48\}$
    $= -42x + 108 - 360y - 384$
    $= -42x - 360y - 276$

41. $-12 - (-19) = -12 + 19 = 7$

43. $-\frac{11}{5} - (-\frac{17}{10})$

$= -\frac{11}{5} + \frac{17}{10}$

$= -\frac{22}{10} + \frac{17}{10}$

$= -\frac{5}{10}$

$= -\frac{1}{2}$

45. $-4[3(x - y - z) - 3(2x + y - 5z)]$

$= 4[3x - 3y - 3z - 6x - 3y + 15z]$

$= -4[-3x - 6y + 12z]$

$= 12x + 24y - 48z$

47. $0.01\{0.1(x-2y)-[0.001(3x+y)-(0.2x-0.1y)]\}-(x-y)$

$= 0.01\{0.1x-0.2y-[0.003x+0.001y-0.2x+0.1y]\}-x+y$

$= 0.01\{0.1x-0.2y-0.003x-0.001y+0.2x-0.1y\}-x+y$

$= 0.001x-0.002y-0.00003x-0.00001y+0.002x-0.001y$
$\qquad\qquad\qquad\qquad\qquad\qquad -x+y$

$= (0.001 - 0.00003 + 0.002 - 1)x +$
$\qquad (-0.002 - 0.00001 - 0.001 + 1)y$

$= -0.99703x + 0.99699y$

Exercise Set 1.7

1. $\underbrace{4\cdot4\cdot4\cdot4\cdot4}_{5 \text{ factors}} = 4^5$

3. $\underbrace{5\cdot5\cdot5\cdot5\cdot5\cdot5}_{6 \text{ factors}} = 5^6$

5. $\underbrace{m\cdot m\cdot m\cdot m}_{4 \text{ factors}} = m^4$

7. $\underbrace{3a\cdot3a\cdot3a\cdot3a}_{4 \text{ factors}} = (3a)^4$

9. There are 2 factors of 5, 3 factors of c, and 4 factors of d.
$5\cdot5\cdot c\cdot c\cdot c\cdot d\cdot d\cdot d\cdot d = 5^2c^3d^4$

11. $2^5 = 2\cdot2\cdot2\cdot2\cdot2$, or 32

13. $(-3)^4 = (-3)\cdot(-3)\cdot(-3)\cdot(-3)$, or 81

15. $x^4 = x\cdot x\cdot x\cdot x$, or xxxx

17. $(-4b)^3 = (-4b)(-4b)(-4b)$, or -64bbb

19. $(ab)^4 = (ab)(ab)(ab)(ab)$

21. $5^1 = 5$ (For any a, $a^1 = a$)

23. $(3z)^0 = 1$ (For any nonzero a, $a^0 = 1$)

25. $(\sqrt{8})^0 = 1$ (For any nonzero a, $a^0 = 1$)

27. $(\frac{7}{8})^1 = \frac{7}{8}$ (For any a, $a^1 = a$)

29. $6^{-3} = \frac{1}{6^3}$, or $\frac{1}{216}$

31. $9^{-5} = \frac{1}{9^5}$, or $\frac{1}{59,049}$

33. $(-11)^{-1} = \frac{1}{(-11)^1} = \frac{1}{-11} = -\frac{1}{11}$

35. $\frac{1}{3^4} = 3^{-4}$

37. $\frac{1}{10^3} = 10^{-3}$

39. $\frac{1}{(-16)^2} = (-16)^{-2}$

41. $\frac{240}{-30} = -\frac{240}{30} = -8$

43. $3.64 \div (-26) = \frac{3.64}{-26} = -\frac{3.64}{26} = -0.14$

45. $-5^2 = -(5^2) = -25$
$(-5)^2 = (-5)(-5) = 25$
Thus, $-5^2 = (-5)^2$ is false.

47. $-x^2 = -1\cdot x\cdot x$
$(-x)^2 = -x\cdot-x = -1\cdot(-1)\cdot x\cdot x = x\cdot x$
Thus, $-1\cdot x\cdot x \neq x\cdot x$ so $-x^2$ and $(-x)^2$ are not equivalent.

49. $x^3a^{-3}b^3d^{-4} = \frac{a^{-3}d^{-4}}{x^{-3}b^{-3}}$

51. $(-2)^0 - (-2)^3 - (-2)^{-1} + (-2)^4 - (-2)^{-2}$

$= (-2)^0 - (-2)^3 - \frac{1}{(-2)^1} + (-2)^4 - \frac{1}{(-2)^2}$

$= 1 - (-8) - (-\frac{1}{2}) + 16 - \frac{1}{4}$

$= 1 + 8 + \frac{1}{2} + 16 - \frac{1}{4}$

$= 25 + \frac{1}{4}$

$= 25\frac{1}{4}$, or $\frac{101}{4}$

53. $\dfrac{(-8)^{-2} \cdot (8 - 8^0)}{2^{-6}}$

    $= \dfrac{2^6(8 - 1)}{(-8)^2}$

    $= \dfrac{64 \cdot 7}{64}$

    $= 7$

55. Substitute 1 for x and -2 for y.

    $(x - y)(x^{y-x} - y^{x-y})$

    $= [1 - (-2)][1^{-2-1} - (-2)^{1-(-2)}]$

    $= 3[1^{-3} - (-2)^3]$

    $= 3[1 - (-8)]$

    $= 3 \cdot 9$

    $= 27$

Exercise Set 1.8

1. $5^6 \cdot 5^3 = 5^{6+3} = 5^9$

3. $8^{-6} \cdot 8^2 = 8^{-6+2} = 8^{-4}$

5. $8^{-2} \cdot 8^{-4} = 8^{-2+(-4)} = 8^{-6}$

7. $b^2 \cdot b^{-5} = b^{2+(-5)} = b^{-3}$

9. $a^{-3} \cdot a^4 \cdot a^2 = a^{-3+4+2} = a^3$

11. $(2x)^3(3x)^2$

    $= 8x^3 \cdot 9x^2$

    $= 8 \cdot 9 \cdot x^3 \cdot x^2$

    $= 72x^{3+2}$

    $= 72x^5$

13. $(14m^2n^3)(-2m^3n^2)$

    $= 14 \cdot (-2) \cdot m^2 \cdot m^3 \cdot n^3 \cdot n^2$

    $= -28m^{2+3}n^{3+2}$

    $= -28m^5n^5$

15. $(-2x^{-3})(7x^{-8})$

    $= -2 \cdot 7 \cdot x^{-3} \cdot x^{-8}$

    $= -14x^{-3+(-8)}$

    $= -14x^{-11}$, or $-\dfrac{14}{x^{11}}$

17. $\dfrac{6^8}{6^3} = 6^{8-3} = 6^5$

19. $\dfrac{4^3}{4^{-2}} = 4^{3-(-2)} = 4^{3+2} = 4^5$

21. $\dfrac{10^{-3}}{10^6} = 10^{-3-6} = 10^{-3+(-6)} = 10^{-9}$

23. $\dfrac{9^{-4}}{9^{-6}} = 9^{-4-(-6)} = 9^{-4+6} = 9^2$

25. $\dfrac{a^3}{a^{-2}} = a^{3-(-2)} = a^{3+2} = a^5$

27. $\dfrac{9a^2}{(-3a)^2} = \dfrac{9a^2}{9a^2} = 1$ $[(-3a)(-3a) = 9a^2]$

29. $\dfrac{-24x^6y^7}{18x^{-3}y^9} = \dfrac{-24}{18} x^{6-(-3)}y^{7-9}$

    $= -\dfrac{24}{18} x^{6+3}y^{-2}$

    $= -\dfrac{4}{3} x^9y^{-2}$, or $-\dfrac{4x^9}{3y^2}$

31. $\dfrac{-18x^{-2}y^3}{-12x^{-5}y^5} = \dfrac{-18}{-12} x^{-2-(-5)}y^{3-5}$

    $= \dfrac{18}{12} x^{-2+5}y^{-2}$

    $= \dfrac{3}{2} x^3y^{-2}$, or $\dfrac{3x^3}{2y^2}$

33. $(4^3)^2 = 4^{3 \cdot 2} = 4^6$

35. $(8^4)^{-3} = 8^{4(-3)} = 8^{-12}$

37. $(6^{-4})^{-3} = 6^{-4(-3)} = 6^{12}$

39. $(3x^2y^2)^3 = 3^3(x^2)^3(y^2)^3$

    $= 27x^{2 \cdot 3}y^{2 \cdot 3}$

    $= 27x^6y^6$

41. $(-2x^3y^{-4})^{-2} = (-2)^{-2}(x^3)^{-2}(y^{-4})^{-2}$

    $= \dfrac{1}{(-2)^2} x^{3(-2)}y^{-4(-2)}$

    $= \dfrac{1}{4} x^{-6}y^8$, or $\dfrac{y^8}{4x^6}$

43. $(-6a^{-2}b^3c)^{-2}$

    $= (-6)^{-2}(a^{-2})^{-2}(b^3)^{-2}c^{-2}$

    $= \dfrac{1}{(-6)^2} a^{-2(-2)}b^{3(-2)}c^{-2}$

    $= \dfrac{1}{36} a^4b^{-6}c^{-2}$, or $\dfrac{a^4}{36b^6c^2}$

45. $\left[\dfrac{4^{-3}}{3^4} \right]^3 = \dfrac{(4^{-3})^3}{(3^4)^3} = \dfrac{4^{-3 \cdot 3}}{3^{4 \cdot 3}} = \dfrac{4^{-9}}{3^{12}}$, or $\dfrac{1}{4^9 \cdot 3^{12}}$

47. $\left[\dfrac{2x^3y^{-2}}{3y^{-3}} \right]^3 = \dfrac{(2x^3y^{-2})^3}{(3y^{-3})^3}$

    $= \dfrac{2^3(x^3)^3(y^{-2})^3}{3^3(y^{-3})^3}$

    $= \dfrac{8x^9y^{-6}}{27y^{-9}}$

    $= \dfrac{8}{27} x^9y^{-6-(-9)}$

    $= \dfrac{8}{27} x^9y^3$

49. $9x - (-4y + 8) + (10x - 12)$

    $= 9x + 4y - 8 + 10x - 12$

    $= 19x + 4y - 20$

51. $\dfrac{(2^{-2})^{-4} \cdot (2^3)^{-2}}{(2^{-2})^2 \cdot (2^5)^{-3}} = \dfrac{2^8 \cdot 2^{-6}}{2^{-4} \cdot 2^{-15}}$

$= \dfrac{2^{8+(-6)}}{2^{-4+(-15)}}$

$= \dfrac{2^2}{2^{-19}}$

$= 2^{2-(-19)}$

$= 2^{21}$

53. $\left[\dfrac{(-3x^{-2}y^5)^{-3}}{(2x^4y^{-8})^{-2}}\right]^2$

$= \dfrac{[(-3x^{-2}y^5)^{-3}]^2}{[(2x^4y^{-8})^{-2}]^2}$

$= \dfrac{(-3x^{-2}y^5)^{-6}}{(2x^4y^{-8})^{-4}}$

$= \dfrac{(-3)^{-6}(x^{-2})^{-6}(y^5)^{-6}}{2^{-4}(x^4)^{-4}(y^{-8})^{-4}}$

$= \dfrac{2^4}{(-3)^6} \cdot \dfrac{x^{12}y^{-30}}{x^{-16}y^{32}}$

$= \dfrac{16}{729} x^{12-(-16)}y^{-30-32}$

$= \dfrac{16}{729} x^{28}y^{-62}$, or $\dfrac{16x^{28}}{729y^{62}}$

55. $(a^n \cdot a^{2n})^4$

$= (a^{n+2n})^4$

$= (a^{3n})^4$

$= a^{3n \cdot 4}$

$= a^{12n}$

57. $(x^{z+y} \cdot x^{z-y})^2$

$= (x^{z+y+z-y})^2$

$= (x^{2z})^2$

$= x^{2z \cdot 2}$

$= x^{4z}$

59. $\left[\dfrac{(2x^ay^b)^3}{(-2x^ay^b)^2}\right]^2$

$= \left[\dfrac{(2x^ay^b)^3}{(2x^ay^b)^2}\right]^2$ $[(-2x^ay^b)^2 = (2x^ay^b)^2]$

$= [(2x^ay^b)^{3-2}]^2$

$= (2x^ay^b)^2$

$= 2^2(x^a)^2(y^b)^2$

$= 4x^{2a}y^{2b}$

Exercise Set 1.9

1. $[10 - 3(6 - 1)]$

$= [10 - 3 \cdot 5]$

$= [10 - 15]$

$= -5$

3. $9[8 - 7(5 - 2)]$

$= 9[8 - 7 \cdot 3]$

$= 9[8 - 21]$

$= 9[-13]$

$= -117$

5. $[5(8 - 6) + 12] - [24 - (8 - 4)]$

$= [5 \cdot 2 + 12] - [24 - 4]$

$= [10 + 12] - [24 - 4]$

$= 22 - 20$

$= 2$

7. $[64 \div (-4)] \div (-2)$

$= -16 \div (-2)$

$= 8$

9. $17(-24) + 50$

$= -408 + 50$

$= -358$

11. $2^3 + 2^4 - 20 \cdot 30$

$= 8 + 16 - 600$

$= 24 - 600$

$= -576$

13. $5^3 + 36 \cdot 72 - (18 + 25 \cdot 4)$

$= 5^3 + 36 \cdot 72 - (18 + 100)$

$= 5^3 + 36 \cdot 72 - 118$

$= 125 + 36 \cdot 72 - 118$

$= 125 + 2592 - 118$

$= 2599$

15. $(13 \cdot 2 - 8 \cdot 4)^2$

$= (26 - 32)^2$

$= (-6)^2$

$= 36$

17. $4000 \cdot (1 + 0.12)^3$

$= 4000(1.12)^3$

$= 4000(1.404928)$

$= 5619.712$

19. $(20 \cdot 4 + 13 \cdot 8)^2 - (39 \cdot 59)^3$

$= (80 + 104)^2 - (2301)^3$

$= 184^2 - 2301^3$

$\approx 33{,}856 - 12{,}182{,}876{,}000$

                     $(2301^3 \approx 12{,}182{,}876{,}000)$

$\approx -12{,}182{,}842{,}144$

21. $a^2 - 2ab + b^2 = A\verb|^|2 - 2*A*B + B\verb|^|2$

23. $\dfrac{3(4 - b)}{d} = 3*(4 - B)/D$

25. $\dfrac{a}{b} + \dfrac{c}{d}$ = A/B + C/D

27. 17*A + 8 = 17a + 8

29. 5*A^2 - 8 = $5a^2 - 8$

31. (A + B)^3 = $(a + b)^3$

33. Substitute 78 for ℓ and 36 for w.
    P = 2ℓ + 2w, or 2(ℓ + w)
    2ℓ + 2w = 2·78 + 2·36 = 156 + 72 = 228
    2(ℓ + w) = 2(78 + 36) = 2·114 = 228

    The perimeter is 228 ft.

    A = ℓw
    A = 78·36, or 2808 ft².

35. Phrase: Two times y plus three times x
    Algebraic expression: 2y + 3x

37. $(-x)^2 = (-x)(-x) = (-1)x(-1)x = x^2$
    Thus, $(-x^2) = x^2$ is true.

Exercise Set 2.1

1. $\qquad$ x + 5 = 14 $\qquad$ Check:
    x + 5 + (-5) = 14 + (-5) $\qquad$ x + 5 = 14
    $\qquad$ x + 0 = 9 $\qquad$ 9 + 5 | 14
    $\qquad$ x = 9 $\qquad$ 14 |

The solution is 9.

3. $\qquad$ -22 = x - 18 $\qquad$ Check:
    -22 + 18 = x - 18 + 18 $\qquad$ -22 = x - 18
    $\qquad$ -4 = x + 0 $\qquad$ -22 | -4 - 18
    $\qquad$ -4 = x $\qquad$ | -22

The solution is -4.

5. $\qquad$ -8 + y = 15 $\qquad$ Check:
    8 + (-8) + y = 8 + 15 $\qquad$ -8 + y = 15
    $\qquad$ 0 + y = 23 $\qquad$ -8 + 23 | 15
    $\qquad$ y = 23 $\qquad$ 15 |

The solution is 23.

7. $\qquad$ -12 + z = -51
    12 + (-12) + z = 12 + (-51)
    $\qquad$ 0 + z = -39
    $\qquad$ z = -39

The number -39 checks, so it is the solution.

9. $\qquad$ p - 2.96 = 83.9
    p - 2.96 + 2.96 = 83.9 + 2.96
    $\qquad$ p + 0 = 86.86
    $\qquad$ p = 86.86

The number 86.86 checks, so it is the solution.

11. $\qquad$ $-\frac{3}{8} + x = -\frac{5}{24}$

    $\frac{3}{8} + (-\frac{3}{8}) + x = \frac{3}{8} + (-\frac{5}{24})$

    $0 + x = \frac{3}{8} \cdot \frac{3}{3} + (-\frac{5}{24})$

    $x = \frac{9}{24} + (-\frac{5}{24})$

    $x = \frac{4}{24}$

    $x = \frac{1}{6}$

The number $\frac{1}{6}$ checks, so it is the solution.

13. $\qquad$ 5x = 20 $\qquad$ Check:
    $\frac{1}{5} \cdot 5x = \frac{1}{5} \cdot 20$ $\qquad$ 5x = 20

    $1 \cdot x = \frac{20}{5}$ $\qquad$ 5·4 | 20
    $\qquad$ 20 |

    x = 4

The solution is 4.

15. $\qquad$ -4x = 88 $\qquad$ Check:
    $-\frac{1}{4} \cdot (-4x) = -\frac{1}{4} \cdot 88$ $\qquad$ -4x = 88

    $1 \cdot x = -\frac{88}{4}$ $\qquad$ -4(-22) | 88
    $\qquad$ 88 |

    x = -22

The solution is -22.

17. $\qquad$ 4 = 24t $\qquad$ Check:
    $\frac{1}{24} \cdot 4 = \frac{1}{24} \cdot 24t$ $\qquad$ 4 = 24t

    $\frac{4}{24} = 1 \cdot t$ $\qquad$ 4 | $24 \cdot \frac{1}{6}$

    $\frac{1}{6} = t$ $\qquad$ | 4

The solution is $\frac{1}{6}$.

19. $\qquad$ -3z = -96
    $-\frac{1}{3} \cdot (-3z) = -\frac{1}{3} \cdot (-96)$

    $1 \cdot z = \frac{96}{3}$

    z = 32

The number 32 checks, so it is the solution.

21. $\qquad$ 4.8y = -28.8
    $\frac{1}{4.8} \cdot (4.8y) = \frac{1}{4.8} \cdot (-28.8)$

    $1 \cdot y = -\frac{28.8}{4.8}$

    $y = -6$ $\qquad$ $(-\frac{28.8}{4.8} \cdot \frac{10}{10} = -\frac{288}{48} = -6)$

The number -6 checks, so it is the solution.

23. $\qquad$ $\frac{3}{2} t = -\frac{1}{4}$

    $\frac{2}{3} \cdot \frac{3}{2} t = \frac{2}{3} \cdot (-\frac{1}{4})$

    $1 \cdot t = -\frac{2}{12}$

    $t = -\frac{1}{6}$

The number $-\frac{1}{6}$ checks, so it is the solution.

25. $\qquad$ 4x - 12 = 60 $\qquad$ Check:
    4x - 12 + 12 = 60 + 12 $\qquad$ 4x - 12 = 60
    $\qquad$ 4x = 72 $\qquad$ 4·18 - 12 | 60
    $\frac{1}{4} \cdot 4x = \frac{1}{4} \cdot 72$ $\qquad$ 72 - 12 |
    $\qquad$ | 60
    $\qquad$ $x = \frac{72}{4}$

    $\qquad$ x = 18

The solution is 18.

27.
$$5x - 10 = 45$$
$$5x - 10 + 10 = 45 + 10$$
$$5x = 55$$
$$\frac{1}{5} \cdot 5x = \frac{1}{5} \cdot 55$$
$$x = \frac{55}{5}$$
$$x = 11$$

Check:

$5x - 10 = 45$	
$5 \cdot 11 - 10$	45
$55 - 10$	
	45

The solution is 11.

29.
$$9t + 4 = -104$$
$$9t + 4 + (-4) = -104 + (-4)$$
$$9t = -108$$
$$\frac{1}{9} \cdot 9t = \frac{1}{9} \cdot (-108)$$
$$t = -\frac{108}{9}$$
$$t = -12$$

Check:

$9t + 4 = -104$	
$9(-12) + 4$	-104
$-108 + 4$	
	-104

The solution is -12.

31.
$$-\frac{7}{3}x + \frac{2}{3} = -18, \qquad LCM = 3$$
$$3\left(-\frac{7}{3}x + \frac{2}{3}\right) = 3(-18) \qquad \text{(Multiplying by 3 to clear fractions)}$$
$$-7x + 2 = -54$$
$$-7x = -56 \qquad \text{(Adding -2)}$$
$$x = \frac{-56}{-7} \qquad \text{(Multiplying by } -\frac{1}{7})$$
$$x = 8$$

The number 8 checks. It is the solution.

33.
$$\frac{6}{5}x + \frac{4}{10}x = \frac{32}{10}, \qquad LCM = 10$$
$$10\left(\frac{6}{5}x + \frac{4}{10}x\right) = 10 \cdot \frac{32}{10} \qquad \text{(Multiplying by 10 to clear fractions)}$$
$$12x + 4x = 32$$
$$16x = 32 \qquad \text{(Collecting like terms)}$$
$$x = \frac{32}{16} \qquad \text{(Multiplying by } \frac{1}{16})$$
$$x = 2$$

The number 2 checks. It is the solution.

35.
$$0.9y - 0.7y = 4.2$$
$$10(0.9y - 0.7y) = 10(4.2) \qquad \text{(Multiplying by 10 to clear fractions)}$$
$$9y - 7y = 42$$
$$2y = 42 \qquad \text{(Collecting like terms)}$$
$$y = \frac{42}{2} \qquad \text{(Multiplying by } \frac{1}{2})$$
$$y = 21$$

The number 21 checks, so it is the solution.

37.
$$8x + 48 = 3x - 12$$
$$5x + 48 = -12 \qquad \text{(Adding -3x)}$$
$$5x = -60 \qquad \text{(Adding -48)}$$
$$x = \frac{-60}{5} \qquad \text{(Multiplying by } \frac{1}{5})$$
$$x = -12$$

The number -12 checks, so it is the solution.

39.
$$7y - 1 = 23 - 5y$$
$$12y - 1 = 23 \qquad \text{(Adding 5y)}$$
$$12y = 24 \qquad \text{(Adding 1)}$$
$$y = \frac{24}{12} \qquad \text{(Multiplying by } \frac{1}{12})$$
$$y = 2$$

The number 2 checks. It is the solution.

41.
$$4x - 3 = 5 + 12x$$
$$-3 = 5 + 8x \qquad \text{(Adding -4x)}$$
$$-8 = 8x \qquad \text{(Adding -5)}$$
$$\frac{-8}{8} = x \qquad \text{(Multiplying by } \frac{1}{8})$$
$$-1 = x$$

The number -1 checks, so it is the solution.

43.
$$5 - 4a = a - 13$$
$$5 = 5a - 13 \qquad \text{(Adding 4a)}$$
$$18 = 5a \qquad \text{(Adding 13)}$$
$$\frac{18}{5} = a \qquad \text{(Multiplying by } \frac{1}{5})$$

The number $\frac{18}{5}$ checks. It is the solution.

45.
$$3m - 7 = -7 - 4m - m$$
$$3m - 7 = -7 - 5m \qquad \text{(Collecting like terms)}$$
$$3m = -5m \qquad \text{(Adding 7)}$$
$$8m = 0 \qquad \text{(Adding 5m)}$$
$$m = \frac{0}{8} \qquad \text{(Multiplying by } \frac{1}{8})$$
$$m = 0$$

The number 0 checks, so it is the solution.

47.
$$5x + 3 = 11 - 4x + x$$
$$5x + 3 = 11 - 3x \qquad \text{(Collecting like terms)}$$
$$8x + 3 = 11 \qquad \text{(Adding 3x)}$$
$$8x = 8 \qquad \text{(Adding -3)}$$
$$x = \frac{8}{8} \qquad \text{(Multiplying by } \frac{1}{8})$$
$$x = 1$$

The number 1 checks, so it is the solution.

49. $-7 + 9x = 9x - 7$

   $-7 = -7$ (Adding $-9x$)

   The equation $-7 = -7$ is true. Replacing x by any real number gives a true sentence. Thus, any real number is a solution.

51. $6y - 8 = 9 + 6y$

   $-8 = 9$ (Adding $-6y$)

   The equation $-8 = 9$ is false. No matter what number we try for x we get a false sentence. Thus, the equation has no solution.

53. $(6x^5y^{-4})(-3x^{-3}y^{-7})$

   $= 6 \cdot (-3) \cdot x^5 \cdot x^{-3} \cdot y^{-4} \cdot y^{-7}$

   $= -18x^{5+(-3)}y^{-4+(-7)}$

   $= -18x^2y^{-11}$, or $-\dfrac{18x^2}{y^{11}}$

55. $-4(3x - 2y + z)$

   $= -4 \cdot 3x - (-4) \cdot 2y + (-4) \cdot z$

   $= -12x + 8y - 4z$

57.

   $$\frac{3x}{2} + \frac{5x}{3} - \frac{13x}{6} - \frac{2}{3} = \frac{5}{6}, \qquad LCM = 6$$

   $$6\left(\frac{3x}{2} + \frac{5x}{3} - \frac{13x}{6} - \frac{2}{3}\right) = 6 \cdot \frac{5}{6}$$

   (Multiplying by 6 to clear fractions)

   $3 \cdot 3x + 2 \cdot 5x - 1 \cdot 13x - 2 \cdot 2 = 1 \cdot 5$

   $9x + 10x - 13x - 4 = 5$

   $6x - 4 = 5$ (Collecting like terms)

   $6x = 9$ (Adding 4)

   $x = \dfrac{9}{6}$ (Mulitplying by $\frac{1}{6}$)

   $x = \dfrac{3}{2}$

   The number $\dfrac{3}{2}$ checks, so it is the solution.

59. $-12 - 3x + 3 + 5x + 2 = 4 + 6x - 18 - 4x + 8$

   $2x - 7 = 2x - 6$

   $-7 = -6$ (Adding $-2x$)

   The equation $-7 = -6$ is false. No matter what number we try for x we get a false sentence. Thus the equation has no solution.

61. $43.008z = 1.201135$

   $z = \dfrac{1.201135}{43.008}$ (Multiplying by $\frac{1}{43.008}$)

   $z \approx 0.027928$

1. $2(x + 6) = 8x$

   $2x + 12 = 8x$ (Removing parentheses)

   $12 = 6x$ (Adding $-2x$)

   $2 = x$ (Multiplying by $\frac{1}{6}$)

   The solution is 2.

3. $80 = 10(3t + 2)$

   $80 = 30t + 20$ (Removing parentheses)

   $60 = 30t$ (Adding -20)

   $2 = t$ (Multiplying by $\frac{1}{30}$)

   The solution is 2.

5. $180(n - 2) = 900$

   $180n - 360 = 900$ (Removing parentheses)

   $180n = 1260$ (Adding 360)

   $n = \dfrac{1260}{180}$ (Multiplying by $\frac{1}{180}$)

   $n = 7$

   The solution is 7.

7. $5y - (2y - 10) = 25$

   $5y - 2y + 10 = 25$ (Removing parentheses)

   $3y + 10 = 25$ (Collecting like terms)

   $3y = 15$ (Adding -10)

   $y = 5$ (Multiplying by $\frac{1}{3}$)

   The solution is 5.

9. $7(3x + 6) = 11 - (x + 2)$

   $21x + 42 = 11 - x - 2$ (Removing parentheses)

   $21x + 42 = 9 - x$ (Collecting like terms)

   $22x + 42 = 9$ (Adding x)

   $22x = -33$ (Adding -42)

   $x = -\dfrac{33}{22}$ (Multiplying by $\frac{1}{22}$)

   $x = -\dfrac{3}{2}$

   The solution is $-\dfrac{3}{2}$.

11. $\dfrac{1}{8}(16y + 8) - 17 = -\dfrac{1}{4}(8y - 16)$

   $2y + 1 - 17 = -2y + 4$ (Removing parentheses)

   $2y - 16 = -2y + 4$ (Collecting like terms)

   $4y - 16 = 4$ (Adding $2y$)

   $4y = 20$ (Adding 16)

   $y = 5$ (Multiplying by $\frac{1}{4}$)

   The solution is 5.

13. $(x + 2)(x - 5) = 0$

$x + 2 = 0$ or $x - 5 = 0$ (Principle of zero products)

$x = -2$ or $x = 5$

The solutions are -2 and 5.

15. $(y - 8)(y - 9) = 0$

$y - 8 = 0$ or $y - 9 = 0$ (Principle of zero products)

$y = 8$ or $y = 9$

The solutions are 8 and 9.

17. $(2x - 3)(3x - 2) = 0$

$2x - 3 = 0$ or $3x - 2 = 0$

$2x = 3$ or $3x = 2$

$x = \frac{3}{2}$ or $x = \frac{2}{3}$

The solutions are $\frac{3}{2}$ and $\frac{2}{3}$.

19. $m(m - 8) = 0$

$m = 0$ or $m - 8 = 0$

$m = 0$ or $m = 8$

The solutions are 0 and 8.

21. $0 = (2x + 8)(3x - 9)$

$2x + 8 = 0$ or $3x - 9 = 0$

$2x = -8$ or $3x = 9$

$x = -4$ or $x = 3$

The solutions are -4 and 3.

23. $(0.5x + 55)(1.2x - 24) = 0$

$0.5x + 55 = 0$ or $1.2x - 24 = 0$

$0.5x = -55$ or $1.2x = 24$

$x = \frac{-55}{0.5}$ or $x = \frac{24}{1.2}$

$x = -110$ or $x = 20$

The solutions are -110 and 20.

25. $\frac{7}{8} + \left(-\frac{5}{6}\right)$

$= \frac{7}{8} \cdot \frac{3}{3} + \left(-\frac{5}{6} \cdot \frac{4}{4}\right)$

$= \frac{21}{24} + \left(-\frac{20}{24}\right)$

$= \frac{1}{24}$

27. $\frac{1}{2} - \frac{2}{3}$

$= \frac{1}{2} \cdot \frac{3}{3} - \frac{2}{3} \cdot \frac{2}{2}$

$= \frac{3}{6} - \frac{4}{6}$

$= -\frac{1}{6}$

29. $2x - 4 - (x + 1) - 3(x - 2) =$
$$6(2x - 3) - 3(6x - 1) - 8$$
$2x - 4 - x - 1 - 3x + 6 = 12x - 18 - 18x + 3 - 8$

$-2x + 1 = -6x - 23$

$4x + 1 = -23$

$4x = -24$

$x = -6$

The solution is -6.

31. $\frac{1}{7}(a - 3)(7a + 4)(a + 2) = 0$

$a - 3 = 0$ or $7a + 4 = 0$ or $a + 2 = 0$

$a = 3$ or $7a = -4$ or $a = -2$

$a = 3$ or $a = -\frac{4}{7}$ or $a = -2$

The solutions are 3, $-\frac{4}{7}$, and -2.

Exercise Set 2.3

1. We first make a drawing.

We let x represent the length of one piece and x + 4 the other.

Length of one piece plus length of other is 12.

$$x + (x + 4) = 12$$

We solve:

$x + x + 4 = 12$

$2x + 4 = 12$

$2x = 8$

$x = 4$

If the length of one piece is 4 in., then the length of the other is 4 + 4, or 8 in. The total length is 4 + 8, or 12 in. The lengths check.

The lengths of the pieces are 4 in. and 8 in.

3. It is helpful to make a drawing.

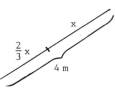

We let x represent the longer piece and $\frac{2}{3}$ x represent the length of the shorter piece.

Length of one piece   plus   length of other   is 4 m.

$$x + \frac{2}{3}x = 4$$

We solve the equation.

$$x + \frac{2}{3}x = 4$$

$$\frac{3}{3}x + \frac{2}{3}x = 4$$

$$\frac{5}{3}x = 4$$

$$\frac{3}{5} \cdot \frac{5}{3}x = \frac{3}{5} \cdot 4$$

$$x = \frac{12}{5}, \text{ or } 2\frac{2}{5}$$

If $x = \frac{12}{5}$, then $\frac{2}{3} \cdot \frac{12}{5} = \frac{8}{5}$, or $1\frac{3}{5}$. The sum of the lengths is $2\frac{2}{5} + 1\frac{3}{5}$ or 4 m. The lengths do check.

The lengths of the pieces are $2\frac{2}{5}$ m and $1\frac{3}{5}$ m.

5. We let c represent the cost. The cost is $2.50 per day plus $1.75 per hour. The cost of a 7-hr babysitting job translates to the following equation:

c = 2.50 + 1.75(7)

c = 2.50 + 12.25

c = 14.75

In this problem the check consists of repeating the calculations.

The cost is $14.75 for a 7-hr babysitting job.

7. We let c represent the cost. The cost is $16 per day plus 15¢ (or $0.15) per mile. The cost of a 290-mi one-day trip translates to the following equation:

c = 16 + 0.15(290)

c = 16 + 43.5

c = 59.5

Checking in this problem consists of repeating the calculation.

The cost of a 290-mi one-day trip is $59.50.

9. Eight plus   five times a number   is   seven times the number.

$$8 + 5 \cdot x = 7 \cdot x$$

We let x represent the number.

We solve:

$$8 + 5x = 7x$$

$$8 = 2x$$

$$4 = x$$

If the number is 4, then eight plus five times the number is 8 + 5·4, or 28, and seven times the number is 7·4, or 28. The value checks.

The number is 4.

11. Five   more than   three times a number   is   ten less than six times the number.

$$5 + 3x = 6x - 10$$

We let x represent the number.

We solve:

$$5 + 3x = 6x - 10$$

$$5 = 3x - 10$$

$$15 = 3x$$

$$5 = x$$

If the number is 5, then five more than three times the number is 5 + 3·5, or 20, and ten less than six times the number is 6·5 - 10, or 20. The value checks.

The number is 5.

13. We let x represent the former price.

Former price   minus   24% times   former price   is   sale price.

$$x - 24\% \cdot x = \$34.20$$

We now solve the equation.

$$x - 24\%x = 34.20$$

$$1x - 0.24x = 34.20$$

$$0.76x = 34.20$$

$$x = \frac{34.20}{0.76}$$

$$x = 45$$

If the former price is $45, then 24%·$45 is $10.80 and the sale price is 45 - 10.80, or $34.20. The value checks.

The former price is $45.

15. We let x represent the amount of the loan.

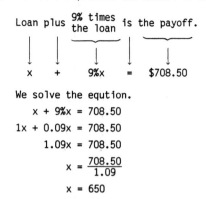

Loan plus 9% times the loan is the payoff.

$$x + 9\%x = \$708.50$$

We solve the eqution.

$$x + 9\%x = 708.50$$
$$1x + 0.09x = 708.50$$
$$1.09x = 708.50$$
$$x = \frac{708.50}{1.09}$$
$$x = 650$$

If $650 was borrowed, then 9%·650, or $58.50, is the simple interest owed for the loan. The payoff was 650 + 58.50, or $708.50. The amount checks.

The original amount borrowed was $650.

17. We draw a picture. We use x for the measure of the first angle. The second angle is three times the first, so its measure will be 3x. The third angle is 12° less than twice the first, so its measure will be 2x - 12.

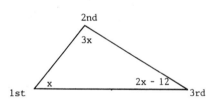

The measure of the angles of a triangle add up to 180°.

Measure of 1st angle + Measure of 2nd angle + Measure of 3rd angle is 180°.

$$x + 3x + (2x - 12) = 180$$

We solve:

$$x + 3x + 2x - 12 = 180$$
$$6x - 12 = 180$$
$$6x = 192$$
$$x = 32$$

The angles will then have measures as follows:
1st angle: x = 32°
2nd angle: 3x = 3·32, or 96°
3rd angle: 2x - 12 = 2·32 - 12, or 52°

These add up to 180° so they give an answer to the problem. The angles are 32°, 96°, and 52°.

19. We first draw a picture.

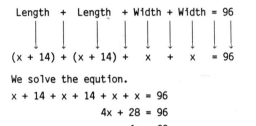

We let x represent the width. Then x + 14 represents the length. The perimeter is 96 m.

Length + Length + Width + Width = 96

$$(x + 14) + (x + 14) + x + x = 96$$

We solve the eqution.

$$x + 14 + x + 14 + x + x = 96$$
$$4x + 28 = 96$$
$$4x = 68$$
$$x = 17$$

If the width is 17 m, then the length is 17 + 4, or 31 m. The perimeter is 2·31 + 2·17, or 96 m. The answer checks.

The dimensions are 31 m and 17 m.

21. Consecutive integers are next to each other like 7, 8, and 9, or -7, -6, and -5. We let x represent the first integer. Then the next two are x + 1 and x + 1 + 1, or x + 2. We translate.

First integer plus twice the second integer plus three times the third is 80

$$x + 2(x + 1) + 3(x + 2) = 80$$

We solve the eqution.

$$x + 2(x + 1) + 3(x + 2) = 80$$
$$x + 2x + 2 + 3x + 6 = 80$$
$$6x + 8 = 80$$
$$6x = 72$$
$$x = 12$$

If x = 12, then x + 1 = 13 and x + 2 = 14. The sum of 12 plus 2·13 plus 3·14 is 12 + 26 + 42, or 80. The numbers check.

The consecutive integers are 12, 13, and 14.

23. We let x represent the old salary. Then 20%x represents the raise.

Old salary plus raise is new salary.

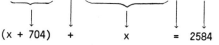

$$x + 20\%x = 9600$$

We solve the eqution.

x + 20%x = 9600

1x = 0.2x = 9600

1.2x = 9600

$x = \dfrac{9600}{1.2}$

x = 8000

If the old salary is $8000, the raise is 20%(8000), or $1600. The new salary would be 8000 + 1600, or $9600. The value check.

The old salary was $8000.

25. Tuition plus room and board is $2584.

$$(x + 704) + x = 2584$$

We let x represent the cost for room and board. Then x + 704 represents the tuition cost.

We solve the equation.

x + 704 + x = 2584

2x + 704 = 2584

2x = 1880

x = 940

When x = $940, x + 704 = 940 + 704, or $1644. The total cost is 940 + 1644, or $2584. The amounts check.

The tuition cost is $1644.

27. 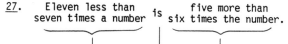 Eleven less than seven times a number is five more than six times the number.

$$7x - 11 = 6x + 5$$

We let x represent the number.

We solve:

7x - 11 = 6x + 5

x - 11 = 5

x = 16

Eleven less than seven times 16 is 7·16 - 11, or 101. Five more than six times 16 is 6·16 + 5, or 101. The numbers check.

The number is 16.

29. Consecutive odd integers are like 11 and 13, or -9 and -7. Let x represent the first odd integer, then x + 2 represents the next odd integer.

First integer plus second integer is 137.

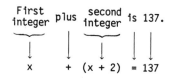

$$x + (x + 2) = 137$$

We solve the equation.

x + x + 2 = 137

2x + 2 = 137

2x = 135

x = 67.5

The number 67.5 is not an odd integer. There is no solution to the problem.

This problem could also be solved as follows. The sum of any two odd integers is always even. Thus, the sum can never be 137. There is no solution.

31. Let x represent the score on the sixth test. The average of the six scores is

$$\frac{93 + 89 + 72 + 80 + 96 + x}{6}.$$

This gives us an equation. The average is 88%.

$$\frac{93 + 89 + 72 + 80 + 96 + x}{6} = 88$$

93 + 89 + 72 + 80 + 96 + x = 6·88

430 + x = 528

x = 98

When the score on the sixth test is 98, the average is (93 + 89 + 72 + 80 + 96 + 98)/6, or 88. The value checks.

The sixth test score is 98%.

33. Let x represent the first number. Then $3x - 6$ represents the second and $\frac{2}{3}(3x - 6) + 2$ represents the third. The sum of the three numbers is 172.

We translate:

$$x + (3x - 6) + [\frac{2}{3}(3x - 6) + 2] = 172$$

We solve:

$$x + 3x - 6 + 2x - 4 + 2 = 172$$
$$6x - 8 = 172$$
$$6x = 180$$
$$x = 30$$

Thus, the three numbers are:

First: $x = 30$
Second: $3x - 6 = 3 \cdot 30 - 6 = 84$
Third: $\frac{2}{3}(3x - 6) + 2 = \frac{2}{3} \cdot 84 + 2 = 56 + 2 = 58$

The sum of the three numbers is $30 + 84 + 58$, or 172. The value checks.

The largest number is 84.

35. It helps to organize the information in a table. We let x represent the number of gallons of freshwater that must be added.

	Amount	Percentage of salt	Amount of salt
Seawater	2000	7.5%	7.5%(2000), or 150
Freshwater	x	0%	0%x, or 0
Mixture	2000+x	7%	7%(2000+x)

The last column gives us an equation equating the salt contents.

$$150 + 0 = 7\%(2000 + x)$$
$$150 = 0.07(2000 + x)$$
$$150 = 140 + 0.07x$$
$$10 = 0.07x$$
$$\frac{10}{0.07} = x$$
$$143 \approx x$$

The value checks. The number of gallons of freshwater which must be added is 143.

1. $A = \ell w$

$$A \cdot \frac{1}{w} = \ell w \cdot \frac{1}{w}$$
$$\frac{A}{w} = \ell$$

3. $W = EI$

$$\frac{1}{E} \cdot W = \frac{1}{E} \cdot EI$$
$$\frac{W}{E} = I$$

5. $F = ma$

$$F \cdot \frac{1}{a} = ma \cdot \frac{1}{a}$$
$$\frac{F}{a} = m$$

7. $I = Prt$

$$\frac{1}{Pr} \cdot I = \frac{1}{Pr} \cdot Prt$$
$$\frac{I}{Pr} = t$$

9. $E = mc^2$

$$E \cdot \frac{1}{c^2} = mc^2 \cdot \frac{1}{c^2}$$
$$\frac{E}{c^2} = m$$

11. $P = 2\ell + 2w$

$$P - 2w = 2\ell + 2w - 2w$$
$$P - 2w = 2\ell$$
$$\frac{1}{2}(P - 2w) = \frac{1}{2} \cdot 2\ell$$
$$\frac{P - 2w}{2} = \ell$$

13. $c^2 = a^2 + b^2$

$$c^2 - b^2 = a^2 + b^2 - b^2$$
$$c^2 - b^2 = a^2$$

15. $A = \pi r^2$

$$\frac{1}{\pi} \cdot A = \frac{1}{\pi} \cdot \pi r^2$$
$$\frac{A}{\pi} = r^2$$

17. $W = \frac{11}{2}(h - 40)$

$$\frac{2}{11} \cdot W = \frac{2}{11} \cdot \frac{11}{2}(h - 40)$$
$$\frac{2}{11} W = h - 40$$
$$\frac{2}{11} W + 40 = h - 40 + 40$$
$$\frac{2}{11} W + 40 = h$$

19.
$$V = \frac{4}{3}\pi r^3$$
$$V = \frac{4\pi}{3} r^3$$
$$\frac{3}{4\pi} \cdot V = \frac{3}{4\pi} \cdot \frac{4\pi}{3} r^3$$
$$\frac{3V}{4\pi} = r^3$$

21.
$$A = \frac{1}{2} h(c - d)$$
$$2 \cdot A = 2 \cdot \frac{1}{2} h(c - d)$$
$$2A = h(c - d)$$
$$2A = hc - hd$$
$$2A + hd = hc - hd + hd$$
$$2A + hd = hc$$
$$\frac{1}{h}(2A + hd) = \frac{1}{h} \cdot hc$$
$$\frac{2A + hd}{h} = c$$

23.
$$F = \frac{mv^2}{r}$$
$$F = m \cdot \frac{v^2}{r}$$
$$F \cdot \frac{r}{v^2} = m \cdot \frac{v^2}{r} \cdot \frac{r}{v^2}$$
$$\frac{Fr}{v^2} = m$$

25. $\frac{80}{-16} = -\frac{80}{16} = -5$

27. $-\frac{1}{2} \div \frac{1}{4} = -\frac{1}{2} \cdot \frac{4}{1} = -\frac{4}{2} = -2$

29.
$$s = v_1 t + \frac{1}{2} at^2$$
$$s - v_1 t = \frac{1}{2} at^2$$
$$2(s - v_1 t) = at^2$$
$$\frac{2(s - v_1 t)}{t^2} = a$$

31.
$$\frac{P_1 V_1}{T_1} = \frac{P_2 V_2}{T_2}$$
$$\frac{T_1}{P_1} \cdot \frac{P_1 V_1}{T_1} = \frac{T_1}{P_1} \cdot \frac{P_2 V_2}{T_2}$$
$$V_1 = \frac{T_1 P_2 V_2}{P_1 T_2}$$

33.

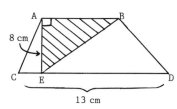

Triangle ABE is a right triangle. We first find the length of $\overline{AB}$. The formula for the area of a triangle is $\frac{1}{2}$ bh. We know the area is 20 cm² and the height is 8 cm. We can substitute to find the base, which is $\overline{AB}$.

$$\text{Area} = \frac{1}{2} bh$$
$$20 = \frac{1}{2} \cdot b \cdot 8 \qquad \text{(Substituting)}$$
$$20 = 4b$$
$$5 = b$$

The length of $\overline{AB}$ is 5 cm.

The formula for the area of a trapezoid is $\frac{1}{2} h(b_1 + b_2)$, where h is the height and b_1 and b_2 are the bases. We can substitute 8 for h, 5 for b_1, and 13 for b_2 and solve for the area.

$$\text{Area} = \frac{1}{2} h(b_1 + b_2)$$
$$\text{Area} = \frac{1}{2} \cdot 8 \cdot (5 + 13) \qquad \text{(Substituting)}$$
$$= 4(18)$$
$$= 72$$

The area of the trapezoid is 72 cm².

Exercise Set 2.5

1.

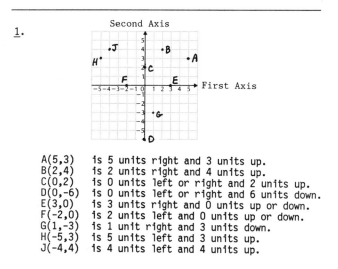

A(5,3) is 5 units right and 3 units up.
B(2,4) is 2 units right and 4 units up.
C(0,2) is 0 units left or right and 2 units up.
D(0,-6) is 0 units left or right and 6 units down.
E(3,0) is 3 units right and 0 units up or down.
F(-2,0) is 2 units left and 0 units up or down.
G(1,-3) is 1 unit right and 3 units down.
H(-5,3) is 5 units left and 3 units up.
J(-4,4) is 4 units left and 4 units up.

3.

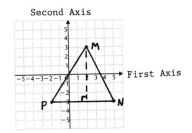

Second Axis / First Axis

A triangle is formed. The area of a triangle is found by using the formula A = $\frac{1}{2}$ bh. In this triangle the base and height are respectively 7 units and 6 units.

A = $\frac{1}{2}$ bh = $\frac{1}{2} \cdot 7 \cdot 6 = \frac{42}{2}$ = 21 square units

5. We substitute 10 for x and 3 for y.

$$\begin{array}{c|c} 3x - 7y = 9 & \\ \hline 3 \cdot 10 - 7 \cdot 3 & 9 \\ 30 - 21 & \\ 9 & \end{array}$$

The equation becomes true: (10,3) is a solution.

7. We substitute 4 for x and -2 for y.

$$\begin{array}{c|c} 4y - 5x = 7 + 3x & \\ \hline 4(-2) - 5(4) & 7 + 3(4) \\ -8 - 20 & 7 + 12 \\ -28 & 19 \end{array}$$

The equation becomes false: (4,-2) is not a solution.

9. We substitute 2 for p and 3 for q.

$$\begin{array}{c|c} 2p + q = 5 & \\ \hline 2 \cdot 2 + 3 & 5 \\ 4 + 3 & \\ 7 & \end{array}$$

The equation becomes false: (2,3) is not a solution.

11. Graph: y = 5x

We choose any number for x and then determine y. We find several ordered pairs in this manner, plot them, and draw the line.

When x = 0, y = 5·0 = 0.

When x = -1, y = 5(-1) = -5.

When x = 1, y = 5·1 = 5.

When x = $\frac{1}{2}$, y = 5 · $\frac{1}{2}$ = $\frac{5}{2}$, or 2 $\frac{1}{2}$.

11. (continued)

x	y	(x,y)
0	0	(0,0)
-1	-5	(-1,-5)
1	5	(1,5)
$\frac{1}{2}$	$\frac{5}{2}$	($\frac{1}{2},\frac{5}{2}$)

y = 5x

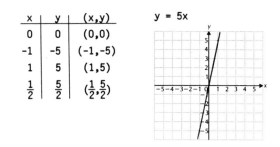

13. Graph: y = -3x

We choose any number for x and then determine y. We find several ordered pairs in this manner, plot them, and draw the line.

When x = 0, y = -3·0 = 0.

When x = -2, y = -3(-2) = 6.

When x = 1, y = -3·1 = -3.

When x = 2, y = -3·2 = -6.

x	y	(x,y)
0	0	(0,0)
-2	6	(-2,6)
1	-3	(1,-3)
2	-6	(2,-6)

y = -3x

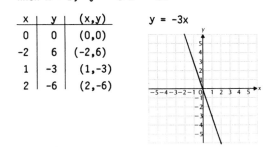

15. Graph: y = x + 3

We choose any number for x and then determine y. We find several ordered pairs in this manner, plot them, and draw the line.

When x = -4, y = -4 + 3 = -1.

When x = -1, y = -1 + 3 = 2.

When x = 0, y = 0 + 3 = 3.

When x = 2, y = 2 + 3 = 5.

x	y	(x,y)
-4	-1	(-4,-1)
-1	2	(-1,2)
0	3	(0,3)
2	5	(2,5)

y = x + 3

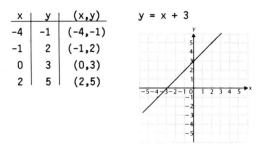

17. Graph: $y = \frac{1}{4}x + 2$

We choose any number for x and then determine y. We find several ordered pairs in this manner, plot them, and draw the line.

When $x = -4$, $y = \frac{1}{4}(-4) + 2 = -1 + 2 = 1$.

When $x = 0$, $y = \frac{1}{4} \cdot 0 + 2 = 0 + 2 = 2$.

When $x = 2$, $y = \frac{1}{4} \cdot 2 + 2 = \frac{1}{2} + 2 = 2\frac{1}{2}$.

When $x = 4$, $y = \frac{1}{4} \cdot 4 + 2 = 1 + 2 = 3$.

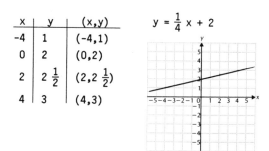

x	y	(x,y)
-4	1	(-4,1)
0	2	(0,2)
2	$2\frac{1}{2}$	$(2,2\frac{1}{2})$
4	3	(4,3)

$y = \frac{1}{4}x + 2$

19. Graph: $y = -x$

We choose any number for x and then determine y. We find several ordered pairs, plot them, and draw the line.

When $x = -5$, $y = -(-5) = 5$.

When $x = -3$, $y = -(-3) = 3$.

When $x = 0$, $y = -(0) = 0$.

When $x = 2$, $y = -(2) = -2$.

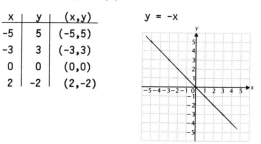

x	y	(x,y)
-5	5	(-5,5)
-3	3	(-3,3)
0	0	(0,0)
2	-2	(2,-2)

$y = -x$

21. Graph: $y = x - 5$

We choose any number for x and then determine y. We find several ordered pairs, plot them, and draw the line.

When $x = -1$, $y = -1 - 5 = -6$.

When $x = 1$, $y = 1 - 5 = -4$.

When $x = 3$, $y = 3 - 5 = -2$.

When $x = 6$, $y = 6 - 5 = 1$.

21. (continued)

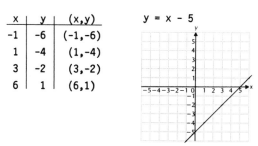

x	y	(x,y)
-1	-6	(-1,-6)
1	-4	(1,-4)
3	-2	(3,-2)
6	1	(6,1)

$y = x - 5$

23. $(-3.4)(-2.2) = 7.48$

The product of two negative numbers is positive.

25. $-5(-6)(-7)4$

$= 30(-28)$

$= -840$

27. There are three possible locations for the fourth vertex. They are (-1,-2), (13,10), and (-19,-2), pictured below.

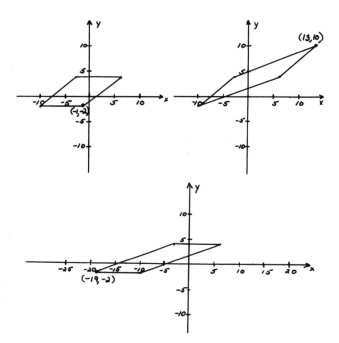

29. a) We substitute $-\frac{1}{3}$ for x and $\frac{1}{4}$ for y.

$$-\frac{3}{2}x - 3y = -\frac{1}{4}$$

$$
\begin{array}{c|c}
-\frac{3}{2}(-\frac{1}{3}) - 3(\frac{1}{4}) & -\frac{1}{4} \\
\frac{1}{2} - \frac{3}{4} & \\
-\frac{1}{4} &
\end{array}
$$

The equation becomes true; $(-\frac{1}{3},\frac{1}{4})$ <u>is</u> a solution.

b) We substitute $-\frac{1}{3}$ for x and $\frac{1}{4}$ for y.

$$8y - 15x = \frac{7}{2}$$

$$
\begin{array}{c|c}
8(\frac{1}{4}) - 15(-\frac{1}{3}) & \frac{7}{2} \\
2 + 5 & \\
7 &
\end{array}
$$

The equation becomes false; $(-\frac{1}{3},\frac{1}{4})$ <u>is not</u> a solution.

c) We substitute $-\frac{1}{3}$ for x and $\frac{1}{4}$ for y.

$$0.16y = -0.09x + 0.1$$

$$
\begin{array}{c|c}
0.16(\frac{1}{4}) & -0.09(-\frac{1}{3}) + 0.1 \\
0.04 & 0.03 + 0.1 \\
& 0.13
\end{array}
$$

The equations becomes false; $(-\frac{1}{3},\frac{1}{4})$ <u>is not</u> a solution.

d) We substitute $-\frac{1}{3}$ for x and $\frac{1}{4}$ for y.

$$2(-y + 2) - \frac{1}{4}(3x - 1) = 4$$

$$
\begin{array}{c|c}
2(-\frac{1}{4} + 2) - \frac{1}{4}[3(-\frac{1}{3}) - 1] & 4 \\
2(\frac{7}{4}) - \frac{1}{4}(-2) & \\
\frac{14}{4} + \frac{2}{4} & \\
\frac{16}{4} & \\
4 &
\end{array}
$$

The eqution becomes true; $(-\frac{1}{3},\frac{1}{4})$ <u>is</u> a solution.

1. $y = 4x + 5$

$$y = mx + b$$

The slope is 4, and the y-intercept is (0,5).

3. $y = -2x - 6$

$$y = mx + b$$

The slope is -2, and the y-intercept is (0,-6).

5. $y = -\frac{3}{8}x - 0.2$

$$y = mx + b$$

The slope is $-\frac{3}{8}$, and the y-intercept is (0,-0.2).

7. $y = 15.3x + 4.04$

$$y = mx + b$$

The slope is 15.3, and the y-intercept is (0,4.04).

9. Graph: $y = \frac{5}{2}x + 1$

The y-intercept is (0,1). We plot this point.

The slope is $\frac{5}{2}$. It tells us that from the y-intercept the line slants <u>up</u> 5 units for every 2 units to the <u>right</u>. Then in this direction from the y-intercept (0,1) we get the point (2,6).

Note that $\frac{5}{2}$ can be expressed as $\frac{-5}{-2}$. From the y-intercept (0,1) we can also move <u>down</u> 5 units for every 2 units to the <u>left</u>. This gives us the point (-2,-4). We join these points with a line to complete the graph.

$y = \frac{5}{2}x + 1$

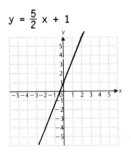

11. Graph: $y = -\frac{5}{2}x - 4$

   The y-intercept is (0,-4). We plot this point.

   The slope is $-\frac{5}{2}$, or $\frac{-5}{2}$. It tells us that from the y-intercept the line slants <u>down</u> 5 units for every 2 units to the <u>right</u>. Then in this direction from the y-intercept (0,-4) we get the point (2,-9).

   Note that $\frac{-5}{2}$ can be expressed as $\frac{5}{-2}$. From the y-intercept (0,-4) we can also move <u>up</u> 5 units for every 2 units to the <u>left</u>. This gives us the point (-2,1). Ccontinuing from (-2,1) we can again move <u>up</u> 5 units and 2 units to the <u>left</u> giving us the point (-4,6). We join these points with a line to complete the graph.

   $y = -\frac{5}{2}x - 4$

   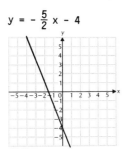

13. Graph: $y = 2x - 5$

   The y-intercept is (0,-5). We plot this point.

   The slope is 2, or $\frac{2}{1}$. This tells us that from the y-intercept the line slants <u>up</u> 2 units for every 1 unit to the <u>right</u>. Then in this direction from the y-intercept (0,-5) we get the point (1,-3). Continuing from (1,-3) we can again move <u>up</u> 2 units and 1 unit to the <u>right</u> giving us the point (2,-1).

   Note that $\frac{2}{1}$ can be expressed as $\frac{-2}{-1}$. From the y-intercept (0,-5) we can also move <u>down</u> 2 units and 1 unit to the <u>left</u>. This gives us the point (-1,-7). We join these points with a line to complete the graph.

   $y = 2x - 5$

   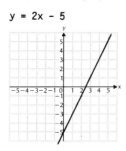

15. Graph: $y = \frac{1}{3}x + 6$

   The y-intercept is (0,6). We plot this point.

   The slope is $\frac{1}{3}$. This tells us that from the y-intercept the line slants <u>up</u> 1 unit for every 3 units to the <u>right</u>. Then in this direction from the y-intercept (0,6) we get the point (3,7). Note that $\frac{1}{3}$ can also be expressed as $\frac{-1}{-3}$. From the y-intercept (0,6) we can also move <u>down</u> 1 unit for every 3 units to the <u>left</u>. This gives us the point (-3,5). Continuing from (-3,5) we can again move <u>down</u> 1 unit and 3 units to the <u>left</u> giving us the point (-6,4). We join these points with a line to complete the graph.

   $y = \frac{1}{3}x + 6$

   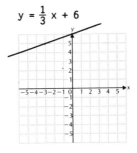

17. Graph: $y = -0.25x + 2$
   or
   $y = -\frac{1}{4}x + 2$

   The y-intercept is (0,2). We plot this point.

   The slope is $-\frac{1}{4}$, or $\frac{-1}{4}$. This tells us that from the y-intercept the line slants <u>down</u> 1 unit for every 4 units to the <u>right</u>. Then in this direction from the y-intercept (0,2) we get the point (4,1).

   Note that $\frac{-1}{4}$ can be expressed as $\frac{1}{-4}$. From the y-intercept (0,2) we can also move <u>up</u> 1 unit for every 4 units to the <u>left</u>. This gives us the point (-4,3). We join these points with a line and complete the graph.

   $y = -0.25x + 2$

19. Graph: $y = -\frac{3}{4}x$

      or

      $y = -\frac{3}{4}x + 0$

The y-intercept is (0,0). We plot this point.

The slope is $-\frac{3}{4}$, or $\frac{-3}{4}$. This tells us that from the y-intercept the line slants <u>down</u> 3 units for every 4 units to the <u>right</u>. Then in this direction from the y-intercept (0,0) we get the point (4,-3).

Note that $\frac{-3}{4}$ can be expressed as $\frac{3}{-4}$. From the y-intercept (0,0) we can also move <u>up</u> 3 units for every 4 units to the <u>left</u>. This gives us the point (-4,3). We join these points with a line and complete the graph.

$y = -\frac{3}{4}x$

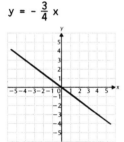

21. Graph: x = 4

Since y is missing, any number for y will do. Thus, all ordered pairs (4,y) are solutions. The graph is a line parallel to the y-axis.

x	y
4	-2
4	1
4	5

x = 4

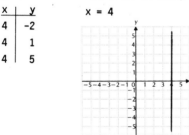

23. Graph: y = -2

Since x is missing, any number for x will do. Thus, all ordered pairs (x,-2) are solutions. The graph is a line parallel to the x-axis.

x	y
-5	-2
0	-2
3	-2

y = -2

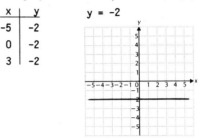

25. Graph: 3x + 15 = 0

            3x = -15

             x = -5

Since y is missing, any number for y will do. Thus, all ordered pairs (-5,y) are solutions. The graph is a line parallel to the y-axis.

x	y
-5	-2
-5	0
-5	4

3x + 15 = 0

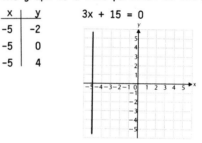

27. To show that the equation is equivalent to an equation y = mx + b, we solve for y.

$3x + 5y + 15 = 0$

        $5y = -3x - 15$

        $y = -\frac{3}{5}x - 3$

Since we have an equation y = mx + b, we know that the graph is a straight line. The slope is $-\frac{3}{5}$, and the y-intercept is (0,-3). The equation is <u>linear</u>.

29. Since there is no y in the equation, we solve for x to see if we get an equation x = c.

$3x - 12 = 0$

      $3x = 12$

       $x = 4$

Since we have an equation x = c, we know the equation is <u>linear</u>. The line is vertical (parallel to the y-axis). There is no slope and no y-intercept.

31. The equation $2x + 4y^2 = 19$ is <u>not</u> <u>linear</u> because of y^2 in the term $4y^2$. It is <u>not</u> equivalent to an equation $y = mx + b$.

33. The equation $5x - 4xy = 12$ is <u>not</u> <u>linear</u> because of the product xy in the term $-4xy$. It is not equivalent to an equation $y = mx + b$.

35. $-6(2a - 5b)$

= $-6 \cdot 2a - (-6)5b$

= $-12a - (-30b)$

= $-12a + 30b$

37. $-2x + 6y - 8x - 10 + 3y - 40$

= $(-2 - 8)x + (6 + 3)y + (-10 - 40)$

= $-10x + 9y - 50$

39. $2x + 5y + 2 = 5x - 10y - 8$

$\quad\quad 5y + 2 = 3x - 10y - 8$ (Adding $-2x$)

$\quad\quad 15y + 2 = 3x - 8$ (Adding $10y$)

$\quad\quad 15y = 3x - 10$ (Adding -2)

$\quad\quad y = \frac{3}{15}x - \frac{10}{15}$ (Multiplying by $\frac{1}{15}$)

$\quad\quad y = \frac{1}{5}x - \frac{2}{3}$

The slope is $\frac{1}{5}$. The y-intercept is $(0, -\frac{2}{3})$.

41. $0.4y - 0.004x = -0.04$

$\quad\quad 0.4y = 0.004x - 0.04$ (Adding $0.004x$)

$\quad\quad y = \frac{0.004x}{0.4} - \frac{0.04}{0.4}$

$\quad\quad\quad\quad$ (Multiplying by $\frac{1}{0.4}$)

$\quad\quad y = 0.01x - 0.1$

The slope is 0.01. The y-intercept is $(0, -0.1)$.

Exercise Set 2.7

1. Graph $5y = -15 + 3x$.

To find the y-intercept, let $x = 0$.

$5y = -15 + 3x$

$5y = -15 + 3 \cdot 0$ (Substituting 0 for x)

$5y = -15$

$y = -3$

Thus, $(0, -3)$ is the y-intercept.

To find the x-intercept, let $y = 0$.

$5y = -15 + 3x$

$5 \cdot 0 = -15 + 3x$ (Substituting 0 for y)

$15 = 3x$

$5 = x$

Thus, $(5, 0)$ is the x-intercept.

1. (continued)

Plot these points and draw the line. A third point should be used as a check.

$5y = -15 + 3x$

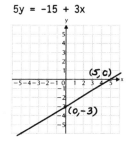

3. $6x - 7 + 3y = 9x - 2y + 8$

$\quad\quad -3x + 5y = 15$

Graph $-3x + 5y = 15$.

To find the y-intercept, let $x = 0$.

$-3x + 5y = 15$

$-3 \cdot 0 + 5y = 15$ (Substituting 0 for x)

$\quad\quad 5y = 15$

$\quad\quad y = 3$

Thus, $(0, 3)$ is the y-intercept.

To find the x-intercpet, let $y = 0$.

$-3x + 5y = 15$

$-3x + 5 \cdot 0 = 15$ (Substituting 0 for y)

$\quad\quad -3x = 15$

$\quad\quad x = -5$

Thus, $(-5, 0)$ is the x-intercept.

Plot these points and draw the line. A third point should be used as a check.

$-3x + 5y = 15$

5. $1.4y - 3.5x = -9.8$

$14y - 34x = -98$ (Multiplying by 10)

$2y - 5x = -14$ (Multiplying by $\frac{1}{7}$)

Graph $2y - 5x = -14$.

To find the y-intercept, let $x = 0$.

$2y - 5x = -14$

$2y - 5 \cdot 0 = -14$ (Substituting 0 for x)

$2y = -14$

$y = -7$

Thus, $(0,-7)$ is the y-intercept.

To find the x-intercept, let $y = 0$.

$2y - 5x = -14$

$2 \cdot 0 - 5x = -14$ (Substituting 0 for y)

$-5x = -14$

$x = \frac{14}{5}$

Thus, $(\frac{14}{5},0)$ is the x-intercept.

Plot these points and draw the line. A third point should be used as a check.

$1.4y - 3.5x = -9.8$

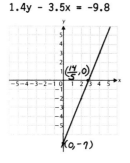

7. Let $(3,8) = (x_1,y_1)$ and $(9,-4) = (x_2,y_2)$.

Slope $= \frac{y_2 - y_1}{x_2 - x_1} = \frac{-4 - 8}{9 - 3} = \frac{-12}{6} = -2$

or $= \frac{y_1 - y_2}{x_1 - x_2} = \frac{8 - (-4)}{3 - 9} = \frac{12}{-6} = -2$

Either way, we get -2.

9. Let $(-8,-7) = (x_1,y_1)$ and $(-9,-12) = (x_2,y_2)$.

Slope $= \frac{y_2 - y_1}{x_2 - x_1} = \frac{-12 - (-7)}{-9 - (-8)} = \frac{-5}{-1} = 5$

or $= \frac{y_1 - y_2}{x_1 - x_2} = \frac{-7 - (-12)}{-8 - (-9)} = \frac{5}{1} = 5$

Either way, we get 5.

11. Let $(-16.3,12.4) = (x_1,y_1)$ and $(-5.2,8.7) = (x_2,y_2)$.

Slope $= \frac{y_2 - y_1}{x_2 - x_1} = \frac{8.7 - 12.4}{-5.2 - (-16.3)} = \frac{-3.7}{11.1} = -\frac{37}{111}$

$= -\frac{1}{3}$

or $= \frac{y_1 - y_2}{x_1 - x_2} = \frac{12.4 - 8.7}{-16.3 - (-5.2)} = \frac{3.7}{-11.1} = -\frac{37}{111}$

$= -\frac{1}{3}$

Either way we get $-\frac{1}{3}$.

13. Let $(3.2,-12.8) = (x_1,y_1)$ and $(3.2,2.4) = (x_2,y_2)$.

Slope $= \frac{y_2 - y_1}{x_2 - x_1} = \frac{2.4 - (-12.8)}{3.2 - 3.2} = \frac{15.2}{0}$

or $= \frac{y_1 - y_2}{x_1 - x_2} = \frac{-12.8 - 2.4}{3.2 - 3.2} = \frac{-15.2}{0}$

Since we cannot divide by 0, the slope of the line through $(3.2,-12.8)$ and $(3.2,2.4)$ is undefined (does not exist). The line is vertical.

15. $3x = 12 + y$

$3x - 12 = y$

$y = 3x - 12$ $\quad (y = mx + b)$

The slope is 3. The line is slanted.

17. $5x - 6 = 15$

$5x = 21$

$x = \frac{21}{5}$

When y is missing, the line is parallel to the y-axis. The line is vertical and does <u>not</u> have a slope.

19. $5y = 6$

$y = \frac{6}{5}$

When x is missing, the line is parallel to the x-axis. The line is horizontal and has a slope of 0.

21. $y - 6 = 14$

$y = 20$

When x is missing, the line is parallel to the x-axis. The line is horizontal and has a slope of 0.

23. $12 - 4x = 9 + x$

$3 = 5x$

$\frac{3}{5} = x$

When y is missing, the line is parallel to the y-axis. The line is vertical and does <u>not</u> have a slope.

25. $2y - 4 = 35 + x$

   $2y = x + 39$

   $y = \frac{1}{2}x + \frac{39}{2}$ ($y = mx + b$)

   The slope is $\frac{1}{2}$. The line is slanted.

27. $3y + x = 3y + 2$

   $x = 2$

   When y is missing, the line is parallel to the y-axis. The line is vertical and does <u>not</u> have a slope.

29. $3y - 2x = 5 + 9y - 2x$

   $3y = 5 + 9y$

   $0 = 5 + 6y$

   $-5 = 6y$

   $-\frac{5}{6} = y$

   When x is missing, the line is parallel to the x-axis. The line is horizontal and has a slope of 0.

31. $2y - 7x = 10 - 3x$

   $2y = 10 + 4x$

   $y = 5 + 2x$

   $y = 2x + 5$ ($y = mx + b$)

   The slope is 2. The line is slanted.

33. $(-2x^{-4}y^6)^5 = (-2)^5(x^{-4})^5(y^6)^5 = -32x^{-20}y^{30}$

   $\text{or} = -\frac{32y^{30}}{x^{20}}$

35. $\frac{-4a^5b^{-7}}{5a^{-12}b^8} = -\frac{4}{5}a^{5-(-12)}b^{-7-8}$

   $= -\frac{4}{5}a^{17}b^{-15}, \text{ or } -\frac{4a^{17}}{5b^{15}}$

37. a) Let $(5b, -6c) = (x_1, y_1)$ and $(b, -c) = (x_2, y_2)$.

   Slope $= \frac{y_2 - y_1}{x_2 - x_1} = \frac{-c - (-6c)}{b - 5b} = \frac{5c}{-4b} = -\frac{5c}{4b}$

   b) Let $(b, d) = (x_1, y_1)$ and $(b, d + e) = (x_2, y_2)$.

   Slope $= \frac{y_2 - y_1}{x_2 - x_1} = \frac{(d + e) - d}{b - b} = \frac{e}{0}$

   Since we cannot divide by 0, the slope is undefined (does not exist). The line is vertical.

37. (continued)

   c) $(c + f, a + d) = (x_1, y_1)$
      $(c - f, -a - d) = (x_2, y_2)$

   Slope $= \frac{y_2 - y_1}{x_2 - x_1} = \frac{(-a - d) - (a + d)}{(c - f) - (c + f)}$

   $= \frac{-a - d - a - d}{c - f - c - f}$

   $= \frac{-2a - 2d}{-2f}$

   $= \frac{-2(a + d)}{-2f}$

   $= \frac{a + d}{f}$

39. We first make a drawing.

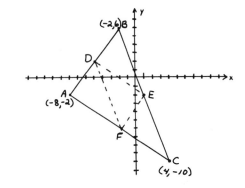

   Let D = midpoint of $\overline{AB}$.
      E = midpoint of $\overline{BC}$.
      F = midpoint of $\overline{AC}$.

   First we use the midpoint formula to calculate the coordinates of the midpoints.

   $(\frac{x_1 + x_2}{2}, \frac{y_1 + y_2}{2})$ (Midpoint formula)

   $D = (\frac{-8 + (-2)}{2}, \frac{-2 + 6}{2}) = (-5, 2)$

   $E = (\frac{-2 + 4}{2}, \frac{6 + (-10)}{2}) = (1, -2)$

   $F = (\frac{-8 + 4}{2}, \frac{-2 + (-10)}{2}) = (-2, -6)$

   Next we find the slopes of the side of triangle DEF.

   Slope of $\overline{DE} = \frac{-2 - 2}{1 - (-5)} = \frac{-4}{6} = -\frac{2}{3}$

   Slope of $\overline{EF} = \frac{-6 - (-2)}{-2 - 1} = \frac{-4}{-3} = \frac{4}{3}$

   Slope of $\overline{DF} = \frac{-6 - 2}{-2 - (-5)} = \frac{-8}{3} = -\frac{8}{3}$

Exercise Set 2.8

1. $y - y_1 = m(x - x_1)$ (Point-slope equation)

    $y - 2 = 4(x - 3)$ (Substituting 4 for m, 3 for x_1, and 2 for y_1)

    $y - 2 = 4x - 12$

    $y = 4x - 10$

3. $y - y_1 = m(x - x_1)$ (Point-slope equation)

    $y - 7 = -2(x - 4)$ (Substituting -2 for m, 4 for x_1, and 7 for y_1)

    $y - 7 = -2x + 8$

    $y = -2x + 15$

5. $y - y_1 = m(x - x_1)$ (Point-slope equation)

    $y - (-4) = 3[x - (-2)]$ (Substituting 3 for m, -2 for x_1, and -4 for y_1)

    $y + 4 = 3x + 6$

    $y = 3x + 2$

7. $y - y_1 = m(x - x_1)$ (Point-slope equation)

    $y - 0 = -2(x - 8)$ (Substituting -2 for m, 8 for x_1, and 0 for y_1)

    $y = -2x + 16$

9. $y - y_1 = m(x - x_1)$ (Point-slope equation)

    $y - (-7) = 0(x - 0)$ (Substituting 0 for m, 0 for x_1, and -7 for y_1)

    $y + 7 = 0$

    $y = -7$

11. $y - y_1 = \dfrac{y_2 - y_1}{x_2 - x_1}(x - x_1)$ (Two-point equation)

    Let $(1,4) = (x_1,y_1)$ and $(5,6) = (x_2,y_2)$.

    $y - 4 = \dfrac{6 - 4}{5 - 1}(x - 1)$ (Substituting)

    $y - 4 = \dfrac{2}{4}(x - 1)$

    $y - 4 = \dfrac{1}{2}(x - 1)$

    $y - \dfrac{8}{2} = \dfrac{1}{2}x - \dfrac{1}{2}$

    $y = \dfrac{1}{2}x + \dfrac{7}{2}$

13. $y - y_1 = \dfrac{y_2 - y_1}{x_2 - x_1}(x - x_1)$ (Two-point equation)

    Let $(-1,-1) = (x_1,y_1)$ and $(2,2) = (x_2,y_2)$.

    $y - (-1) = \dfrac{2 - (-1)}{2 - (-1)}[x - (-1)]$ (Substituting)

    $y + 1 = \dfrac{3}{3}(x + 1)$

    $y + 1 = x + 1$

    $y = x$

15. $y - y_1 = \dfrac{y_2 - y_1}{x_2 - x_1}(x - x_1)$ (Two-point equation)

    Let $(-2,0) = (x_1,y_1)$ and $(0,5) = (x_2,y_2)$.

    $y - 0 = \dfrac{5 - 0}{0 - (-2)}[x - (-2)]$ (Substituting)

    $y = \dfrac{5}{2}(x + 2)$

    $y = \dfrac{5}{2}x + 5$

17. $y - y_1 = \dfrac{y_2 - y_1}{x_2 - x_1}(x - x_1)$ (Two-point equation)

    Let $(-2,-3) = (x_1,y_1)$ and $(-4,-6) = (x_2,y_2)$.

    $y - (-3) = \dfrac{-6 - (-3)}{-4 - (-2)}[x - (-2)]$ (Substituting)

    $y + 3 = \dfrac{-3}{-2}(x + 2)$

    $y + 3 = \dfrac{3}{2}(x + 2)$

    $y + 3 = \dfrac{3}{2}x + 3$

    $y = \dfrac{3}{2}x$

19. $y - y_1 = \dfrac{y_2 - y_1}{x_2 - x_1}(x - x_1)$ (Two-point equation)

    Let $(0,0) = (x_1,y_1)$ and $(5,2) = (x_2,y_2)$.

    $y - 0 = \dfrac{2 - 0}{5 - 0}(x - 0)$ (Substituting)

    $y = \dfrac{2}{5}x$

21. First solve the equation for y and determine the slope of the given line.

    $x + 2y = 6$ (Given line)

    $2y = -x + 6$

    $y = -\dfrac{1}{2}x + 3$

The slope of the given line is $-\dfrac{1}{2}$.

The slope of every line parallel to the given line must also be $-\dfrac{1}{2}$. We find the equation of the line with slope $-\dfrac{1}{2}$ and containing the point $(3,7)$.

    $y - y_1 = m(x - x_1)$ (Point-slope equation)

    $y - 7 = -\dfrac{1}{2}(x - 3)$ (Substituting)

    $y - \dfrac{14}{2} = -\dfrac{1}{2}x + \dfrac{3}{2}$

    $y = -\dfrac{1}{2}x + \dfrac{17}{2}$

23. First solve the equation for y and determine the slope of the given line.

$5x - 7y = 8$ (Given line)

$5x - 8 = 7y$

$\frac{5}{7}x - \frac{8}{7} = y$

$y = \frac{5}{7}x - \frac{8}{7}$

The slope of the given line is $\frac{5}{7}$.

The slope of every line parallel to the given line must also be $\frac{5}{7}$. We find the equation of the line with slope $\frac{5}{7}$ and containing the point $(2,-1)$.

$y - y_1 = m(x - x_1)$ (Point-slope equation)

$y - (-1) = \frac{5}{7}(x - 2)$ (Substituting)

$y + \frac{7}{7} = \frac{5}{7}x - \frac{10}{7}$

$y = \frac{5}{7}x - \frac{17}{7}$

25. First solve the equtaion for y and determine the slope of the given line.

$2x + y = 3$

$y = -2x + 3$

The slope of the given line is -2.

Two lines are perpendicular if the product of their slopes is -1. The slope of every line perpendicular to the given line is $\frac{1}{2}$.

$-2 \cdot \frac{1}{2} = -1$

We find the equation of the line with slope $\frac{1}{2}$ and containing the point $(2,5)$.

$y - y_1 = m(x - x_1)$ (Point-slope equation)

$y - 5 = \frac{1}{2}(x - 2)$ (Substituting)

$y - 5 = \frac{1}{2}x - 1$

$y = \frac{1}{2}x + 4$

27. First solve the equation for y and determine the slope of the given line.

$3x + 4y = 5$ (Given line)

$4y = -3x + 5$

$y = -\frac{3}{4}x + \frac{5}{4}$

The slope of the given line is $-\frac{3}{4}$.

Two lines are perpendicular if the product of their slopes is -1. The slope of every line perpendicular to the given line is $\frac{4}{3}$.

$-\frac{3}{4} \cdot \frac{4}{3} = -1$

27. (continued)

We find the equation of the line with slope $\frac{4}{3}$ and containing the point $(3,-2)$.

$y - y_1 = m(x - x_1)$ (Point-slope equation)

$y - (-2) = \frac{4}{3}(x - 3)$ (Substituting)

$y + 2 = \frac{4}{3}x - 4$

$y = \frac{4}{3}x - 6$

29. $-43.5 + (-5.8) = -49.3$

The sum of two negative numbers is negative.

31. $-43.5(-5.8) = 252.3$

The product of two negative numbers is positive.

33. The slope of the line containing $(-1,4)$ and $(2,-3)$ is $\frac{-3 - 4}{2 - (-1)}$, or $-\frac{7}{3}$. We find a line whose slope is $-\frac{7}{3}$ and containing the point $(4,-2)$.

$y - y_1 = m(x - x_1)$ (Point-slope equation)

$y - (-2) = -\frac{7}{3}(x - 4)$ (Substituting)

$y + 2 = -\frac{7}{3}x + \frac{28}{3}$

$y = -\frac{7}{3}x + \frac{22}{3}$

35. We first find the slope of each line.

$5y = ax + 5$ $\frac{1}{4}y = \frac{1}{10}x - 1$

$y = \frac{a}{5}x + 1$ $5y = 2x - 20$

The slope is $\frac{a}{5}$. $y = \frac{2}{5}x - 4$

The slope is $\frac{2}{5}$.

Parallel lines have equal slopes.

Thus, $\frac{a}{5} = \frac{2}{5}$, or $a = 2$.

37. The slope of the line determined by $(-3,0)$ and $(0,\frac{2}{5})$ is

$\frac{\frac{2}{5} - 0}{0 - (-3)} = \frac{\frac{2}{5}}{3} = \frac{2}{5} \cdot \frac{1}{3} = \frac{2}{15}$.

We use the point-slope equation substituting $\frac{2}{15}$ for m and either $(-3,0)$ or $(0,\frac{2}{5})$ for (x_1,y_1).

$y - y_1 = m(x - x_1)$ (Point-slope equation)

$y - 0 = \frac{2}{15}[x - (-3)]$ (Substituting)

$y = \frac{2}{15}(x + 3)$

$y = \frac{2}{15}x + \frac{2}{5}$

Exercise Set 2.9

1. a) We use the two-point equation and the data points (0,72) and (20,75). These points are in the form (t,E).

$$E - E_1 = \frac{E_2 - E_1}{t_2 - t_1} (t - t_1)$$

$$E - 72 = \frac{75 - 72}{20 - 0} (t - 0) \qquad \text{(Substituting)}$$

$$E - 72 = \frac{3}{20} t$$

$$E = 0.15t + 72$$

b) In 1990, t = 40 (1990 - 1950 = 40).

$$E = 0.15(40) + 72$$
$$= 6 + 72$$
$$= 78$$

The life expectancy of females in 1990 is 78 years.

In 1998, t = 48 (1998 - 1950 = 48).

$$E = 0.15(48) + 72$$
$$= 7.2 + 72$$
$$= 79.2$$

The life expectancy of females in 1998 is 79.2 years.

3. a) We need two data points of the form (W,H). When W = 165, H = 70. This gives us our first data point, (165,70). When W = 145, H = 67. This gives us our second data point (145,67). We use the two-point equation.

$$H - H_1 = \frac{H_2 - H_1}{W_2 - W_1} (W - W_1)$$

$$H - 70 = \frac{67 - 70}{145 - 165} (W - 165) \qquad \text{(Substituting)}$$

$$H - 70 = \frac{3}{20} (W - 165)$$

$$H - 70 = 0.15(W - 165)$$

$$H - 70 = 0.15W - 24.75$$

$$H = 0.15W + 45.25$$

b) Substitute 130 for W in the linear equation obtained in part a).

$$H = 0.15(130) + 45.25$$
$$= 19.5 + 45.25$$
$$= 64.75$$

We estimate the height of an average-size person weighing 130 lb will be 64.75 in.

5. a) We need two data-points of the form (t,R). When t = 0, (1930 - 1930 = 0), R = 3.85. This gives us our first data point, (0,3.85). When t = 20, (1950 - 1930 = 20), R = 3.70. This gives us our second data point, (20,3.70). We use the two-point equation.

$$R - R_1 = \frac{R_2 - R_1}{t_2 - t_1} (t - t_1)$$

$$R - 3.85 = \frac{3.70 - 3.85}{20 - 0} (t - 0) \quad \text{(Substituting)}$$

$$R - 3.85 = \frac{-0.15}{20} t$$

$$R - 3.85 = -0.0075t$$

$$R = -0.0075t + 3.85$$

b) In 1988, t = 58 (1988 - 1930 = 58).

$$R = -0.0075(58) + 3.85$$
$$= -0.435 + 3.85$$
$$= 3.415$$

The record in 1988 will be 3.415 minutes.

In 1992, t = 62 (1992 - 1930 = 62).

$$R = -0.0075(62) + 3.85$$
$$= -0.465 + 3.85$$
$$= 3.385$$

The record in 1992 will be 3.385 minutes.

c) We substitute 3.3 for R and solve for t.

$$R = -0.0075t + 3.85$$

$$3.3 = -0.0075t + 3.85 \qquad \text{(Substituting)}$$

$$-0.55 = -0.0075t$$

$$\frac{-0.55}{-0.0075} = t$$

$$73.3 \approx t$$

In approximately 73.3 years (or in the year 2004), the record will be 3.3 minutes.

7. a) We need two data points of the form (m,C). When m = 2, C = 1.75. This gives us our first data point, (2,1.75). When m = 3, C = 2. This gives us our second data point, (3,2). We use the two-point equation.

$$C - C_1 = \frac{C_2 - C_1}{m_2 - m_1} (m - m_1)$$

$$C - 1.75 = \frac{2 - 1.75}{3 - 2} (m - 2) \qquad \text{(Substituting)}$$

$$C - 1.75 = \frac{0.25}{1} (m - 2)$$

$$C - 1.75 = 0.25m - 0.5$$

$$C = 0.25m + 1.25$$

b) Substitute 7 for m in the linear equation obtained in part a) and solve for C.

$$C = 0.25 \cdot 7 + 1.25$$
$$C = 1.75 + 1.25$$
$$C = 3$$

The cost of a 7-mile ride is $3.

9. We want to express V in terms of t. We need two
   data points of the form (t,V). When t = 0,
   V = $5200. This gives us our first data point,
   (0,5200). When t = 2, V = $4225. This gives us
   our second data point, (2,4225). We use the
   two-point equation.

$$V - V_1 = \frac{V_2 - V_1}{t_2 - t_1}(t - t_1)$$

$$V - 5200 = \frac{4225 - 5200}{2 - 0}(t - 0) \quad \text{(Substituting)}$$

$$V - 5200 = \frac{-975}{2}t$$

$$V - 5200 = -487.5t$$

$$V = -487.5t + 5200$$

We substitute 8 for t.

$$V = -487.5(8) + 5200$$
$$= -3900 + 5200$$
$$= 1300$$

The value after 8 years is $1300.

11. We use the two-point equation and the data points
    (18,100) and (20,100.00356) to determine a linear
    equation that fits the situation. We let L
    represent the length and T represent the tempera-
    ture.

$$L - L_1 = \frac{L_2 - L_1}{T_2 - T_1}(T - T_1)$$

$$L - 100 = \frac{100.00356 - 100}{20 - 18}(T - 18) \quad \text{(Substituting)}$$

$$L - 100 = \frac{0.00356}{2}(T - 18)$$

$$L - 100 = 0.00178(T - 18)$$

$$L - 100 = 0.00178T - 0.03204$$

$$L = 0.00178T + 99.96796$$

We substitute 40 for T.

$$L = 0.00178(40) + 99.96796$$
$$= 0.0712 + 99.96796$$
$$= 100.03916$$

The length of the pipe at 40° C is 100.03916 cm.

We substitute 0 for T.

$$L = 0.00178(0) + 99.96796$$
$$= 99.96796$$

The length of the pipe at 0° C is 99.96796 cm.

Exercise Set 3.1

1. We use alphabetical order for the variables. We replace x by 1 and y by 2.

4x - y = 2	
4·1 - 2	2
4 - 2	
2	

10x - 3y = 4	
10·1 - 3·2	4
10 - 6	
4	

The ordered pair (1,2) makes both equations true, so it _is_ a solution of the system.

3. We use alphabetical order for the variables. We replace x by -1 and y by -2.

x + 3y = -7	
-1 + 3(-2)	-7
-1 - 6	
-7	

3x - 2y = 12	
3(-1) - 2(-2)	12
-3 + 4	
1	

The ordered pair (-1,-2) is not a solution of 3x - 2y = 12. Therefore it _is not_ a solution of the system of equations.

5. We replace a by 2 and b by -7.

3a + b = -1	
3·2 + (-7)	-1
6 - 7	
-1	

2a - 3b = -8	
2·2 - 3·(-7)	-8
4 + 21	
25	

The ordered pair (2,-7) is not a solution of 2a - 3b = -8. Therefore it _is not_ a solution of the system of equations.

7. We replace s by 1 and t by 5.

s + t = 6	
1 + 5	6
6	

t = 2s + 3	
5	2·1 + 3
	2 + 3
	5

The ordered pair (1,5) makes both equations true, so it _is_ a solution of the system.

9. Graph both lines on the same set of axes. The x and y-intercepts of the line x + y = 4 are (4,0) and (0,4). Plot these points and draw the line they determine. The x and y-intercepts of the line x - y = 2 are (2,0) and (0,-2). Plot these points and draw the line they determine.

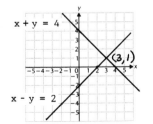

9. (continued)

The solution (point of intersection) seems to be the point (3,1).

Check:

x + y = 4	
3 + 1	4
4	

x - y = 2	
3 - 1	2
2	

The solution is (3,1).

11. Graph both lines on the same set of axes.

Graph 2x - y = 4.

The x and y-intercepts are (2,0) and (0,-4). Plot these points and draw the line they determine.

Graph 5x - y = 13.

When x = 2,
5·2 - y = 13
10 - y = 13
-y = 3
y = -3

When x = 4,
5·4 - y = 13
20 - y = 13
-y = -7
y = 7

Plot the points (2,-3) and (4,7) and draw the line they determine.

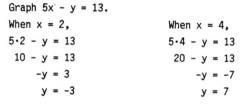

The solution (point of intersection) seems to be the point (3,2).

Check:

2x - y = 4	
2·3 - 2	4
6 - 2	
4	

5x - y = 13	
5·3 - 2	13
15 - 2	
13	

The solution is (3,2).

13. Graph both lines on the same set of axes.

Graph 4x - y = 9.

When x = 3,   When x = 1,
4·3 - y = 9   4·1 - y = 9
12 - y = 9   4 - y = 9
   -y = -3   -y = 5
    y = 3   y = -5

Plot the points (3,3) and (1,-5) and draw the line they determine.

Graph x - 3y = 16.

When x = 4,   When x = 1,
4 - 3y = 16   1 - 3y = 16
  -3y = 12   -3y = 15
    y = -4   y = -5

Plot the points (4,-4) and (1,-5) and draw the line they determine.

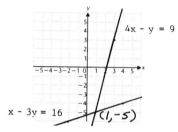

The solution seems to be the point (1,-5).

Check:

The solution is (1,-5).

15. Graph both lines on the same set of axes. The a and b-intercepts of a = 1 + b are (1,0) and (0,-1). Plot these points and draw the line they determine. The a and b-intercepts of b = -2a + 5 are $(\frac{5}{2},0)$ and (0,5). Plot these points and draw the line they determine.

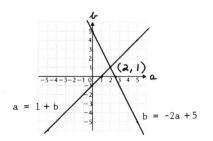

15. (continued)

The solution seems to be the point (2,1).

Check:

a = 1 + b			b = -2a + 5	
2	1 + 1		1	-2·2 + 5
	2			-4 + 5
				1

The solution is (2,1).

17. Graph both lines on the same set of axes.

Graph 2u + v = 3.

When u = 0, v = 3. When u = 1, v = 1. Plot the points (0,3) and (1,1) and draw the line they determine.

Graph 2u = v + 7.

When u = 1, v = -5. when u = 3, v = -1. Plot the points (1,-5) and (3,-1) and draw the line they determine.

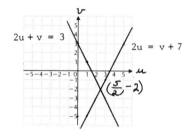

The solution seems to be $(\frac{5}{2},-2)$.

Check:

2u + v = 3			2u = v + 7	
$2 \cdot \frac{5}{2} + (-2)$	3		$2 \cdot \frac{5}{2}$	-2 + 7
5 - 2			5	5
3				

The solution is $(\frac{5}{2},-2)$.

19. Graph both lines on the same set of axes.

Graph y = -x - 1.

When x = 0, y = -1. When x = 2, y = -3. Plot the points (0,-1) and (2,-3) and draw the line they determine.

Graph 4x - 3y = 18.

When x = 0, y = -6. When x = 3, y = -2. Plot the points (0,-6) and (3,-2) and draw the line they determine.

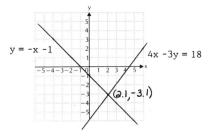

At first glance, the solution seems to be (2,-3), but (2,-3) is not a solution of 4x - 3y = 18.

$$\begin{array}{c|c} 4x - 3y = 18 & \\ \hline 4(2) - 3(-3) & 18 \\ 8 + 9 & \\ 17 & \end{array}$$

We now try (2.1,-3.1).

$$\begin{array}{c|c} y = -x - 1 & \\ \hline -3.1 & -2.1 - 1 \\ & -3.1 \end{array} \qquad \begin{array}{c|c} 4x - 3y = 18 & \\ \hline 4(2.1) - 3(-3.1) & 18 \\ 8.4 + 9.3 & \\ 17.7 & \end{array}$$

This is closer, but not exact. Graphing is not perfectly accurate, so solving by graphing may give only approximate answers. Thus, the solution is about (2.1,-3.1).

21. Graph both lines on the same set of axes.

Graph 6x - 2y = 2.

When x = 0, y = -1. When x = -1, y = -4. Plot the points (0,-1) and (-1,-4) and draw the line they determine.

Graph 9x - 3y = 1.

When x = 1, y = $\frac{8}{3}$. When x = -1, y = $-\frac{10}{3}$. Plot the points $(1,\frac{8}{3})$ and $(-1,-\frac{10}{3})$ and draw the line they determine.

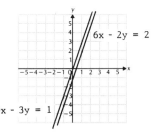

The lines are parallel. There is _no_ solution.

23. Graph both lines on the same set of axes.

Graph 2x - 3y = 6.

The x and y-intercepts are (3,0) and (0,-2). Plot these points and draw the line they determine.

Graph 3y - 2x = -6.

The x and y-intercepts are (3,0) and (0,-2). This equation has exactly the same graph as 2x - 3y = 6.

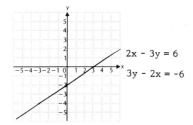

The system has an infinite set of solutions.

25. 3x + 4 = x - 2
         2x = -6
          x = -3

27. 5y + 2 - 6y - 7 = 14
          -y - 5 = 14
              -y = 19
               y = -19

29.   Q = $\frac{1}{4}$(a - b)

         4Q = a - b

     4Q + b = a

          b = a - 4Q

31. We first make a drawing letting h represent the height.

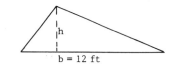

The formula for the area of a triangle is A = $\frac{1}{2}$ bh.

A = $\frac{1}{2}$ bh

156 = $\frac{1}{2}$ · 12·h   (Substituting 156 for A and 12 for b)

156 = 6h

 26 = h

The height should be 26 ft.

33. Let x represent the number of years Mrs. Ng has taught and y represent the number of years Mr. Ng has taught. Then x - 2 represents the number of years Mrs. Ng had taught two years ago and y - 2 represents the number of years Mr. Ng had taught two years ago.

We translate to a system of equations.

In total they have 46 years of service.

$$x + y = 46$$

Two years ago, Mrs. Ng had taught 2.5 times as many years as Mr. Ng.

$$x - 2 = 2.5(y - 2)$$

The resulting system of equations is

$$x + y = 46$$
$$x - 2 = 2.5(y - 2)$$

Exercise Set 3.2

1.
$$3x + 5y = 3 \qquad (1)$$
$$x = 8 - 4y \qquad (2)$$

We substitute 8 - 4y for x in the first equation and solve for y.

$$3x + 5y = 3 \qquad (1)$$
$$3(8 - 4y) + 5y = 3 \qquad \text{(Substituting)}$$
$$24 - 12y + 5y = 3$$
$$24 - 7y = 3$$
$$-7y = -21$$
$$y = 3$$

Next we substitute 3 for y in either equation of the original system and solve for x.

$$x = 8 - 4y \qquad (2)$$
$$x = 8 - 4 \cdot 3 \qquad \text{(Substituting)}$$
$$x = 8 - 12$$
$$x = -4$$

We check the ordered pair (-4,3).

$3x + 5y = 3$		$x = 8 - 4y$	
$3(-4) + 5 \cdot 3$	3	-4	$8 - 4 \cdot 3$
$-12 + 15$			$8 - 12$
3			-4

Since (-4,3) checks, it is the solution.

3.
$$2x + 3y = 10 \qquad (1)$$
$$4x - 9y = 10 \qquad (2)$$

We solve the first equation for x.

$$2x + 3y = 10 \qquad (1)$$
$$2x = -3y + 10$$
$$x = -\frac{3}{2}y + 5$$

We now substitute $-\frac{3}{2}y + 5$ for x in the second equation and solve for y.

$$4x - 9y = 10 \qquad (2)$$
$$4 \cdot (-\frac{3}{2}y + 5) - 9y = 10 \qquad \text{(Substituting)}$$
$$-6y + 20 - 9y = 10$$
$$-15y = -10$$
$$y = \frac{10}{15}$$
$$y = \frac{2}{3}$$

Next we substitute $\frac{2}{3}$ for y in either equation of the original system and solve for x.

$$2x + 3y = 10 \qquad (1)$$
$$2x + 3(\frac{2}{3}) = 10 \qquad \text{(Substituting)}$$
$$2x + 2 = 10$$
$$2x = 8$$
$$x = 4$$

We check the ordered pair $(4, \frac{2}{3})$.

$2x + 3y = 10$		$4x - 9y = 10$	
$2(4) + 3(\frac{2}{3})$	10	$4(4) - 9(\frac{2}{3})$	10
$8 + 2$		$16 - 6$	
10		10	

Since $(4, \frac{2}{3})$ checks, it is the solution.

5.
$$5m + n = 8 \qquad (1)$$
$$3m - 4n = 14 \qquad (2)$$

We solve the first equation for n.

$$5m + n = 8 \qquad (1)$$
$$n = 8 - 5m$$

We substitute 8 - 5m for n in the second equation and solve for m.

$$3m - 4n = 14 \qquad (2)$$
$$3m - 4(8 - 5m) = 14 \qquad \text{(Substituting)}$$
$$3m - 32 + 20m = 14$$
$$23m - 32 = 14$$
$$23m = 46$$
$$m = 2$$

5. (continued)

Now we substitute 2 for m in either equation of the original system and solve for n.

$5m + n = 8$ (1)

$5 \cdot 2 + n = 8$ (Substituting)

$10 + n = 8$

$n = -2$

We obtain $(2,-2)$. This checks, so it is the solution.

7. $4x + 12y = 4$ (1)

$-5x + y = 11$ (2)

We solve the second equation for y.

$-5x + y = 11$ (2)

$y = 5x + 11$

We substitute $5x + 11$ for y in the first equation and solve for x.

$4x + 12y = 4$ (1)

$4x + 12(5x + 11) = 4$ (Substituting)

$4x + 60x + 132 = 4$

$64x + 132 = 4$

$64x = -128$

$x = -2$

Now substitute -2 for x in either equation of the original system and solve for y.

$-5x + y = 11$ (2)

$-5(-2) + y = 11$ (Substituting)

$10 + y = 11$

$y = 1$

We obtain $(-2,1)$. This checks, so it is the solution.

9. $x + 3y = 7$

$\underline{-x + 4y = 7}$

$0 + 7y = 14$ (Adding)

$7y = 14$

$y = 2$

Substitute 2 for y in one of the original equations and solve for x.

$x + 3y = 7$

$x + 3 \cdot 2 = 7$ (Substituting)

$x + 6 = 7$

$x = 1$

We check the ordered pair $(1,2)$.

$x + 3y = 7$		$-x + 4y = 7$	
$1 + 3 \cdot 2$	7	$-1 + 4 \cdot 2$	7
$1 + 6$		$-1 + 8$	
7		7	

Since $(1,2)$ checks, it is the solution.

11. $9x + 3y = -3$

$\underline{2x - 3y = -8}$

$11x + 0 = -11$ (Adding)

$11x = -11$

$x = -1$

Substitute -1 for x in one of the original equations and solve for y.

$9x + 3y = -3$

$9(-1) + 3y = -3$ (Substituting)

$-9 + 3y = -3$

$3y = 6$

$y = 2$

We check the ordered pair $(-1,2)$.

$9x + 3y = -3$		$2x - 3y = -8$	
$9(-1) + 3 \cdot 2$	-3	$2(-1) - 3 \cdot 2$	-8
$-9 + 6$		$-2 - 6$	
-3		-8	

Since $(-1,2)$ checks, it is the solution.

13. $x - 3y = 4$

$2x + 5y = 8$

We multiply by -2 on both sides of the first equation and then add.

$-2x + 6y = -8$ (Multiplying by -2)

$\underline{2x + 5y = 8}$

$11y = 0$ (Adding)

$y = 0$

Substitute 0 for y in one of the original equations and solve for x.

$x - 3y = 4$

$x - 3 \cdot 0 = 4$ (Substituting)

$x - 0 = 4$

$x = 4$

We obtain $(4,0)$. This checks, so it is the solution.

15. $5r - 3s = 24$

$3r + 5s = 28$

We mutliply twice to make two terms become additive inverses.

$25r - 15s = 120$ (Multiplying by 5)

$\underline{9r + 15s = 84}$ (Multiplying by 3)

$34r \quad\quad = 204$ (Adding)

$r = 6$

15. (continued)

Substitute 6 for r in one of the original equations and solve for s.

$3r + 5s = 28$

$3 \cdot 6 + 5s = 28$ (Substituting)

$18 + 5s = 28$

$5s = 10$

$s = 2$

We obtain (6,2). This checks, so it is the solution.

17. $5x + 3y = 19$

$2x - 5y = 11$

We multiply twice to make two terms become additive inverses.

$25x + 15y = 95$ (Multiplying by 5)

$\underline{6x - 15y = 33}$ (Multiplying by 3)

$31x \qquad = 128$ (Adding)

$x = \frac{128}{31}$

Substitute $\frac{128}{31}$ for x in one of the original equations and solve for y.

$5x + 3y = 19$

$5 \cdot \frac{128}{31} + 3y = 19$ (Substituting)

$\frac{640}{31} + 3y = \frac{589}{31}$

$3y = -\frac{51}{31}$

$\frac{1}{3} \cdot 3y = \frac{1}{3} \cdot (-\frac{51}{31})$

$y = -\frac{17}{31}$

We obtain $(\frac{128}{31}, -\frac{17}{31})$. This checks, so it is the solution.

19. $\frac{3}{5} x - y = 52$

$6x - \frac{5}{4} y = 170$

We multiply each equation by the LCM of the denominators to clear fractions.

$5(\frac{3}{5} x - y) = 5(52)$ (Multiplying by 5)

$4(6x - \frac{5}{4} y) = 4(170)$ (Multiplying by 4)

We solve the resulting system.

$3x - 5y = 260$

$24x - 5y = 680$

19. (continued)

We multiply by -1 on both sides of the first equation and then add.

$-3x + 5y = -260$ (Multiplying by -1)

$\underline{24x - 5y = 680}$

$21x \qquad = 420$ (Adding)

$x = 20$

Substitute 20 for x in one of the equations in which the fractions were cleared and solve for y.

$3x - 5y = 260$

$3 \cdot 20 - 5y = 260$ (Substituting)

$60 - 5y = 260$

$-5y = 200$

$y = -40$

We obtain (20,-40). This checks, so it is the solution.

21. $0.3x - 0.2y = 4$

$0.2x + 0.3y = 1$

We first multiply each equation by 10 to clear decimals.

$3x - 2y = 40$

$2x + 3y = 10$

We use the multiplication principle with both equations of the resulting system.

$9x - 6y = 120$ (Multiplying by 3)

$\underline{4x + 6y = 20}$ (Multiplying by 2)

$13x \qquad = 140$ (Adding)

$x = \frac{140}{13}$

Substitute $\frac{140}{13}$ for x in one of the equations in which the decimals were cleared and solve for y.

$2x + 3y = 10$

$2 \cdot \frac{140}{13} + 3y = 10$ (Substituting)

$\frac{280}{13} + 3y = \frac{130}{13}$

$3y = -\frac{150}{13}$

$y = -\frac{50}{13}$

We obtain $(\frac{140}{13}, -\frac{50}{13})$. This checks, so it is the solution.

23. $\frac{1}{2}$ x + $\frac{1}{3}$ y = 4

$\frac{1}{4}$ x + $\frac{1}{3}$ y = 3

We first multiply each equation by the LCM of the denominators to clear fractions.

3x + 2y = 24   (Multiplying by 6)

3x + 4y = 36   (Multiplying by 12)

We multiply by -1 on both sides of the first equation and then add.

-3x - 2y = -24   (Multiplying by -1)

 3x + 4y = 36

    2y = 12   (Adding)

     y = 6

Substitute 6 for y in one of the equations in which the fractions were cleared and solve for x.

 3x + 2y = 24

3x + 2·6 = 24   (Substituting)

3x + 12 = 24

   3x = 12

    x = 4

We obtain (4,6). This checks, so it is the solution.

25. 5x - 9y = 7

7y - 3x = -5

We first write the second equation in the form Ax + By = C.

 5x - 9y = 7

-3x + 7y = -5

We use the multiplication principle with both equations and then add.

 15x - 27y = 21   (Multiplying by 3)

-15x + 35y = -25   (Multiplying by 5)

     8y = -4   (Adding)

      y = -$\frac{1}{2}$

Substitute -$\frac{1}{2}$ for y in one of the original equations and solve for x.

   5x - 9y = 7

5x - 9(-$\frac{1}{2}$) = 7   (Substituting)

   5x + $\frac{9}{2}$ = $\frac{14}{2}$

      5x = $\frac{5}{2}$

       x = $\frac{1}{2}$

We obtain ($\frac{1}{2}$,-$\frac{1}{2}$). This checks, so it is the solution.

27. 1.3x - 0.2y = 12

0.4x +   17y = 89

We multiply on both sides of each equation by 10 to clear decimals.

13x -   2y = 120

4x + 170y = 890

We multiply the first equation of the resulting system by 85 and then add.

1105x - 170y = 10,200   (Multiplying by 85)

   4x + 170y =   890

1109x   = 11,090   (Adding)

     x = 10

Substitute 10 for x in either one of the equations in which the decimals were cleared and solve for y.

   4x + 170y = 890

4·10 + 170y = 890   (Substituting)

  40 + 170y = 890

     170y = 850

        y = 5

We obtain (10,5). This checks, so it is the solution.

29. $\frac{1}{8}$ x + $\frac{3}{5}$ y = $\frac{19}{2}$

  -$\frac{3}{10}$ x - $\frac{7}{20}$ y = -1

We multiply each equation by the LCM of the denominators to clear fractions.

 5x + 24y = 380   (Multiplying by 40)

-6x - 7y = -20   (Multiplying by 20)

We use the multiplication principle with both equations of the resulting system.

  35x + 168y = 2660   (Multiplying by 7)

-144x - 168y = -480   (Multiplying by 24)

-109x   = 2180   (Adding)

     x = -20

Substitute -20 for x in one of the equations in which fractions were cleared and solve for y.

    5x + 24y = 380

5(-20) + 24y = 380

 -100 + 24y = 380

      24y = 480

       y = 20

We obtain (-20,20). This checks, so it is the solution.

31.   I = Prt

17.60 = 320·r · $\frac{1}{2}$ (Substituting 17.60 for I,
                                        320 for P and $\frac{1}{2}$ for t)

17.60 = 160r

$\frac{17.60}{160}$ = r

 0.11 = r

The rate of interest is 11%.

33. $\frac{x + y}{2} - \frac{x - y}{5} = 1$

$\frac{x - y}{2} + \frac{x + y}{6} = -2$

We multiply each equation by the LCM of the
denominators to clear fractions.

5(x + y) - 2(x - y) = 10   (Multiplying by 10)

5x + 5y - 2x + 2y = 10

3x + 7y = 10

3(x - y) + (x + y) = -12   (Multiplying by 6)

3x - 3y + x + y = -12

4x - 2y = -12

2x - y = -6

We solve the resulting system.

3x + 7y = 10

2x - y = -6

We multiply the second equation by 7 and then add.

3x + 7y = 10

$\underline{14x - 7y = -42}$ (Multiplying by 7)

17x   = -32

x = $-\frac{32}{17}$

Substitute $-\frac{32}{17}$ for x in either of the equations
in which fractions were cleared and solve for y.

2x - y = -6

$2(-\frac{32}{17})$ - y = -6   (Substituting)

$-\frac{64}{17}$ - y = $-\frac{102}{17}$

-y = $-\frac{38}{17}$

y = $\frac{38}{17}$

We obtain $(-\frac{32}{17}, \frac{38}{17})$. This checks, so it is the
solution.

35. ax + by = -26

bx - ay = 7

Since (-4,-3) is a solution of the system, we
replace x by -4 and y by -3 in each equation and
solve the resulting system for a and b.

-4a - 3b = -26   or   -4a - 3b = -26

-4b + 3a = 7   3a - 4b = 7

We use the multiplication principle with each
equation and then add.

-12a - 9b = -78   (Multiplying by 3)

$\underline{12a - 16b = 28}$ (Multiplying by 4)

-25b = -50   (Adding)

b = 2

Substitute 2 for b in either equation and solve
for a.

3a - 4b = 7

3a - 4·2 = 7   (Substituting)

3a - 8 = 7

3a = 15

a = 5

We obtain (5,2). This checks, so a = 5 and
b = 2.

Exercise Set 3.3

1. We let x represent the first number and y represent
the second number.

First number plus second number is -42.

x   +   y   =   -42

First number minus second number is 52.

x   -   y   =   52

The resulting system of equations is

x + y = -42

x - y = 52

We use the addition method.

x + y = -42

$\underline{x - y = 52}$

2x   = 10   (Adding)

x = 5

Next we substitute 5 for x in one of the original
equations and solve for y.

x + y = -42

5 + y = -42   (Substituting)

y = -47

The sum of the numbers is 5 + (-47), or -42. The
first number minus the second number is 5 - (-47),
or 52. The numbers check.

The numbers are 5 and -47.

3. We let x represent the larger number and y represent the smaller number.

Larger number minus smaller number is 16.

$$x - y = 16$$

Three times the larger number is nine times the smaller number.

$$3 \cdot x = 9 \cdot y$$

The resulting system is

$$x - y = 16$$
$$3x = 9y$$

We solve the second equation for x and use the substitution method.

$$3x = 9y$$
$$x = 3y$$

We substitute 3y for x in the first equation and solve for y.

$$x - y = 16$$
$$3y - y = 16 \qquad \text{(Substituting)}$$
$$2y = 16$$
$$y = 8$$

We substitute 8 for y in one of the original equations and solve for x.

$$x - y = 16$$
$$x - 8 = 16 \qquad \text{(Substituting)}$$
$$x = 24$$

The larger number minus the smaller number is 24 - 8, or 16. Three times the larger number is nine times the smaller number ($3 \cdot 24 = 9 \cdot 8 = 72$). The numbers check.

The numbers are 24 and 8.

5. We first make a drawing.

We let ℓ represent the length and w the width.

The formula for perimeter is $P = 2\ell + 2w$.

The perimeter is 628 m.

$$2\ell + 2w = 628$$

The length equals the width plus 6 m.

$$\ell = w + 6$$

5. (continued)

The resulting system is

$$2\ell + 2w = 628$$
$$\ell = w + 6$$

We use the substitution method.

We substitute w + 6 for ℓ in the first equation and solve for w.

$$2\ell + 2w = 628$$
$$\text{or} \quad \ell + w = 314 \qquad \text{(Multiplying by } \tfrac{1}{2}\text{)}$$
$$w + 6 + w = 314 \qquad \text{(Substituting)}$$
$$2w + 6 = 314$$
$$2w = 308$$
$$w = 154$$

Next we substitute 154 for w in one of the original equations and solve for ℓ.

$$\ell = w + 6$$
$$\ell = 154 + 6 \qquad \text{(Substituting)}$$
$$\ell = 160$$

The length is 6 more than the width: $160 = 154 + 6$. The perimeter is $2(160) + 2(154)$, or 628. The values check.

The length is 160 m, and the width is 154 m.

7. List the information in a table.

Sweatshirt	Cost per shirt	Number sold	Money taken in
White	$ 9.95	x	$ 9.95x
Yellow	$10.50	y	$10.50y
	Total	30	$310.60

We let x represent the number of white sweatshirts sold and y represent the number of yellow sweatshirts sold.

The total number of sweatshirts sold was 30, so

$$x + y = 30$$

The total amount received was $310.60, so

$$9.95x + 10.50y = 310.60$$
$$\text{or} \quad 995x + 1050y = 31{,}060 \qquad \text{(Multiplying by 100)}$$

The resulting system of equtions is

$$x + y = 30$$
$$995x + 1050y = 31{,}060$$

We multiply the first equation by −995 and then add.

$$-995x - 995y = -29{,}850 \qquad \text{(Multiplying by −995)}$$
$$\underline{995x + 1050y = \quad 31{,}060}$$
$$55y = \quad 1210 \qquad \text{(Adding)}$$
$$y = 22$$

7. (continued)

Next we substitute 22 for y in one of the original equations and solve for x.

x + y = 30

x + 22 = 30   (Substituting)

x = 8

The total number of sweatshirts sold was 8 white ones plus 22 yellow ones, or 30. The total receipts were 9.95(8) + 10.50(22), or 79.6 + 231, or $310.60. The values check.

Thus, 8 white sweatshirts and 22 yellow sweatshirts were sold.

9. We can arrange the information in a table.

Type of meal	Amount of meal	Percent of protein	Amount of protein in meal
Soybean	x	16%	16%x
Corn	y	9%	9%y
Mixture	350	12%	12%×350 or 42

We let x represent the number of pounds of soybean meal and y represent the number of pounds of corn meal.

Since the total is 350 pounds, we have

x + y = 350

The amount of protein in the mixture is to be 12% of 350, or 42 pounds. The amounts of protein from the two meals are 16%x and 9%y. Thus

16%x + 9%y = 42

or 0.16x + 0.09y = 42

or   16x + 9y = 4200

The resulting system is

x + y = 350

16x + 9y = 4200

We multiply the first equation by -9 and then add.

-9x - 9y = -3150   (Multiplying by -9)

16x + 9y = 4200

7x   = 1050   (Adding)

x = 150

We substitute 150 for x in one of the original equations and solve for y.

x + y = 350

150 + y = 350   (Substituting)

y = 200

We consider x = 150 and y = 200. The sum is 350. Now 16% of 150 is 24, and 9% of 200 is 18. These add up to 42. The numbers check.

Thus, 150 pounds of soybean meal and 200 pounds of corn meal should be mixed.

11. We organize the information in a table.

	Principal	Rate	Time	Interest
1st investment	x	14%	1 yr	7%x
2nd investment	y	16%	1 yr	8%y
Total	$8800			$663

We let x represent one investment and y the other investment.

The investments total $8800. This gives us one equation.

x + y = 8800

The amounts of interest from the investments are 7%x and 8%y. They total $663. This gives us a second equation.

7%x + 8%y = 663

or 0.07x + 0.08y = 663

or   7x + 8y = 66,300

The resulting system is

x + y = 8800

7x + 8y = 66,300

We multiply the first equation by -7 and then add.

-7x - 7y = -61,600   (Multiplying by -7)

7x + 8y = 66,300

y = 4700   (Adding)

Next we substitute 4700 for y in one of the original equations and solve for x.

x + y = 8800

x + 4700 = 8800   (Substituting)

x = 4100

The sum of the investments is 4100 + 4700, or $8800. The amounts of interest earned are 7% of 4100, or $287, and 8% of 4700, or $376. The total interest earned is 287 + 376, or $663. The values check.

Thus, $4100 is invested at 7% and $4700 is invested at 8%.

13. We organize the information in a table.

	Principal	Rate	Time	Interest
Investment @5%	x	5%	1 yr	5%x
Investment @6%	y, or x + 10,000	6%	1 yr	6%y
Total				$3900

We let x represent one investment and y represent the other. The investment at 6% is $10,000 more than the investment at 5%. This gives us one equation.

y = x + 10,000

The amounts of interest from the investments are 5%x and 6%y. They total $3900. This gives us a second equation.

$$5\%x + 6\%y = 3900$$

or 0.05x + 0.06y = 3900

or   5x + 6y = 390,000

The resulting system is

y = x + 10,000

5x + 6y = 390,000

We substitute x + 10,000 for y in the second equation and solve for x.

$$5x + 6y = 390,000$$

5x + 6(x + 10,000) = 390,000   (Substituting)

  5x + 6x + 60,000 = 390,000

    11x + 60,000 = 390,000

          11x = 330,000

            x = 30,000

Next we substitute 30,000 for x in either one of the original equations and solve for y.

y = x + 10,000

y = 30,000 + 10,000   (Substituting)

y = 40,000

One investment ($40,000) is $10,000 more than the other ($30,000). The amounts of interest earned are 5%·30,000, or $1500, and 6%·40,000, or $2400. The total interest earned is 1500 + 2400, or $3900. The values check.

Thus, $30,000 is invested at 5% and $40,000 is invested at 6%.

15. We let d represent the number of dimes and q the number of quarters. The total number of coins is 412. This gives us one equation.

d + q = 412

The value of the dimes is 10d, in cents. The value of the quarters is 25q, in cents. The total value is $61, or 6100 cents. Now we have a second equation.

10d + 25q = 6100

15. (continued)

We have a system of equations to solve.

d + q = 412

10d + 25q = 6100

We multiply on both sides of the first equation by -10 and then add.

-10d - 10q = -4120   (Multiplying by -10)

 10d + 25q = 6100

      15q = 1980   (Adding)

        q = 132

Substitute 132 for q in one of the original equations and solve for d.

  d + q = 412

d + 132 = 412   (Substituting)

      d = 280

If there are 280 dimes and 132 quarters, there are 412 coins. The total value of the coins is 280(0.10) + 132(0.25), or 28 + 33, or $61. The values check.

There are 280 dimes and 132 quarters.

17. It helps to organize information in a table. We let x represent the number of liters of the solution that is 80% acid and y represent the number of liters of the solution that is 30% acid.

	Amt. of solution	Percent of acid	Amt. of acid in solution
Solution (80% acid)	x	80%	80%x
Solution (30% acid)	y	30%	30%y
Mixture	200L	62%	62%·200, or 124L

The total number of liters in the mixture is 200. This gives us one equation.

x + y = 200

The amounts of acid from the solutions are 80%x and 30%y. They total 62%·200, or 124 liters. This gives us a second equation.

  80%x + 30%y = 124

or 0.8x + 0.3y = 124

or   8x + 3y = 1240

The resulting system is

x + y = 200

8x + 3y = 1240

We multiply on both sides of the first equation by -3 and then add.

-3x - 3y = -600   (Multiplying by -3)

 8x + 3y = 1240

 5x   = 640   (Adding)

      x = 128

17. (continued)

We substitute 128 for x in one of the original equations and solve for y.

$x + y = 200$

$128 + y = 200$ (Substituting)

$y = 72$

If $x = 128$, the number of liters of the 80% solution, and $y = 72$, the number of liters of the 30% solution, the total number of liters in the mixture is $128 + 72$, or 200. The total amount of acid in the mixture is $80\% \cdot 128 + 30\% \cdot 72$, or $102.4 + 21.6$, or 124 liters. The values check.

Thus, 128 liters of the 80%-acid solution and 72 liters of the 30%-acid solution should be used.

19. Let x represent Ann's age now and y represent her son's age now. Then $x - 10$ and $y - 10$ represent their ages ten years ago. We translate to a system of equations.

Now, Ann is twice as old as her son.

$x = 2y$

Ten years ago, Ann was three times as old as her son.

$x - 10 = 3(y - 10)$

or

$x - 10 = 3y - 30$

or

$x - 3y = -20$

The resulting system is

$x = 2y$

$x - 3y = -20$

Substitute 2y for x in the second equation and solve for y.

$x - 3y = -20$

$2y - 3y = -20$

$-y = -20$

$y = 20$

Next substitute 20 for y in either of the equations and solve for x.

$x = 2y$

$x = 2 \cdot 20$ (Substituting)

$x = 40$

If Ann is 40 and her son 20, she is now twice as old as her son. Ten years ago when Ann was 30 and her son 10, Ann was three times as old as her son. The values check.

Now, Ann is 40 and her son is 20.

21. We make a table to organize the information. We let x represent John's age now and y represent Sue's age now.

	Age now	Age four years ago
John	x	x − 4
Sue	y	y − 4

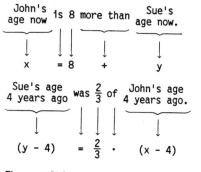

The resulting system is

$x = 8 + y$

$y - 4 = \frac{2}{3}(x - 4)$

We substitute $8 + y$ for x in the second equation and solve for y.

$y - 4 = \frac{2}{3}(x - 4)$

$y - 4 = \frac{2}{3}(8 + y - 4)$ (Substituting)

$y - 4 = \frac{2}{3}(4 + y)$

$y - \frac{12}{3} = \frac{8}{3} + \frac{2}{3}y$

$\frac{1}{3}y = \frac{20}{3}$

$y = 20$

Next we substitute 20 for y in one of the original equations and solve for x.

$x = 8 + y$

$x = 8 + 20$ (Substituting)

$x = 28$

John, who is 28, is 8 years older than his sister Sue, who is 20. Four years ago, John was 24 and Sue 16, and 16 is $\frac{2}{3}$ of 24. The numbers check.

Now John is 28 years old, and Sue is 20 years old.

23. We first make a drawing.

We let ℓ represent the length and w the width. The formula for perimeter is P = 2ℓ + 2w.

The perimeter is 86 in.

$$2ℓ + 2w = 86$$

The length is 19 in. greater than the width.

$$ℓ = 19 + w$$

The resulting system is

$$2ℓ + 2w = 86$$
$$ℓ = 19 + w$$

We use the substitution method.

We substitute 19 + w for ℓ in the first equation and solve for w.

$$2ℓ + 2w = 86$$
or $ℓ + w = 43$ (Multiplying by $\frac{1}{2}$)
$19 + w + w = 43$ (Substituting)
$2w + 19 = 43$
$2w = 24$
$w = 12$

Next we substitute 12 for w in one of the original equations and solve for ℓ.

$$ℓ = 19 + w$$
$ℓ = 19 + 12$ (Substituting)
$ℓ = 31$

The perimeter is 2·31 + 2·12, or 86. The length is 19 more than the width: 31 = 19 + 12. The values check.

The length is 31 in. and the width is 12 in.

25. List the information in a table.

Pens	Cost per pen	Number sold	Money taken in
$8.50 kind	$8.50	x	$8.50x
$9.75 kind	$9.75	y	$9.75y
	Total	45	$398.75

25. (continued)

We let x represent the number of $8.50 pens sold and y represent the number of $9.75 pens sold.

The total number of pens sold was 45, so
$$x + y = 45$$

The total amount received was $398.75, so
$$8.50x + 9.75y = 398.75$$
or $850x + 975y = 39,875$ (Multiplying by 100)

The resulting system of equations is
$$x + y = 45$$
$$850x + 975y = 39,875$$

We use the addition method.

We multiply the first equation by -850 and then add.

$-850x - 850y = -38,250$ (Multiplying by -850)
$\underline{850x + 975y = 39,875}$
$125y = 1625$ (Adding)
$y = 13$

Next we substitute 13 for y in one of the original equations and solve for x.

$$x + y = 45$$
$x + 13 = 45$ (Substituting)
$x = 32$

The total number of pens sold was 32 + 13, or 45. The total receipts were 8.50(32) + 9.75(13), or 272 + 126.75, or $398.75. The values check.

Thus, 32 of the $8.50 pens and 13 of the $9.75 pens were sold.

27. It is helpful to organize the information in a table.

	Principal	Rate	Time	Interest
1st investment	x	6%	1 yr	6%x
2nd investment	y	5%	1 yr	5%y
Total	$1150			$65.75

We let x represent one investment and y the other investment.

The investments total $1150. This gives us one equation.
$$x + y = 1150$$

The amounts of interest from the investments are 6%x and 5%y. They total $65.75. This gives us a second equation.

$$6\%x + 5\%y = 65.75$$
or $0.06x + 0.05y = 65.75$
or $6x + 5y = 6575$

27. (continued)

The resulting system is

x + y = 1150

6x + 5y = 6575

We multiply the first equation by -5 and then add.

-5x - 5y = -5750   (Multiplying by -5)

6x + 5y = 6575

x   =   825   (Adding)

We substitute 825 for x in one of the original equations and solve for y.

x + y = 1150

825 + y = 1150   (Substituting)

y = 325

The sum of the investments is 825 + 325, or $1150. The amounts of interest earned are 6% of 825, or $49.50, and 5% of 325, or $16.25. The total interest earned is 49.50 + 16.25, or $65.75. The values check.

Thus, $825 was invested at 6% and $325 was invested at 5%.

29. We first make a drawing.

16 liters - x liters + x liters = 16 liters

We let x represent the number of liters which should be drained and replaced. The original amount of antifreeze is 30%·16. The amount of antifreeze drained is 30%·x. The amount of antifreeze added is 100%·x, or x. The resulting amount of antifreeze is 50%·16.

From the drawing we get

30%(16) - 30%x + x = 50%(16)

0.3(16) - 0.3x + x = 0.5(16)

4.8 + 0.7x = 8

0.7x = 3.2

$x = \frac{3.2}{0.7}$

$x = \frac{32}{7}$, or $4\frac{4}{7}$

We check:

$30\%(16) - 30\%(\frac{32}{7}) + \frac{32}{7} = 4.8 + 0.7(\frac{32}{7}) =$
$4.8 + 3.2 = 8; 50\%(16) = 8.$ The value checks.

Thus $4\frac{4}{7}$ L should be drained and replaced.

31. Let x represent the number of years Bert Ng has taught and y represent the number of years Sally Ng has taught. Then two years ago they had taught x - 2 and y - 2 years respectively. We translate to a system of equations.

They have taught a total of 46 years.

x + y = 46

Two years ago, Bert Ng had taught 2.5 times as many years as Sally.

x - 2 = 2.5(y - 2)

or   x - 2 = 2.5y - 5

or x - 2.5y = -3

We solve the resulting system.

x + y = 46

x - 2.5y = -3

We multiply the second equation by -1 and then add.

x +   y = 46

-x + 2.5y = 3   (Multiplying by -1)

3.5y = 49   (Adding)

$y = \frac{49}{3.5}$

y = 14

We substitute 14 for y in either of the original equations and solve for x.

x + y = 46

x + 14 = 46

x = 32

The total number of years is 32 + 14, or 46. The number 32 is 2.5 × 14. The values check.

Bert Ng has taught 32 years, and Sally Ng has taught 14 years.

33. Two angles are supplementary if the sum of their measures is 180°. We let x and y represent the angles.

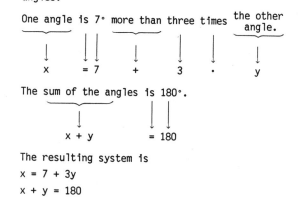

The resulting system is

x = 7 + 3y

x + y = 180

33. (continued)

We substitute 7 + 3y for x in the second equation and solve for y.

$$x + y = 180$$
$$7 + 3y + y = 180 \qquad \text{(Substituting)}$$
$$4y + 7 = 180$$
$$4y = 173$$
$$y = \frac{173}{4}, \text{ or } 43\frac{1}{4}$$

Next we substitute $\frac{173}{4}$ for y in one of the original equations and solve for x.

$$x = 7 + 3y$$
$$x = 7 + 3 \cdot \frac{173}{4} \qquad \text{(Substituting)}$$
$$x = \frac{28}{4} + \frac{519}{4}$$
$$x = \frac{547}{4}, \text{ or } 136\frac{3}{4}$$

The measure of $136\frac{3}{4}°$ is 7° more than three times the measure of $43\frac{1}{4}°$.

$$\frac{547}{4} = 7 + 3 \cdot \frac{173}{4} = \frac{28}{4} + \frac{519}{4} = \frac{547}{4}$$

The sum of the two angles is $136\frac{3}{4}° + 43\frac{1}{4}°$, or 180°. The values check.

The larger of the two angles is $136\frac{3}{4}°$.

35.
Let x represent the numerator of the fraction and y the denominator. We translate to a system of equations.

The numerator is 12 more than the denominator.

$$x = y + 12$$

The sum of the numerator and the denominator is 5 more than three times the denominator.

$$x + y = 5 + 3y, \text{ or } x - 2y = 5$$

We substitute y + 12 for x in the second equation and solve for y.

$$x - 2y = 5$$
$$y + 12 - 2y = 5 \qquad \text{(Substituting)}$$
$$12 - y = 5$$
$$-y = -7$$
$$y = 7$$

We substitute 7 for y in one of the equations and solve for x.

$$x = y + 12$$
$$x = 7 + 12 \qquad \text{(Substituting)}$$
$$x = 19$$

35. (continued)

If x = 19 and y = 7, the fraction is $\frac{19}{7}$. The The numerator is 12 more than the denominator. The sum of the numerator and the denominator, 19 + 7, or 26, is 5 more than three times the denominator: $26 = 5 + 3\cdot7$. The values check.

The fraction is $\frac{19}{7}$. Thus, the reciprocal of the fraction is $\frac{7}{19}$.

Exercise Set 3.4

1. We replace x by 1, y by -2 and z by 3.

$$\begin{array}{c|c} x + y + z = 2 & \\ 1 + (-2) + 3 & 2 \\ 2 & \end{array} \qquad \begin{array}{c|c} x - 2y - z = 2 & \\ 1 - 2(-2) - 3 & 2 \\ 1 + 4 - 3 & \\ 2 & \end{array}$$

$$\begin{array}{c|c} 3x + 2y + z = 2 & \\ 3\cdot1 + 2(-2) + 3 & 2 \\ 3 - 4 + 3 & \\ 2 & \end{array}$$

Since (1,-2,3) is a solution of each equation, it is a solution of the system.

3.
$$x + y + z = 6 \qquad (1)$$
$$2x - y + 3z = 9 \qquad (2)$$
$$-x + 2y + 2z = 9 \qquad (3)$$

We add equations (1) and (2) to eliminate y.

$$\begin{array}{ll} x + y + z = 6 & (1) \\ \underline{2x - y + 3z = 9} & (2) \\ 3x + 4z = 15 & (4) \quad \text{(Adding)} \end{array}$$

We multiply equation (2) by 2 and add to equation (3) to eliminate y.

$$\begin{array}{ll} 4x - 2y + 6z = 18 & \text{[Multiplying equation (2) by 2]} \\ \underline{-x + 2y + 2z = 9} & (3) \\ 3x + 8z = 27 & (5) \quad \text{(Adding)} \end{array}$$

We solve the resulting system of equations, (4) and (5), for x and z.

$$3x + 4z = 15 \qquad (4)$$
$$3x + 8z = 27 \qquad (5)$$

$$\begin{array}{ll} -3x - 4z = -15 & \text{[Multiplying equation (4) by -1]} \\ \underline{3x + 8z = 27} & (5) \\ 4z = 12 & \text{(Adding)} \\ z = 3 \end{array}$$

3. (continued)

Substitute 3 for z in either equation (4) or equation (5) and solve for x.

$$3x + 4z = 15 \qquad (4)$$
$$3x + 4 \cdot 3 = 15 \qquad \text{(Substituting)}$$
$$3x + 12 = 15$$
$$3x = 3$$
$$x = 1$$

We now substitute 1 for x and 3 for z in one of the original three equations and solve for y.

$$x + y + z = 6 \qquad (1)$$
$$1 + y + 3 = 6 \qquad \text{(Substituting)}$$
$$y + 4 = 6$$
$$y = 2$$

We obtain (1,2,3). This checks, so it is the solution.

5.
$$2x - y - 3z = -1 \qquad (1)$$
$$2x - y + z = -9 \qquad (2)$$
$$x + 2y - 4z = 17 \qquad (3)$$

We multiply equation (1) by 2 and add to equation (3) to eliminate y.

$$4x - 2y - 6z = -2 \qquad \text{[Multiplying equation (1) by 2]}$$
$$\underline{x + 2y - 4z = 17} \qquad (3)$$
$$5x \qquad - 10z = 15 \qquad (4) \quad \text{(Adding)}$$

or

$$x - 2y = 3$$

We multiply equation (2) by 2 and add to equation (3) to eliminate y.

$$4x - 2y + 2z = -18 \qquad \text{[Multiplying equation (2) by 2]}$$
$$\underline{x + 2y - 4z = 17} \qquad (3)$$
$$5x \qquad - 2z = -1 \qquad (5) \quad \text{(Adding)}$$

We solve the resulting system of equations, (4) and (5), for x and z.

$$x - 2z = 3 \qquad (4)$$
$$5x - 2z = -1 \qquad (5)$$

$$-x + 2z = -3 \qquad \text{[Multiplying equation (4) by -1]}$$
$$\underline{5x - 2z = -1} \qquad (5)$$
$$4x \qquad = -4 \qquad \text{(Adding)}$$
$$x = -1$$

Substitute -1 for x in either equation (4) or equation (5) and solve for z.

$$x - 2z = 3 \qquad (4)$$
$$-1 - 2z = 3 \qquad \text{(Substituting)}$$
$$-2z = 4$$
$$z = -2$$

5. (continued)

We now substitute -1 for x and -2 for z in one of the original three equations and solve for y.

$$x + 2y - 4z = 17 \qquad (3)$$
$$-1 + 2y - 4(-2) = 17 \qquad \text{(Substituting)}$$
$$2y + 7 = 17$$
$$2y = 10$$
$$y = 5$$

We obtain (-1,5,-2). This checks, so it is the solution.

7.
$$2x - 3y + z = 5 \qquad (1)$$
$$x + 3y + 8z = 22 \qquad (2)$$
$$3x - y + 2z = 12 \qquad (3)$$

We add equations (1) and (2) to eliminate y.

$$2x - 3y + z = 5 \qquad (1)$$
$$\underline{x + 3y + 8z = 22} \qquad (2)$$
$$3x \qquad + 9z = 27 \qquad (4) \quad \text{(Adding)}$$

or

$$x + 3z = 9$$

We multiply equation (3) by 3 and add to equation (2) to eliminate y.

$$x + 3y + 8z = 22 \qquad (2)$$
$$\underline{9x - 3y + 6z = 36} \qquad \text{[Multiplying equation (3) by 3]}$$
$$10x \qquad + 14z = 58 \qquad (5) \quad \text{(Adding)}$$

or

$$5x + 7z = 29$$

We solve the resulting system of equations, (4) and (5), for x and z.

$$x + 3x = 9 \qquad (4)$$
$$5x + 7z = 29 \qquad (5)$$

$$-5x - 15z = -45 \qquad \text{[Multiplying equation (4) by -5]}$$
$$\underline{5x + 7z = 29} \qquad (5)$$
$$-8z = -16 \qquad \text{(Adding)}$$
$$z = 2$$

Substitute 2 for z in either equation (4) or equation (5) and solve for x.

$$x + 3z = 9 \qquad (4)$$
$$x + 3 \cdot 2 = 9 \qquad \text{(Substituting)}$$
$$x + 6 = 9$$
$$x = 3$$

We now substitute 3 for x and 2 for z in one of the original three equations and solve for y.

$$3x - y + 2z = 12 \qquad (3)$$
$$3 \cdot 3 - y + 2 \cdot 2 = 12 \qquad \text{(Substituting)}$$
$$9 - y + 4 = 12$$
$$13 - y = 12$$
$$-y = -1$$
$$y = 1$$

We obtain (3,1,2). This checks, so it is the solution.

<u>9.</u> $3a - 2b + 7c = 13$ (1)
      $a + 8b - 6c = -47$ (2)
      $7a - 9b - 9c = -3$ (3)

We multiply equation (2) by -3 and add to equation (1) to eliminate a.

$3a - 2b + 7c = 13$ (1)

<u>$-3a - 24b + 18c = 141$</u>   [Multiplying equation (2) by -3]

$-26b + 25c = 154$ (4) (Adding)

We multiply equation (2) by -7 and add to equation (3) to eliminate a.

$-7a - 56b + 42c = 329$ [Multiplying equation (2) by -7]

<u>$7a - 9b - 9c = -3$</u>   (3)

$-65b + 33c = 326$ (5) (Adding)

We solve the resulting system of equations, (4) and (5), for b and c.

$-26b + 25c = 154$ (4)
$-65b + 33c = 326$ (5)

$130b - 125c = -770$ [Multiplying equation (4) by -5]

<u>$-130b + 66c = 652$</u>   [Multiplying equation (5) by 2]

$-59c = -118$ (Adding)

$c = 2$

Substitute 2 for c in either equation (4) or equation (5) and solve for b.

$-26b + 25c = 154$ (4)
$-26b + 25 \cdot 2 = 154$ (Substituting)
$-26b + 50 = 154$
$-26b = 104$
$b = -4$

We now substitute -4 for b and 2 for c in one of the original three equations and solve for a.

$a + 8b - 6c = -47$ (2)
$a + 8(-4) - 6(2) = -47$ (Substituting)
$a - 32 - 12 = -47$
$a - 44 = -47$
$a = -3$

We obtain (-3,-4,2). This checks, so it is the solution.

<u>11.</u> $2x + 3y + z = 17$ (1)
      $x - 3y + 2z = -8$ (2)
      $5x - 2y + 3z = 5$ (3)

We multiply equation (1) by -2 and add to equation (2) to eliminate z.

$-4x - 6y - 2z = -34$ [Multiplying equation (1) by -2]

<u>$x - 3y + 2z = -8$</u>   (2)

$-3x - 9y = -42$ (4) (Adding)

or

$x + 3y = 14$

We multiply equation (1) by -3 and add to equation (3) to eliminate z.

$-6x - 9y - 3z = -51$ [Multiplying equation (1) by -3]

<u>$5x - 2y + 3z = 5$</u>   (3)

$-x - 11y = -46$ (5) (Adding)

or

$x + 11y = 46$

We solve the resulting system of equations, (4) and (5), for x and y.

$x + 3y = 14$ (4)
$x + 11y = 46$ (5)

$-x - 3y = -14$ [Multiplying equation (4) by -1]

<u>$x + 11y = 46$</u>   (5)

$8y = 32$ (Adding)

$y = 4$

Substitute 4 for y in either equation (4) or equation (5) and solve for x.

$x + 3y = 14$ (4)
$x + 3 \cdot 4 = 14$ (Substituting)
$x + 12 = 14$
$x = 2$

We now substitute 2 for x and 4 for y in one of the original three equations and solve for z.

$2x + 3y + z = 17$ (1)
$2 \cdot 2 + 3 \cdot 4 + z = 17$ (Substituting)
$4 + 12 + z = 17$
$16 + z = 17$
$z = 1$

We obtain (2,4,1). This checks, so it is the solution.

13. $2x + y + z = -2$ (1)
    $2x - y + 3z = 6$ (2)
    $3x - 5y + 4z = 7$ (3)

We add equations (1) and (2) to eliminate y.

$2x + y + z = -2$ (1)
$\underline{2x - y + 3z = 6}$ (2)
$4x \quad\quad + 4z = 4$ (4) (Adding)

or

$x + z = 1$

We multiply equation (1) by 5 and add to equation (3) to eliminate y.

$10x + 5y + 5z = -10$ [Multiplying equation (1) by 5]

$\underline{3x - 5y + 4z = 7}$ (3)
$13x \quad\quad + 9z = -3$ (5) (Adding)

We solve the resulting system of equations, (4) and (5), for x and z.

$x + z = 1$ (4)
$13x + 9z = -3$ (5)

$-9x - 9z = -9$ [Multiplying equation (4) by -9]
$\underline{13x + 9z = -3}$ (5)
$4x \quad\quad = -12$ (Adding)
$x = -3$

Substitute -3 for x in either equation (4) or equation (5) and solve for z.

$x + z = 1$ (4)
$-3 + z = 1$ (Substituting)
$z = 4$

We now substitute -3 for x and 4 for z in one of the three original equations and solve for y.

$2x + y + z = -2$ (1)
$2(-3) + y + 4 = -2$ (Substituting)
$-6 + y + 4 = -2$
$y - 2 = -2$
$y = 0$

We obtain (-3,0,4). This checks, so it is the solution.

15. $x + y + z = 57$ (1)
    $-2x + y \quad\quad = 3$ (2)
    $x \quad\quad - z = 6$ (3)

We add equations (1) and (3) to eliminate z.

$x + y + z = 57$ (1)
$\underline{x \quad\quad - z = 6}$ (3)
$2x + y \quad\quad = 63$ (4) (Adding)

We now solve the resulting system of equations, (2) and (4), for x and y.

$-2x + y = 3$ (2)
$\underline{2x + y = 63}$ (4)
$2y = 66$ (Adding)
$y = 33$

Substitute 33 for y in either equation (2) or equation (4) and solve for x.

$2x + y = 63$ (4)
$2x + 33 = 63$ (Substituting)
$2x = 30$
$x = 15$

We now substitute 15 for x in equation (3) and solve for z.

$x - z = 6$ (3)
$15 - z = 6$ (Substituting)
$-z = -9$
$z = 9$

We obtain (15,33,9). This checks, so it is the solution.

17. $2a - 3b \quad\quad = 2$ (1)
    $7a \quad\quad + 4c = \frac{3}{4}$ (2)
    $-3b + 2c = 1$ (3)

We multiply equation (1) by -1 and add to equation (3) to eliminate b.

$-2a + 3b \quad\quad = -2$ [Multiplying equation (1) by -1]

$\underline{-3b + 2c = 1}$ (3)
$-2a \quad\quad + 2c = -1$ (4) (Adding)

We now solve the resulting system of equations, (2) and (4), for a and c.

$7a + 4c = \frac{3}{4}$ (2)
$-2a + 2c = -1$ (4)

$7a + 4c = \frac{3}{4}$ (2)

$\underline{4a - 4c = 2}$ [Multiplying equation (4) by -2]
$11a \quad\quad = \frac{11}{4}$ (Adding)

$a = \frac{1}{4}$

17. (continued)

Substitute $\frac{1}{4}$ for a in either equation (2) or equation (4) and solve for c.

$$-2a + 2c = -1 \qquad (4)$$
$$-2\left(\frac{1}{4}\right) + 2c = -1 \qquad \text{(Substituting)}$$
$$-\frac{1}{2} + 2c = -\frac{2}{2}$$
$$2c = -\frac{1}{2}$$
$$c = -\frac{1}{4}$$

We now substitute $\frac{1}{4}$ for a in equation (1) and solve for b.

$$2a - 3b = 2 \qquad (1)$$
$$2 \cdot \frac{1}{4} - 3b = 2 \qquad \text{(Substituting)}$$
$$\frac{1}{2} - 3b = \frac{4}{2}$$
$$-3b = \frac{3}{2}$$
$$b = -\frac{1}{2}$$

We obtain $\left(\frac{1}{4}, -\frac{1}{2}, -\frac{1}{4}\right)$. This checks, so it is the solution.

19.
$$x + y + z = 180 \qquad (1)$$
$$y = 2 + 3x \qquad (2)$$
$$z = 80 + x \qquad (3)$$

Substitute $2 + 3x$ for y and $80 + x$ for z in equation (1) and solve for x.

$$x + y + z = 180 \qquad (1)$$
$$x + 2 + 3x + 80 + x = 180 \qquad \text{(Substituting)}$$
$$5x + 82 = 180$$
$$5x = 98$$
$$x = \frac{98}{5}$$

Substitute $\frac{98}{5}$ for x in equation (2) and solve for y.

$$y = 2 + 3x \qquad (2)$$
$$y = 2 + 3 \cdot \frac{98}{5} \qquad \text{(Substituting)}$$
$$y = \frac{10}{5} + \frac{294}{5}$$
$$y = \frac{304}{5}$$

19. (continued)

Substitute $\frac{98}{5}$ for x in equation (3) and solve for z.

$$z = 80 + x \qquad (3)$$
$$z = 80 + \frac{98}{5}$$
$$z = \frac{400}{5} + \frac{98}{5}$$
$$z = \frac{498}{5}$$

We obtain $\left(\frac{98}{5}, \frac{304}{5}, \frac{498}{5}\right)$. This checks, so it is the solution.

21.
$$F = \frac{1}{2}t(c - d)$$
$$2F = t(c - d)$$
$$\frac{2F}{t} = c - d$$
$$\frac{2F}{t} + d = c$$
$$\text{or} \quad c = \frac{2F + dt}{t}$$

23.
$$w - 2x + y - 2z = -7 \qquad (1)$$
$$4w + x + 2y - z = -1 \qquad (2)$$
$$2w + 4x + y - 2z = 5 \qquad (3)$$
$$w + x - 2y - z = 3 \qquad (4)$$

Add equations (2) and (4) to eliminate y.

$$4w + x + 2y - z = -1 \qquad (2)$$
$$\underline{w + x - 2y - z = 3} \qquad (4)$$
$$5w + 2x \qquad\quad - 2z = 2 \qquad (5) \text{ (Adding)}$$

Multiply equation (1) by 2 and add to equation (4) to eliminate y.

$$2w - 4x + 2y - 4z = -14 \qquad \text{[Multiplying equation (1) by 2]}$$
$$\underline{w + x - 2y - z = 3} \qquad (4)$$
$$3w - 3x \qquad\quad - 5z = -11 \qquad (6) \text{ (Adding)}$$

Multiply equation (3) by 2 and add to equation (4) to eliminate y.

$$4w + 8x + 2y - 4z = 10 \qquad \text{[Multiplying equation (3) by 2]}$$
$$\underline{w + x - 2y - z = 3} \qquad (4)$$
$$5w + 9x \qquad\quad - 5z = 13 \qquad (7) \text{ (Adding)}$$

Solve the resulting system.

$$5w + 2x - 2z = 2 \qquad (5)$$
$$3w - 3x - 5z = -11 \qquad (6)$$
$$5w + 9x - 5z = 13 \qquad (7)$$

23. (continued)

Multiply equation (6) by -1 and add to equation (7) to eliminate z.

$-3w + 3x + 5z = 11$ [Multiplying equation (6) by -1]

$\underline{5w + 9x - 5z = 13}$ (7)

$2w + 12x \quad\quad = 24$ (8) (Adding)

or

$w + 6x = 12$

Multiply equation (5) by 5 and equation (6) by -2 and then add to eliminate z.

$25w + 10x - 10z = 10$ [Multiplying equation (5) by 5]

$\underline{-6w + 6x + 10z = 22}$ [Multiplying equation (6) by -2]

$19w + 16x \quad\quad = 32$ (9) (Adding)

Solve the resulting system for w and x.

$w + 6x = 12$ (8)

$19w + 16x = 32$ (9)

Multiply equation (8) by -19 and add to equation (9) to eliminate w and solve for x.

$-19w - 114x = -228$ [Multiplying equation (8) by -19]

$\underline{19w + 16x = 32}$ (9)

$-98x = -196$ (Adding)

$x = 2$

Substitute 2 for x in either equation (8) or equation (9) and solve for w.

$w + 6x = 12$ (8)

$w + 6 \cdot 2 = 12$ (Substituting)

$w + 12 = 12$

$w = 0$

Substitute 0 for w and 2 for x in either equation (5), equation (6), or equation (7), and solve for z.

$5w + 2x - 2z = 2$ (5)

$5 \cdot 0 + 2 \cdot 2 - 2z = 2$ (Substituting)

$4 - 2z = 2$

$-2z = -2$

$z = 1$

Substitute 0 for w, 2 for x, and 1 for z in any one of the original four equtions and solve for y.

$w - 2x + y - 2z = -7$ (1)

$0 - 2 \cdot 2 + y - 2 \cdot 1 = -7$ (Substituting)

$-4 + y - 2 = -7$

$y - 6 = -7$

$y = -1$

We obtain $(w,x,y,z) = (0,2,-1,1)$. This checks, so it is the solution.

1. We let x represent the first number, y the second number, and z the third number.

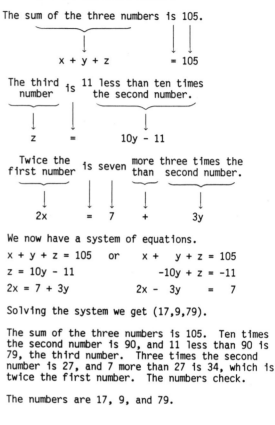

The sum of the three numbers is 105.

$$x + y + z = 105$$

The third number is 11 less than ten times the second number.

$$z = 10y - 11$$

Twice the first number is seven more than three times the second number.

$$2x = 7 + 3y$$

We now have a system of equations.

$x + y + z = 105$ or $x + y + z = 105$

$z = 10y - 11$ $-10y + z = -11$

$2x = 7 + 3y$ $2x - 3y \quad = 7$

Solving the system we get (17,9,79).

The sum of the three numbers is 105. Ten times the second number is 90, and 11 less than 90 is 79, the third number. Three times the second number is 27, and 7 more than 27 is 34, which is twice the first number. The numbers check.

The numbers are 17, 9, and 79.

3. We let x represent the first number, y the second number, and z the third number.

The sum of the three numbers is 5.

$$x + y + z = 5$$

The first number minus the second plus the third is 1.

$$x - y + z = 1$$

The first number minus the third is 3 more than the second.

$$x - z = y + 3$$

We now have a system of equations.

$x + y + z = 5$ or $x + y + z = 5$

$x - y + z = 1$ $x - y + z = 1$

$x - z = y + 3$ $x - y - z = 3$

Solving the system we get (4,2,-1).

3. (continued)

The sum of the numbers is 5. The first minus the second plus the third is 4 - 2 + (-1), or 1. The first minus the third is 5, which is three more than the second. The numbers check.

The numbers are 4, 2, and -1.

5. We first make a drawing.

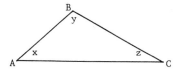

We let x, y, and z represent the measures of angles A, B, and C, respectively. The measures of the angles of a triangle add up to 180°.

The sum of the measures is 180°.

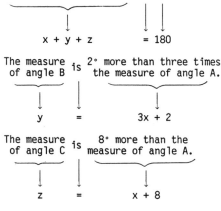

$x + y + z = 180$

The measure of angle B is 2° more than three times the measure of angle A.

$y = 3x + 2$

The measure of angle C is 8° more than the measure of angle A.

$z = x + 8$

We now have a system of equations.

$x + y + z = 180$

$y = 3x + 2$

$z = x + 8$

Solving the system we get (34, 104, 42).

The sum of the numbers is 180, so that checks. Three times the measure of angle A is 3·34, or 102°, and 2° added to 102° is 104°, the measure of angle B. The measure of angle C, 42°, is 8° more than 34°, the measure of angle A. These values check.

Angles A, B, and C measure 34°, 104°, and 42°, respectively.

7. We first make a drawing.

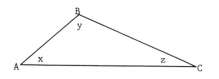

7. (continued)

We let x, y, and z represent the measures of angles A, B, and C, respectively. The measures of the angles of a triangle add up to 180°.

The sum of the measures is 180°.

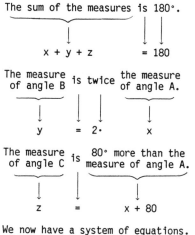

$x + y + z = 180$

The measure of angle B is twice the measure of angle A.

$y = 2 \cdot x$

The measure of angle C is 80° more than the measure of angle A.

$z = x + 80$

We now have a system of equations.

$x + y + z = 180$

$y = 2x$

$z = x + 80$

Solving the system we get (25,50,105).

The sum of the numbers is 180, so that checks. The measure of angle B, 50°, is twice 25°, the measure of angle A. The measure of angle C, 105°, is 80° more than 25°, the measrue of angle A. The values check.

Angles A, B, and C measure 25°, 50°, and 105°, respectively.

9. We let x, y, and z represent the amount Paula took in on Thursday, Friday, and Saturday, respectively.

The sum of the amounts for all three days is $66.

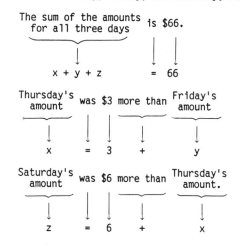

$x + y + z = 66$

Thursday's amount was $3 more than Friday's amount

$x = 3 + y$

Saturday's amount was $6 more than Thursday's amount.

$z = 6 + x$

9. (continued)

We now have a system of equations.

$x + y + z = 66$

$x = 3 + y$

$z = 6 + x$

Solving the system we get (21,18,27).

The sum of the three numbers is 66, so that checks. Thursday's amount, $21, is $3 more than $18, Friday's amount. Saturday's amount, $27, is $6 more than $21, Thursday's amount. The values check.

Paula sold $21 on Thursday, $18 on Friday, and $27 on Saturday.

11.

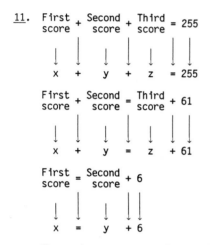

We now have a system of equations.

$x + y + z = 255$

$x + y = z + 61$

$x = y + 6$

Solving the system we get (82,76,97).

The sum of the three scores is 255. The sum of the first two scores, 82 + 76, or 158, is 61 more than 97, the third score. The first score, 82, is 6 more than 76, the second score. The numbers check.

The three scores are 82, 76, and 97.

13. It helps to organize the information in a table.

Machines Working	A	B	C	A + B	B + C	A, B, & C
Weekly Production	x	y	z	3400	4200	5700

We let x, y, and z represent the weekly productions of the individual machines.

From the table, we obtain three equations.

$x + y + z = 5700$ (All three machines working)

$x + y = 3400$ (A and B working)

$ y + z = 4200$ (B and C working)

Solving the system we get (1500,1900,2300).

The sum of the weekly productions of machines A, B, and C is 5700. The sum of the weekly productions of machines A and B is 1500 + 1900, or 3400. The sum of the weekly productions of machines B and C is 1900 + 2300, or 4200. The numbers check.

In a week Machine A can polish 1500 lenses, Machine B can polish 1900 lenses, and Machine C can polish 2300 lenses.

15. It helps to organize the information in a table.

Pumps Working	A	B	C	A + B	A + C	A, B, & C
Gallons Per hour	x	y	z	2200	2400	3700

We let x, y, and z represent the number of gallons per hour which can be pumped by pumps A, B, and C respectively.

From the table, we obtain three equations.

$x + y + z = 3700$ (All three pumps working)

$x + y = 2200$ (A and B working)

$x + z = 2400$ (A and C working)

Solving the system we get (900,1300,1500).

The sum of the gallons per hour pumped by each pump when all three are pumping is 900 + 1300 + 1500, or 3700. The sum of the gallons per hour pumped when only pump A and pump B are pumping is 900 + 1300, or 2200. The sum of the gallons per hour pumped when only pump A and pump C are pumping is 900 + 1500, or 2400. The numbers check.

The pumping capacities of pumps A, B, and C are respectively 900, 1300, and 1500 gallons per hour.

17. We organize the information in a table. We let x, y, and z represent the investments at 8%, 6%, and 9% respectively.

Investment	Amount invested	Interest rate	Interest earned
@ 8%	x	8%	8%x
@ 6%	y	6%	6%y
@ 9%	z	9%	9%z
Total	$80,000		$6300

We translate to a system of equations.

The total amount invested was $80,000.

$x + y + z = 80{,}000$

The total interest earned was $6300.

$$8\%x + 6\%y + 9\%z = 6300$$
$$0.08x + 0.06y + 0.09z = 6300$$

or $\quad\quad 8x + 6y + 9z = 630{,}000$

The interest from the first investment was four times the interest from the second.

$$8\%x = 4(6\%y)$$
$$0.08x = 4(0.06y)$$
$$0.08x = 0.24y$$
$$8x = 24y$$

or $\;x = 3y$

We now have a system of equations.

$x + y + z = 80{,}000$

$8x + 6y + 9z = 630{,}000$

$x = 3y$

Solving the system we get (45,000, 15,000, 20,000).

The sum of the three investments is 45,000 + 15,000 + 20,000, or $80,000. The total interest earned from all three investments was 8%(45,000) + 6%(15,000) + 9%(20,000), or 3600 + 900 + 1800, or $6300. The interest from the first investment, $3600, was four times the interest from the second, $3600 = 4·$900. The values check.

The investments are $45,000 at 8%, $15,000 at 6%, and $20,000 at 9%.

19. We know the thousand's digit must be 1. The United States did not exist as a union until the 1700's, and we have not reached the year 2000.

$\underline{1}\ \underline{x}\ \underline{y}\ \underline{z}$

We let x represent the hundred's digit, y the ten's digit, and z the one's digit. Since z is a multiple of 3, we know that z must be 3, 6, or 9. We have the following possibilities:

$\underline{1}\ \underline{x}\ \underline{y}\ \underline{3}$ $\quad\quad$ $\underline{1}\ \underline{x}\ \underline{y}\ \underline{6}$ $\quad\quad$ $\underline{1}\ \underline{x}\ \underline{y}\ \underline{9}$

We also know that z is one more than x.

When z = 3, x = 2.

When z = 6, x = 5.

When z = 9, x = 8.

Now the possibilities are:

$\underline{1}\ \underline{2}\ \underline{y}\ \underline{3}$ $\quad\quad$ $\underline{1}\ \underline{5}\ \underline{y}\ \underline{6}$ $\quad\quad$ $\underline{1}\ \underline{8}\ \underline{y}\ \underline{9}$

Since the sum of the digits must be 24 and y is a multiple of 3 (3, 6, or 9), only $\underline{1}\ \underline{8}\ \underline{y}\ \underline{9}$ is a possibility.

$$1 + 8 + y + 9 = 24$$
$$y = 6$$

Thus, the year is 1869.

Exercise Set 3.6

1. $\begin{vmatrix} 2 & 7 \\ 1 & 5 \end{vmatrix} = 2\cdot5 - 1\cdot7 = 10 - 7 = 3$

3. $\begin{vmatrix} 6 & -9 \\ 2 & 3 \end{vmatrix} = 6\cdot3 - 2\cdot(-9) = 18 + 18 = 36$

5. $\begin{vmatrix} 0 & 2 & 0 \\ 3 & -1 & 1 \\ 1 & -2 & 2 \end{vmatrix}$

$= 0\begin{vmatrix} -1 & 1 \\ -2 & 2 \end{vmatrix} - 3\begin{vmatrix} 2 & 0 \\ -2 & 2 \end{vmatrix} + 1\begin{vmatrix} 2 & 0 \\ -1 & 1 \end{vmatrix}$

$= 0[-1\cdot2 - (-2)\cdot1] - 3[2\cdot2 - (-2)\cdot0] +$
$\quad\quad\quad\quad\quad\quad\quad\quad\quad 1[2\cdot1 - (-1)\cdot0]$

$= 0\cdot0 - 3\cdot4 + 1\cdot2$

$= 0 - 12 + 2$

$= -10$

7. $\begin{vmatrix} -1 & -2 & -3 \\ 3 & 4 & 2 \\ 0 & 1 & 2 \end{vmatrix}$

$= -1\begin{vmatrix} 4 & 2 \\ 1 & 2 \end{vmatrix} - 3\begin{vmatrix} -2 & -3 \\ 1 & 2 \end{vmatrix} + 0\begin{vmatrix} -2 & -3 \\ 4 & 2 \end{vmatrix}$

$= -1[4\cdot2 - 1\cdot2] - 3[-2\cdot2 - 1(-3)] + 0[-2\cdot2 - 4(-3)]$

$= -1\cdot6 - 3\cdot(-1) + 0\cdot8$

$= -6 + 3 + 0$

$= -3$

9. $\begin{vmatrix} 3 & 2 & -2 \\ -2 & 1 & 4 \\ -4 & -3 & 3 \end{vmatrix}$

$= 3\begin{vmatrix} 1 & 4 \\ -3 & 3 \end{vmatrix} - (-2)\begin{vmatrix} 2 & -2 \\ -3 & 3 \end{vmatrix} + (-4)\begin{vmatrix} 2 & -2 \\ 1 & 4 \end{vmatrix}$

$= 3[1\cdot3 - (-3)\cdot4] + 2[2\cdot3 - (-3)(-2)] -$
$\qquad\qquad\qquad 4[2\cdot4 - 1(-2)]$

$= 3\cdot15 + 2\cdot0 - 4\cdot10$

$= 45 + 0 - 40$

$= 5$

11. $3x - 4y = 6$
     $5x + 9y = 10$

We compute D, D_x, and D_y.

$D = \begin{vmatrix} 3 & -4 \\ 5 & 9 \end{vmatrix} = 27 - (-20) = 47$

$D_x = \begin{vmatrix} 6 & -4 \\ 10 & 9 \end{vmatrix} = 54 - (-40) = 94$

$D_y = \begin{vmatrix} 3 & 6 \\ 5 & 10 \end{vmatrix} = 30 - 30 = 0$

Then,

$x = \dfrac{D_x}{D} = \dfrac{94}{47} = 2$

and

$y = \dfrac{D_y}{D} = \dfrac{0}{47} = 0$

The solution is (2,0).

13. $-2x + 4y = 3$
     $3x - 7y = 1$

We compute D, D_x, and D_y.

$D = \begin{vmatrix} -2 & 4 \\ 3 & -7 \end{vmatrix} = 14 - 12 = 2$

$D_x = \begin{vmatrix} 3 & 4 \\ 1 & -7 \end{vmatrix} = -21 - 4 = -25$

$D_y = \begin{vmatrix} -2 & 3 \\ 3 & 1 \end{vmatrix} = -2 - 9 = -11$

Then,

$x = \dfrac{D_x}{D} = \dfrac{-25}{2} = -\dfrac{25}{2}$

and

$y = \dfrac{D_y}{D} = \dfrac{-11}{2} = -\dfrac{11}{2}$

The solution is $(-\dfrac{25}{2}, -\dfrac{11}{2})$.

15. $3x + 2y - z = 4$
     $3x - 2y + z = 5$
     $4x - 5y - z = -1$

We compute D, D_x, D_y, and D_z.

$D = \begin{vmatrix} 3 & 2 & -1 \\ 3 & -2 & 1 \\ 4 & -5 & -1 \end{vmatrix}$

$= 3\begin{vmatrix} -2 & 1 \\ -5 & -1 \end{vmatrix} - 3\begin{vmatrix} 2 & -1 \\ -5 & -1 \end{vmatrix} + 4\begin{vmatrix} 2 & -1 \\ -2 & 1 \end{vmatrix}$

$= 3(7) - 3(-7) + 4(0)$

$= 21 + 21 + 0$

$= 42$

$D_x = \begin{vmatrix} 4 & 2 & -1 \\ 5 & -2 & 1 \\ -1 & -5 & -1 \end{vmatrix}$

$= 4\begin{vmatrix} -2 & 1 \\ -5 & -1 \end{vmatrix} - 5\begin{vmatrix} 2 & -1 \\ -5 & -1 \end{vmatrix} + (-1)\begin{vmatrix} 2 & -1 \\ -2 & 1 \end{vmatrix}$

$= 4(7) - 5(-7) - 1(0)$

$= 28 + 35 - 0$

$= 63$

15. (continued)

$$D_y = \begin{vmatrix} 3 & 4 & -1 \\ 3 & 5 & 1 \\ 4 & -1 & -1 \end{vmatrix}$$

$$= 3\begin{vmatrix} 5 & 1 \\ -1 & -1 \end{vmatrix} - 3\begin{vmatrix} 4 & -1 \\ -1 & -1 \end{vmatrix} + 4\begin{vmatrix} 4 & -1 \\ 5 & 1 \end{vmatrix}$$

$$= 3(-4) - 3(-5) + 4(9)$$

$$= -12 + 15 + 36$$

$$= 39$$

$$D_z = \begin{vmatrix} 3 & 2 & 4 \\ 3 & -2 & 5 \\ 4 & -5 & -1 \end{vmatrix}$$

$$= 3\begin{vmatrix} -2 & 5 \\ -5 & -1 \end{vmatrix} - 3\begin{vmatrix} 2 & 4 \\ -5 & -1 \end{vmatrix} + 4\begin{vmatrix} 2 & 4 \\ -2 & 5 \end{vmatrix}$$

$$= 3(27) - 3(18) + 4(18)$$

$$= 81 - 54 + 72$$

$$= 99$$

Then,

$$x = \frac{D_x}{D} = \frac{63}{42} = \frac{3}{2},$$

$$y = \frac{D_y}{D} = \frac{39}{42} = \frac{13}{14},$$

and

$$z = \frac{D_z}{D} = \frac{99}{42} = \frac{33}{14}$$

The solution is $(\frac{3}{2}, \frac{13}{14}, \frac{33}{14})$.

17. $2x - 3y + 5z = 27$
    $x + 2y - z = -4$
    $5x - y + 4z = 27$

We compute D, D_x, D_y, and D_z.

$$D = \begin{vmatrix} 2 & -3 & 5 \\ 1 & 2 & -1 \\ 5 & -1 & 4 \end{vmatrix}$$

$$= 2\begin{vmatrix} 2 & -1 \\ -1 & 4 \end{vmatrix} - 1\begin{vmatrix} -3 & 5 \\ -1 & 4 \end{vmatrix} + 5\begin{vmatrix} -3 & 5 \\ 2 & -1 \end{vmatrix}$$

$$= 2(7) - 1(-7) + 5(-7)$$

$$= 14 + 7 - 35$$

$$= -14$$

17. (continued)

$$D_x = \begin{vmatrix} 27 & -3 & 5 \\ -4 & 2 & -1 \\ 27 & -1 & 4 \end{vmatrix}$$

$$= 27\begin{vmatrix} 2 & -1 \\ -1 & 4 \end{vmatrix} - (-4)\begin{vmatrix} -3 & 5 \\ -1 & 4 \end{vmatrix} + 27\begin{vmatrix} -3 & 5 \\ 2 & -1 \end{vmatrix}$$

$$= 27(7) + 4(-7) + 27(-7)$$

$$= 189 - 28 - 189$$

$$= -28$$

$$D_y = \begin{vmatrix} 2 & 27 & 5 \\ 1 & -4 & -1 \\ 5 & 27 & 4 \end{vmatrix}$$

$$= 2\begin{vmatrix} -4 & -1 \\ 27 & 4 \end{vmatrix} - 1\begin{vmatrix} 27 & 5 \\ 27 & 4 \end{vmatrix} + 5\begin{vmatrix} 27 & 5 \\ -4 & -1 \end{vmatrix}$$

$$= 2(11) - 1(-27) + 5(-7)$$

$$= 22 + 27 - 35$$

$$= 14$$

$$D_z = \begin{vmatrix} 2 & -3 & 27 \\ 1 & 2 & -4 \\ 5 & -1 & 27 \end{vmatrix}$$

$$= 2\begin{vmatrix} 2 & -4 \\ -1 & 27 \end{vmatrix} - 1\begin{vmatrix} -3 & 27 \\ -1 & 27 \end{vmatrix} + 5\begin{vmatrix} -3 & 27 \\ 2 & -4 \end{vmatrix}$$

$$= 2(50) - 1(-54) + 5(-42)$$

$$= 100 + 54 - 210$$

$$= -56$$

Then,

$$x = \frac{D_x}{D} = \frac{-28}{-14} = 2,$$

$$y = \frac{D_y}{D} = \frac{14}{-14} = -1,$$

and

$$z = \frac{D_z}{D} = \frac{-56}{-14} = 4$$

The solution is $(2,-1,4)$.

19. $r - 2s + 3t = 6$
    $2r - s - t = -3$
    $r + s + t = 6$

We compute D, D_r, D_s, and D_t.

$$D = \begin{vmatrix} 1 & -2 & 3 \\ 2 & -1 & -1 \\ 1 & 1 & 1 \end{vmatrix}$$

$$= 1\begin{vmatrix} -1 & -1 \\ 1 & 1 \end{vmatrix} - 2\begin{vmatrix} -2 & 3 \\ 1 & 1 \end{vmatrix} + 1\begin{vmatrix} -2 & 3 \\ -1 & -1 \end{vmatrix}$$

$$= 1(0) - 2(-5) + 1(5)$$
$$= 0 + 10 + 5$$
$$= 15$$

$$D_r = \begin{vmatrix} 6 & -2 & 3 \\ -3 & -1 & -1 \\ 6 & 1 & 1 \end{vmatrix}$$

$$= 6\begin{vmatrix} -1 & -1 \\ 1 & 1 \end{vmatrix} - (-3)\begin{vmatrix} -2 & 3 \\ 1 & 1 \end{vmatrix} + 6\begin{vmatrix} -2 & 3 \\ -1 & -1 \end{vmatrix}$$

$$= 6(0) + 3(-5) + 6(5)$$
$$= 0 - 15 + 30$$
$$= 15$$

$$D_s = \begin{vmatrix} 1 & 6 & 3 \\ 2 & -3 & -1 \\ 1 & 6 & 1 \end{vmatrix}$$

$$= 1\begin{vmatrix} -3 & -1 \\ 6 & 1 \end{vmatrix} - 2\begin{vmatrix} 6 & 3 \\ 6 & 1 \end{vmatrix} + 1\begin{vmatrix} 6 & 3 \\ -3 & -1 \end{vmatrix}$$

$$= 1(3) - 2(-12) + 1(3)$$
$$= 3 + 24 + 3$$
$$= 30$$

$$D_t = \begin{vmatrix} 1 & -2 & 6 \\ 2 & -1 & -3 \\ 1 & 1 & 6 \end{vmatrix}$$

$$= 1\begin{vmatrix} -1 & -3 \\ 1 & 6 \end{vmatrix} - 2\begin{vmatrix} -2 & 6 \\ 1 & 6 \end{vmatrix} + 1\begin{vmatrix} -2 & 6 \\ -1 & -3 \end{vmatrix}$$

$$= 1(-3) - 2(-18) + 1(12)$$
$$= -3 + 36 + 12$$
$$= 45$$

19. (continued)

Then,

$$r = \frac{D_r}{D} = \frac{15}{15} = 1,$$

$$s = \frac{D_s}{D} = \frac{30}{15} = 2,$$

and

$$t = \frac{D_t}{D} = \frac{45}{15} = 3$$

The solution is $(1,2,3)$.

21. $0.5x - 2.34 + 2.4x = 7.8x - 9$
    $2.9x - 2.34 = 7.8x - 9$
    $6.66 = 4.9x$

$$\frac{6.66}{4.9} = x$$

$$\frac{666}{490} = x$$

$$\frac{333}{245} = x$$

23. We first make a drawing.

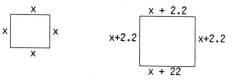

Let x represent the length of a side of the smaller square and $x + 2.2$ the length of a side of the larger square. The perimeter of the smaller square is $4x$. The perimeter of the larger square is $4(x + 2.2)$. The sum of the two perimeters is 32.8 ft. We have an equation.

$4x + 4(x + 2.2) = 32.8$
$4x + 4x + 8.8 = 32.8$
$8x = 24$
$x = 3$

If $x = 3$ ft, then $x + 2.2 = 5.2$ ft. The perimeters are $4 \cdot 3$, or 12 ft, and $4(5.2)$, or 20.8 ft. The sum of the two perimeters is $12 + 20.8$, or 32.8 ft. The length of the wire is 32.8 ft. The values check.

The wire should be cut into two pieces measuring 12 ft and 20.8 ft.

25. $\begin{vmatrix} 2 & x & -1 \\ -1 & 3 & 2 \\ -2 & 1 & 1 \end{vmatrix} = -12$

$2\begin{vmatrix} 3 & 2 \\ 1 & 1 \end{vmatrix} - (-1)\begin{vmatrix} x & -1 \\ 1 & 1 \end{vmatrix} + (-2)\begin{vmatrix} x & -1 \\ 3 & 2 \end{vmatrix} = -12$

$$2(1) + 1(x + 1) - 2(2x + 3) = -12$$
$$2 + x + 1 - 4x - 6 = -12$$
$$-3x - 3 = -12$$
$$-3x = -9$$
$$x = 3$$

27. $\begin{vmatrix} x & y & 1 \\ x_1 & y_1 & 1 \\ x_2 & y_2 & 1 \end{vmatrix} = 0$

is equivalent to

$x\begin{vmatrix} y_1 & 1 \\ y_2 & 1 \end{vmatrix} - x_1\begin{vmatrix} y & 1 \\ y_2 & 1 \end{vmatrix} + x_2\begin{vmatrix} y & 1 \\ y_1 & 1 \end{vmatrix} = 0$

or

$$x(y_1 - y_2) - x_1(y - y_2) + x_2(y - y_1) = 0$$

or

$$xy_1 - xy_2 - x_1y + x_1y_2 + x_2y - x_2y_1 = 0$$

An equation of the line through (x_1, y_1) and (x_2, y_2) is

$$y - y_1 = \frac{y_2 - y_1}{x_2 - x_1}(x - x_1)$$

which is equivalent to

$$(x_2 - x_1)(y - y_1) = (y_2 - y_1)(x - x_1)$$

or

$$x_2y - x_2y_1 - x_1y + x_1y_1 = y_2x - y_2x_1 - y_1x + y_1x_1$$

or

$$x_2y - x_2y_1 - x_1y - xy_2 + x_1y_2 + xy_1 = 0$$

Exercise Set 3.7

1. C = 45x + 600,000   R = 65x

a) P = R - C
       = 65x - (45x + 600,000)
       = 65x - 45x - 600,000
       = 20x - 600,000

b) We set R = C and solve for x.
       R = C
    65x = 45x + 600,000
    20x = 600,000
      x = 30,000

Thus, 30,000 units must be produced and sold in order to break even.

3. C = 10x + 120,000   R = 60x

a) P = R - C
       = 60x - (10x + 120,000)
       = 60x - 10x - 120,000
       = 50x - 120,000

b) We set R = C and solve for x.
       R = C
    60x = 10x + 120,000
    50x = 120,000
      x = 2400

Thus, 2400 units must be produced and sold in order to break even.

5. C = 20x + 10,000   R = 100x

a) P = R - C
       = 100x - (20x + 10,000)
       = 100x - 20x - 10,000
       = 80x - 10,000

b) We set R = C and solve for x.
        R = C
    100x = 20x + 10,000
     80x = 10,000
       x = 125

Thus, 125 units must be produced and sold in order to break even.

7. D = 2000 - 60P   S = 460 + 94P

We set D = S and solve for P.
2000 - 60P = 460 + 94P
      1540 = 154P
        10 = P

The equilibrium price, P_E, is $\underline{\$10}$ per unit.

To find the equilibrium quantity we substitute P_E into either D or S.
D = 2000 - 60P
D = 2000 - 60(10)   (Substituting 10 for P)
  = 2000 - 600
  = 1400

The equilibrium quantity is $\underline{1400}$ units.

The equilibrium point is ($10, 1400).

9. D = 760 - 13P   S = 430 + 2P

We set D = S and solve for P.

$$760 - 13P = 430 + 2P$$
$$330 = 15P$$
$$22 = P$$

The equilibrium price, P_E, is <u>$22</u> per unit.

To find the equilibrium quantity we substitute P_E into either D or S.

S = 430 + 2P

S = 430 + 2(22)   (Substituting 22 for P)

  = 430 + 44

  = 474

The equilibrium quantity is <u>474</u> units.

The equilibrium point is ($22,474).

11. D = 7500 - 25P   S = 6000 + 5P

We set D = S and solve for P.

$$7500 - 25P = 6000 + 5P$$
$$1500 = 30P$$
$$50 = P$$

The equilibrium price, P_E, is <u>$50</u> per unit.

To find the equilibrium quantity we substitute P_E into either D or S.

D = 7500 - 25P

D = 7500 - 25(50)   (Substituting 50 for P)

  = 7500 - 1250

  = 6250

The equilibrium quantity is <u>6250</u> units.

The equilibrium point is ($50,6250).

13. a) C = 40x + 22,500

   b) R = 85x

   c) P = R - C

       = 85x - (40x + 22,500)

       = 85x - 40x - 22,500

       = 45x - 22,500

   d) P = 45(3000) - 22,500

       = 135,000 - 22,500

       = 112,500

The company will realize a profit of $112,500.

   e) We set R = C and solve for x.

      85x = 40x + 22,500

      45x = 22,500

        x = 500

Thus, 500 lamps must be produced and sold to break even.

15. 4a - 8 - (6 - 3a)

  = 4a - 8 - 6 + 3a

  = 7a - 14

17. $\frac{1}{2}$(12x - 8) + $\frac{1}{2}$(26x + 48) - 19

  = 6x - 4 + 13x + 24 - 19

  = 19x + 1

19. [8(x - 3) + 7x] - {8[4(3y - 4) - (9y + 10)] - 42}

  = [8x - 24 + 7x] - {8[12y - 16 - 9y - 10] -42}

  = [15x - 24] - {8[3y - 26] - 42}

  = 15x - 24 - {24y - 208 - 42}

  = 15x - 24 - {24y - 250}

  = 15x - 24 - 24y + 250

  = 15x - 24y + 226

Exercise Set 3.8

1. x + 2y = 6   or   x + 2y = 6

   2x = 8 - 4y   2x + 4y = 8

We attempt to find a solution.

-2x + 4y = -12   (Multiplying by -2)

<u> 2x + 4y = 8</u>

      0 = -4   (Adding)

The last equation says that $0 \cdot x + 0 \cdot y = -4$. There are no numbers x and y for which this is true, so there is no solution. The system is <u>inconsistent</u>.

3. y - x = 4   or   -x + y = 4

   x + 2y = 2   x + 2y = 2

We attempt to find a solution.

-x + y = 4

<u> x + 2y = 2</u>

   3y = 6   (Adding)

    y = 2

We substitute 2 for y and solve for x.

  x + 2y = 2

x + 2(2) = 2   (Substituting)

  x + 4 = 2

     x = -2

The solution is (-2,2). If a system has a solution, it is <u>consistent</u>.

5. x - 3 = y   or   x - y = 3
   2x - 2y = 6   2x - 2y = 6

We attempt to find a solution.

   -2x + 2y = -6   (Multiplying by -2)
   <u>2x - 2y = 6</u>
        0 = 0   (Adding)

The last equation says that $0 \cdot x + 0 \cdot y = 0$. This is true for <u>all</u> numbers x and y, so there is an infinite number of solutions to the system. Since a system is consistent if it has a solution, this system is <u>consistent</u>.

7. x   + z = 0   (1)
   x + y + 2z = 3   (2)
       y + z = 2   (3)

We attempt to find a solution. If we multiply equation (2) by -1 and add it to equation (3) we get -x - z = -1. If we add this equation to equation (1), we get 0 = -1. This last equation says that $0 \cdot x + 0 \cdot y + 0 \cdot z = -1$. There are no numbers x, y, and z for which this is true, so there is no solution. The system is <u>inconsistent</u>.

9. x   + z = 0   (1)
   x + y   = 1   (2)
       y + z = 1   (3)

We attempt to find a solution. We multiply equation (1) by -1 and add it to equation (2).

   -x   - z = 0   [Multiplying equation (1) by -1]
   <u>x + y   = 1</u>   (2)
       y - z = 1   (4) (Adding)

We now solve the resulting system for y and z.

   y + z = 1   (3)
   <u>y - z = 1</u>   (4)
   2y   = 2   (Adding)
    y = 1

We substitute 1 for y in equation (3) and solve for z.

   y + z = 1   (3)
   1 + z = 1   (Substituting)
       z = 0

We substitute 1 for y in equation (2) and solve for x.

   x + y = 1   (2)
   x + 1 = 1   (Substituting)
       x = 0

The solution is (0,1,0). If a system has a solution, it is <u>consistent</u>.

11. See the solution to Exercise 5 above. The last equation says that $0 \cdot x + 0 \cdot y = 0$. This is true for all numbers x and y. The system is <u>dependent</u>.

13. See the solution to Exercise 3 above. We did not obtain equations identical or equivalent, so the system is <u>independent</u>.

15. 2x + 3y = 1
    x + 1.5y = 0.5

We attempt to find a solution. We multiply the second equation by -2.

    2x + 3y = 1
    <u>-2x - 3y = -1</u>   (Multiplying by -2)
        0 = 0   (Adding)

The last equation says that $0 \cdot x + 0 \cdot y = 0$. This is true for all x and y. The system is <u>dependent</u>.

17. See the solution to Exercise 9 above. We did not obtain equations identical or equivalent, so the system is <u>independent</u>.

19. x + y + z = 1   (1)
    -x + 2y + z = 2   (2)
    2x - y   = -1   (3)

We attempt to find a solution. We multiply equation (1) by -1 and add it to equation (2).

    x + y + z = 1   (1)
    -2x + y   = 1   (2)
    2x - y   = -1   (3)

We multiply equation (2) by -1.

    x + y + z = 1   (1)
    2x - y   = -1   (2)
    2x - y   = -1   (3)

The system of three equations is equivalent to a system of two equations. The system is <u>dependent</u>.

21. Let m represent the number of miles beyond the first $\frac{1}{2}$ mile. The cost of each additional $\frac{1}{4}$ mile is 30¢. Thus the cost of each additional mile is 4(30¢), or $1.20. The total cost of the taxi ride is $1 for the first $\frac{1}{2}$ mile and $1.20 × m for the additional miles, or 1 + 1.20m, which is $5.20. We now have an equation.

    1 + 1.20m = 5.20
        1.20m = 4.20
            m = $\frac{4.20}{1.20}$
            m = $\frac{42}{12}$
            m = 3.5

If m = 3.5, the total cost of the trip is 1 + (1.20)3.5, or $5.20. The value checks.

Thus, it is $\frac{1}{2}$ mile + $3\frac{1}{2}$ miles, or 4 miles, from Johnson Street to Elm Street.

23. There is no solution. The sum of any two even
    integers is also even. Thus, the sum cannot
    be 139.

Exercise Set 4.1

1. $x > -4$

   a) Since $4 > -4$ is true, 4 is a solution.
   b) Since $0 > -4$ is true, 0 is a solution.
   c) Since $-4 > -4$ is false, -4 is not a solution.
   d) Since $6 > -4$ is true, 6 is a solution.

3. $x - 2 \geqslant 6$

   a) Since $-4 - 2 \geqslant 6$ (or $-6 \geqslant 6$) is false, -4 is not a solution.
   b) Since $0 - 2 \geqslant 6$ (or $-2 \geqslant 6$) is false, 0 is not a solution.
   c) Since $4 - 2 \geqslant 6$ (or $2 \geqslant 6$) is false, 4 is not a solution.
   d) Since $8 - 2 \geqslant 6$ (or $6 \geqslant 6$) is true, 8 is a solution.

5. $t - 8 > 2t - 3$

   a) Since $0 - 8 > 2 \cdot 0 - 3$ (or $-8 > -3$) is false, 0 is not a solution.
   b) Since $-8 - 8 > 2(-8) - 3$ (or $-16 > -19$) is true, -8 is a solution.
   c) Since $-9 - 8 > 2(-9) - 3$ (or $-17 > -20$) is true, -9 is a solution.
   d) Since $-3 - 8 > 2(-3) - 3$ (or $-11 > -9$) is false, -3 is not a solution.

7. $$x - 7 > 5$$
   $$x - 7 + 7 > 5 + 7 \qquad \text{(Adding 7)}$$
   $$x > 12$$

   The solution set is $\{x | x > 12\}$.

9. $$x - 3 \geqslant -1$$
   $$x - 3 + 3 \geqslant -1 + 3 \qquad \text{(Adding 3)}$$
   $$x \geqslant 2$$

   The solution set is $\{x | x \geqslant 2\}$.

11. $$x - \frac{3}{4} \leqslant \frac{11}{8}$$
    $$x - \frac{3}{4} + \frac{3}{4} \leqslant \frac{11}{8} + \frac{3}{4} \qquad \text{(Adding } \frac{3}{4})$$
    $$x \leqslant \frac{11}{8} + \frac{6}{8}$$
    $$x \leqslant \frac{17}{8}$$

    The solution set is $\{x | x \leqslant \frac{17}{8}\}$.

13. $$5.3 < x + 2.4$$
    $$5.3 - 2.4 < x + 2.4 - 2.4 \qquad \text{(Adding } -2.4)$$
    $$2.9 < x$$

    The solution set is $\{x | x > 2.9\}$.

15. $$3x - 2 \leqslant 2x + 1$$
    $$3x - 2 + 2 \leqslant 2x + 1 + 2 \qquad \text{(Adding 2)}$$
    $$3x \leqslant 2x + 3$$
    $$3x - 2x \leqslant 2x + 3 - 2x \qquad \text{(Adding } -2x)$$
    $$x \leqslant 3$$

    The solution set is $\{x | x \leqslant 3\}$.

17. $$2y - 12 > y - 7$$
    $$2y - 12 + 12 > y - 7 + 12 \qquad \text{(Adding 12)}$$
    $$2y > y + 5$$
    $$2y - y > y + 5 - y \qquad \text{(Adding } -y)$$
    $$y > 5$$

    The solution set is $\{y | y > 5\}$.

19. $$5(r + 7) \geqslant 4r + 5$$
    $$5r + 35 \geqslant 4r + 5$$
    $$5r + 35 - 35 \geqslant 4r + 5 - 35 \qquad \text{(Adding } -35)$$
    $$5r \geqslant 4r - 30$$
    $$5r - 4r \geqslant 4r - 30 - 4r \qquad \text{(Adding } -4r)$$
    $$r \geqslant -30$$

    The solution set is $\{r | r \geqslant -30\}$.

21. $$3x \leqslant 18$$
    $$\frac{1}{3} \cdot 3x \leqslant \frac{1}{3} \cdot 18 \qquad \text{(Multiplying by } \frac{1}{3})$$
    $$x \leqslant 6$$

    The solution set is $\{x | x \leqslant 6\}$.

23. $$-3y > \frac{3}{8}$$
    $$-\frac{1}{3}(-3y) < -\frac{1}{3}(\frac{3}{8}) \qquad \text{(Multiplying by } -\frac{1}{3} \text{ and reversing the inequality symbol)}$$
    $$y < -\frac{1}{8}$$

    The solution set is $\{y | y < -\frac{1}{8}\}$.

25. $$9t < -81$$
    $$\frac{1}{9}(9t) < \frac{1}{9}(-81) \qquad \text{(Multiplying by } \frac{1}{9})$$
    $$t < -9$$

    The solution set is $\{t | t < -9\}$.

27. $$-0.3x < -18$$
    $$\frac{1}{-0.3}(-0.3x) > \frac{1}{-0.3}(-18) \qquad \text{(Multiplying by } \frac{1}{-0.3} \text{ and reversing the inequality symbol)}$$
    $$x > \frac{18}{0.3}$$
    $$x > 60$$

    The solution set is $\{x | x > 60\}$.

29.
$$-8.1 \geqslant -9x$$
$$-\tfrac{1}{9}(-8.1) \leqslant -\tfrac{1}{9}(-9x) \qquad \text{(Multiplying by } -\tfrac{1}{9}$$
$$\text{and reversing the inequality symbol)}$$
$$0.9 \leqslant x$$

The solution set is $\{x \mid x \geqslant 0.9\}$.

31.
$$-\tfrac{3}{4}x \geqslant -\tfrac{5}{8}$$
$$-\tfrac{4}{3}(-\tfrac{3}{4}x) \leqslant -\tfrac{4}{3}(-\tfrac{5}{8}) \qquad \text{(Multiplying by } -\tfrac{4}{3}$$
$$\text{and reversing the inequality symbol)}$$
$$x \leqslant \tfrac{20}{24}$$
$$x \leqslant \tfrac{5}{6}$$

The solution set is $\{x \mid x \leqslant \tfrac{5}{6}\}$.

33.
$$5y + 2y \leqslant -21$$
$$7y \leqslant -21 \qquad \text{(Collecting like terms)}$$
$$\tfrac{1}{7} \cdot 7y \leqslant \tfrac{1}{7}(-21) \qquad \text{(Multiplying by } \tfrac{1}{7})$$
$$y \leqslant 3$$

The solution set is $\{y \mid y \leqslant -3\}$.

35.
$$-4 + 5 \geqslant -\tfrac{1}{3}x$$
$$1 \geqslant -\tfrac{1}{3}x \qquad \text{(Collecting like terms)}$$
$$-3 \cdot 1 \leqslant -3(-\tfrac{1}{3}x) \quad \text{(Multiplying by } -3 \text{ and}$$
$$\text{reversing the inequality symbol)}$$
$$-3 \leqslant x$$

The solution set is $\{x \mid x \geqslant -3\}$.

37. Graph: $5y - 10 = 2x$

x	y	
0	2	(y-intercept)
-5	0	(x-intercept)
5	4	

$5y - 10 = 2x$

39. $|-16| = 16$

41.
$$x + 9,479,756 \leqslant -8,579,243$$
$$x + 9,479,756 - 9,479,756 \leqslant -8,579,243 - 9,479,756$$
$$\text{(Adding } -9,479,756)$$
$$x \leqslant -18,058,999$$

The solution set is $\{x \mid x \leqslant -18,058,999\}$.

43. For any real numbers a, b, c, and d, if a < b and c < d, then a - c < b - d.

This statement is false.

Let a = 10, b = 12, c = 3, and d = 7.

If 10 < 12 and 3 < 7, then $10 - 3 \not< 12 - 7$.

Exercise Set 4.2

1.
$$2x - 7 \geqslant 5x - 5$$
$$-2x + 2x - 7 \geqslant -2x + 5x - 5 \qquad \text{(Adding } -2x)$$
$$-7 \geqslant 3x - 5$$
$$-7 + 5 \geqslant 3x - 5 + 5 \qquad \text{(Adding 5)}$$
$$-2 \geqslant 3x$$
$$\tfrac{1}{3}(-2) \geqslant \tfrac{1}{3} \cdot 3x \qquad \text{(Multiplying by } \tfrac{1}{3})$$
$$-\tfrac{2}{3} \geqslant x$$

The solution set is $\{x \mid x \leqslant -\tfrac{2}{3}\}$.

3.
$$2x + 7 < 19$$
$$2x + 7 - 7 < 19 - 7 \qquad \text{(Adding } -7)$$
$$2x < 12$$
$$\tfrac{1}{2} \cdot 2x < \tfrac{1}{2} \cdot 12 \qquad \text{(Multiplying by } \tfrac{1}{2})$$
$$x < 6$$

The solution set is $\{x \mid x < 6\}$.

5.
$$8x - 9 < 3x - 11$$
$$8x - 9 + 9 < 3x - 11 + 9 \qquad \text{(Adding 9)}$$
$$8x < 3x - 2$$
$$-3x + 8x < -3x + 3x - 2 \qquad \text{(Adding } -3x)$$
$$5x < -2$$
$$\tfrac{1}{5} \cdot 5x < \tfrac{1}{5}(-2) \qquad \text{(Multiplying by } \tfrac{1}{5})$$
$$x < -\tfrac{2}{5}$$

The solution set is $\{x \mid x < -\tfrac{2}{5}\}$.

7.
$$0.9x > 1.8 - 0.1x$$
$$0.9x + 0.1x > 1.8 - 0.1x + 0.1x \qquad \text{(Adding 0.1x)}$$
$$x > 1.8$$

The solution set is $\{x \mid x > 1.8\}$.

9.
$$0.4x + 5 \le 1.2x - 4$$
$$0.4x + 5 + 4 \le 1.2x - 4 + 4 \qquad \text{(Adding 4)}$$
$$0.4x + 9 \le 1.2x$$
$$-0.4x + 0.4x + 9 \le -0.4x + 1.2x \qquad \text{(Adding -0.4x)}$$
$$9 \le 0.8x$$
$$\frac{1}{0.8}(9) \le \frac{1}{0.8}(0.8x) \qquad \text{(Multiplying by } \frac{1}{0.8})$$
$$\frac{90}{8} \le x$$
$$\frac{45}{4} \le x$$

The solution set is $\{x \mid x \ge \frac{45}{4}\}$.

11.
$$3x - \frac{1}{8} \le \frac{3}{8} + 2x$$
$$3x - \frac{1}{8} + \frac{1}{8} \le \frac{3}{8} + 2x + \frac{1}{8} \qquad \text{(Adding } \frac{1}{8})$$
$$3x \le 2x + \frac{1}{2}$$
$$-2x + 3x \le -2x + 2x + \frac{1}{2} \qquad \text{(Adding -2x)}$$
$$x \le \frac{1}{2}$$

The solution set is $\{x \mid x \le \frac{1}{2}\}$.

13. We let m represent the number of miles traveled in a day. Then the total rental cost for a day is $(13.95 + 0.10 m). The total cost for a day must be less than or equal to $76. This translates to the following inequality.

$$13.95 + 0.10m \le 76$$

We solve the inequality.

$$0.10m \le 62.05 \qquad \text{(Adding -13.95}$$
$$m \le \frac{62.05}{0.10} \qquad \text{(Multiplying by } \frac{1}{0.10})$$
$$m \le 620.5$$

If you travel 620.5 miles, the total cost is 13.95 + 0.10(620.5), or 13.95 + 62.05 = $76. Any mileage less than 620.5 miles will also stay within the budget.

Thus, mileage less than or equal to 620.5 miles allows you to stay within budget.

15. Listing information in a table is helpful.

Test	Score
Test 1	91
Test 2	86
Test 3	73
Test 4	79
Test 5	S
Total	400 or more

15. (continued)

We let S represent the score on the fifth test. We can easily get an inequality from the table.

$$91 + 86 + 73 + 79 + S \ge 400$$

Solving the inequality we get:

$$329 + S \ge 400 \qquad \text{(Collecting like terms)}$$
$$S \ge 71 \qquad \text{(Adding -329)}$$

If you get 71 on the fifth test, your total score will be 91 + 86 + 73 + 79 + 71, or 400. Any higher score will also give you at least a B.

17. Listing information in a table is helpful.

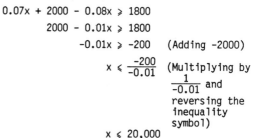

Amount invested	Rate of Interest	Interest earned
x	7%	0.07x
(25,000 - x)	8%	0.08(25,000 - x)
Total $25,000		$1800 or more

We let x represent the amount invested at 7%. Then 25,000 - x represents the amount invested at 8%. The interest earned from the 7% investment is 0.07x. The interest earned from the 8% investment is 0.08(25,000 - x).

The total interest earned from both investments must be greater than or equal to $1800. This translates to the following inequality:

$$0.07x + 0.08(25,000 - x) \ge 1800$$

We solve the inequality.

$$0.07x + 2000 - 0.08x \ge 1800$$
$$2000 - 0.01x \ge 1800$$
$$-0.01x \ge -200 \qquad \text{(Adding -2000)}$$
$$x \le \frac{-200}{-0.01} \qquad \text{(Multiplying by } \frac{1}{-0.01} \text{ and reversing the inequality symbol)}$$
$$x \le 20,000$$

For x = 20,000, 7%(20,000) = 0.07(20,000), or $1400, and 8%(25,000 - 20,000) = 0.08(5000), or $400. The total interest earned is 1400 + 400, or $1800. We also calculate for some amount less than $20,000 and for some amount greater than $20,000.

For x = $15,000   7%(15,000) = 0.07(15,000), or $1050, and 8%(25,000 - 15,000) = 0.08(10,000), or $800. The total interest earned is 1050 + 800, or $1850. For x = $22,000, 7%(22,000) = 0.07(22,000), or $1540, and 8%(25,000 - 22,000) = 0.08(3000), or $240. The total interest earned is 1540 + 240, or $1780. For these values the inequality, x ≤ 20,000, gives correct results.

To make at least $1800 interest per year, $20,000 is the most that can be invested at 7%.

19. We make a table of information.

Plan A: Monthly Income	Plan B: Monthly Income
$500 salary	$750 salary
4% of sales	5% of sales over $8000
Total: 500 + 4% of sales	Total: 750 + 5% of sales over 8000

We write an inequality stating that the income from Plan B is greater than the income from Plan A. We let S represent gross sales. Then S - 8000 represents gross sales over 8000.

$$750 + 5\%(S - 8000) > 500 + 4\%S$$

We solve the inequality.

$$750 + 0.05S - 400 > 500 + 0.04S$$
$$350 + 0.05S > 500 + 0.04S$$
$$0.01S > 150$$
$$S > \frac{150}{0.01}$$
$$S > 15{,}000$$

We calculate for x = $15,000 and for some amount greater than $15,000 and some amount less than $15,000.

When x = $15,000, income from Plan A is equal to the income from Plan B.

Plan A:
500 + 4%(15,000)
500 + 0.04(15,000)
500 + 600
$1100

Plan B:
750 + 5%(15,000 - 8000)
750 + 0.05(7000)
750 + 350
$1100

When x = $16,000, income from Plan B is greater than the income from Plan A.

Plan A:
500 + 4%(16,000)
500 + 0.04(16,000)
500 + 640
$1140

Plan B:
750 + 5%(16,000 - 8000)
750 + 0.05(8000)
750 + 400
$1150

When x = $14,000, income from Plan B is less than the income from Plan A.

Plan A:
500 + 4%(14,000)
500 + 0.04(14,000)
500 + 560
$1060

Plan B:
750 + 5%(14,000 - 8000)
750 + 0.05(6000)
750 + 300
$1050

For these values, the inequality S > 15,000 gives correct values.

Plan A is better than Plan B when gross sales are greater than $15,000.

21. Graph on a plane: 3x = -9, or x = -3.

x	y
-3	-2
-3	0
-3	5

3x = -9, or x = -3

23. $5(x + 4) = 2(x - 7)$

$$5x + 20 = 2x - 14$$
$$3x + 20 = -14 \qquad \text{(Adding -2x)}$$
$$3x = -34 \qquad \text{(Adding -20)}$$
$$x = -\frac{34}{3} \qquad \text{(Multiplying by } \tfrac{1}{3})$$

25. $4(3y - 2) \geqslant 9(2y + 5)$

$$12y - 8 \geqslant 18y + 45$$
$$-6y - 8 \geqslant 45 \qquad \text{(Adding -18y)}$$
$$-6y \geqslant 53 \qquad \text{(Adding 8)}$$
$$y \leqslant -\frac{53}{6} \qquad \text{(Multiplying by } -\tfrac{1}{6} \text{ and}$$
$$\text{reversing the inequality symbol)}$$

The solution set is $\{y | y \leqslant -\frac{53}{6}\}$.

27. $2(0.5 - 3y) + y > (4y - 0.2)8$

$$1 - 6y + y > 32y - 1.6$$
$$1 - 5y > 32y - 1.6$$
$$2.6 - 5y > 32y \qquad \text{(Adding 1.6)}$$
$$2.6 > 37y \qquad \text{(Adding 5y)}$$
$$\frac{2.6}{37} > y \qquad \text{(Multiplying by } \tfrac{1}{37})$$
$$\frac{26}{370} > y$$

The solution set is $\{y | y < \frac{26}{370}\}$.

Exercise Set 4.3

1. Using the roster method, the name of the set of even whole numbers less than 10 is

   {0, 2, 4, 6, 8}.

3. $(x + 5)(x - 5) = 0$

   $$x + 5 = 0 \text{ or } x - 5 = 0$$
   $$x = -5 \text{ or } \qquad x = 5$$

   The solution set is {-5, 5}.

5. Set builder notation for the set of real numbers greater than -3 is

{x|x > -3}.

7. Set builder notation for the set of positive real numbers is

{x|x > 0}.

9. {1, 5, 8} ⊂ {1, 2, 5, 7, 8} is true because each member of the first set is also a member of the second.

11. {1, 2, 3, 4, 5} ⊂ {2, 3, 4} is false because there is at least one member (here there are two, 1 and 5) of the first set that is not a member of the second.

13. {3, 8, 13} ⊂ {6, 8, 25, 38} is false because there is at least one member (here there are two, 3 and 13) of the first set that is not a member of the second.

15. ∅ ⊂ {1, 2} is true because the empty set is a subset of every set.

17. {x|x > 3} ⊂ {x|x > 2} is true because any number greater than 3 is also greater than 2.

19. {x|x < 5} ⊂ {x|x ≤ 5} is true because any number less than 5 is also less than or equal to 5.

21. The subsets of {-4, 7} are:

{-4, 7}   Every set is a subset of itself.

{-4}
{7}   There are two subsets with one member each.

∅   The empty set is a subset of any set.

23. Find {5, 6, 7, 8} ∩ {4, 6, 8, 10}.

The numbers 6 and 8 are common to the two sets, so the intersection is {6, 8}.

25. Find {4, 5, 6, 7, 8} ∪ {1, 4, 6, 11}.

The numbers in either or both sets are 1, 4, 5, 6, 7, 8, and 11, so the union is {1, 4, 5, 6, 7, 8, 11}.

27. Find {2, 4, 6, 8} ∩ {1, 3, 5}.

There are no members common to the two sets, so the intersection is the empty set, ∅.

29. Find {1, 2, 3, 4} ∩ {1, 2, 3, 4}.

The numbers 1, 2, 3, and 4 are common to the two sets, so the intersection is {1, 2, 3, 4}.

31. The empty set is a set without any members. The union of two empty sets is also empty.

∅ ∪ ∅ = ∅

33. Graph: x < -1

The solution set is {x|x < -1}. The solutions are those numbers less than -1. They are shown on the graph by shading all points to the left of -1. Since the inequality involves <, we use an open circle to show that -1 is not part of the graph.

$$\overset{\qquad\quad\ominus}{\underset{-3\ -2\ -1\ \ 0\ \ 1\ \ 2\ \ 3}{\longleftarrow\mkern-8mu\vert\mkern8mu\vert\mkern8mu\vert\mkern8mu\vert\mkern8mu\vert\mkern8mu\vert\mkern8mu\vert\longrightarrow}}$$

35. Graph: 4 ≤ y, or y ≥ 4

The solution set is {y|y ≥ 4}. The solutions are shown on the graph by shading the point for 4 and all points to the right of 4. Since the inequality involves ≥, we use a solid circle to show that 4 is part of the graph.

$$\underset{-3\ -2\ -1\ \ 0\ \ 1\ \ 2\ \ 3\ \ 4\ \ 5}{\longleftarrow\mkern-8mu\vert\mkern8mu\vert\mkern8mu\vert\mkern8mu\vert\mkern8mu\vert\mkern8mu\vert\mkern8mu\vert\mkern4mu\bullet\!\!\longrightarrow}$$

37. Graph: -3x ≤ 18

x ≥ -6

The solution set is {x|x ≥ -6}. The solutions are shown on the graph by shading the point for -6 and all points to the right of -6. Since the inequality involves ≥, we use a solid circle to show that -6 is part of the graph.

$$\underset{-7\ -6\ -5\ -4\ -3\ -2\ -1\ \ 0\ \ 1\ \ 2}{\longleftarrow\mkern-8mu\vert\mkern4mu\bullet\!\!\longrightarrow}$$

39. Graph: x - 7 > -5

x > 2

The solution set is {x|x > 2}. The solutions are those numbers greater than 2. They are shown on the graph by shading all points to the right of 2. Since the inequality involves >, we use an open circle to show that 2 is not part of the graph.

$$\underset{-3\ -2\ -1\ \ 0\ \ 1\ \ 2\ \ 3}{\longleftarrow\mkern-8mu\vert\mkern8mu\vert\mkern8mu\vert\mkern8mu\vert\mkern8mu\vert\mkern4mu\ominus\!\!\longrightarrow}$$

41. Graph: 6x + 11 ≤ 14x + 3

8 ≤ 8x

1 ≤ x

The solution set is {x|x ≥ 1}. The solutions are shown on the graph by shading the point 1 and all points to the right of 1. Since the inequality involves ≥, we use a solid circle to show that 1 is part of the graph.

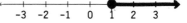

$$\underset{-3\ -2\ -1\ \ 0\ \ 1\ \ 2\ \ 3}{\longleftarrow\mkern-8mu\vert\mkern8mu\vert\mkern8mu\vert\mkern8mu\vert\mkern4mu\bullet\!\!\longrightarrow}$$

43. We let x represent the number of coach seats and y represent the number of first-class seats.

The total number of seats is 152.

x + y = 152   (1)

The number of coach seats is five more than six times the number of first-class seats.

x = 5 + 6y   (2)

We solve the system of equations. Here we use the substitution method, substituting 5 + 6y for x in equation (1) and solving for x.

$$x + y = 152 \qquad (1)$$
$$5 + 6y + y = 152 \qquad \text{(Substituting)}$$
$$5 + 7y = 152$$
$$7y = 147$$
$$y = 21$$

Next we substitute 21 in either of the original equations and solve for x.

$$x = 5 + 6y \qquad (2)$$
$$x = 5 + 6(21) \qquad \text{(Substituting)}$$
$$= 5 + 126$$
$$= 131$$

The values x = 131 and y = 21 check. Thus, there are 131 coach seats and 21 first-class seats.

45. (x + 4)(x - 2) = 0

x + 4 = 0 or x - 2 = 0
   x = -4 or   x = 2

The solutions are -4 and 2.

47. E = {..., -4, -2, 0, 2, 4, 6, ...}
D = {..., -5, -3, -1, 1, 3, 5, ...}

Find E ∩ D.

There are no members common to both sets.
Thus, E ∩ D = ∅.

49. Q = {1, 2, 3, 4}
E = {..., -4, -2, 0, 2, 4, 6, ...}

Find Q ∩ E.

The numbers 2 and 4 are common to the two sets.
Thus, Q ∩ E = {2, 4}.

1. Graph: 1 < x < 6

The word "and" corresponds to intersection. The solution set is the intersection of the solution sets of 1 < x and x < 6.

$\{x \mid 1 < x < 6\} = \{x \mid 1 < x\} \cap \{x \mid x < 6\}$

The graph is the intersection of the individual graphs.

$\{x \mid 1 < x\}$

$\{x \mid x < 6\}$

$\{x \mid 1 < x < 6\}$

3. Graph: -3 ⩾ y ⩾ -6

The solution set is the intersection of the solution sets -3 ⩾ y and y ⩾ -6.

$\{y \mid -3 \geqslant y \geqslant -6\} = \{y \mid -3 \geqslant y\} \cap \{y \mid y \geqslant -6\}$

The graph is the intersection of the individual graphs.

$\{y \mid -3 \geqslant y\}$
or $\{y \mid y \leqslant -3\}$

$\{y \mid y \geqslant -6\}$
or $\{y \mid -6 \leqslant y\}$

$\{y \mid -3 \geqslant y \geqslant -6\}$
or $\{y \mid -6 \leqslant y \leqslant -3\}$

5.
$$-2 < x + 2 < 8$$
$$-2 - 2 < x + 2 - 2 < 8 - 2 \qquad \text{(Adding -2)}$$
$$-4 < x < 6$$

The solution set is {x | -4 < x < 6}.

7.
$$1 < 2y + 5 \leqslant 9$$
$$1 - 5 < 2y + 5 - 5 \leqslant 9 - 5 \qquad \text{(Adding -5)}$$
$$-4 < 2y \leqslant 4$$
$$\frac{1}{2}(-4) < \frac{1}{2} \cdot 2y \leqslant \frac{1}{2} \cdot 4 \qquad \text{(Multiplying by } \frac{1}{2}\text{)}$$
$$-2 < y \leqslant 2$$

The solution set is {y | -2 < y ⩽ 2}.

9.
$$-10 \leqslant -3x + 5 \leqslant -1$$
$$-10 - 5 \leqslant -3x + 5 - 5 \leqslant -1 - 5 \qquad \text{(Adding -5)}$$
$$-15 \leqslant -3x \leqslant -6$$
$$-\frac{1}{3}(-15) \geqslant -\frac{1}{3}(-3x) \geqslant -\frac{1}{3}(-6)$$

(Multiplying by $-\frac{1}{3}$ and reversing the inequality sign)

$$5 \geqslant x \geqslant 2$$

The solution set is {x | 5 ⩾ x ⩾ 2}, or {x | 2 ⩽ x ⩽ 5}.

11. Graph: x < -1 or x > 1

    The word "or" corresponds to union. The solution set is the <u>union</u> of the individual solution sets.

    $\{x|x < -1 \text{ or } x > 1\} = \{x|x < -1\} \cup \{x|x > 1\}$

    The graph is the union of the individual graphs.

    $\{x|x < -1\}$

    $\{x|x > 1\}$

    $\{x|x < -1 \text{ or } x > 1\}$

13. Graph: x ⩽ -3 or x > 1

    The solution set is the <u>union</u> of the individual solution sets.

    $\{x|x \leqslant -3\}$

    $\{x|x > 1\}$

    $\{x|x \leqslant -3 \text{ or } x > 1\}$

15. $\begin{array}{lll} x + 7 \leqslant -2 & \text{or} & x + 7 \geqslant 2 \\ x + 7 - 7 \leqslant -2 - 7 & \text{or} & x + 7 - 7 \geqslant 2 - 7 \\ x \leqslant -9 & \text{or} & x \geqslant -5 \end{array}$

    The solution set is $\{x|x \leqslant -9 \text{ or } x \geqslant -5\}$.

17. $\begin{array}{lll} 2x - 8 \leqslant -3 & \text{or} & x - 8 \geqslant 3 \\ 2x - 8 + 8 \leqslant -3 + 8 & \text{or} & x - 8 + 8 \geqslant 3 + 8 \\ 2x \leqslant 5 & \text{or} & x \geqslant 11 \\ x \leqslant \frac{5}{2} & \text{or} & x \geqslant 11 \end{array}$

    The solution set is $\{x|x \leqslant \frac{5}{2} \text{ or } x \geqslant 11\}$.

19. $\begin{array}{lll} 3x - 9 < -5 & \text{or} & x - 9 > 6 \\ 3x - 9 + 9 < -5 + 9 & \text{or} & x - 9 + 9 > 6 + 9 \\ 3x < 4 & \text{or} & x > 15 \\ x < \frac{4}{3} & \text{or} & x > 15 \end{array}$

    The solution set is $\{x|x < \frac{4}{3} \text{ or } x > 15\}$.

21. $\begin{array}{lll} -2x - 2 < -6 & \text{or} & -2x - 2 > 6 \\ -2x - 2 + 2 < -6 + 2 & \text{or} & -2x - 2 + 2 > 6 + 2 \\ -2x < -4 & \text{or} & -2x > 8 \\ -\frac{1}{2}(-2x) > -\frac{1}{2}(-4) & \text{or} & -\frac{1}{2}(-2x) < -\frac{1}{2}(8) \\ x > 2 & \text{or} & x < -4 \end{array}$

    The solution set is $\{x|x < -4 \text{ or } x > 2\}$.

23. $2x - 3y = 7$
     $3x + 2y = -10$

    We solve using the addition method.

    $\begin{array}{ll} 4x - 6y = 14 & \text{(Multiplying by 2)} \\ \underline{9x + 6y = -30} & \text{(Multiplying by 3)} \\ 13x \quad\quad = -16 & \\ x = -\frac{16}{13} & \end{array}$

    Next we substitute $-\frac{16}{13}$ for x in either of the original equations and solve for y.

    $3x + 2y = -10$

    $3(-\frac{16}{13}) + 2y = -10$

    $-\frac{48}{13} + 2y = -\frac{130}{13}$

    $2y = -\frac{82}{13}$

    $y = -\frac{41}{13}$

    The values check. The solution is $(-\frac{16}{13}, -\frac{41}{13})$.

25. $(2x + 3)(x - 4) = 0$

    $\begin{array}{ll} 2x + 3 = 0 & \text{or } x - 4 = 0 \\ 2x = -3 & \text{or} \quad x = 4 \\ x = -\frac{3}{2} & \text{or} \quad x = 4 \end{array}$

    The solutions are $-\frac{3}{2}$ and 4.

27. $4a - 2 \leqslant a + 1 \leqslant 3a + 4$

    $\begin{array}{lll} 4a - 2 \leqslant a + 1 & \text{and} & a + 1 \leqslant 3a + 4 \\ 3a \leqslant 3 & \text{and} & -2a \leqslant 3 \\ a \leqslant 1 & \text{and} & a \geqslant -\frac{3}{2} \end{array}$

    The solution set is the <u>intersection</u> of $\{a|a \leqslant 1\}$ and $\{a|a \geqslant -\frac{3}{2}\}$.

    The solution set is $\{a|-\frac{3}{2} \leqslant a \leqslant 1\}$.

29. $-\frac{2}{15} \leqslant \frac{2}{3}x - \frac{2}{5} \leqslant \frac{2}{15}$

    $-\frac{2}{15} + \frac{2}{5} \leqslant \frac{2}{3}x - \frac{2}{5} + \frac{2}{5} \leqslant \frac{2}{15} + \frac{2}{5}$

    $\frac{4}{15} \leqslant \frac{2}{3}x \leqslant \frac{8}{15}$

    $\frac{3}{2} \cdot \frac{4}{15} \leqslant \frac{3}{2} \cdot \frac{2}{3}x \leqslant \frac{3}{2} \cdot \frac{8}{15}$

    $\frac{2}{5} \leqslant x \leqslant \frac{4}{5}$

    The solution set is $\{x|\frac{2}{5} \leqslant x \leqslant \frac{4}{5}\}$.

31. 2x + 3 ⩽ x - 6   or   3x - 2 ⩽ 4x + 5
         x ⩽ -9   or   -x ⩽ 7
         x ⩽ -9   or   x ⩾ -7

The solution set is {x|x ⩽ -9 or x ⩾ -7}.

Exercise Set 4.5

1. The distance between -8 and -42 is
   |-8 - (-42)| = |-8 + 42| = |34| = 34.

   The distance can also be found as follows.
   |-42 - (-8)| = |-42 + 8| = |-34| = 34

3. The distance between 26 and 15 is
   |26 - 15| = |11| = 11.

   The distance can also be found as follows.
   |15 - 26| = |-11| = 11

5. The distance between -9 and 24 is
   |-9 - 24| = |-33| = 33.

   The distance can also be found as follows.
   |24 - (-9)| = |33| = 33

7. The distance between -2 and 0 is
   |-2 - 0| = |-2| = 2.

   The distance can also be found as follows.
   |0 - (-2)| = |2| = 2

9. |3x - 9| = 12

   We use Property 1.
   3x - 9 = -12   or   3x - 9 = 12
      3x = -3   or   3x = 21   (Adding 9)
       x = -1   or   x = 7   (Multiplying by $\frac{1}{3}$)

   The solution set is {-1, 7}.

   The graph is as follows.

   ← | -2 ● -1 | 0 | 1 | 2 | 3 | 4 | 5 | 6 ● 7 | 8 →

11. |x| < 3

    We use Property 2. The solutions are those numbers x such that -3 < x < 3.
    The solution set is {x|-3 < x < 3}.

    The graph is as follows.

    ← | -4 ⊕ -3 -2 -1 0 1 2 ⊕ 3 | 4 →

13. |x| ⩾ 2

    We use Property 3. The solutions are those numbers x such that x ⩽ -2 or x ⩾ 2.
    The solution set is {x|x ⩽ -2 or x ⩾ 2}.

    The graph is as follows.

    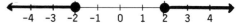

    ← -4 -3 ●-2 -1 0 1 ●2 3 4 →

15. |x - 3| < 12

    -12 < x - 3 < 12   (Using Property 2)
     -9 < x < 15   (Adding 3)

    The solution set is {x|-9 < x < 15}.

17. |2x + 3| ⩽ 4

    -4 ⩽ 2x + 3 ⩽ 4   (Using Property 2)
    -7 ⩽ 2x ⩽ 1   (Adding -3)
    $-\frac{7}{2}$ ⩽ x ⩽ $\frac{1}{2}$ (Multiplying by $\frac{1}{2}$)

    The solution set is {x|$-\frac{7}{2}$ ⩽ x ⩽ $\frac{1}{2}$}.

19. |2y - 7| > 5

    2y - 7 < -5   or   2y - 7 > 5   (Using Property 3)
       2y < 2   or   2y > 12   (Adding 7)
        y < 1   or   y > 6   (Multiplying by $\frac{1}{2}$)

    The solution set is {y|y < 1 or y > 6}.

21. |4x - 9| ⩾ 14

    4x - 9 ⩽ -14   or   4x - 9 ⩾ 14   (Using Property 3)
       4x ⩽ -5   or   4x ⩾ 23   (Adding 9)
        x ⩽ $-\frac{5}{4}$ or   x ⩾ $\frac{23}{4}$ (Multiplying by $\frac{1}{4}$)

    The solution set is {x|x ⩽ $-\frac{5}{4}$ or x ⩾ $\frac{23}{4}$}.

23. |3 - 4x| < 21

    -21 < 3 - 4x < 21   (Using Property 2)
    -24 < -4x < 18   (Adding -3)
      6 > x > $-\frac{9}{2}$ (Multiplying by $-\frac{1}{4}$ and reversing the inequality symbol).

    The solution set is {x|6 > x > $-\frac{9}{2}$}.

25. $\left|\frac{1}{2} + 3x\right| \geqslant 12$

$\frac{1}{2} + 3x \leqslant -12 \quad$ or $\quad \frac{1}{2} + 3x \geqslant 12$

(Using Property 3)

$3x \leqslant -\frac{25}{2} \quad$ or $\quad 3x \geqslant \frac{23}{2}$ (Adding $-\frac{1}{2}$)

$x \leqslant -\frac{25}{6} \quad$ or $\quad x \geqslant \frac{23}{6}$

(Multiplying by $\frac{1}{6}$)

The solution set is $\{x | x \leqslant -\frac{25}{6}$ or $x \geqslant \frac{23}{6}\}$.

27. It helps to make a drawing. We let ℓ represent the length and w the width.

We translate to a system of equations.

The perimeter is 628 m.

$2\ell + 2w = 628$, or $\ell + w = 314 \qquad$ (1)

The length is 6 m greater than the width.

$\ell = 6 + w \qquad$ (2)

We substitute $6 + w$ for ℓ in the first equation and solve for w.

$\ell + w = 314 \qquad$ (1)

$6 + w + w = 314 \qquad$ (Substituting)

$6 + 2w = 314$

$2w = 308$

$w = 154$

Substitute 154 for w in either of the original equations and solve for ℓ.

$\ell = 6 + w \qquad$ (2)

$\ell = 6 + 154 \qquad$ (Substituting)

$\ell = 160$

If $\ell = 160$ and $w = 154$, the length is 6 more than the width and the perimeter is $2(160) + 2(154)$, or 628. The values check. The length is 160 m, and the width is 154 m. Thus, the area is 160×154, or 24,640 m².

29. $\left|\frac{2x - 1}{3}\right| \leqslant 1$

$-1 \leqslant \frac{2x - 1}{3} \leqslant 1 \qquad$ (Using Property 2)

$-3 \leqslant 2x - 1 \leqslant 3 \qquad$ (Multiplying by 3)

$-2 \leqslant 2x \leqslant 4 \qquad$ (Adding 1)

$-1 \leqslant x \leqslant 2 \qquad$ (Multiplying by $\frac{1}{2}$)

The solution set is $\{x | -1 \leqslant x \leqslant 2\}$.

31. $|3x - 4| > -2$

From the definition of absolute value we know that $|3x - 4| \geqslant 0$.

Thus, $|3x - 4| > -2$ is true for all x. The solution set is the set of all reals.

33. $2 \leqslant |x - 1| \leqslant 5$

$2 \leqslant |x - 1| \quad$ and $\quad |x - 1| \leqslant 5$.

The solution set is the intersection of the individual solution sets.

$2 \leqslant |x - 1| \quad$ (or $|x - 1| \geqslant 2$)

$x - 1 \leqslant -2 \quad$ or $\quad x - 1 \geqslant 2 \qquad$ (Using Property 3)

$x \leqslant -1 \quad$ or $\quad x \geqslant 3 \qquad$ (Adding 1)

The solution set is $\{x | x \leqslant -1$ or $x \geqslant 3\}$.

$|x - 1| \leqslant 5$

$-5 \leqslant x - 1 \leqslant 5 \qquad$ (Using Property 2)

$-4 \leqslant x \leqslant 6 \qquad$ (Adding 1)

The solution set is $\{x | -4 \leqslant x \leqslant 6\}$.

The solution set of $2 \leqslant |x - 1| \leqslant 5$ is

$\{x | x \leqslant -1$ or $x \geqslant 3\} \cap \{x | -4 \leqslant x \leqslant 6\}$

$= \{x | -4 \leqslant x \leqslant -1$ or $3 \leqslant x \leqslant 6\}$.

35. $|x - 1| - 2 = |2x - 5|$

$|x - 1| = 2 + |2x - 5|$

Using Property 1, we get

$x - 1 = 2 + |2x - 5| \quad$ or $\quad x - 1 = -2 - |2x - 5|$

$x - 3 = |2x - 5| \quad$ or $\quad x + 1 = -|2x - 5|$

$x - 3 = |2x - 5| \quad$ or $\quad -x - 1 = |2x - 5|$

Again using Property 1, we get

$2x - 5 = x - 3 \quad$ or $\quad 2x - 5 = -x + 3$

$x = 2 \qquad$ or $\qquad 3x = 8$

$x = 2 \qquad$ or $\qquad x = \frac{8}{3}$

or

$2x - 5 = -x - 1 \quad$ or $\quad 2x - 5 = x + 1$

$3x = 4 \qquad$ or $\qquad x = 6$

$x = \frac{4}{3} \qquad$ or $\qquad x = 6$

The possible solutions are $\frac{4}{3}$, 2, $\frac{8}{3}$, and 6. None of these numbers check. Thus, there is no solution.

<u>37</u>. $\left|\frac{5}{9} + 3x\right| < \frac{1}{6}$

$-\frac{1}{6} < \frac{5}{9} + 3x < \frac{1}{6}$ (Using Property 2)

$-\frac{3}{18} < \frac{10}{18} + 3x < \frac{3}{18}$

$-\frac{13}{18} < 3x < -\frac{7}{18}$ (Adding $-\frac{10}{18}$)

$-\frac{13}{54} < x < -\frac{7}{54}$ (Multiplying by $\frac{1}{3}$)

The solution set is $\{x| -\frac{13}{54} < x < -\frac{7}{54}\}$.

Exercise Set 4.6

<u>1</u>. We replace x by -2 and y by 1.

$$\frac{4x + 5y < 1}{\begin{array}{c|c} 4(-2) + 5(1) & 1 \\ -8 + 5 & \\ -3 & \end{array}}$$

Since -3 < 1 is true, (-2,1) is a solution.

<u>3</u>. We replace x by 2 and y by 2.

$$\frac{y \geqslant 3x - 4}{\begin{array}{c|c} 2 & 3\cdot2 - 4 \\ & 6 - 4 \\ & 2 \end{array}}$$

Since $2 \geqslant 2$ is true, (2,2) is a solution.

<u>5</u>. Graph: y > 2x

a) We first graph the line y = 2x. Three of the points on the line are (0,0), (2,4), and (-1,-2). Since the inequality symbol is >, we draw the line dashed.

y = 2x

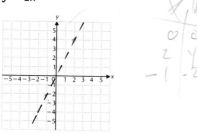

<u>5</u>. (continued)

b) We determine which half-plane to shade by trying some point off the line. We cannot use (0,0) since it is on the line. Let us use (3,2) as a check. Since 2 > 2·3 (or 2 > 6) is false, (3,2) is not in the graph. We shade the other half-plane. The graph consists of the shaded half-plane but not the dashed line.

y > 2x

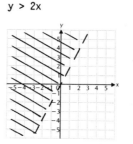

<u>7</u>. Graph: y ≤ x + 1

a) We first graph the line y = x + 1. Three of the points on the line are (0,1), (-4,-3), and (3,4). Since the inequality symbol is ≤, we draw it solid.

y = x + 1

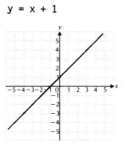

b) We determine which half-plane to shade by trying some point off the line. The point (0,0) is easy to check. Since 0 ≤ 0 + 1 (or 0 ≤ 1) is true, (0,0) is in the graph. We shade that half-plane. The graph consists of the shaded half-plane and the solid line as well.

y ≤ x + 1

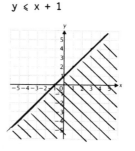

9. Graph: x + y < 4

    a) We first graph the line x + y = 4. The inter-
        cepts are (0,4) and (4,0). Since the inequal-
        ity symbol is <, we draw the line dashed.

        x + y = 4

        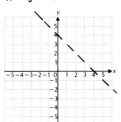

    b) We determine which half-plane to shade by
        trying some point off the line. The point
        (0,0) is easy to check. Since 0 + 0 < 4
        (or 0 < 4) is true, (0,0) is in the graph.
        We shade that half-plane. The graph consists
        of the shaded half-plane but not the dashed
        line.

        x + y < 4

        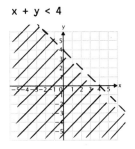

11. Graph: 3x + 4y ⩾ 12

    a) We first graph the line 3x + 4y = 12. The
        intercepts are (0,3) and (4,0). Since the
        inequality symbol is ⩾, we draw the line
        solid.

        3x + 4y = 12

        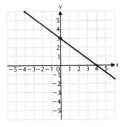

11. (continued)

    b) We determine which half-plane to shade by
        trying some point off the line. The point
        (0,0) is easy to check. Since
        3·0 + 4·0 ⩾ 12 (or 0 ⩾ 12) is false, (0,0) is
        not in the graph. We shade the other half-
        plane. The graph consists of the shaded
        half-plane and the solid line as well.

        3x + 4y ⩾ 12

        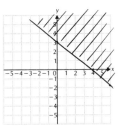

13. Graph: 7x + 2y ⩽ 21

    a) We first graph the line 7x + 2y = 21.
        The intercepts are (3,0) and $(0,\frac{21}{2})$. Other
        points on the line are (1,7), $(2, \frac{7}{2})$, and
        $(4,- \frac{7}{2})$. Since the inequality symbol is ⩽,
        we draw the line solid.

        7x + 2y = 21

        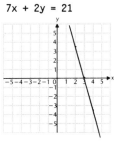

    b) We determine which half-plane to shade by
        trying some point off the line. The point
        (0,0) is easy to check. Since 7·0 + 2·0 ⩽ 21
        (or 0 ⩽ 21) is true, (0,0) is in the graph.
        We shade that half-plane. The graph consists
        of the shaded half-plane and the solid line
        as well.

        7x + 2y ⩽ 21

        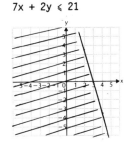

15. Graph: x < -4

   a) We first graph the line x = -4. It is
      parallel to the y-axis and has (-4,0) as its
      x-intercept. Since the inequality symbol
      is <, we draw the line dashed.

      x = -4

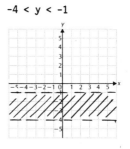

   b) We determine which half-plane to shade by
      trying some point off the line. The point
      (0,0) is easy to check. Since 0 < -4 is
      false, (0,0) is not in the graph. We shade
      the other half-plane. The graph consists of
      the shaded half-plane but not the dashed line.

      x < -4

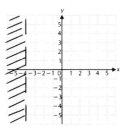

17. Graph: -4 < y < -1

   Think of this as a system of inequalities.

   -4 < y   and   y < -1

   First graph the line -4 = y. Since the inequality
   symbol is <, we draw it dashed. Since any point
   above this line has a y-coordinate greater than
   -4, we shade the upper half-plane. Next graph the
   line y = -1. Since the inequality symbol is <, we
   draw it dashed. Since any point below this line
   has a y-coordinate less than -1, we shade the
   lower half-plane.

   -4 < y   y < -1

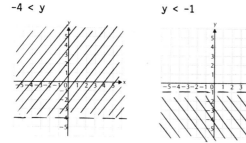

17. (continued)

   Then we shade the intersection of the graphs. The
   inequality -4 < y < -1 means -4 < y and y < -1.
   The y-coordinate of each point in the solution
   must satisfy both requirements: greater than -4
   and less than -1.

   -4 < y < -1

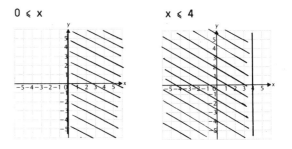

19. Graph: 0 ⩽ x ⩽ 4

   Think of this as a system of inequalities.

   0 ⩽ x   and   x ⩽ 4

   First graph the line 0 = x. Since the inequality
   symbol is ⩽, we draw it solid. Since any point
   to the right of the line has an x-coordinate
   greater than 0, we shade the right half-plane.
   Next graph the line x = 4. Since the inequality
   symbol is ⩽, we draw it solid. Since any point
   to the left of this line has an x-coordinate
   less than 4, we shade the left half-plane.

   0 ⩽ x   x ⩽ 4

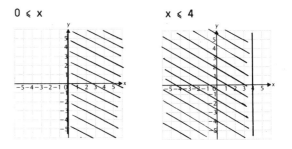

Then shade the intersection of the graphs. The
inequality 0 ⩽ x ⩽ 4 means 0 ⩽ x and x ⩽ 4. The
x-coordinate of each point in the solution must
satisfy both requirements: greater than or equal
to 0 and less than or equal to 4.

   0 ⩽ x ⩽ 4

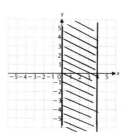

21. $(3x - 4)(x + 1) = 0$

$3x - 4 = 0$ or $x + 1 = 0$

$3x = 4$ or $x = -1$

$x = \frac{4}{3}$ or $x = -1$

The solutions are $\frac{4}{3}$ and -1.

23. Let x represent the number of field goals and y represent the number of free throws.

We translate to a system of equations.

The number of field goals plus the number of free throws was 18.

$x + y = 18$ (1)

The total number of points scored was 30.

$2x + y = 30$ (2)

We solve the system using the addition method.

$-x - y = -18$ [Multiplying (1) by -1]

$\underline{2x + y = 30}$ (2)

$x = 12$ (Adding)

Next we substitute 12 for x in either of the original equations and solve for y.

$x + y = 18$ (1)

$12 + y = 18$ (Substituting)

$y = 6$

If she makes 12 field goals and 6 free throws, she scores 18 times and earns $2 \times 12 + 1 \times 6$, or 30 points. The values check.

The player made 12 field goals and 6 free throws.

25. Graph: $y \leqslant |x|$

We first graph $y = |x|$. Since the inequality symbol is $\leqslant$, we draw the graph solid.

x	y
0	0
2	2
-2	2
5	5
-5	5

$y = |x|$

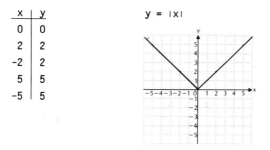

Note that in $y \leqslant |x|$, y is by itself. We interpret the graph of the inequality as the set of all ordered pairs (x,y) where the second coordinate y is less than or equal to the absolute value of the first. Decide below which pairs satisfy the inequality and which do not.

25. (continued)

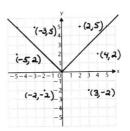

We see that any pair below the graph of $y = |x|$ is a solution as well as those in the graph of $y = |x|$. The graph is as follows.

$y \leqslant |x|$

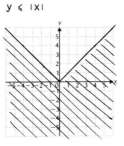

27. Graph this system: $x + y \leqslant 3$

$ x - y \leqslant 1$

We first graph the individual inequalities.

$x + y \leqslant 3$ $x - y \leqslant 1$

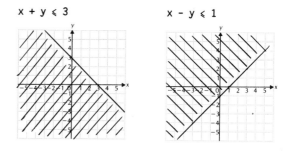

We now find the intersection of the two graphs.

$x + y \leqslant 3$

$x - y \leqslant 1$

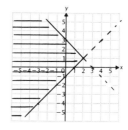

<u>29.</u> Graph this system: $y - x \leqslant 2$

$x - y \leqslant 2$

$2 \leqslant y \leqslant 3$

We first graph the individual inequalities.

$y - x \leqslant 2$ $x - y \leqslant 2$

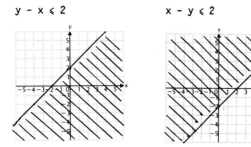

$2 \leqslant y \leqslant 3$

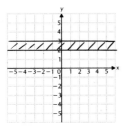

We now find the intersection of the three graphs.

$y - x \leqslant 2$
$x - y \leqslant 2$
$2 \leqslant y \leqslant 3$

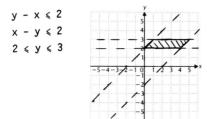

Exercise Set 5.1

1. We replace x by –1.

    $8x^2 - 2x - 5$

    $= 8(-1)^2 - 2(-1) - 5$

    $= 8 + 2 - 5$

    $= 5$

3. We replace x by –1 and y by 2.

    $18xy - 8x^3 - y + 50$

    $= 18(-1)(2) - 8(-1)^3 - 2 + 50$

    $= -36 + 8 - 2 + 50$

    $= 20$

5. We replace n by 12.

    $n^2 - n$

    $= 12^2 - 12$

    $= 144 - 12$

    $= 132$

    There are 132 games played.

7. We replace r by 1.2, h by 4.7, and π by 3.14.

    $2\pi rh + 2\pi r^2$

    $= 2(3.14)(1.2)(4.7) + 2(3.14)(1.2)^2$

    $= 35.4192 + 9.0432$

    $= 44.4624$

    The area of the can is about 44.5 in.

9. We first find an equivalent polynomial with plus signs.

    $5x^3 + 7x^2 - 3x - 9 = 5x^3 + 7x^2 + (-3x) + (-9)$

    The terms are $5x^3$, $7x^2$, $-3x$, and -9.
    The coefficients are 5, 7, –3, and –9.

11. We first find an equivalent polynomial with plus signs.

     $-3xyz + 7x^2y^2 - 5xy^2z + 4xyz^2$

     $= -3xyz + 7x^2y^2 + (-5xy^2z) + 4xyz^2$

     The terms are $-3xyz$, $7x^2y^2$, $-5xy^2z$, and $4xyz^2$.
     The coefficients are –3, 7, –5, and 4.

13. $x^4 - 7$

     There are no terms with x^3, x^2, or x.
     The missing terms are the x^3-term, the x^2-term, and the x-term.

15. $x^3 - x^2 + 2$

     There is no term with x.
     The missing term is the x-term.

17. $x^2 + 3x^5 - x^3y^4 - 7$

     $= x^2 + 3x^5 + (-x^3y^4) + (-7)$

Term	Degree	
x^2	2	
$3x^5$	5	
$-x^3y^4$	7	(3 + 4 = 7)
–7	0	($-7 = -7x^0$)

     The degree of the polynomial is 7, the degree of the term of highest degree.
     The leading term is $-x^3y^4$, the term of highest degree.
     The leading coefficient is –1, the coefficient of the leading term.

19. $x^5 + 3x^2y^4 - 5xy + 4x - 3$

     $= x^5 + 3x^2y^4 + (-5xy) + 4x + (-3)$

Term	Degree	
x^5	5	
$3x^2y^4$	6	(2 + 4 = 6)
$-5xy$	2	($-5xy = -5x^1y^1$; 1 + 1 = 2)
$4x$	1	($4x = 4x^1$)
–3	0	($-3 = -3x^0$)

     The degree of the polynomial is 6, the degree of the term of highest degree.
     The leading term is $3x^2y^4$, the term of highest degree.
     The leading coefficient is 3, the coefficient of the leading term.

21. $6x^2 - 14 - 7x^2 + 24 + 3x^2$

     $= (6 - 7 + 3)x^2 + (-14 + 24)$

     $= 2x^2 + 10$

23. $5x - 4y - 2x + 5y$

     $= (5 - 2)x + (-4 + 5)y$

     $= 3x + 1y$

     $= 3x + y$

25. $5a + 7 - 4 + 2a - 6a + 3$

     $= (5 + 2 - 6)a + (7 - 4 + 3)$

     $= 1a + 6$

     $= a + 6$

27. $8x^2 - 3xy + 12y^2 + x^2 - y^2 + 5xy + 4y^2$

     $= (8 + 1)x^2 + (-3 + 5)xy + (12 - 1 + 4)y^2$

     $= (9x^2 + 2xy + 15y^2$

29. $4x^2y - 3y + 2xy^2 - 5x^2y + 7y + 7xy^2$

  $= (4 - 5)x^2y + (-3 + 7)y + (2 + 7)xy^2$

  $= -x^2y + 4y + 9xy^2$

31. $x - 3x^2 + 1 + x^3$

  $= x^3 - 3x^2 + x + 1$ (Decending order)

33. $a - a^3 + 5a^5 - 9 + 6a^2$

  $= 5a^5 - a^3 + 6a^2 + a - 9$ (Decending order)

35. $2y^3 - y + y^4 - 7 + 3y^2$

  $= -7 - y + 3y^2 + 2y^3 + y^4$ (Ascending order)

37. $x^2 - x + 5x^5 - 9x^3 + 18x^4$

  $= -x + x^2 - 9x^3 + 18x^4 + 5x^5$ (Ascending order)

39. $x^2y^2 + x^3y - xy^3 + 1$

  $= -xy^3 + x^2y^2 + x^3y + 1$ (Decending powers of y)

41. $-9x^3y + 3xy^3 + x^2y^2 + 2x^4$

  $= 3xy^3 + x^2y^2 - 9x^3y + 2x^4$ (Ascending powers
                                     of x)

43. $16 - z^2$ is a binomial.

45. $34xy^2$ is a monomial.

47. $3(y - 2) = 3 \cdot y - 3 \cdot 2 = 3y - 6$

49. We replace x by 10

  $0.0001x^3 + 0.001x^2 - 0.01x + 0.1$

  $= 0.0001(10^3) + 0.001(10^2) - 0.01(10) + 0.1$

  $= 0.1 + 0.1 - 0.1 + 0.1$

  $= 0.2$

51. $0.00976x^2y^2 - 0.0805x^3y + 0.80149x^2y^2 +$

                         $0.00943x^3y$

  $= (0.00976 + 0.80149)x^2y^2 + (-0.0805 + 0.00943)x^3y$

  $= 0.81125x^2y^2 - 0.07107x^3y$

Exercise Set 5.2

---

1. $(3x^2 + 5y^2 + 6) + (2x^2 - 3y^2 - 1)$

  $= (3 + 2)x^2 + (5 - 3)y^2 + (6 - 1)$

  $= 5x^2 + 2y^2 + 5$

3. $(2a + 3b - c) + (4a - 2b + 2c)$

  $= (2 + 4)a + (3 - 2)b + (-1 + 2)c$

  $= 6a + b + c$

5. $(a^2 - 3b^2 + 4c^2) + (-5a^2 + 2b^2 - c^2)$

  $= (1 - 5)a^2 + (-3 + 2)b^2 + (4 - 1)c^2$

  $= -4a^2 - b^2 + 3c^2$

7. $(x^2 + 2x - 3xy - 7) + (-3x^2 - x + 2xy + 6)$

  $= (1 - 3)x^2 + (2 - 1)x + (-3 + 2)xy + (-7 + 6)$

  $= -2x^2 + x - xy - 1$

9. $(7x^2y - 3xy^2 + 4xy) + (-2x^2y - xy^2 + xy)$

  $= (7 - 2)x^2y + (-3 - 1)xy^2 + (4 + 1)xy$

  $= 5x^2y - 4xy^2 + 5xy$

11. $(2r^2 + 12r - 11) + (6r^2 - 2r + 4) + (r^2 - r - 2)$

  $= (2 + 6 + 1)r^2 + (12 - 2 - 1)r + (-11 + 4 - 2)$

  $= 9r^2 + 9r - 9$

13. $-(5x^3 - 7x^2 + 3x - 6)$

  $= -5x^3 + 7x^2 - 3x + 6$ ("Changing the sign"
                                   of every term inside
                                   parentheses)

15. $(8x - 4) - (-5x + 2)$

  $= (8x - 4) + (5x - 2)$

  $= 13x - 6$

17. $(-3x^2 + 2x + 9) - (x^2 + 5x - 4)$

  $= (-3x^2 + 2x + 9) + (-x^2 - 5x + 4)$

  $= -4x^2 - 3x + 13$

19. $(5a - 2b + c) - (3a + 2b - 2c)$

  $= (5a - 2b + c) + (-3a - 2b + 2c)$

  $= 2a - 4b + 3c$

21. $(3x^2 - 2x - x^3) - (5x^2 - 8x - x^3)$

  $= (3x^2 - 2x - x^3) + (-5x^2 + 8x + x^3)$

  $= -2x^2 + 6x$

23. $(5a^2 + 4ab - 3b^2) - (9a^2 - 4ab + 2b^2)$

  $= (5a^2 + 4ab - 3b^2) + (-9a^2 + 4ab - 2b^2)$

  $= -4a^2 + 8ab - 5b^2$

25. $(\frac{2}{3}xy^2 + \frac{1}{3}x^2y^2 + 12.3) -$

                   $(\frac{4}{5}xy^2 - \frac{1}{2}x^2y^2 + 25.01)$

  $= (\frac{2}{3}xy^2 + \frac{1}{3}x^2y^2 + 12.3) +$

                   $(-\frac{4}{5}xy^2 + \frac{1}{2}x^2y^2 - 25.01)$

  $= (\frac{2}{3} - \frac{4}{5})xy^2 + (\frac{1}{3} + \frac{1}{2})x^2y^2 + (12.3 - 25.01)$

  $= (\frac{10}{15} - \frac{12}{15})xy^2 + (\frac{2}{6} + \frac{3}{6})x^2y^2 + (-12.71)$

  $= -\frac{2}{15}xy^2 + \frac{5}{6}x^2y^2 - 12.71$

27. $10x + 15y - 5$

  $= 5 \cdot 2x + 5 \cdot 3y - 5 \cdot 1$

  $= 5(2x + 3y - 1)$

29. $(x^3)^4 = x^{3 \cdot 4} = x^{12}$

31. $\frac{2}{3}(18a^2 - 33ab + 3b^2) - \frac{3}{4}(20a^2 + 44ab + 56b^2)$

= $(12a^2 - 22ab + 2b^2) + (-15a^2 - 33ab - 42b^2)$

= $-3a^2 - 55ab - 40b^2$

33. $(0.06u^2 + 0.003v^2) - (v^2 - 0.6u^2) -$
$$(0.003u^2 - 6v^2)$$

= $(0.06u^2 + 0.003v^2) + (-v^2 + 0.6u^2) +$
$$(-0.003u^2 + 6v^2)$$

= $(0.06 + 0.6 - 0.003)u^2 + (0.003 - 1 + 6)v^2$

= $0.657u^2 + 5.003v^2$

Exercise Set 5.3

1. $2y^2(5y) = (2\cdot5)(y^2\cdot y) = 10y^3$

3. $5x(-4x^2y) = 5(-4)(x\cdot x^2)y = -20x^3y$

5. $2x^3y^2(-5x^2y^4) = 2(-5)(x^3\cdot x^2)(y^2\cdot y^4) = -10x^5y^6$

7. $2x(3 - x)$
= $2x\cdot3 - 2x\cdot x$
= $6x - 2x^2$

9. $-3ab(a + b)$
= $-3ab\cdot a + (-3ab)\cdot b$
= $-3a^2b - 3ab^2$

11. $5cd(3c^2d - 5cd^2)$
= $5cd\cdot3c^2d - 5cd\cdot5cd^2$
= $15c^3d^2 - 25c^2d^3$

13. $(2x + 3)(3x - 4)$
= $2x(3x - 4) + 3(3x - 4)$
= $2x\cdot3x - 2x\cdot4 + 3\cdot3x - 3\cdot4$
= $6x^2 - 8x + 9x - 12$
= $6x^2 + x - 12$

15. $(s + 3t)(s - 3t)$
= $s(s - 3t) + 3t(s - 3t)$
= $s\cdot s - s\cdot3t + 3t\cdot s - 3t\cdot3t$
= $s^2 - 3st + 3st - 9t^2$
= $s^2 - 9t^2$

17. $(x - y)(x - y)$
= $x(x - y) - y(x - y)$
= $x\cdot x - x\cdot y - y\cdot x + y\cdot y$
= $x^2 - xy - xy + y^2$
= $x^2 - 2xy + y^2$

19. $(y + 8x)(2y - 7x)$
= $y(2y - 7x) + 8x(2y - 7x)$
= $y\cdot2y - y\cdot7x + 8x\cdot2y - 8x\cdot7x$
= $2y^2 - 7xy + 16xy - 56x^2$
= $2y^2 + 9xy - 56x^2$

21. $(a^2 - 2b^2)(a^2 - 3b^2)$
= $a^2(a^2 - 3b^2) - 2b^2(a^2 - 3b^2)$
= $a^2\cdot a^2 - a^2\cdot3b^2 - 2b^2\cdot a^2 + 2b^2\cdot3b^2$
= $a^4 - 3a^2b^2 - 2a^2b^2 + 6b^4$
= $a^4 - 5a^2b^2 + 6b^4$

23.
$$
\begin{array}{ll}
x^2 + 4x + 16 & \\
\underline{\qquad\qquad x - 4} & \\
x^3 + 4x^2 + 16x & \text{(Multiplying by x)} \\
\underline{\qquad -4x^2 - 16x - 64} & \text{(Multiplying by -4)} \\
x^3 \qquad\qquad\qquad - 64 & \text{(Adding)}
\end{array}
$$

The product is $x^3 - 64$.

25.
$$
\begin{array}{ll}
x^2 - xy + y^2 & \\
\underline{\qquad\qquad x + y} & \\
x^3 - x^2y + xy^2 & \text{(Multiplying by x)} \\
\underline{\qquad x^2y - xy^2 + y^3} & \text{(Multiplying by y)} \\
x^3 \qquad\qquad\qquad + y^3 & \text{(Adding)}
\end{array}
$$

The product is $x^3 + y^3$.

27.
$$
\begin{array}{ll}
a^2 + 4a - 5 & \\
\underline{\qquad a^2 + a - 1} & \\
a^4 + 4a^3 - 5a^2 & \text{(Multiplying by } a^2) \\
\quad\;\; a^3 + 4a^2 - 5a & \text{(Multiplying by a)} \\
\underline{\qquad\qquad -a^2 - 4a + 5} & \text{(Multiplying by -1)} \\
a^4 + 5a^3 - 2a^2 - 9a + 5 & \text{(Adding)}
\end{array}
$$

29.
$$
\begin{array}{lll}
4a^2b - 2ab + 3b^2 & & \\
\underline{\qquad\qquad ab - 2b + a} & & \\
4a^3b^2 - 2a^2b^2 + 3ab^3 & & ① \\
\quad -8a^2b^2 \qquad + 4ab^2 - 6b^3 & & ② \\
\underline{\qquad\qquad\quad 3ab^2 \qquad + 4a^3b - 2a^2b} & & ③ \\
4a^3b^2 - 10a^2b^2 + 3ab^3 + 7ab^2 - 6b^3 + 4a^3b - 2a^2b & & ④
\end{array}
$$

① Multiplying by ab

② Multiplying by $-2b$

③ Multiplying by a

④ Adding

31. $x + 2y + z = 4$ (1)
$2x + y - z = 2$ (2)
$x + y + z = 7$ (3)

Adding equations (1) and (2) we get

$3x + 3y = 6$, or $x + y = 2$

Adding equations (2) and (3) we get

$3x + 2y = 9$

We solve the resulting system.
$x + y = 2$ (4)
$3x + 2y = 9$ (5)

$-2x - 2y = -4$ [Multiplying (4) by -2]
$\underline{3x + 2y = 9}$ (5)
$x = 5$ (Adding)

We now substitute 5 for x in either equation (4) or equation (5) and solve for y.
$x + y = 2$ (4)
$5 + y = 2$ (Substituting)
$y = -3$

Finally we substitute -3 for y and 5 for x in any one of the original three equations and solve for z.
$x + y + z = 7$ (3)
$5 + (-3) + z = 7$ (Substituting)
$2 + z = 7$
$z = 5$

The ordered triple (5,-3,5) checks and is the solution.

33. $|2x + 4| > 10$

$2x + 4 < -10$ or $2x + 4 > 10$
$2x < -14$ or $2x > 6$
$x < -7$ or $x > 3$

The solution set is $\{x | x < -7 \text{ or } x > 3\}$.

35. $(-8s^3t)(2s^5 - 3s^3t^4 + st^7 - t^{10})$
$= -8s^3t(2s^5) - (-8s^3t)3s^3t^4 +$
$\qquad\qquad\qquad (-8s^3t)st^7 - (-8s^3t)t^{10}$
$= -16s^8t + 24s^6t^5 - 8s^4t^8 + 8s^3t^{11}$

37. The area of the base is $x \cdot x$, or x^2.
The area of each side is $x \cdot h$, of xh.
The area of all 4 sides is 4xh.
The total outside area of the box is $x^2 + 4xh$.

1. $(a + 2)(a + 3)$
$= a^2 + 3a + 2a + 6$ (FOIL)
$= a^2 + 5a + 6$

3. $(y + 3)(y - 2)$
$= y^2 - 2y + 3y - 6$ (FOIL)
$= y^2 + y - 6$

5. $(b - \frac{1}{3})(b - \frac{1}{2})$
$= b^2 - \frac{1}{2}b - \frac{1}{3}b + \frac{1}{6}$ (FOIL)
$= b^2 - \frac{3}{6}b - \frac{2}{6}b + \frac{1}{6}$
$= b^2 - \frac{5}{6}b + \frac{1}{6}$

7. $(2x + 9)(x + 2)$
$= 2x^2 + 4x + 9x + 18$ (FOIL)
$= 2x^2 + 13x + 18$

9. $(2x - 3y)(2x + y)$
$= 4x^2 + 2xy - 6xy - 3y^2$ (FOIL)
$= 4x^2 - 4xy - 3y^2$

11. $(1.3x - 4y)(2.5x + 7y)$
$= 3.25x^2 + 9.1xy - 10yx - 28y^2$ (FOIL)
$= 3.25x^2 - 0.9xy - 28y^2$

13. $(x + 3)^2$
$= x^2 + 2 \cdot x \cdot 3 + 3^2$ $[(A + B)^2 = A^2 + 2AB + B^2]$
$= x^2 + 6x + 9$

15. $(2a + \frac{1}{3})^2$
$= (2a)^2 + 2(2a)(\frac{1}{3}) + (\frac{1}{3})^2$
$\qquad\qquad [(A + B)^2 = A^2 + 2AB + B^2]$
$= 4a^2 + \frac{4}{3}a + \frac{1}{9}$

17. $(x - 2y)^2$
$= x^2 - 2(x)(2y) + (2y)^2$
$\qquad\qquad [(A - B)^2 = A^2 - 2AB + B^2]$
$= x^2 - 4xy + 4y^2$

19. $(2x^2 - 3y^2)^2$
$= (2x^2)^2 - 2(2x^2)(3y^2) + (3y^2)^2$
$\qquad\qquad [(A - B)^2 = A^2 - 2AB + B^2]$
$= 4x^4 - 12x^2y^2 + 9y^4$

21. $(a^2b^2 + 1)^2$
$= (a^2b^2)^2 + 2(a^2b^2) \cdot 1 + 1^2$
$\qquad\qquad [(A + B)^2 = A^2 + 2AB + B^2]$
$= a^4b^4 + 2a^2b^2 + 1$

23. $(20a - 0.16b)^2$

$= (20a)^2 - 2(20a)(0.16b) + (0.16b)^2$

$= 400a^2 - 6.4ab + 0.0256b^2$

25. $(c + 2)(c - 2)$

$= c^2 - 2^2$　　　$[(A + B)(A - B) = A^2 - B^2]$

$= c^2 - 4$

27. $(2a + 1)(2a - 1)$

$= (2a)^2 - 1^2$　　　$[(A + B)(A - B) = A^2 - B^2]$

$= 4a^2 - 1$

29. $(3m - 2n)(3m + 2n)$

$= (3m)^2 - (2n)^2$　　　$[(A - B)(A + B) = A^2 - B^2]$

$= 9m^2 - 4n^2$

31. $(-yz + x^2)(yz + x^2)$

$= (x^2 - yz)(x^2 + yz)$

$= (x^2)^2 - (yz)^2$　　　$[(A - B)(A + B) = A^2 - B^2]$

$= x^4 - y^2z^2$

33. Let x, y, and z represent the number of suitcases produced per day by machines A, B, and C, respectively. We translate to a system of equations.

When all three work, they produce 222 per day.
$x + y + z = 222$　　　(1)

When only A and B work, they produce 159 per day.
$x + y = 159$　　　(2)

When only B and C work, they produce 147 per day.
$y + z = 147$　　　(3)

This system can be easily solved using the substitution method.

Substitute 159 for x + y in equation (1) and solve for z.
$x + y + z = 222$
$159 + z = 222$
$z = 63$

Next substitute 147 for y + z in equation (1) and solve for x.
$x + y + z = 222$
$x + 147 = 222$
$x = 75$

Finally substitute 75 for x in equation (2) and solve for y.
$x + y = 159$
$75 + y = 159$
$y = 84$

33. (continued)

If A produces 75 per day, B 84 per day and C 63 a day, then together they produce 75 + 84 + 63, or 222, per day. When only A and B are working, they produce 75 + 84, or 159, per day. When only B and C are working, they produce 84 + 63, or 147, per day. The values check.

The daily productions of machines A, B, and C are 75, 84, and 63, respectively.

35. $[x + y + 1][x^2 - x(y + 1) + (y + 1)^2]$

Let A = x and B = y + 1, then rewrite the problem and multiply.

$[A + B][A^2 - AB + B^2]$

$= (A \cdot A^2 - A \cdot AB + A \cdot B^2) + (B \cdot A^2 - B \cdot AB + B \cdot B^2)$

$= A^3 - A^2B + AB^2 + A^2B - AB^2 + B^3$

$= A^3 + B^3$

Replace A by x and B by y + 1 and simplify.

$x^3 + (y + 1)^3$

$= x^3 + (y + 1)(y + 1)^2$

$= x^3 + (y + 1)(y^2 + 2y + 1)$

$= x^3 + y^3 + 2y^2 + y + y^2 + 2y + 1$

$= x^3 + y^3 + 3y^2 + 3y + 1$

37. $(3x^a - \frac{5}{11})^2$

$= (3x^a)^2 - 2(3x^a)(\frac{5}{11}) + (\frac{5}{11})^2$

$= 9x^{2a} - \frac{30}{11}x^a + \frac{25}{121}$

39. $(x - 1)(x^2 + x + 1)(x^3 + 1)$

$= (x^3 + x^2 + x - x^2 - x - 1)(x^3 + 1)$

$= (x^3 - 1)(x^3 + 1)$

$= x^6 - 1$

Exercise Set 5.4A

1. $(4x - y)(2x - y)$

$= 8x^2 - 4xy - 2xy + y^2$　　　(FOIL)

$= 8x^2 - 6xy + y^2$

3. $(2c + 7d)^2$

$= (2c)^2 + 2(2c)(7d) + (7d^2)$

　　　　　　$[(A + B)^2 = A^2 + 2AB + B^2]$

$= 4c^2 + 28cd + 49d^2$

5. $(-2d + 3c)(2d + 3c)$

$= (3c - 2d)(3c + 2d)$

$= (3c)^2 - (2d)^2$　　　$[(A - B)(A + B) = A^2 - B^2]$

$= 9c^2 - 4d^2$

7. $(x^2 + 2y)(2x^2 - y)$

   $= 2x^4 - x^2y + 4x^2y - 2y^2$ (FOIL)

   $= 2x^4 + 3x^2y - 2y^2$

9. $(2m^2 - n^2)(m^2 + 3n^2)$

   $= 2m^4 + 6m^2n^2 - m^2n^2 - 3n^4$ (FOIL)

   $= 2m^4 + 5m^2n^2 - 3n^4$

11. $(3x - 4y)^2$

   $= (3x)^2 - 2(3x)(4y) + (4y)^2$

   $\qquad\qquad\qquad\qquad [(A - B)^2 = A^2 - 2AB + B^2]$

   $= 9x^2 - 24xy + 16y^2$

13. $(a^2 + b)(a^2 - b)$

   $= (a^2)^2 - b^2$ $[(A + B)(A - B) = A^2 - B^2]$

   $= a^4 - b^2$

15. $(\frac{1}{5} - x)(\frac{1}{5} + x)$

   $= (\frac{1}{5})^2 - x^2$ $[(A - B)(A + B) = A^2 - B^2]$

   $= \frac{1}{25} - x^2$

17. $(2x^2 + 3y^2)(4x^2 - 5y^2)$

   $= 8x^4 - 10x^2y^2 + 12x^2y^2 - 15y^4$ (FOIL)

   $= 8x^4 + 2x^2y^2 - 15y^4$

19. $(\frac{1}{2}x - 6)^2$

   $= (\frac{1}{2}x)^2 - 2(\frac{1}{2}x)(6) + 6^2$

   $\qquad\qquad\qquad [(A - B)^2 = A^2 - 2AB + B^2]$

   $= \frac{1}{4}x^2 - 6x + 36$

21. $(x + 1)(x - 1)(x^2 + 1)$

   $= (x^2 - 1)(x^2 + 1)$

   $= x^4 - 1$

23. $(a + b)(a - b)(a^2 - b^2)$

   $= (a^2 - b^2)(a^2 - b^2)$

   $= (a^2)^2 - 2(a^2)(b^2) + (b^2)^2$

   $= a^4 - 2a^2b^2 + b^4$

25. $(a + b + 1)(a + b - 1)$

   $= [(a + b) + 1][(a + b) - 1]$

   $= (a + b)^2 - 1^2$

   $= a^2 + 2ab + b^2 - 1$

27. $(2x + 3y + 4)(2x + 3y - 4)$

   $= [(2x + 3y) + 4][(2x + 3y) - 4]$

   $= (2x + 3y)^2 - 4^2$

   $= 4x^2 + 12xy + 9y^2 - 16$

29.   Let d represent the number of rolls of dimes, n the number of rolls of nickels, and q the number of rolls of quarters.

We translate to a system of equations.

The total number of rolls is 13.

$d + n + q = 13$

The total value of the rolls is $89.

$0.10(50d) + 0.05(40n) + 0.25(40q) = 89$

or

$5d + 2n + 10q = 89$

The number of rolls of dimes is three more than the number of rolls of nickels.

$d = n + 3$

We solve the resulting system of equations.

$d + n + q = 13$ (1)

$5d + 2n + 10q = 89$ (2)

$d = n + 3$ (3)

Substitute n + 3 for d in each of the first two equations.

$(n + 3) + n + q = 13$ (1)

$\qquad 2n + q = 10$ (4)

$5(n + 3) + 2n + 10q = 89$ (2)

$\quad 5n + 15 + 2n + 10q = 89$

$\qquad\qquad 7n + 10q = 74$ (5)

We solve the resulting system of two equations [(4) and (5)] for n and q.

$-20n - 10q = -100$ [Multiplying equation (4)

$\qquad\qquad\qquad\qquad$ by -10

$\underline{\quad 7n + 10q = \quad 74}$ (5)

$-13n \qquad = -26$ (Adding)

$\qquad n = 2$

Substitute 2 for n in either equation (4) or equation (5) and solve for q.

$\quad 2n + q = 10$ (4)

$2 \cdot 2 + q = 10$

$\quad 4 + q = 10$

$\qquad q = 6$

Now we substitute 2 for n in equation (3) and solve for d.

$d = n + 3$ (3)

$d = 2 + 3$

$d = 5$

If there are 5 rolls of dimes, 2 rolls of nickels and 6 rolls of quarters, the total number of rolls is 5 + 2 + 6, or 13. The total value is

$\quad 0.10(50 \cdot 5) + 0.05(40 \cdot 2) + 0.25(40 \cdot 6)$

$= 25 + 4 + 60$

$= \$89$

The values check. There are 5 rolls of dimes, 2 rolls of nickels, and 6 rolls of quarters.

31. $(x^a + y^b)(x^a - y^b)(x^{2a} + y^{2b})$

    $= (x^{2a} - y^{2b})(x^{2a} + y^{2b})$

    $= x^{4a} - y^{4b}$

33. $(x - \frac{1}{7})(x^2 + \frac{1}{7}x + \frac{1}{49})$

    $= x^3 + \frac{1}{7}x^2 + \frac{1}{49}x - \frac{1}{7}x^2 - \frac{1}{49}x - \frac{1}{343}$

    $= x^3 - \frac{1}{343}$

35. $(x^{a-b})(x^{a+b})$

    $= x^{(a-b)+(a+b)}$

    $= x^{2a}$

37. $(4x^2 + 2xy + y^2)(4x^2 - 2xy + y^2)$

    $= [(4x^2 + y^2) + 2xy][(4x^2 + y^2) - 2xy]$

    $= (4x^2 + y^2)^2 - (2xy)^2$

    $= 16x^4 + 8x^2y^2 + y^4 - 4x^2y^2$

    $= 16x^4 + 4x^2y^2 + y^4$

Exercise Set 5.5

1. $4a^2 + 2a$

   $= 2a \cdot 2a + 2a \cdot 1$

   $= 2a(2a + 1)$

3. $3y^2 - 3y - 9$

   $= 3 \cdot y^2 - 3 \cdot y - 3 \cdot 3$

   $= 3(y^2 - y - 3)$

5. $6x^2 - 3x^4$

   $= 3x^2 \cdot 2 - 3x^2 \cdot x^2$

   $= 3x^2(2 - x^2)$

7. $4ab - 6ac + 12ad$

   $= 2a \cdot 2b - 2a \cdot 3c + 2a \cdot 6d$

   $= 2a(2b - 3c + 6d)$

9. $10a^4 + 15a^2 - 25a - 30$

   $= 5 \cdot 2a^4 + 5 \cdot 3a^2 - 5 \cdot 5a - 5 \cdot 6$

   $= 5(2a^4 + 3a^2 - 5a - 6)$

11. $a(b - 2) + c(b - 2)$

    $= (a + c)(b - 2)$

13. $(x - 2)(x + 5) + (x - 2)(x + 8)$

    $= (x - 2)[(x + 5) + (x + 8)]$

    $= (x - 2)(2x + 13)$

15. $a^2(x - y) + a^2(x - y)$

    $= 2a^2(x - y)$

17. $ac + ad + bc + bd$

    $= a(c + d) + b(c + d)$

    $= (a + b)(c + d)$

19. $b^3 - b^2 + 2b - 2$

    $= b^2(b - 1) + 2(b - 1)$

    $= (b^2 + 2)(b - 1)$

21. $y^4 - 8y^3 + 2y - 16$

    $= y^3(y - 8) + 2(y - 8)$

    $= (y^3 + 2)(y - 8)$

23. $x^2 - 16$

    $= x^2 - 4^2$

    $= (x + 4)(x - 4)$ $[A^2 - B^2 = (A + B)(A - B)]$

25. $6x^2 - 6y^2$

    $= 6(x^2 - y^2)$

    $= 6(x + y)(x - y)$ $[A^2 - B^2 = (A + B)(A - B)]$

27. $4xy^4 - 4xz^4$

    $= 4x(y^4 - z^4)$

    $= 4x[(y^2)^2 - (z^2)^2]$

    $= 4x(y^2 + z^2)(y^2 - z^2)$ $[A^2 - B^2 = (A + B)(A - B)]$

    $= 4x(y^2 + z^2)(y + z)(y - z)$

              $[A^2 - B^2 = (A + B)(A - B)]$

29. $9a^4 - 25a^2b^4$

    $= a^2(9a^2 - 25b^4)$

    $= a^2[(3a)^2 - (5b^2)^2]$

    $= a^2(3a + 5b^2)(3a - 5b^2)$

              $[A^2 - B^2 = (A + B)(A - B)]$

31. $\frac{1}{25} - x^2$

    $= (\frac{1}{5})^2 - x^2$

    $= (\frac{1}{5} + x)(\frac{1}{5} - x)$ $[A^2 - B^2 = (A + B)(A - B)]$

33. $0.04x^2 - 0.09y^2$

    $= (0.2x)^2 - (0.3y)^2$

    $= (0.2x + 0.3y)(0.2x - 0.3y)$

              $[A^2 - B^2 = (A + B)(A - B)]$

35. $\begin{array}{ll} x - y + z = 6 & (1) \\ 2x + y - z = 0 & (2) \\ x + 2y + z = 3 & (3) \end{array}$

Adding equations (1) and (2) we get

$3x = 6$, or $x = 2$ (4)

Adding equations (2) and (3) we get

$3x + 3y = 3$, or $x + y = 1$ (5)

Solving the resulting system of equations, (4) and (5), we get $x = 2$ and $y = -1$. We substitute these values in any one of the original equations and solve for z.

$\begin{array}{ll} x - y + z = 6 & (1) \\ 2 - (-1) + z = 6 & \text{(Substituting)} \\ 3 + z = 6 & \\ z = 3 & \end{array}$

The solution of the original system is $(2, -1, 3)$.

37. $|5 - 7x| \leqslant 9$

$-9 \leqslant 5 - 7x \leqslant 9$ (Property 2)

$-14 \leqslant -7x \leqslant 4$ (Adding -5)

$2 \geqslant x \geqslant -\dfrac{4}{7}$ (Multiplying by $-\dfrac{1}{7}$ and reversing the inequality symbol)

The solution set is $\{x| -\dfrac{4}{7} \leqslant x \leqslant 2\}$.

39. $(x - h)^2 - h^2$
$= [(x - h) + h][(x - h) - h]$
$= x(x - 2h)$

41. $\dfrac{1}{2}n^2 - \dfrac{3}{2}n = \dfrac{1}{2}n(n - 3)$

Replace n by 5.

$\dfrac{1}{2} \cdot 5 \cdot (5 - 3) = \dfrac{1}{2} \cdot 5 \cdot 2 = 5$

A polygon with 5 sides has 5 diagonals.

Exercise Set 5.6

1. $y^2 - 6y + 9$
$= y^2 - 2 \cdot y \cdot 3 + 3^2$
$= (y - 3)^2$ $[A^2 - 2AB + B^2 = (A - B)^2]$

3. $x^2 - 14x + 49$
$= x^2 - 2 \cdot x \cdot 7 + 7^2$
$= (x - 7)^2$ $[A^2 - 2AB + B^2 = (A - B)^2]$

5. $-18y^2 + y^3 + 81y$
$= y^3 - 18y^2 + 81y$
$= y(y^2 - 18y + 81)$
$= y(y^2 - 2 \cdot y \cdot 9 + 9^2)$
$= y(y - 9)^2$ $[A^2 - 2AB + B^2 = (A - B)^2]$

7. $12a^2 + 36a + 27$
$= 3(4a^2 + 12a + 9)$
$= 3[(2a)^2 + 2 \cdot 2a \cdot 3 + 3^2]$
$= 3(2a + 3)^2$ $[A^2 + 2AB + B^2 = (A + B)^2]$

9. $2x^2 - 40x + 200$
$= 2(x^2 - 20x + 100)$
$= 2(x^2 - 2 \cdot x \cdot 10 + 10^2)$
$= 2(x - 10)^2$ $[A^2 - 2AB + B^2 = (A - B)^2]$

11. $0.25x^2 + 0.30x + 0.09$
$= (0.5x)^2 + 2(0.5x)(0.3) + (0.3)^2$
$= (0.5x + 0.3)^2$ $[A^2 + 2AB + B^2 = (A + B)^2]$

13. $x^2 + 9x + 20$

We look for two numbers whose product is 20 and whose sum is 9. Since both 9 and 20 are positive, we need to consider only positive factors.

Pairs of factors	Sums of factors
1, 20	21
2, 10	12
* 4, 5	9

The numbers we want are 4 and 5.

$x^2 + 9x + 20 = (x + 4)(x + 5)$

15. $2y^2 - 16y + 32$
$= 2(y^2 - 8y + 16)$ (Removing the common factor)

We now factor $y^2 - 8y + 16$. We look for two numbers whose product is 16 and whose sum is -8. Since the constant term is positive and the coefficient of the middle term is negative, we look for a factorization of 16 in which both factors are negative.

Pairs of factors	Sums of factors
-1, -16	-17
-2, -8	-10
* -4, -4	-8

The numbers we want are -4 and -4.

$y^2 - 8y + 16 = (y - 4)(y - 4)$

We must not forget to include the common factor 2.

$2y^2 - 16y + 32 = 2(y - 4)(y - 4)$, or $2(y - 4)^2$

17. $x^2 - 27 - 6x$

= $x^2 - 6x - 27$ (Changing the order)

We look for two numbers whose product is -27 and whose sum is -6. Since the constant term is negative, we look for a factorization of -27 in which one factor is positive and one factor is negative. Their sum must be -6.

Pairs of factors	Sums of factors
1, -27	-26
-1, 27	26
* 3, -9	-6
-3, 9	6

The numbers we want are 3 and -9.

$x^2 - 6x - 27 = (x + 3)(x - 9)$

19. $32y + 4y^2 - y^3$

= $-y^3 + 4y^2 + 32y$ (Changing the order)

= $-y(y^2 - 4y - 32)$ (Removing the common factor)

We now factor $y^2 - 4y - 32$. We look for two numbers whose product is -32 and whose sum is -4. Since the constant term is negative, we look for a factorization of -32 in which one factor is positive and one factor is negative. Their sum must be -4.

Pairs of factors	Sums of factors
1, -32	-31
-1, 32	31
2, -16	-14
-2, 16	14
* 4, -8	-4
-4, 8	4

The numbers we want are 4 and -8.

$y^2 - 4y - 32 = (y + 4)(y - 8)$

We must not forget to include the common factor -y.

$-y^3 + 4y^2 + 32y = -y(y + 4)(y - 8)$, or
$\qquad\qquad\qquad\quad y(4 + y)(8 - y)$

21. $15 + t^2 + 8t$

= $t^2 + 8t + 15$ (Changing the order)

We look for two numbers whose product is 15 and whose sum is 8. Since both 8 and 15 are positive, we need to consider only positive factors.

Pairs of factors	Sums of factors
1, 15	16
* 3, 5	8

The numbers we want are 3 and 5.

$t^2 + 8t + 15 = (t + 3)(t + 5)$

23. $x^4 + 11x^2 - 80$

= $(x^2)^2 + 11x^2 - 80$

The first term of each factor will be x^2. We look for two numbers whose product is -80 and whose sum is 11. Since the constant term is negative, we look for a factorization of -80 in which one factor is negative. Their sum must be 11.

Pairs of factors	Sums of factors
1, -80	-79
-1, 80	79
2, -40	-38
-2, 40	38
4, -20	-16
-4, 20	16
5, -16	-11
* -5, 16	11
8, -10	-2
-8, 10	2

The numbers we want are -5 and 16.

$x^4 + 11x^2 - 80 = (x^2 - 5)(x^2 + 16)$

25. $3x^2 - 16x - 12$

There is no common factor other than 1 or -1.

Multiply the leading coefficient and the constant, 3 and -12: 3(-12) = -36.

Factor -36 so that the sum of the factors is -16. The desired factorization is -18·2.

Split the middle term and factor by grouping.

$3x^2 - 16x - 12 = 3x^2 - 18x + 2x - 12$
$\qquad\qquad\quad = 3x(x - 6) + 2(x - 6)$
$\qquad\qquad\quad = (3x + 2)(x - 6)$

27. $6x^3 - 15x - x^2$

= $6x^3 - x^2 - 15x$ (Changing the order)

= $x(6x^2 - x - 15)$ (Removing the common factor)

We now factor $6x^2 - x - 15$.

Multiply the leading coefficient and the constant, 6 and -15: 6(-15) = -90.

Factor -90 so that the sum of the factors is -1. The desired factorization is -10·9.

Split the middle term and factor by grouping.

$6x^2 - x - 15 = 6x^2 - 10x + 9x - 15$
$\qquad\qquad\quad = 2x(3x - 5) + 3(3x - 5)$
$\qquad\qquad\quad = (2x + 3)(3x - 5)$

We must not forget to include the common factor x.

$6x^3 - x^2 - 15x = x(2x + 3)(3x - 5)$

29. $3a^2 - 10a + 8$

There is no common factor other than 1 or -1.

Multiply the leading coefficient and the constant, 3 and 8: $3 \cdot 8 = 24$.

Factor 24 so that the sum of the factors is -10. The desired factorization is $-6 \cdot (-4)$.

Split the middle term and factor by grouping.
$$3a^2 - 10a + 8 = 3a^2 - 6a - 4a + 8$$
$$= 3a(a - 2) - 4(a - 2)$$
$$= (3a - 4)(a - 2)$$

31. $35y^2 + 34y + 8$

There is no common factor other than 1 or -1.

Multiply the leading coefficient and the constant, 35 and 8: $35 \cdot 8 = 280$.

Factor 280 so that the sum of the factors is 34. The desired factorization is $14 \cdot 20$.

Split the middle term and factor by grouping.
$$35y^2 + 34y + 8 = 35y^2 + 14y + 20y + 8$$
$$= 7y(5y + 2) + 4(5y + 2)$$
$$= (7y + 4)(5y + 2)$$

33. $4t + 10t^2 - 6$
$$= 10t^2 + 4t - 6 \qquad \text{(Changing the order)}$$
$$= 2(5t^2 + 2t - 3) \qquad \text{(Removing the common factor)}$$

We now factor $5t^2 + 2t - 3$.

Multiply the leading coefficient and the constant, 5 and -3: $5 \cdot (-3) = -15$.

Factor -15 so that the sum of the factors is 2. The desired factorization is $-3 \cdot 5$.

Split the middle term and factor by grouping.
$$5t^2 + 2t - 3 = 5t^2 - 3t + 5t - 3$$
$$= t(5t - 3) + 1(5t - 3)$$
$$= (t + 1)(5t - 3)$$

We must not forget to include the common factor 2.
$$10t^2 + 4t - 6 = 2(t + 1)(5t - 3)$$

35. $8x^2 - 16 - 28x$
$$= 8x^2 - 28x - 16 \qquad \text{(Changing the order)}$$
$$= 4(2x^2 - 7x - 4) \qquad \text{(Removing the common factor)}$$

We now factor $2x^2 - 7x - 4$.

Multiply the leading coefficient and the constant, 2 and -4: $2 \cdot (-4) = -8$.

Factor -8 so that the sum of the factors is -7. The desired factorization is $-8 \cdot 1$.

35. (continued)

Split the middle term and factor by grouping.
$$2x^2 - 7x - 4 = 2x^2 - 8x + x - 4$$
$$= 2x(x - 4) + 1(x - 4)$$
$$= (2x + 1)(x - 4)$$

We must include the common factor 4.
$$8x^2 - 28x - 16 = 4(2x + 1)(x - 4)$$

37. $12x^3 - 31x^2 + 20x$
$$= x(12x^2 - 31x + 20) \qquad \text{(Removing the common factor)}$$

We now factor $12x^2 - 31x + 20$.

Multiply the leading coefficient and the constant, 12 and 20: $12 \cdot 20 = 240$.

Factor 240 so that the sum of the factors is -31. The desired factorization is $-15 \cdot (-16)$.

Split the middle term and factor by grouping.
$$12x^2 - 31x + 20 = 12x^2 - 15x - 16x + 20$$
$$= 3x(4x - 5) - 4(4x - 5)$$
$$= (3x - 4)(4x - 5)$$

We must include the common factor x.
$$12x^3 - 31x^2 + 20x = x(3x - 4)(4x - 5)$$

39. $14x^4 - 19x^3 - 3x^2$
$$= x^2(14x^2 - 19x - 3) \qquad \text{(Removing the common factor)}$$

We now factor $14x^2 - 19x - 3$.

Multiply the leading coefficient and the constant, 14 and -3: $14 \cdot (-3) = -42$.

Factor -42 so that the sum of the factors is -19. The desired factorization is $-21 \cdot 2$.

Split the middle term and factor by grouping.
$$14x^2 - 19x - 3 = 14x^2 - 21x + 2x - 3$$
$$= 7x(2x - 3) + 1(2x - 3)$$
$$= (7x + 1)(2x - 3)$$

We must include the common factor x^2.
$$14x^4 - 19x^3 - 3x^2 = x^2(7x + 1)(2x - 3)$$

41. $x^2 - 3x + 7$

We look for two numbers whose product is 7 and whose sum is -3. Since the constant term is positive and the coefficient of the middle term is negative, we look for a factorization of 7 in which both factors are negative.

Pairs of factors	Sums of factors
-1, -7	-8

There are no such factors whose sum is -3. Thus, the trinomial $x^2 - 3x + 7$ cannot be factored into polynomials with real number coefficients.

43. $2x^2 + xy - 6y^2$

The variable in the first term of each binomial factor will be x. The variable in the second term of each binomial factor will be y.

(x   y)(x   y)

There is no common factor other than 1 or -1.

Multiply the coefficients of the x^2 and y^2 terms, 2 and -6: 2(-6) = -12.

Factor -12 so that the sum of the factors is 1. The desired factorization is -3·4.

Split the middle term and factor by grouping.

$2x^2 + xy - 6y^2 = 2x^2 - 3xy + 4xy - 6y^2$
$\qquad\qquad\qquad = x(2x - 3y) + 2y(2x - 3y)$
$\qquad\qquad\qquad = (x + 2y)(2x - 3y)$

45. $x^4 - 50x^2 + 49$
$= (x^2)^2 - 50x^2 + 49$
$= (x^2 - 1)(x^2 - 49)$
$= (x + 1)(x - 1)(x + 7)(x - 7)$

47. $x^2 + \frac{3}{5} x - \frac{4}{25}$

$= (x + \frac{4}{5})(x - \frac{1}{5})$

$\left[\frac{4}{5} \cdot (- \frac{1}{5}) = - \frac{4}{25}; \frac{4}{5} + (- \frac{1}{5}) = \frac{3}{5} \right]$

49. $72a^2 + 284a - 160$
$= 4(18a^2 + 71a - 40)$
$= 4(2a - 1)(9a + 40)$

51. $x^{2a} + 5x^a - 24$
$= (x^a)^2 + 5x^a - 24$
$= (x^a + 8)(x^a - 3)$

Exercise Set 5.7

1. $a^2 + 2ab + b^2 - 9$
$= (a^2 + 2ab + b^2) - 9$
$= (a + b)^2 - 3^2$
$= [(a + b) + 3][(a + b) - 3]$
$= (a + b + 3)(a + b - 3)$

3. $r^2 - 2r + 1 - 4s^2$
$= (r^2 - 2r + 1) - 4s^2$
$= (r - 1)^2 - (2s)^2$
$= [(r - 1) + 2s][(r - 1) - 2s]$
$= (r + 2s - 1)(r - 2s - 1)$

5. $2m^2 + 4mn + 2n^2 - 50b^2$
$= 2(m^2 + 2mn + n^2 - 25b^2)$
$= 2[(m^2 + 2mn + n^2) - 25b^2]$
$= 2[(m + n)^2 - (5b)^2]$
$= 2[(m + n) + 5b][(m + n) - 5b]$
$= 2(m + n + 5b)(m + n - 5b)$

7. $9 - (a^2 + 2ab + b^2)$
$= 3^2 - (a + b)^2$
$= [3 + (a + b)][3 - (a + b)]$
$= (3 + a + b)(3 - a - b)$

9. What must be added to $x^2 + 16x$ in order to make it a trinomial square? We take half the coefficient of x and square it.
$x^2 + 16x$
$\quad \longrightarrow$ Half of 16 is 8, and $8^2 = 64$.
We add 64.

$x^2 + 16x + 64$ is a trinomial square.
It is equivalent to $(x + 8)^2$.

11. What must be added to $x^2 - 4.2x$ in order to make it a trinomial square? We take half of the coefficient of x and square it.
$x^2 - 4.2x$
$\quad \longrightarrow$ Half of 4.2 is 2.1, and $(2.1)^2 = 4.41$. We add 4.41.

$x^2 - 4.2x + 4.41$ is a trinomial square.
It is equivalent to $(x - 2.1)^2$.

13. What must be added to $x^2 + \frac{2}{3} bx$ in order to make it a trinomial square? We take half of the coefficient of x and square it.
$x^2 + (\frac{2}{3} b)x$
$\quad \longrightarrow$ Half of $\frac{2}{3}$ b is $\frac{1}{3}$ b, and $(\frac{1}{3} b)^2 = \frac{1}{9} b^2$. We add $\frac{1}{9}$ b^2.

$x^2 + \frac{2}{3} bx + \frac{1}{9} b^2$ is a trinomial square.
It is equivalent to $(x + \frac{1}{3} b)^2$.

15. $x^2 + 24x + 119$
$= x^2 + 24x + 119 + (144 - 144)$
Half of 24 is 12, and $12^2 = 144$.
We add 0, naming it 144 - 144.

$= (x^2 + 24x + 144) + 119 - 144$
$= (x^2 + 24x + 144) - 25$
$= (x + 12)^2 - 5^2$
$= (x + 12 + 5)(x + 12 - 5)$
$= (x + 17)(x + 7)$

17. $x^2 - 26x + 105$

$= x^2 - 26x + 105 + (169 - 169)$

Half of -26 is -13, and $(-13)^2 = 169$.
We add 0, naming it 169 - 169.

$= (x^2 - 26x + 169) + 105 - 169$

$= (x^2 - 26x + 169) - 64$

$= (x - 13)^2 - 8^2$

$= (x - 13 + 8)(x - 13 - 8)$

$= (x - 5)(x - 21)$

19. $2x^2 + 56x + 342$

$= 2(x^2 + 28x + 171)$

$= 2[x^2 + 28x + 171 + (196 - 196)]$

Half of 28 is 14, and $14^2 = 196$.
We add 0, naming it 196 - 196.

$= 2[(x^2 + 28x + 196) + 171 - 196]$

$= 2[(x^2 + 28x + 196) - 25]$

$= 2[(x + 14)^2 - 5^2]$

$= 2(x + 14 + 5)(x + 14 - 5)$

$= 2(x + 19)(x + 9)$

21. $2x^2 - 32ax + 96a^2$

$= 2(x^2 - 16ax + 48a^2)$

$= 2[x^2 - 16ax + 48a^2 + (64a^2 - 64a^2)]$

Half of -16a is -8a, and $(-8a)^2 = 64a^2$.
We add 0, naming it $64a^2 - 64a^2$.

$= 2[(x^2 - 16ax + 64a^2) + 48a^2 - 64a^2]$

$= 2[(x^2 - 16ax + 64a^2) - 16a^2]$

$= 2[(x - 8a)^2 - (4a)^2]$

$= 2(x - 8a + 4a)(x - 8a - 4a)$

$= 2(x - 4a)(x - 12a)$

23. $x^2 + 2.6x + 0.69$

$= x^2 + 2.6x + (1.69 - 1.69) + 0.69$

$= (x^2 + 2.6x + 1.69) - 1$

$= (x + 1.3)^2 - 1^2$

$= (x + 1.3 + 1)(x + 1.3 - 1)$

$= (x + 2.3)(x + 0.3)$

25. $x^2 + \frac{3}{5}x + \frac{2}{25}$

$= x^2 + \frac{3}{5}x + \left(\frac{9}{100} - \frac{9}{100}\right) + \frac{2}{25}$

$= \left(x^2 + \frac{3}{5}x + \frac{9}{100}\right) + \left(-\frac{9}{100} + \frac{8}{100}\right)$

$= \left(x + \frac{3}{10}\right)^2 - \left(\frac{1}{10}\right)^2 \qquad \left(-\frac{1}{100} = -\left(\frac{1}{10}\right)^2\right)$

$= \left[\left(x + \frac{3}{10}\right) + \frac{1}{10}\right]\left[\left(x + \frac{3}{10}\right) - \frac{1}{10}\right]$

$= \left(x + \frac{4}{10}\right)\left(x + \frac{2}{10}\right)$

$= \left(x + \frac{2}{5}\right)\left(x + \frac{1}{5}\right)$

27.
$$x + 3z = 47 \qquad (1)$$
$$y - z = 14 \qquad (2)$$
$$2x + y = 43 \qquad (3)$$

First solve equation (2) for y.

$y - z = 14$

$\quad y = z + 14$

Substitute z + 14 for y in equation (3).

$\quad 2x + y = 43 \qquad (3)$

$2x + z + 14 = 43 \qquad$ (Substituting)

$\quad 2x + z = 29 \qquad (4)$

We now solve the resulting system of two equations for x and z.

$\quad x + 3z = 47 \qquad (1)$

$2x + \ z = 29 \qquad (4)$

Here we use the addition method.

$-2x - 6z = -94 \qquad$ [Multiplying (1) by -2]

$\underline{\ 2x + \ z = \ 29} \qquad (4)$

$\quad\quad -5z = -65 \qquad$ (Adding)

$\quad\quad\quad z = 13$

Substitute 13 for z in equation (1) and solve for x.

$\quad x + 3z = 47 \qquad (1)$

$x + 3 \cdot 13 = 47 \qquad$ (Substituting)

$\quad x + 39 = 47$

$\quad\quad\quad x = 8$

Substitute 13 for z in equation (2) and solve for y.

$\quad y - z = 14 \qquad (2)$

$y - 13 = 14$

$\quad\quad y = 27$

The ordered triple (8,27,13) checks and is the solution.

29. $x^{2a} + 14x^a + 45$

$= (x^a)^2 + 14x^a + 45$

$= (x^a)^2 + 14x^a + (49 - 49) + 45$

$= [(x^a)^2 + 14x^a + 49] - 4$

$= (x^a + 7)^2 - 2^2$

$= (x^a + 7 + 2)(x^a + 7 - 2)$

$= (x^a + 9)(x^a + 5)$

31. $x^2 + 4.482x - 7.403544$

$= x^2 + 4.482x - 7.403544 + (5.022081 - 5.022081)$

Half of 4.482 is 2.241, and $(2.241)^2 = 5.022081$.
We add 0, naming it 5.022081 - 5.022081.

$= (x^2 + 4.482x + 5.022081) - 7.403544 - 5.022081$

$= (x^2 + 4.482x + 5.022081) - 12.425625$

$= (x + 2.241)^2 - (3.525)^2$

$= (x + 2.241 + 3.525)(x + 2.241 - 3.525)$

$= (x + 5.766)(x - 1.284)$

Exercise Set 5.8

1. $x^3 + 8$
    $= x^3 + 2^3$
    $= (x + 2)(x^2 - x \cdot 2 + 2^2)$
    $\quad\quad\quad [A^3 + B^3 = (A + B)(A^2 - AB + B^2)]$
    $= (x + 2)(x^2 - 2x + 4)$

3. $2y^3 - 128$
    $= 2(y^3 - 64)$
    $= 2(y^3 - 4^3)$
    $= 2(y - 4)(y^2 + y \cdot 4 + 4^2)$
    $\quad\quad\quad [A^3 - B^3 = (A - B)(A^2 + AB + B^2)]$
    $= 2(y - 4)(y^2 + 4y + 16)$

5. $24a^3 + 3$
    $= 3(8a^3 + 1)$
    $= 3[(2a)^3 + 1^3]$
    $= 3(2a + 1)[(2a)^2 - 2a \cdot 1 + 1^2]$
    $\quad\quad\quad [A^3 + B^3 = (A + B)(A^2 - AB + B^2)]$
    $= 3(2a + 1)(4a^2 - 2a + 1)$

7. $8 - 27b^3$
    $= 2^3 - (3b)^3$
    $= (2 - 3b)[2^2 + 2 \cdot 3b + (3b)^2]$
    $\quad\quad\quad [A^3 - B^3 = (A - B)(A^2 + AB + B^2)]$
    $= (2 - 3b)(4 + 6b + 9b^2)$

9. $8x^3 + 27$
    $= (2x)^3 + 3^3$
    $= (2x + 3)[(2x)^2 - 2x \cdot 3 + 3^2]$
    $= (2x + 3)(4x^2 - 6x + 9)$

11. $a^3 + \frac{1}{8}$
    $= a^3 + (\frac{1}{2})^3$
    $= (a + \frac{1}{2})(a^2 - a \cdot \frac{1}{2} + (\frac{1}{2})^2]$
    $= (a + \frac{1}{2})(a^2 - \frac{1}{2}a + \frac{1}{4})$

13. $rs^3 + 64r$
    $= r(s^3 + 64)$
    $= r(s^3 + 4^3)$
    $= r(s + 4)(s^2 - 4s + 16)$

15. $5x^3 - 40z^3$
    $= 5(x^3 - 8z^3)$
    $= 5[x^3 - (2z)^3]$
    $= 5(x - 2z)(x^2 + 2xz + 4z^2)$

17. $x^3 + 0.001$
    $= x^3 + (0.1)^3$
    $= (x + 0.1)(x^2 - 0.1x + 0.01)$

19. $64x^6 - 8t^6$
    $= 8(8x^6 - t^6)$
    $= 8[(2x^2)^3 - (t^2)^3]$
    $= 8(2x^2 - t^2)(4x^4 + 2x^2t^2 + t^4)$

21. $z^6 - 1$
    $= (z^3)^2 - 1^2$
    $= (z^3 + 1)(z^3 - 1)$
    $= (z + 1)(z^2 - z + 1)(z - 1)(z^2 + z + 1)$

23. $t^6 + 64y^6$
    $= (t^2)^3 + (4y^2)^3$
    $= (t^2 + 4y^2)(t^4 - 4t^2y^2 + 16y^4)$

25. $|x| = 27$
    $x = -27 \quad$ or $\quad x = 27$
    The solution set is $\{-27, 27\}$.

27. $|5x - 6| > 39$
    $5x - 6 < -39 \quad$ or $\quad 5x - 6 > 39$
    $\quad\quad 5x < -33 \quad$ or $\quad\quad 5x > 45$
    $\quad\quad\quad x < -\frac{33}{5} \quad$ or $\quad\quad\quad x > 9$
    The solution set is $\{x | x < -\frac{33}{5}$ or $x > 9\}$.

29. $[(c - d)^3 - d^3]^2$
    $= ([(c - d) - d][(c - d)^2 + (c - d)d + d^2])^2$
    $= ([c - 2d][c^2 - 2cd + d^2 + cd - d^2 + d^2])^2$
    $= ([c - 2d][c^2 - cd + d^2])^2$
    $= (c - 2d)^2(c^2 - cd + d^2)^2$

31. $(a + 2)^3 - (a - 2)^3$
    $= [(a + 2) - (a - 2)][(a + 2)^2 + (a + 2)(a - 2) +$
    $\quad\quad\quad\quad\quad\quad\quad\quad\quad\quad\quad\quad (a - 2)^2]$
    $= 4(a^2 + 4a + 4 + a^2 - 4 + a^2 - 4a + 4)$
    $= 4(3a^2 + 4)$

33. $x^{6a} + y^{3b}$
    $= (x^{2a})^3 + (y^b)^3$
    $= (x^{2a} + y^b)[(x^{2a})^2 - x^{2a}y^b + (y^b)^2]$
    $= (x^{2a} + y^b)(x^{4a} - x^{2a}y^b + y^{2b})$

35. $\frac{8}{27}x^3 - \frac{1}{64}y^3$
    $= (\frac{2}{3}x)^3 - (\frac{1}{4}y)^3$
    $= (\frac{2}{3}x - \frac{1}{4}y)[(\frac{2}{3}x)^2 + \frac{2}{12}xy + (\frac{1}{4}y)^2]$
    $= (\frac{2}{3}x - \frac{1}{4}y)(\frac{4}{9}x^2 + \frac{1}{6}xy + \frac{1}{16}y^2)$

37. $y^4 - 8y^3 - y + 8$
    $= y^3(y - 8) - 1(y - 8)$
    $= (y^3 - 1)(y - 8)$
    $= (y - 1)(y^2 + y + 1)(y - 8)$

Exercise Set 5.9

1. $x^2 - 144$
    $= x^2 - 12^2$ (Difference of squares)
    $= (x + 12)(x - 12)$

3. $2x^2 + 11x + 12$
    $= (2x + 3)(x + 4)$ (Trial and error)

5. $3x^4 - 12$
    $= 3(x^4 - 4)$ (Difference of squares)
    $= 3(x^2 + 2)(x^2 - 2)$

7. $a^2 + 25 + 10a$
    $= a^2 + 10a + 25$ (Trinomial square)
    $= (a + 5)^2$

9. $2x^2 - 10x - 132$
    $= 2(x^2 - 5x - 66)$
    $= 2(x - 11)(x + 6)$ (Trial and error)

11. $9x^2 - 25y^2$
    $= (3x)^2 - (5y)^2$ (Difference of squares)
    $= (3x + 5y)(3x - 5y)$

13. $4c^2 - 4cd + d^2$ (Trinomial square)
    $= (2c - d)^2$

15. $-7x^2 + 2x^3 + 4x - 14$
    $= 2x^3 - 7x^2 + 4x - 14$
    $= x^2(2x - 7) + 2(2x - 7)$ (Factoring by grouping)
    $= (x^2 + 2)(2x - 7)$

17. $250x^3 - 128y^3$
    $= 2(125x^3 - 64y^3)$
    $= 2[(5x)^3 - (4y)^3]$ (Difference of cubes)
    $= 2(5x - 4y)(25x^2 + 20xy + 16y^2)$

19. $8m^3 + m^6 - 20$
    $= (m^3)^2 + 8m^3 - 20$
    $= (m^3 - 2)(m^3 + 10)$ (Trial and error)

21. $ac + cd - ab - bd$
    $= c(a + d) - b(a + d)$ (Factoring by grouping)
    $= (c - b)(a + d)$

23. $m^6 - 1$
    $= (m^3)^2 - 1^2$ (Difference of squares)
    $= (m^3 + 1)(m^3 - 1)$ (Sum and difference of cubes)
    $= (m + 1)(m^2 - m + 1)(m - 1)(m^2 + m + 1)$

25. $x^2 + 6x - y^2 + 9$
    $= x^2 + 6x + 9 - y^2$
    $= (x + 3)^2 - y^2$ (Difference of squares)
    $= [(x + 3) + y][(x + 3) - y]$
    $= (x + y + 3)(x - y + 3)$

27. $36y^2 - 35 + 12y$
    $= 36y^2 + 12y - 35$
    $= (6y - 5)(6y + 7)$ (Trial and error)

29. $a^8 - b^8$
    $= (a^4 + b^4)(a^4 - b^4)$ (Difference of squares)
    $= (a^4 + b^4)(a^2 + b^2)(a^2 - b^2)$ (Difference of squares)
    $= (a^4 + b^4)(a^2 + b^2)(a + b)(a - b)$

31. $a^3b - 16ab^3$
    $= ab(a^2 - 16b^2)$ (Difference of squares)
    $= ab(a + 4b)(a - 4b)$

33. $2x^3 + 6x^2 - 8x - 24$
    $= 2(x^3 + 3x^2 - 4x - 12)$
    $= 2[x^2(x + 3) - 4(x + 3)]$ (Factoring by grouping)
    $= 2(x^2 - 4)(x + 3)$ (Difference of squares)
    $= 2(x + 2)(x - 2)(x + 3)$

35. $16x^3 + 54y^3$
    $= 2(8x^3 + 27y^3)$
    $= 2[(2x)^3 + (3y)^3]$ (Sum of cubes)
    $= 2(2x + 3y)(4x^2 - 6xy + 9y^2)$

37. $3x^2y^2z + 25xyz^2 + 28z^3$
    $= z(3x^2y^2 + 25xyz + 28z^2)$
    $= z(3xy + 4z)(xy + 7z)$

39. $(y - 1)^4 - (y - 1)^2$
    $= (y - 1)^2[(y - 1)^2 - 1]$
    $= (y - 1)^2[(y - 1) + 1][(y - 1) - 1]$
    $= (y - 1)^2(y)(y - 2)$
    $= y(y - 1)^2(y - 2)$

41. $27x^{6s} + 64y^{3t}$
    $= (3x^{2s})^3 + (4y^t)^3$
    $= (3x^{2s} + 4y^t)(9x^{4s} - 12x^{2s}y^t + 16y^{2t})$

43. $4x^2 + 4xy + y^2 - r^2 + 6rs - 9s^2$
    $= (4x^2 + 4xy + y^2) - (r^2 - 6rs + 9s^2)$
    $= (2x + y)^2 - (r - 3s)^2$
    $= [(2x + y) + (r - 3s)][(2x + y) - (r - 3s)]$
    $= (2x + y + r - 3s)(2x + y - r + 3s)$

45. $24x^{2a} - 6$

    $= 6(4x^{2a} - 1)$

    $= 6[(2x^a)^2 - 1^2]$

    $= 6(2x^a + 1)(2x^a - 1)$

47. $1 - \dfrac{x^{27}}{1000}$

    $= 1^3 - (\dfrac{x^9}{10})^3$

    $= (1 - \dfrac{x^9}{10})(1 + \dfrac{x^9}{10} + \dfrac{x^{18}}{100})$

49. $8(a - 3)^2 - 64(a - 3) + 128$

    $= 8[(a - 3)^2 - 8(a - 3) + 16]$

    $= 8[(a - 3) - 4]^2$

    $= 8(a - 7)^2$

Exercise Set 5.10

1. $x^2 + 3x - 28 = 0$

    $(x + 7)(x - 4) = 0$

    $x + 7 = 0$ or $x - 4 = 0$

        $x = -7$ or $x = 4$

    The solutions are -7 and 4.

3. $y^2 - 8y + 16 = 0$

    $(y - 4)(y - 4) = 0$

    $y - 4 = 0$ or $y - 4 = 0$

        $y = 4$ or $y = 4$

    The solution is 4.

5. $9x + x^2 + 20 = 0$

    $x^2 + 9x + 20 = 0$

    $(x + 5)(x + 4) = 0$

    $x + 5 = 0$ or $x + 4 = 0$

        $x = -5$ or $x = -4$

    The solutions are -5 and -4.

7. $x^2 + 8x = 0$

    $x(x + 8) = 0$

    $x = 0$ or $x + 8 = 0$

    $x = 0$ or $x = -8$

    The solutions are 0 and -8.

9. $z^2 = 36$

        $z^2 - 36 = 0$

    $(z + 6)(z - 6) = 0$

    $z + 6 = 0$ or $z - 6 = 0$

        $z = -6$ or $z = 6$

    The solutions are -6 and 6.

11. $x^2 + 14x + 45 = 0$

    $(x + 9)(x + 5) = 0$

    $x + 9 = 0$ or $x + 5 = 0$

        $x = -9$ or $x = -5$

    The solutions are -9 and -5.

13. $p^2 - 11p = -28$

       $p^2 - 11p + 28 = 0$

    $(p - 7)(p - 4) = 0$

    $p - 7 = 0$ or $p - 4 = 0$

       $p = 7$ or $p = 4$

    The solutions are 7 and 4.

15. $2x^2 - 15x = -7$

      $2x^2 - 15x + 7 = 0$

    $(2x - 1)(x - 7) = 0$

    $2x - 1 = 0$ or $x - 7 = 0$

        $2x = 1$ or $x = 7$

        $x = \dfrac{1}{2}$ or $x = 7$

    The solutions are $\dfrac{1}{2}$ and 7.

17. $14 = x(x - 5)$

    $14 = x^2 - 5x$

    $0 = x^2 - 5x - 14$

    $0 = (x + 2)(x - 7)$

    $x + 2 = 0$ or $x - 7 = 0$

        $x = -2$ or $x = 7$

    The solutions are -2 and 7.

19.   We let x represent the number.

    4 times | the square of a number | is 21 | more than | 8 times | the number.

    4   · x^2 $= 21$ $+$ 8   · x

            $4x^2 = 21 + 8x$

    $4x^2 - 8x - 21 = 0$

    $(2x + 3)(2x - 7) = 0$

    $2x + 3 = 0$ or $2x - 7 = 0$

       $2x = -3$ or $2x = 7$

       $x = -\dfrac{3}{2}$ or $x = \dfrac{7}{2}$

    Both numbers check. The solutions for the number are $-\dfrac{3}{2}$ and $\dfrac{7}{2}$.

21. We first make a drawing and label it.

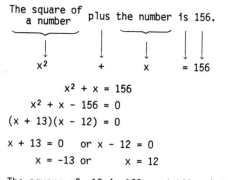

We let w represent the width and ℓ the length. The formula for the area of a rectangle is A = ℓ·w.

We have a system of two equations.

$84 = ℓ·w$

$ℓ = w + 5$

We substitute w + 5 for ℓ in the first equation and solve for w.

$84 = (w + 5)·w$

$84 = w^2 + 5w$

$0 = w^2 + 5w - 84$

$0 = (w - 7)(w + 12)$

$w - 7 = 0$ or $w + 12 = 0$

$w = 7$ or $w = -12$

The number -12 is not a solution because width cannot be negative in this problem. If the width is 7 in. and the length is 5 in. more, or 12, then the area will be 12·7, or 84 in². We have a solution. The table top has length 12 in. and width 7 in.

23. Consecutive odd integers are next to each other like 13 and 15. We let x represent the first odd integer. Then x + 2 represents the next odd integer.

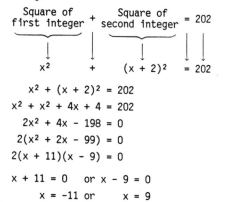

$x^2 + (x + 2)^2 = 202$

$x^2 + x^2 + 4x + 4 = 202$

$2x^2 + 4x - 198 = 0$

$2(x^2 + 2x - 99) = 0$

$2(x + 11)(x - 9) = 0$

$x + 11 = 0$ or $x - 9 = 0$

$x = -11$ or $x = 9$

We only check 9 since the problem asks for consecutive positive odd integers. If x = 9, then x + 2 = 11, and 9 and 11 are consecutive positive odd integers. The sum of the squares of 9 and 11 is 81 + 121, or 202. The numbers check. The integers are 9 and 11.

25. Let x represent the number.

The square of a number plus the number is 156.

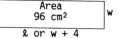

x^2 $+$ x $= 156$

$x^2 + x = 156$

$x^2 + x - 156 = 0$

$(x + 13)(x - 12) = 0$

$x + 13 = 0$ or $x - 12 = 0$

$x = -13$ or $x = 12$

The square of -13 is 169, and 169 + (-13) = 156. The squrae of 12 is 144, and 144 + 12 = 156.

Both numbers check. The solutions for the number are -13 and 12.

27. We first make a drawing and label it.

We let w represent the width and ℓ the length. The formula for the area of a rectangle is A = ℓ·w.

We have a system of equations.

$96 = ℓ·w$

$ℓ = w + 4$

We substitute w + 4 for ℓ in the first equation and solve for w.

$96 = (w + 4)·w$

$96 = w^2 + 4w$

$0 = w^2 + 4w - 96$

$0 = (w + 12)(w - 8)$

$w + 12 = 0$ or $w - 8 = 0$

$w = -12$ or $w = 8$

The number -12 is not a solution because width cannot be negative in the problem. If the width is 8 cm and the length is 4 cm more, or 12, then the area is 12·8, or 96 cm². We have a solution. The length of the top of the work bench is 12 cm and the width is 8 cm.

29. We make a drawing and let x represent the length of a side of the square.

The perimeter is x + x + x + x, or 4x.
The area is x·x, or x².

Perimeter is 4 more than the area.

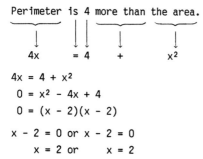

$$4x = 4 + x^2$$
$$0 = x^2 - 4x + 4$$
$$0 = (x - 2)(x - 2)$$

x - 2 = 0 or x - 2 = 0
x = 2 or   x = 2

If the length of a side is 2, the perimeter is 4·2, or 8, the area is 2·2 or 4, and 8 is four more than 4. The value checks. The length of a side is 2.

31. We make a drawing.

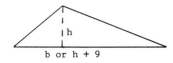

We let h represent the height and b the base. The formula for the area of a triangle is $A = \frac{1}{2}$ bh.

We have a system of equations.
$$56 = \frac{1}{2} \cdot b \cdot h \qquad \text{(Area)}$$
$$b = h + 9$$

We substitute h + 9 for b in the first equation and solve for h.
$$56 = \frac{1}{2} \cdot (h + 9) \cdot h$$
$$112 = (h + 9) \cdot h$$
$$112 = h^2 + 9h$$
$$0 = h^2 + 9h - 112$$
$$0 = (h + 16)(h - 7)$$

h + 16 = 0   or h - 7 = 0
     h = -16 or   h = 7

31. (continued)

We only check 7 since the height cannot be negative. If h = 7, then b = 7 + 9, or 16, and the area is $\frac{1}{2}$ · 16·7, or 56 cm². We have a solution. The height is 7 cm, and the base is 16 cm.

33. Consecutive even integers are next to each other like 8, 10, and 12. We let x represent the first, x + 2 the second, and x + 4 the third.

Square of the first + Square of the third = 136

$$x^2 + (x + 4)^2 = 136$$

$$x^2 + (x + 4)^2 = 136$$
$$x^2 + x^2 + 8x + 16 = 136$$
$$2x^2 + 8x - 120 = 0$$
$$2(x^2 + 4x - 60) = 0$$
$$2(x + 10)(x - 6) = 0$$

x + 10 = 0   or x - 6 = 0
     x = -10 or   x = 6

If x = -10, the consecutive even integers are -10, -8, and -6. The square of -10 is 100; the square of -6 is 36. The sum of 100 and 36 is 136. If x = 6, the consecutive even integers are 6, 8, and 10. The square of 6 is 36; the square of 10 is 100. The sum of 36 and 100 is 136. Both sets check. The three consecutive even integers can be -10, -8, and -6 or 6, 8, and 10.

35.
$$2x - 14 + 9x > -8x + 16 + 10x$$
$$11x - 14 > 2x + 16$$
$$9x > 30$$
$$x > \frac{30}{9}$$
$$x > \frac{10}{3}$$

The solution set is $\{x \mid x > \frac{10}{3}\}$.

37.
$$(x + 6)(x - 3) + b = (x - 5)(x - 2) - 3b$$
$$x^2 + 3x - 18 + b = x^2 - 7x + 10 - 3b$$
$$3x - 18 + b = -7x + 10 - 3b$$
$$10x = 28 - 4b$$
$$x = \frac{28 - 4b}{10}$$
$$x = \frac{14 - 2b}{5}$$

<u>39</u>. We first make a drawing.

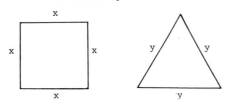

Let x represent the length of a side of the square. Then 4x represents the perimeter of the square. Let y represent the length of a side of the equilateral triangle. Then 3y represents the perimeter of the triangle. We translate to a system of equations.

The area of the square is 9 cm².

x·x = 9, or x² = 9, or x = 3 or -3.

The perimeter of the square is equal to the perimeter of the triangle.

$4x = 3y$, or $y = \frac{4}{3}x$

Since the length of a side of the square must be positive, we only consider x = 3. Substituting 3 for x in the second equation we get $\frac{4}{3} \cdot 3$, or 4 cm for the length of a side of the triangle.

<u>41</u>. We let x and y represent the numbers.

The sum of the numbers is 17. This gives us one equation.

x + y = 17

The sum of their squares is 205. This gives us a second equation.

x² + y² = 205

We solve the system.

x + y = 17

x² + y² = 205

We solve the first equation for y.

x + y = 17

   y = 17 - x

We substitute 17 - x for y in the second equation and solve for x.

$$x^2 + y^2 = 205$$
$$x^2 + (17 - x)^2 = 205$$
$$x^2 + 289 - 34x + x^2 = 205$$
$$2x^2 - 34x + 84 = 0$$
$$2(x^2 - 17x + 42) = 0$$
$$2(x - 14)(x - 3) = 0$$

x - 14 = 0 or x - 3 = 0

   x = 14 or   x = 3

If x = 14, y = 17 - 14, or 3. If x = 3, y = 17 - 3, or 14. The sum of the numbers is 14 + 3, or 17. The sum of their squares is 196 + 9, or 205. The numbers check. The numbers are 14 and 3.

<u>43</u>. We first make a drawing and let x represent the uniform width around the pool.

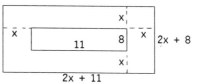

The dimensions of the pool are 11 and 8. The dimensions of the yard are 2x + 11 and 2x + 8.

We translate to an equation.

The area of the backyard is 1120 m².

(2x + 11)(2x + 8) = 1120

We solve the equation.

$$4x^2 + 38x + 88 = 1120$$
$$2x^2 + 19x + 44 = 560$$
$$2x^2 + 19x - 516 = 0$$
$$(2x + 43)(x - 12) = 0$$

2x + 43 = 0   or x - 12 = 0

   $x = -\frac{43}{2}$ or   x = 12

We only check 12 since the width cannot be negative. If x = 12, then the length is 2·12 + 11, or 35 m and the width is 2·12 + 8, or 32 m. The area is 35·32, or 1120 m². The values check. The width of the strip is 12 m.

Exercise Set 5.11

<u>1</u>. The correspondence <u>is not</u> a function because the members New York and Los Angeles of the domain are each matched to more than one member of the range.

<u>3</u>. The correspondence <u>is</u> a function, even though -4, -5, and -6 are each matched to 5. Each member of the domain is matched to exactly one member of the range.

<u>5</u>. g(x) = -2x - 4

   g(-3) = -2(-3) - 4   (Substituting the input, -3)

      = 6 - 4

      = 2

<u>7</u>. g(x) = -2x - 4

   $g(\frac{3}{2}) = -2 \cdot \frac{3}{2} - 4$ (Substituting the input, $\frac{3}{2}$)

      = -3 - 4

      = -7

9. $h(x) = 3x^2$

$h(-1) = 3(-1)^2$ (Substituting the input, -1)
$= 3 \cdot 1$
$= 3$

11. $h(x) = 3x^2$

$h(2) = 3 \cdot 2^2$ (Substituting the input, 2)
$= 3 \cdot 4$
$= 12$

13. $P(x) = x^3 - x$

$P(2) = 2^3 - 2$ (Substituting the input, 2)
$= 8 - 2$
$= 6$

15. $P(x) = x^3 - x$

$P(-1) = (-1)^3 - (-1)$ (Substituting the input, -1)
$= -1 + 1$
$= 0$

17. $Q(x) = x^4 - 2x^3 + x^2 - x + 2$

$Q(-2) = (-2)^4 - 2(-2)^3 + (-2)^2 - (-2) + 2$
(Substituting the input, -2)
$= 16 + 16 + 4 + 2 + 2$
$= 40$

19. $Q(x) = x^4 - 2x^3 + x^2 - x + 2$

$Q(0) = 0^4 - 2 \cdot 0^3 + 0^2 - 0 + 2$
(Substituting the input, 0)
$= 0 - 0 + 0 - 0 + 2$
$= 2$

21. $D(t) = 2t + 115$

$D(0) = 2 \cdot 0 + 115 = 0 + 115 = 115$
The stopping distance at $0°F$ is 115 ft.

$D(-20) = 2(-20) + 115 = -40 + 115 = 75$
The stopping distance at $-20°F$ is 75 ft.

$D(10) = 2 \cdot 10 + 115 = 20 + 115 = 135$
The stopping distance at $10°F$ is 135 ft.

$D(32) = 2 \cdot 32 + 115 = 64 + 115 = 179$
The stopping distance at $32°F$ is 179 ft.

23. $V(r) = \frac{4}{3} \pi r^3$

$V(6377) = \frac{4}{3}(3.14)(6377)^3$

$\approx \frac{4}{3}(3.14)(2.593 \times 10^{11})$

$\approx (4.187)(2.593 \times 10^{11})$

$\approx 10.857 \times 10^{11}$

$\approx 1.09 \times 10^{12}$

25. $f(x) = 5x^2 + 4x$

a) $f(0) = 5 \cdot 0^2 + 4 \cdot 0 = 0 + 0 = 0$
b) $f(-1) = 5(-1)^2 + 4(-1) = 5 - 4 = 1$
c) $f(3) = 5 \cdot 3^2 + 4 \cdot 3 = 45 + 12 = 57$
d) $f(a) = 5a^2 + 4a$
e) $f(a + h) = 5(a + h)^2 + 5(a + h)$
$= 5(a^2 + 2ah + h^2) + 5a + 5h$
$= 5a^2 + 10ah + 5h^2 + 5a + 5h$

27. $f(x) = 2|x| + 3x$

a) $f(1) = 2|1| + 3 \cdot 1 = 2 + 3 = 5$
b) $f(-2) = 2|-2| + 3(-2) = 4 - 6 = -2$
c) $f(-4) = 2|-4| + 3(-4) = 8 - 12 = -4$
d) $f(2y) = 2|2y| + 3(2y) = 4|y| + 6y$
e) $f(a + h) = 2|a + h| + 3(a + h)$
$= 2|a + h| + 3a + 3h$

29. Graph: $f(x) = -2x - 3$

We find ordered pairs $(x, f(x))$, plot them, and connect the points.

x	$f(x)$
0	-3
-2	1
1	-5

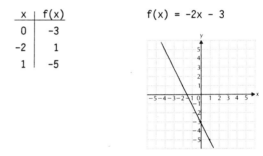

$f(x) = -2x - 3$

31. Graph: $h(x) = |x|$

We find ordered pairs $(x, h(x))$, plot them, and connect the points.

x	$h(x)$
-4	4
-1	1
0	0
2	2
5	5

$h(x) = |x|$

33. Graph: f(x) = -5

    We find ordered pairs (x,f(x)), plot them, and connect the points.

x	f(x)
-3	-5
0	-5
1	-5
4	-5

    f(x) = -5

    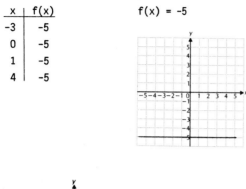

35.

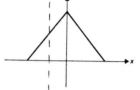

The graph <u>is</u> the graph of a function. It does pass the vertical line test. No vertical line intersects the graph more than once.

37.

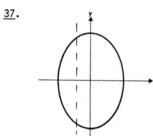

The graph <u>is not</u> the graph of a function. It does not pass the vertical line test. It is possible for a vertical line to intersect the graph more than once.

39. f(x) = x + 3   g(x) = x - 3

    (f + g)(x) = f(x) + g(x) = (x + 3) + (x - 3) = 2x

    (f - g)(x) = f(x) - g(x) = (x + 3) - (x - 3)

    $\qquad\qquad\qquad$ = x + 3 - x + 3

    $\qquad\qquad\qquad$ = 6

    fg(x) = f(x)·g(x) = (x + 3)(x - 3) = x² - 9

    (f/g)(x) = $\frac{f(x)}{g(x)}$ = $\frac{x + 3}{x - 3}$

    ff(x) = f(x)·f(x) = (x + 3)(x + 3) = x² + 6x + 9

41. f(x) = 2x² - 3x + 1   g(x) = x³

    (f + g)(x) = f(x) + g(x) = (2x² - 3x + 1) + x³

    $\qquad\qquad\qquad$ = x³ + 2x² - 3x + 1

    (f - g)(x) = f(x) - g(x) = (2x² - 3x + 1) - x³

    $\qquad\qquad\qquad$ = -x³ + 2x² - 3x + 1

    fg(x) = f(x)·g(x) = (2x² - 3x + 1)(x³)

    $\qquad\qquad\qquad$ = 2x⁵ - 3x⁴ + x³

    (f/g)(x) = $\frac{f(x)}{g(x)}$ = $\frac{2x² - 3x + 1}{x³}$

    ff(x) = f(x)·f(x) = (2x² - 3x + 1)(2x² - 3x + 1)

    $\qquad\qquad\qquad$ = 4x⁴ - 6x³ + 2x² - 6x³ + 9x² -

    $\qquad\qquad\qquad\qquad\qquad$ 3x + 2x² - 3x + 1

    $\qquad\qquad\qquad$ = 4x⁴ - 12x³ + 13x² - 6x + 1

43. f(x) = -5x²   g(x) = 4x³

    (f + g)(x) = f(x) + g(x) = -5x² + 4x³ = 4x³ - 5x²

    (f - g)(x) = f(x) - g(x) = -5x² - 4x³ = -4x³ - 5x²

    fg(x) = f(x)·g(x) = -5x²·4x³ = -20x⁵

    (f/g)(x) = $\frac{f(x)}{g(x)}$ = $\frac{-5x²}{4x³}$ = $-\frac{5}{4x}$

    ff(x) = f(x)·f(x) = -5x²(-5x²) = 25x⁴

45. f(x) = 20   g(x) = -5

    (f + g)(x) = f(x) + g(x) = 20 + (-5) = 15

    (f - g)(x) = f(x) - g(x) = 20 - (-5) = 25

    fg(x) = f(x)·g(x) = 20(-5) = -100

    (f/g)(x) = $\frac{f(x)}{g(x)}$ = $\frac{20}{-5}$ = -4

    ff(x) = f(x)·f(x) = 20·20 = 400

47. $3x - 4y - 2z = 7$ (1)

    $x + 2y - z = 5$ (2)

    $2x + z = -1$ (3)

Multiply equation (2) by 2 and add equations (1) and (2).

$3x - 4y - 2z = 7$ (1)

$\underline{2x + 4y - 2z = 10}$ [Multiplying (2) by 2]

$5x - 4z = 17$ (4)

Solve the resulting system of two equations, (3) and (4), for x and z.

$8x + 4z = -4$ [Multiplying equation (3) by 4]

$\underline{5x - 4z = 17}$ (4)

$13x = 13$

$x = 1$

Substitute 1 for x in either equation (3) or (4) and solve for z.

$2x + z = -1$ (3)

$2 \cdot 1 + z = -1$ (Substituting)

$z = -3$

Substitute 1 for x and -3 for z in either equation (1) or (2) and solve for y.

$x + 2y - z = 5$ (2)

$1 + 2y - (-3) = 5$ (Substituting)

$2y + 4 = 5$

$2y = 1$

$y = \frac{1}{2}$

The ordered triple $(1, \frac{1}{2}, -3)$ checks and is the solution.

49. $\left| \frac{1}{2} x - 6 \right| < 1$

$-1 < \frac{1}{2} x - 6 < 1$ (Property 2)

$5 < \frac{1}{2} x < 7$

$10 < x < 14$

The solution set is $\{x | 10 < x < 14\}$.

51. $f(x) = x^2$

$f(x + h) = (x + h)^2 = x^2 + 2xh + h^2$

$\dfrac{f(x + h) - f(x)}{h} = \dfrac{(x^2 + 2xh + h^2) - (x^2)}{h}$

$= \dfrac{2xh + h^2}{h}$

$= \dfrac{h(2x + h)}{h}$

$= 2x + h$

53. We have two ordered pairs:

(4,32) and (7,38)

The slope of the line determined by these points is

$\dfrac{38 - 32}{7 - 4} = \dfrac{6}{3} = 2$.

Thus, $m = 2$ and $f(x) = 2x + b$.

We substitute either (4,32) or (7,38) in the equation and solve for b.

$f(x) = 2x + b$

$32 = 2 \cdot 4 + b$

$32 = 8 + b$

$24 = b$

The function is $f(x) = 2x + 24$.

$f(8) = 2 \cdot 8 + 24 = 16 + 24$, or 40

Size 8 in the USA corresponds to size 40 in Italy.

Exercise Set 6.1

1. a) $\dfrac{3a^2 - 16}{5a - 20}$

The sensible replacements are all those real numbers which do <u>not</u> make the denominator 0. To find them, we first find the ones which do make the denominator 0. We set the denominator equal to 0 and solve.

$$5a - 20 = 0$$
$$5a = 20$$
$$a = 4$$

The sensible replacements are all real numbers except 4.

b) $\dfrac{x^3 - x^2 + x + 2}{x^2 + 11x + 28}$

We first set the denominator equal to 0 and solve.

$$x^2 + 11x + 28 = 0$$
$$(x + 7)(x + 4) = 0 \qquad \text{(Factoring)}$$
$$x + 7 = 0 \ \text{ or } \ x + 4 = 0 \qquad \text{(Principle of zero products)}$$
$$x = -7 \text{ or } \qquad x = -4$$

The sensible replacements are all real numbers except -7 and -4.

3. a) $\dfrac{3x}{3x} \cdot \dfrac{x + 1}{x + 3} = \dfrac{3x(x + 1)}{3x(x + 3)}$

b) $\dfrac{4 - y^2}{6 - y} \cdot \dfrac{-1}{-1} = \dfrac{(4 - y^2)(-1)}{(6 - y)(-1)}$

5. $\dfrac{9y^2}{15y} = \dfrac{3y \cdot 3y}{3y \cdot 5} = \dfrac{3y}{3y} \cdot \dfrac{3y}{5} = \dfrac{3y}{5}$

7. $\dfrac{2a - 6}{2} = \dfrac{2(a - 3)}{2 \cdot 1} = \dfrac{2}{2} \cdot \dfrac{a - 3}{1} = a - 3$

9. $\dfrac{4y - 12}{4y + 12} = \dfrac{4(y - 3)}{4(y + 3)} = \dfrac{4}{4} \cdot \dfrac{y - 3}{y + 3} = \dfrac{y - 3}{y + 3}$

11. $\dfrac{t^2 - 16}{t^2 - 8t + 16} = \dfrac{(t + 4)(t - 4)}{(t - 4)(t - 4)} = \dfrac{t + 4}{t - 4} \cdot \dfrac{t - 4}{t - 4}$

$$= \dfrac{t + 4}{t - 4}$$

13. $\dfrac{x^2 - 16}{x^2} \cdot \dfrac{x^2 - 4x}{x^2 - x - 12}$

$$= \dfrac{(x + 4)(x - 4) \cdot x(x - 4)}{x \cdot x(x - 4)(x + 3)}$$

$$= \dfrac{x(x - 4)}{x(x - 4)} \cdot \dfrac{(x + 4)(x - 4)}{x(x + 3)}$$

$$= \dfrac{x^2 - 16}{x^2 + 3x}$$

15. $\dfrac{y^2 - 16}{2y + 6} \cdot \dfrac{y + 3}{y - 4}$

$$= \dfrac{(y + 4)(y - 4)(y + 3)}{2(y + 3)(y - 4)}$$

$$= \dfrac{(y - 4)(y + 3)}{(y - 4)(y + 3)} \cdot \dfrac{y + 4}{2}$$

$$= \dfrac{y + 4}{2}$$

17. $\dfrac{x^2 - 2x - 35}{2x^3 - 3x^2} \cdot \dfrac{4x^3 - 9x}{7x - 49}$

$$= \dfrac{(x - 7)(x + 5) \cdot x(2x + 3)(2x - 3)}{x \cdot x(2x - 3) \cdot 7(x - 7)}$$

$$= \dfrac{x(x - 7)(2x - 3)}{x(x - 7)(2x - 3)} \cdot \dfrac{(x + 5)(2x + 3)}{x \cdot 7}$$

$$= \dfrac{2x^2 + 13x + 15}{7x}$$

19. $\dfrac{c^3 + 8}{c^2 - 4} \cdot \dfrac{c^2 - 4c + 4}{c^2 - 2c + 4}$

$$= \dfrac{(c + 2)(c^2 - 2c + 4)(c - 2)(c - 2)}{(c + 2)(c - 2)(c^2 - 2c + 4)}$$

$$= \dfrac{(c + 2)(c - 2)(c^2 - 2c + 4)}{(c + 2)(c - 2)(c^2 - 2c + 4)} \cdot \dfrac{c - 2}{1}$$

$$= c - 2$$

21. $\dfrac{x^2 - y^2}{x^3 - y^3} \cdot \dfrac{x^2 + xy + y^2}{x^2 + 2xy + y^2}$

$$= \dfrac{(x + y)(x - y)(x^2 + xy + y^2)}{(x - y)(x^2 + xy + y^2)(x + y)(x + y)}$$

$$= \dfrac{(x + y)(x - y)(x^2 + xy + y^2)}{(x + y)(x - y)(x^2 + xy + y^2)} \cdot \dfrac{1}{x + y}$$

$$= \dfrac{1}{x + y}$$

23. $\dfrac{3y + 15}{y} \div \dfrac{y + 5}{y}$

$$= \dfrac{3y + 15}{y} \cdot \dfrac{y}{y + 5}$$

$$= \dfrac{3(y + 5) \cdot y}{y(y + 5)}$$

$$= \dfrac{y(y + 5)}{y(y + 5)} \cdot \dfrac{3}{1}$$

$$= 3$$

25. $\dfrac{y^2 - 9}{y} \div \dfrac{y + 3}{y + 2}$

$$= \dfrac{y^2 - 9}{y} \cdot \dfrac{y + 2}{y + 3}$$

$$= \dfrac{(y + 3)(y - 3)(y + 2)}{y(y + 3)}$$

$$= \dfrac{y + 3}{y + 3} \cdot \dfrac{(y - 3)(y + 2)}{y}$$

$$= \dfrac{y^2 - y - 6}{y}$$

27. $\dfrac{4a^2 - 1}{a^2 - 4} \div \dfrac{2a - 1}{a - 2}$

$= \dfrac{4a^2 - 1}{a^2 - 4} \cdot \dfrac{a - 2}{2a - 1}$

$= \dfrac{(2a + 1)(2a - 1)(a - 2)}{(a + 2)(a - 2)(2a - 1)}$

$= \dfrac{(2a - 1)(a - 2)}{(2a - 1)(a - 2)} \cdot \dfrac{2a + 1}{a + 2}$

$= \dfrac{2a + 1}{a + 2}$

29. $\dfrac{x^2 - 16}{x^2 - 10x + 25} \div \dfrac{3x - 12}{x^2 - 3x - 10}$

$= \dfrac{x^2 - 16}{x^2 - 10x + 25} \cdot \dfrac{x^2 - 3x - 10}{3x - 12}$

$= \dfrac{(x + 4)(x - 4)(x - 5)(x + 2)}{(x - 5)(x - 5) \cdot 3(x - 4)}$

$= \dfrac{(x - 4)(x - 5)}{(x - 4)(x - 5)} \cdot \dfrac{(x + 4)(x + 2)}{3(x - 5)}$

$= \dfrac{x^2 + 6x + 8}{3x - 15}$

31. $\dfrac{y^3 + 3y}{y^2 - 9} \div \dfrac{y^2 + 5y - 14}{y^2 + 4y - 21}$

$= \dfrac{y^3 + 3y}{y^2 - 9} \cdot \dfrac{y^2 + 4y - 21}{y^2 + 5y - 14}$

$= \dfrac{y(y^2 + 3)(y + 7)(y - 3)}{(y + 3)(y - 3)(y + 7)(y - 2)}$

$= \dfrac{(y + 7)(y - 3)}{(y + 7)(y - 3)} \cdot \dfrac{y(y^2 + 3)}{(y + 3)(y - 2)}$

$= \dfrac{y^3 + 3y}{y^2 + y - 6}$

33. $\dfrac{x^3 - 64}{x^3 + 64} \div \dfrac{x^2 - 16}{x^2 - 4x + 16}$

$= \dfrac{x^3 - 64}{x^3 + 64} \cdot \dfrac{x^2 - 4x + 16}{x^2 - 16}$

$= \dfrac{(x - 4)(x^2 + 4x + 16)(x^2 - 4x + 16)}{(x + 4)(x^2 - 4x + 16)(x + 4)(x - 4)}$

$= \dfrac{(x - 4)(x^2 - 4x + 16)}{(x - 4)(x^2 - 4x + 16)} \cdot \dfrac{x^2 + 4x + 16}{(x + 4)(x + 4)}$

$= \dfrac{x^2 + 4x + 16}{x^2 + 8x + 16}$

35. $\left[\dfrac{r^2 - 4s^2}{r + 2s} \div (r + 2s) \right] \cdot \dfrac{2s}{r - 2s}$

$= \dfrac{r^2 - 4s^2}{r + 2s} \cdot \dfrac{1}{r + 2s} \cdot \dfrac{2s}{r - 2s}$

$= \dfrac{(r + 2s)(r - 2s)(2s)}{(r + 2s)(r + 2s)(r - 2s)}$

$= \dfrac{(r + 2s)(r - 2s)}{(r + 2s)(r - 2s)} \cdot \dfrac{2s}{r + 2s}$

$= \dfrac{2s}{r + 2s}$

37. $-\dfrac{7}{8} \div \dfrac{1}{3} = -\dfrac{7}{8} \cdot \dfrac{3}{1} = -\dfrac{21}{8}$

39. $\dfrac{2}{3} + \left(-\dfrac{7}{9}\right) = \dfrac{2}{3} \cdot \dfrac{3}{3} + \left(-\dfrac{7}{9}\right) = \dfrac{6}{9} + \left(-\dfrac{7}{9}\right) = -\dfrac{1}{9}$

41. $\dfrac{834x}{y - 427.2} \cdot \dfrac{26.3x}{y + 427.2}$

$= \dfrac{(834x)(26.3x)}{(y - 427.2)(y + 427.2)}$

$= \dfrac{21{,}934.2x^2}{y^2 - 182{,}499.84}$

43. $\dfrac{x(x + 1) - 2(x + 3)}{(x + 1)(x + 2)(x + 3)}$

$= \dfrac{x^2 + x - 2x - 6}{(x + 1)(x + 2)(x + 3)}$

$= \dfrac{x^2 - x - 6}{(x + 1)(x + 2)(x + 3)}$

$= \dfrac{(x - 3)(x + 2)}{(x + 1)(x + 2)(x + 3)}$

$= \dfrac{x + 2}{x + 2} \cdot \dfrac{x - 3}{(x + 1)(x + 3)}$

$= \dfrac{x - 3}{x^2 + 4x + 3}$

45. $\dfrac{m^2 - t^2}{m^2 + t^2 + m + t + 2mt}$

$= \dfrac{m^2 - t^2}{(m^2 + 2mt + t^2) + (m + t)}$

$= \dfrac{(m + t)(m - t)}{(m + t)^2 + (m + t)}$

$= \dfrac{(m + t)(m - t)}{(m + t)[(m + t) + 1]}$

$= \dfrac{m + t}{m + t} \cdot \dfrac{m - t}{m + t + 1}$

$= \dfrac{m - t}{m + t + 1}$

47. $\dfrac{x^3 + x^2 - y^3 - y^2}{x^2 - 2xy + y^2}$

$= \dfrac{(x^3 - y^3) + (x^2 - y^2)}{x^2 - 2xy + y^2}$

$= \dfrac{(x - y)(x^2 + xy + y^2) + (x + y)(x - y)}{(x - y)^2}$

$= \dfrac{(x - y)[(x^2 + xy + y^2) + (x + y)]}{(x - y)(x - y)}$

$= \dfrac{x - y}{x - y} \cdot \dfrac{x^2 + xy + y^2 + x + y}{x - y}$

$= \dfrac{x^2 + xy + y^2 + x + y}{x - y}$

49. $\dfrac{x^5 - x^3 + x^2 - 1 - (x^3 - 1)(x + 1)^2}{(x^2 - 1)^2}$

$= \dfrac{x^3(x^2 - 1) + (x^2 - 1) - [(x^3 - 1)(x + 1)^2]}{(x^2 - 1)^2}$

$= \dfrac{x^3(x^2 - 1) + (x^2 - 1) - [(x^2 - 1)(x + 1)(x^2 + x + 1)]}{(x^2 - 1)^2}$

$= \dfrac{(x^2 - 1)[x^3 + 1 - (x + 1)(x^2 + x + 1)]}{(x^2 - 1)^2}$

$= \dfrac{-2x^2 - 2x}{x^2 - 1}$

$= \dfrac{-2x(x + 1)}{(x + 1)(x - 1)}$

$= \dfrac{-2x}{x - 1}$

Exercise Set 6.2

1. $12 = 2\cdot 2\cdot 3$
   $18 = 2\cdot 3\cdot 3$
   LCM $= 2\cdot 2\cdot 3\cdot 3$, or 36

3. $18 = 2\cdot 3\cdot 3$
   $48 = 2\cdot 2\cdot 2\cdot 2\cdot 3$
   LCM $= 2\cdot 2\cdot 2\cdot 2\cdot 3\cdot 3$, or 144

5. $24 = 2\cdot 2\cdot 2\cdot 3$
   $36 = 2\cdot 2\cdot 3\cdot 3$
   LCM $= 2\cdot 2\cdot 2\cdot 3\cdot 3$, or 72

7. $9 = 3\cdot 3$
   $15 = 3\cdot 5$
   $5 = 5$
   LCM $= 3\cdot 3\cdot 5$, or 45

9. $\dfrac{5}{6} + \dfrac{4}{15} = \dfrac{5}{2\cdot 3} + \dfrac{4}{3\cdot 5}$,   LCM $= 2\cdot 3\cdot 5$, or 30

   $= \dfrac{5}{2\cdot 3}\cdot\dfrac{5}{5} + \dfrac{4}{3\cdot 5}\cdot\dfrac{2}{2}$

   $= \dfrac{25}{30} + \dfrac{8}{30}$

   $= \dfrac{33}{30}$

   $= \dfrac{11}{10}$

11. $\dfrac{7}{12} + \dfrac{11}{18} = \dfrac{7}{2\cdot 2\cdot 3} + \dfrac{11}{2\cdot 3\cdot 3}$,   LCM $= 2\cdot 2\cdot 3\cdot 3$, or 36

   $= \dfrac{7}{2\cdot 2\cdot 3}\cdot\dfrac{3}{3} + \dfrac{11}{2\cdot 3\cdot 3}\cdot\dfrac{2}{2}$

   $= \dfrac{21}{36} + \dfrac{22}{36}$

   $= \dfrac{43}{36}$

13. $\dfrac{3}{4} + \dfrac{2}{5} + \dfrac{1}{6} = \dfrac{3}{2\cdot 2} + \dfrac{2}{5} + \dfrac{1}{2\cdot 3}$,   LCM $= 2\cdot 2\cdot 3\cdot 5$, or 60

   $= \dfrac{3}{2\cdot 2}\cdot\dfrac{3\cdot 5}{3\cdot 5} + \dfrac{2}{5}\cdot\dfrac{2\cdot 2\cdot 3}{2\cdot 2\cdot 3} + \dfrac{1}{2\cdot 3}\cdot\dfrac{2\cdot 5}{2\cdot 5}$

   $= \dfrac{45}{60} + \dfrac{24}{60} + \dfrac{10}{60}$

   $= \dfrac{79}{60}$

15. $12x^2y = 2\cdot 2\cdot 3\cdot x\cdot x\cdot y$
   $4xy = 2\cdot 2\cdot x\cdot y$
   LCM $= 2\cdot 2\cdot 3\cdot x\cdot x\cdot y$, or $12x^2y$

17. $y^2 - 9 = (y + 3)(y - 3)$
   $3y + 9 = 3(y + 3)$
   LCM $= 3(y + 3)(y - 3)$

19. $15ab^2 = 3\cdot 5\cdot a\cdot b\cdot b$
   $3ab = 3\cdot a\cdot b$
   $10a^3b = 2\cdot 5\cdot a\cdot a\cdot a\cdot b$
   LCM $= 2\cdot 3\cdot 5\cdot a\cdot a\cdot a\cdot b\cdot b$, or $30a^3b^2$

21. $5y - 15 = t(y - 3)$
   $y^2 - 6y + 9 = (y - 3)(y - 3)$
   LCM $= 5(y - 3)(y - 3)$, or $5(y - 3)^2$

23. $x^2 - 4 = (x + 2)(x - 2)$
   $2 - x = (2 - x)$
   LCM $= (x + 2)(x - 2)$
   or $= (x + 2)(2 - x)$

25. $2r^2 - 5r - 12 = (2r + 3)(r - 4)$
   $3r^2 - 13r + 4 = (3r - 1)(r - 4)$
   $r^2 - 16 = (r + 4)(r - 4)$
   LCM $= (2r + 3)(3r - 1)(r + 4)(r - 4)$

27. $(-3x^4 + x^3 - 2x^2 + 1) - (2x^4 - 3x^2 - 4)$
   $= -3x^4 + x^3 - 2x^2 + 1 - 2x^4 + 3x^2 + 4$
   $= -5x^4 + x^3 + x^2 + 5$

29. $x^2 - 25 = x^2 - 5^2 = (x + 5)(x - 5)$

31. $18 = 2\cdot 3\cdot 3$
   $42 = 2\cdot 3\cdot 7$
   $82 = 2\cdot 41$
   $120 = 2\cdot 2\cdot 2\cdot 3\cdot 5$
   $300 = 2\cdot 2\cdot 3\cdot 5\cdot 5$
   $700 = 2\cdot 2\cdot 5\cdot 5\cdot 7$
   LCM $= 2\cdot 2\cdot 2\cdot 3\cdot 3\cdot 5\cdot 5\cdot 7\cdot 41$, or 516,600

33. $2a^3b^7 = 2\cdot a\cdot a\cdot a\cdot b\cdot b\cdot b\cdot b\cdot b\cdot b\cdot b$
   Other expression $= ?$
   LCM $= 8a^4b^7$, or $2\cdot 2\cdot 2\cdot a\cdot a\cdot a\cdot a\cdot b\cdot b\cdot b\cdot b\cdot b\cdot b\cdot b$

   The other expression must contain three factors
   of 2 and four factors of a, or $8a^4$. It may also
   contain from 0 to 7 factors of b. The possibilities are:

   $8a^4$, $8a^4b$, $8a^4b^2$, $8a^4b^3$, $8a^4b^4$, $8a^4b^5$,
   $8a^4b^6$, or $8a^4b^7$.

Exercise Set 6.3

1. $\dfrac{a - 3b}{a + 5} + \dfrac{a + 5b}{a + b}$

$= \dfrac{a - 3b + a + 5b}{a + b}$

$= \dfrac{2a + 2b}{a + b} = \dfrac{2(a + b)}{a + b}$

$= \dfrac{2}{1} \cdot \dfrac{a + b}{a + b} = 2$

3. $\dfrac{4y + 3}{y - 2} - \dfrac{y - 2}{y - 2}$

$= \dfrac{4y + 3 - (y - 2)}{y - 2}$

$= \dfrac{4y + 3 - y + 2}{y - 2}$

$= \dfrac{3y + 5}{y - 2}$

5. $\dfrac{a^2}{a - b} + \dfrac{b^2}{b - a}$

$= \dfrac{a^2}{a - b} + \dfrac{-1}{-1} \cdot \dfrac{b^2}{b - a}$

$= \dfrac{a^2}{a - b} + \dfrac{-b^2}{a - b}$

$= \dfrac{a^2 - b^2}{a - b} = \dfrac{(a + b)(a - b)}{a - b}$

$= \dfrac{a + b}{1} \cdot \dfrac{a - b}{a - b} = a + b$

7. $\dfrac{3}{x} - \dfrac{8}{-x}$

$= \dfrac{3}{x} - \dfrac{-1}{-1} \cdot \dfrac{8}{-x}$

$= \dfrac{3}{x} - \dfrac{-8}{x}$

$= \dfrac{3 - (-8)}{x}$

$= \dfrac{11}{x}$

9. $\dfrac{2x - 10}{x^2 - 25} - \dfrac{5 - x}{25 - x^2}$

$= \dfrac{2x - 10}{x^2 - 25} - \dfrac{-1}{-1} \cdot \dfrac{5 - x}{25 - x^2}$

$= \dfrac{2x - 10}{x^2 - 25} - \dfrac{x - 5}{x^2 - 25}$

$= \dfrac{2x - 10 - (x - 5)}{x^2 - 25}$

$= \dfrac{2x - 10 - x + 5}{x^2 - 25}$

$= \dfrac{x - 5}{x^2 - 25} = \dfrac{x - 5}{(x + 5)(x - 5)}$

$= \dfrac{x - 5}{x - 5} \cdot \dfrac{1}{x + 5} = \dfrac{1}{x + 5}$

11. $\dfrac{y - 2}{y + 4} + \dfrac{y + 3}{y - 5}$

LCM $= (y + 4)(y - 5)$

$= \dfrac{y - 2}{y + 4} \cdot \dfrac{y - 5}{y - 5} + \dfrac{y + 3}{y - 5} \cdot \dfrac{y + 4}{y + 4}$

$= \dfrac{(y^2 - 7y + 10) + (y^2 + 7y + 12)}{(y + 4)(y - 5)}$

$= \dfrac{2y^2 + 22}{y^2 - y - 20}$

13. $\dfrac{4xy}{x^2 - y^2} + \dfrac{x - y}{x + y}$

$= \dfrac{4xy}{(x + y)(x - y)} + \dfrac{x - y}{x + y}$

LCM $= (x + y)(x - y)$

$= \dfrac{4xy}{(x + y)(x - y)} + \dfrac{x - y}{x + y} \cdot \dfrac{x - y}{x - y}$

$= \dfrac{4xy + x^2 - 2xy + y^2}{(x + y)(x - y)}$

$= \dfrac{x^2 + 2xy + y^2}{(x + y)(x - y)} = \dfrac{(x + y)(x + y)}{(x + y)(x - y)}$

$= \dfrac{x + y}{x + y} \cdot \dfrac{x + y}{x - y} = \dfrac{x + y}{x - y}$

15. $\dfrac{9x + 2}{3x^2 - 2x - 8} + \dfrac{7}{3x^2 + x - 4}$

$= \dfrac{9x + 2}{(3x + 4)(x - 2)} + \dfrac{7}{(3x + 4)(x - 1)}$

LCM $= (3x + 4)(x - 2)(x - 1)$

$= \dfrac{9x + 2}{(3x + 4)(x - 2)} \cdot \dfrac{x - 1}{x - 1} + \dfrac{7}{(3x + 4)(x - 1)} \cdot \dfrac{x - 2}{x - 2}$

$= \dfrac{9x^2 - 7x - 2 + 7x - 14}{(3x + 4)(x - 2)(x - 1)}$

$= \dfrac{9x^2 - 16}{(3x + 4)(x - 2)(x - 1)} = \dfrac{(3x + 4)(3x - 4)}{(3x + 4)(x - 2)(x - 1)}$

$= \dfrac{3x + 4}{3x + 4} \cdot \dfrac{3x - 4}{(x - 2)(x - 1)} = \dfrac{3x - 4}{x^2 - 3x + 2}$

17. $\dfrac{4}{x + 1} + \dfrac{x + 2}{x^2 - 1} + \dfrac{3}{x - 1}$

$= \dfrac{4}{x + 1} + \dfrac{x + 2}{(x + 1)(x - 1)} + \dfrac{3}{x - 1}$

LCM $= (x + 1)(x - 1)$

$= \dfrac{4}{x + 1} \cdot \dfrac{x - 1}{x - 1} + \dfrac{x + 2}{(x + 1)(x - 1)} + \dfrac{3}{x - 1} \cdot \dfrac{x + 1}{x + 1}$

$= \dfrac{4x - 4 + x + 2 + 3x + 3}{(x + 1)(x - 1)}$

$= \dfrac{8x + 1}{x^2 - 1}$

19. $\dfrac{x - 1}{3x + 15} - \dfrac{x + 3}{5x + 25}$

$= \dfrac{x - 1}{3(x + 5)} - \dfrac{x + 3}{5(x + 5)}$

LCM $= 3 \cdot 5(x + 5)$, or $15(x + 5)$

$= \dfrac{x - 1}{3(x + 5)} \cdot \dfrac{5}{5} - \dfrac{x + 3}{5(x + 5)} \cdot \dfrac{3}{3}$

$= \dfrac{5x - 5 - (3x + 9)}{15(x + 5)}$

$= \dfrac{5x - 5 - 3x - 9}{15(x + 5)}$

$= \dfrac{2x - 14}{15x + 75}$

21. $\dfrac{5ab}{a^2 - b^2} - \dfrac{a - b}{a + b}$

$= \dfrac{5ab}{(a + b)(a - b)} - \dfrac{a - b}{a + b}$

LCM $= (a + b)(a - b)$

$= \dfrac{5ab}{(a + b)(a - b)} - \dfrac{a - b}{a + b} \cdot \dfrac{a - b}{a - b}$

$= \dfrac{5ab - (a^2 - 2ab + b^2)}{(a + b)(a - b)}$

$= \dfrac{5ab - a^2 + 2ab - b^2}{(a + b)(a - b)}$

$= \dfrac{-a^2 + 7ab - b^2}{a^2 - b^2}$

23. $\dfrac{3y}{y^2 - 7y + 10} - \dfrac{2y}{y^2 - 8y + 15}$

$= \dfrac{3y}{(y - 5)(y - 2)} - \dfrac{2y}{(y - 5)(y - 3)}$

LCM $= (y - 5)(y - 2)(y - 3)$

$= \dfrac{3y}{(y - 5)(y - 2)} \cdot \dfrac{y - 3}{y - 3} - \dfrac{2y}{(y - 5)(y - 3)} \cdot \dfrac{y - 2}{y - 2}$

$= \dfrac{3y^2 - 9y - (2y^2 - 4y)}{(y - 5)(y - 2)(y - 3)}$

$= \dfrac{3y^2 - 9y - 2y^2 + 4y}{(y - 5)(y - 2)(y - 3)}$

$= \dfrac{y^2 - 5y}{(y - 5)(y - 2)(y - 3)} = \dfrac{y(y - 5)}{(y - 5)(y - 2)(y - 3)}$

$= \dfrac{y - 5}{y - 5} \cdot \dfrac{y}{(y - 2)(y - 3)} = \dfrac{y}{y^2 - 5y + 6}$

25. $\dfrac{y}{y^2 - y - 20} + \dfrac{2}{y + 4}$

$= \dfrac{y}{(y - 5)(y + 4)} + \dfrac{2}{y + 4}$

LCM $= (y - 5)(y + 4)$

$= \dfrac{y}{(y - 5)(y + 4)} + \dfrac{2}{y + 4} \cdot \dfrac{y - 5}{y - 5}$

$= \dfrac{y + 2y - 10}{(y - 5)(y + 4)}$

$= \dfrac{3y - 10}{y^2 - y - 20}$

27. $\dfrac{3y + 2}{y^2 + 5y - 24} + \dfrac{7}{y^2 + 4y - 32}$

$= \dfrac{3y + 2}{(y + 8)(y - 3)} + \dfrac{7}{(y + 8)(y - 4)}$

LCM $= (y + 8)(y - 3)(y - 4)$

$= \dfrac{3y + 2}{(y + 8)(y - 3)} \cdot \dfrac{y - 4}{y - 4} + \dfrac{7}{(y + 8)(y - 4)} \cdot \dfrac{y - 3}{y - 3}$

$= \dfrac{3y^2 - 10y - 8 + 7y - 21}{(y + 8)(y - 3)(y - 4)}$

$= \dfrac{3y^2 - 3y - 29}{(y + 8)(y - 3)(y - 4)}$

29. $\dfrac{3x - 1}{x^2 + 2x - 3} - \dfrac{x + 4}{x^2 - 9}$

$= \dfrac{3x - 1}{(x + 3)(x - 1)} - \dfrac{x + 4}{(x + 3)(x - 3)}$

LCM $= (x + 3)(x - 1)(x - 3)$

$= \dfrac{3x - 1}{(x + 3)(x - 1)} \cdot \dfrac{x - 3}{x - 3} - \dfrac{x + 4}{(x + 3)(x - 3)} \cdot \dfrac{x - 1}{x - 1}$

$= \dfrac{3x^2 - 10x + 3 - (x^2 + 3x - 4)}{(x + 3)(x - 1)(x - 3)}$

$= \dfrac{3x^2 - 10x + 3 - x^2 - 3x + 4}{(x + 3)(x - 1)(x - 3)}$

$= \dfrac{2x^2 - 13x + 7}{(x + 3)(x - 1)(x - 3)}$

31. $\dfrac{1}{x + 1} - \dfrac{x}{x - 2} + \dfrac{x^2 + 2}{x^2 - x - 2}$

$= \dfrac{1}{x + 1} - \dfrac{x}{x - 2} + \dfrac{x^2 + 2}{(x - 2)(x + 1)}$

LCM $= (x + 1)(x - 2)$

$= \dfrac{1}{x + 1} \cdot \dfrac{x - 2}{x - 2} - \dfrac{x}{x - 2} \cdot \dfrac{x + 1}{x + 1} + \dfrac{x^2 + 2}{(x - 2)(x + 1)}$

$= \dfrac{x - 2 - (x^2 + x) + x^2 + 2}{(x + 1)(x - 2)}$

$= \dfrac{x - 2 - x^2 - x + x^2 + 2}{(x + 1)(x - 2)}$

$= \dfrac{0}{(x + 1)(x - 2)} = 0$

33. $\dfrac{x - 1}{x - 2} - \dfrac{x + 1}{x + 2} + \dfrac{x - 6}{x^2 - 4}$

$= \dfrac{x - 1}{x - 2} - \dfrac{x + 1}{x + 2} + \dfrac{x - 6}{(x - 2)(x + 2)}$

LCM $= (x - 2)(x + 2)$

$= \dfrac{x - 1}{x - 2} \cdot \dfrac{x + 2}{x + 2} - \dfrac{x + 1}{x + 2} \cdot \dfrac{x - 2}{x - 2} + \dfrac{x - 6}{(x - 2)(x + 2)}$

$= \dfrac{(x^2 + x - 2) - (x^2 - x - 2) + (x - 6)}{(x - 2)(x + 2)}$

$= \dfrac{x^2 + x - 2 - x^2 + x + 2 + x - 6}{(x - 2)(x + 2)}$

$= \dfrac{3x - 6}{(x - 2)(x + 2)}$

$= \dfrac{3(x - 2)}{(x - 2)(x + 2)}$

$= \dfrac{x - 2}{x - 2} \cdot \dfrac{3}{x + 2}$

$= \dfrac{3}{x + 2}$

35. $\dfrac{4x}{x^2-1} + \dfrac{3x}{1-x} - \dfrac{4}{x-1}$

$= \dfrac{4x}{x^2-1} + \dfrac{-1}{-1} \cdot \dfrac{3x}{1-x} - \dfrac{4}{x-1}$

$= \dfrac{4x}{(x+1)(x-1)} + \dfrac{-3x}{x-1} - \dfrac{4}{x-1}$

LCM $= (x+1)(x-1)$

$= \dfrac{4x}{(x+1)(x-1)} + \dfrac{-3x}{x-1} \cdot \dfrac{x+1}{x+1} - \dfrac{4}{x-1} \cdot \dfrac{x+1}{x+1}$

$= \dfrac{4x - 3x^2 - 3x - 4x - 4}{(x+1)(x-1)}$

$= \dfrac{-3x^2 - 3x - 4}{x^2 - 1}$

37. $8 - 3(a-1) = 2 + 4(3-a)$

$8 - 3a + 3 = 2 + 12 - 4a$

$11 - 3a = 14 - 4a$

$a = 3$

39. $2x^{-2} + 3x^{-2}y^{-2} - 7xy^{-1}$

$= \dfrac{2}{x^2} + \dfrac{3}{x^2y^2} - \dfrac{7x}{y}$

LCM $= x^2y^2$

$= \dfrac{2}{x^2} \cdot \dfrac{y^2}{y^2} + \dfrac{3}{x^2y^2} - \dfrac{7x}{y} \cdot \dfrac{x^2y}{x^2y}$

$= \dfrac{2y^2 + 3 - 7x^3y}{x^2y^2}$

41. $4(y-1)(2y-5)^{-1} + 5(2y+3)(5-2y)^{-1} + (y-4)(2y-5)^{-1}$

$= \dfrac{4(y-1)}{2y-5} + \dfrac{-1}{-1} \cdot \dfrac{5(2y+3)}{5-2y} + \dfrac{y-4}{2y-5}$

$= \dfrac{4y - 4 - 10y - 15 + y - 4}{2y-5}$

$= \dfrac{-5y - 23}{2y-5}$, or $\dfrac{5y+23}{5-2y}$

Exercise Set 6.4

1. $\dfrac{2}{5} + \dfrac{7}{8} = \dfrac{y}{20}$,   LCM $= 40$

$40\left(\dfrac{2}{5} + \dfrac{7}{8}\right) = 40 \cdot \dfrac{y}{20}$

$40 \cdot \dfrac{2}{5} + 40 \cdot \dfrac{7}{8} = 40 \cdot \dfrac{y}{20}$

$16 + 35 = 2y$

$51 = 2y$

$\dfrac{51}{2} = y$

Check:

$\dfrac{2}{5} + \dfrac{7}{8} = \dfrac{y}{20}$

$\dfrac{16}{40} + \dfrac{35}{40} \left|\ \dfrac{\frac{51}{2}}{20}\right.$

$\dfrac{51}{40} \left|\ \dfrac{51}{2} \cdot \dfrac{1}{20}\right.$

$\left|\ \dfrac{51}{40}\right.$

The solution is $\dfrac{51}{2}$.

3. $\dfrac{1}{3} - \dfrac{5}{6} = \dfrac{1}{x}$,   LCM $= 6x$

$6x\left(\dfrac{1}{3} - \dfrac{5}{6}\right) = 6x \cdot \dfrac{1}{x}$

$6x \cdot \dfrac{1}{3} - 6x \cdot \dfrac{5}{6} = 6x \cdot \dfrac{1}{x}$

$2x - 5x = 6$

$-3x = 6$

$x = -2$

Check:

$\dfrac{1}{3} - \dfrac{5}{6} = \dfrac{1}{x}$

$\dfrac{2}{6} - \dfrac{5}{6} \left|\ \dfrac{1}{-2}\right.$

$-\dfrac{3}{6} \left|\ -\dfrac{1}{2}\right.$

$-\dfrac{1}{2} \left|\ \right.$

The solution is -2.

5. $\dfrac{x}{3} - \dfrac{x}{4} = 12$,   LCM $= 12$

$12\left(\dfrac{x}{3} - \dfrac{x}{4}\right) = 12 \cdot 12$

$12 \cdot \dfrac{x}{3} - 12 \cdot \dfrac{x}{4} = 12 \cdot 12$

$4x - 3x = 144$

$x = 144$

Check:

$\dfrac{x}{3} - \dfrac{x}{4} \left|\ 12\right.$

$\dfrac{144}{3} - \dfrac{144}{4} \left|\ 12\right.$

$48 - 36 \left|\ \right.$

$12 \left|\ \right.$

The solution is 144.

7. $y + \dfrac{5}{y} = -6$,   LCM $= y$

$y\left(y + \dfrac{5}{y}\right) = y(-6)$

$y \cdot y + y \cdot \dfrac{5}{y} = -6y$

$y^2 + 5 = -6y$

$y^2 + 6y + 5 = 0$

$(y+5)(y+1) = 0$

$y + 5 = 0$ or $y + 1 = 0$

$y = -5$ or $y = -1$

7. (continued)

Check:

For: -5

$$y + \frac{5}{y} = -6$$

$-5 + \frac{5}{-5}$	-6
$-5 - 1$	
	-6

For: -1

$$y + \frac{5}{y} = -6$$

$-1 + \frac{5}{-1}$	-6
$-1 - 5$	
	-6

The solutions are -5 and -1.

9.
$$\frac{4}{z} + \frac{2}{z} = 3 , \quad LCM = z$$

$$z(\frac{4}{z} + \frac{2}{z}) = z \cdot 3$$

$$z \cdot \frac{4}{z} + z \cdot \frac{2}{z} = 3z$$

$$4 + 2 = 3z$$

$$6 = 3z$$

$$2 = z$$

Check:

$$\frac{4}{z} + \frac{2}{z} = 3$$

$\frac{4}{2} + \frac{2}{2}$	3
$2 + 1$	
	3

The solution is 2.

11.
$$\frac{x - 3}{x + 2} = \frac{1}{5} , \quad LCM = 5(x + 2)$$

$$5(x + 2) \cdot \frac{x - 3}{x + 2} = 5(x + 2) \cdot \frac{1}{5}$$

$$5(x - 3) = x + 2$$

$$5x - 15 = x + 2$$

$$4x = 17$$

$$x = \frac{17}{4}$$

Check:

$$\frac{x - 3}{x + 2} = \frac{1}{5}$$

$\frac{\frac{17}{4} - \frac{12}{4}}{\frac{17}{4} + \frac{8}{4}}$	$\frac{1}{5}$
$\frac{5}{4} \cdot \frac{4}{25}$	
$\frac{1}{5}$	

The solution is $\frac{17}{4}$.

13.
$$\frac{3}{y + 1} = \frac{2}{y - 3} , \quad LCM = (y+1)(y-3)$$

$$(y + 1)(y - 3) \cdot \frac{3}{y + 1} = (y + 1)(y - 3) \cdot \frac{2}{y - 3}$$

$$3(y - 3) = 2(y + 1)$$

$$3y - 9 = 2y + 2$$

$$y = 11$$

Check:

$$\frac{3}{y + 1} = \frac{2}{y - 3}$$

$\frac{3}{11 + 1}$	$\frac{2}{11 - 3}$
$\frac{3}{12}$	$\frac{2}{8}$
$\frac{1}{4}$	$\frac{1}{4}$

The solution is 11.

15.
$$\frac{y - 1}{y - 3} = \frac{2}{y - 3} , \quad LCM = y - 3$$

$$(y - 3) \cdot \frac{y - 1}{y - 3} = (y - 3) \cdot \frac{2}{y - 3}$$

$$y - 1 = 2$$

$$y = 3$$

Check:

$$\frac{y - 1}{y - 3} = \frac{2}{y - 3}$$

$\frac{3 - 1}{3 - 3}$	$\frac{2}{3 - 3}$
$\frac{2}{0}$	$\frac{2}{0}$

We know that 3 is not a solution of the original equation because it results in division by 0. The equation has no solution.

17.
$$\frac{x + 1}{x} = \frac{3}{2} , \quad LCM = 2x$$

$$2x \cdot \frac{x + 1}{x} = 2x \cdot \frac{3}{2}$$

$$2(x + 1) = x \cdot 3$$

$$2x + 2 = 3x$$

$$2 = x$$

Check:

$$\frac{x + 1}{x} = \frac{3}{2}$$

$\frac{2 + 1}{2}$	$\frac{3}{2}$
$\frac{3}{2}$	

The solution is 2.

19. $\dfrac{2}{x} - \dfrac{3}{x} + \dfrac{4}{x} = 5$,   LCM = x

$x\left(\dfrac{2}{x} - \dfrac{3}{x} + \dfrac{4}{x}\right) = x \cdot 5$

$2 - 3 + 4 = 5x$

$3 = 5x$

$\dfrac{3}{5} = x$

Check:

$$\begin{array}{c|c} \dfrac{2}{x} - \dfrac{3}{x} + \dfrac{4}{x} = 5 \\ \hline \dfrac{2}{\frac{3}{5}} - \dfrac{3}{\frac{3}{5}} + \dfrac{4}{\frac{3}{5}} & \dfrac{15}{3} \\ \dfrac{10}{3} - \dfrac{15}{3} + \dfrac{20}{3} & \\ & \dfrac{15}{3} \end{array}$$

The solution is $\dfrac{3}{5}$.

21. $\dfrac{1}{2} - \dfrac{4}{9x} = \dfrac{4}{9} - \dfrac{1}{6x}$,   LCM = 18x

$18x\left(\dfrac{1}{2} - \dfrac{4}{9x}\right) = 18x\left(\dfrac{4}{9} - \dfrac{1}{6x}\right)$

$9x - 8 = 8x - 3$

$x = 5$

Since 5 checks, it is the solution.

23. $\dfrac{60}{x} - \dfrac{60}{x - 5} = \dfrac{2}{x}$,   LCM = x(x - 5)

$x(x - 5)\left(\dfrac{60}{x} - \dfrac{60}{x - 5}\right) = x(x - 5) \cdot \dfrac{2}{x}$

$60(x - 5) - 60x = 2(x - 5)$

$60x - 300 - 60x = 2x - 10$

$-300 = 2x - 10$

$-290 = 2x$

$-145 = x$

Since -145 checks, it is the solution.

25. $\dfrac{7}{5x - 2} = \dfrac{5}{4x}$,   LCM = 4x(5x - 2)

$4x(5x - 2) \cdot \dfrac{7}{5x - 2} = 4x(5x - 2) \cdot \dfrac{5}{4x}$

$4x \cdot 7 = 5(5x - 2)$

$28x = 25x - 10$

$3x = -10$

$x = -\dfrac{10}{3}$

Since $-\dfrac{10}{3}$ checks, it is the solution.

27. $\dfrac{x}{x - 2} + \dfrac{x}{x^2 - 4} = \dfrac{x + 3}{x + 2}$

$\dfrac{x}{x - 2} + \dfrac{x}{(x + 2)(x - 2)} = \dfrac{x + 3}{x + 2}$,   LCM = (x+2)(x-2)

$(x+2)(x-2)\left(\dfrac{x}{x-2} + \dfrac{x}{(x+2)(x-2)}\right) = (x+2)(x-2) \cdot \dfrac{x+3}{x+2}$

$x(x + 2) + x = (x - 2)(x + 3)$

$x^2 + 2x + x = x^2 + x - 6$

$3x = x - 6$

$2x = -6$

$x = -3$

Since -3 checks, it is the solution.

29. $\dfrac{a}{2a - 6} - \dfrac{3}{a^2 - 6a + 9} = \dfrac{a - 2}{3a - 9}$

$\dfrac{a}{2(a - 3)} - \dfrac{3}{(a - 3)(a - 3)} = \dfrac{a - 2}{3(a - 3)}$

LCM = 2·3(a - 3)(a - 3)

$6(a-3)(a-3)\left(\dfrac{a}{2(a-3)} - \dfrac{3}{(a-3)(a-3)}\right) =$

$6(a-3)(a-3) \cdot \dfrac{a-2}{3(a-3)}$

$3a(a - 3) - 2 \cdot 3 \cdot 3 = 2(a - 3)(a - 2)$

$3a^2 - 9a - 18 = 2(a^2 - 5a + 6)$

$3a^2 - 9a - 18 = 2a^2 - 10a + 12$

$a^2 + a - 30 = 0$

$(a + 6)(a - 5) = 0$

a + 6 = 0 or a - 5 = 0

a = -6 or   a = 5

Both -6 and 5 check. The solutions are -6 and 5.

31. $\dfrac{2x + 3}{x - 1} = \dfrac{10}{x^2 - 1} + \dfrac{2x - 3}{x + 1}$

$\dfrac{2x + 3}{x - 1} = \dfrac{10}{(x - 1)(x + 1)} + \dfrac{2x - 3}{x + 1}$

LCM = (x - 1)(x + 1)

$(x-1)(x+1) \cdot \dfrac{2x+3}{x-1} = (x-1)(x+1)\left(\dfrac{10}{(x-1)(x+1)} + \dfrac{2x-3}{x+1}\right)$

$(x + 1)(2x + 3) = 10 + (x - 1)(2x - 3)$

$2x^2 + 5x + 3 = 10 + 2x^2 - 5x + 3$

$5x + 3 = 13 - 5x$

$10x = 10$

$x = 1$

We know that 1 is not a solution of the original equation because it results in division by 0. The equation has no solution.

33. $\dfrac{4}{x + 3} + \dfrac{7}{x^2 - 3x + 9} = \dfrac{108}{x^3 + 27}$

Note: $x^3 + 27 = (x + 3)(x^2 - 3x + 9)$
Thus the LCM is $(x + 3)(x^2 - 3x + 9)$.

$(x + 3)(x^2 - 3x + 9)(\dfrac{4}{x + 3} + \dfrac{7}{x^2 - 3x + 9}) =$

$\qquad (x + 3)(x^2 - 3x + 9)(\dfrac{108}{(x + 3)(x^2 - 3x + 9)})$

$\qquad\qquad 4(x^2 - 3x + 9) + 7(x + 3) = 108$

$\qquad\qquad 4x^2 - 12x + 36 + 7x + 21 = 108$

$\qquad\qquad\qquad\qquad\qquad 4x^2 - 5x + 51 = 0$

$\qquad\qquad\qquad\qquad\qquad (4x - 17)(x + 3) = 0$

$4x - 17 = 0$ or $x + 3 = 0$

$\qquad 4x = 17$ or $\qquad x = -3$

$\qquad x = \dfrac{17}{4}$ or $\qquad x = -3$

We know that -3 is not a solution of the original equation because it results in division by 0. Since $\dfrac{17}{4}$ checks, it is the solution.

35. $\dfrac{3x}{x + 2} + \dfrac{6}{x} + 4 = \dfrac{12}{x^2 + 2x}$

Note: $x^2 + 2x = x(x + 2)$
Thus the LCM is $x(x + 2)$.

$\qquad x(x + 2)(\dfrac{3x}{x + 2} + \dfrac{6}{x} + 4) = x(x + 2) \cdot \dfrac{12}{x(x + 2)}$

$x \cdot 3x + (x + 2) \cdot 6 + x(x + 2) \cdot 4 = 12$

$\qquad 3x^2 + 6x + 12 + 4x^2 + 8x = 12$

$\qquad\qquad\qquad\qquad 7x^2 + 14x = 0$

$\qquad\qquad\qquad\qquad 7x(x + 2) = 0$

$x = 0$ or $x + 2 = 0$

$x = 0$ or $\qquad x = -2$

Neither 0 nor -2 checks. Each results in division by 0. The equation has no solution.

37. $4x^2 - 5x - 51 = (4x - 17)(x + 3)$

39. $1 - t^6$

$= (1 + t^3)(1 - t^3)$

$= (1 + t)(1 - t + t^2)(1 - t)(1 + t + t^2)$

41. $(\dfrac{1}{1 + x} + \dfrac{x}{1 - x}) \div (\dfrac{x}{1 + x} - \dfrac{1}{1 - x}) = -1$

$\dfrac{1 \cdot (1 - x) + x(1 + x)}{(1 + x)(1 - x)} \div \dfrac{x(1 - x) - 1 \cdot (1 + x)}{(1 + x)(1 - x)} = -1$

$\qquad \dfrac{x^2 + 1}{(1 + x)(1 - x)} \cdot \dfrac{(1 + x)(1 - x)}{-x^2 - 1} = -1$

$\qquad\qquad\qquad\qquad \dfrac{x^2 + 1}{-x^2 - 1} = -1$

$\qquad\qquad\qquad\qquad -\dfrac{x^2 + 1}{x^2 + 1} = -1$

$\qquad\qquad\qquad\qquad\qquad\qquad -1 = -1$

We know that 1 and -1 cannot be solutions of the original equation because they result in division by 0. Since -1 = -1 is true, all reals except 1 and -1 are solutions.

43. $\dfrac{7}{x - 9} - \dfrac{7}{x} = \dfrac{63}{x^2 - 9x}$

Note: $x^2 - 9x = x(x - 9)$
Thus the LCM is $x(x - 9)$

$x(x - 9)(\dfrac{7}{x - 9} - \dfrac{7}{x}) = x(x - 9) \cdot \dfrac{63}{x(x - 9)}$

$\qquad\qquad 7x - 7(x - 9) = 63$

$\qquad\qquad 7x - 7x + 63 = 63$

$\qquad\qquad\qquad\qquad 63 = 63$

Since 63 = 63 is true, all reals except 0 and 9 (which result in division by 0) are solutions of the equation.

Exercise Set 6.5

---

1.   Let x represent the number. Then the reciprocal of the number is $\dfrac{1}{x}$.

A number plus 21 times its reciprocal is -10.

$\qquad x \qquad + 21 \quad \cdot \qquad \dfrac{1}{x} \qquad = -10$

We solve the equation.

$\qquad x + \dfrac{21}{x} = -10$,   LCM $= x$

$\qquad x(x + \dfrac{21}{x}) = x(-10)$

$\qquad\qquad x^2 + 21 = -10x$

$\qquad x^2 + 10x + 21 = 0$

$\qquad (x + 3)(x + 7) = 0$

$x + 3 = 0$ or $x + 7 = 0$

$\qquad x = -3$ or $\qquad x = -7$

The possible solutions are -3 and -7.

$x + \dfrac{21}{x} = -10$		$x + \dfrac{21}{x} = -10$	
$-3 + \dfrac{21}{-3}$	-10	$-7 + \dfrac{21}{-7}$	-10
$-3 - 7$		$-7 - 3$	
-10		-10	

Both numbers check. There are two numbers satisfying the conditions of the problem. They are -3 and -7.

3. Let x represent the number. Then the reciprocal of the number is $\frac{1}{x}$.

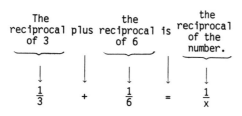

The reciprocal of 3	plus	the reciprocal of 6	is	the reciprocal of the number.
$\frac{1}{3}$	+	$\frac{1}{6}$	=	$\frac{1}{x}$

We solve the equation.

$$\frac{1}{3} + \frac{1}{6} = \frac{1}{x} , \quad LCM = 6x$$

$$6x(\frac{1}{3} + \frac{1}{6}) = 6x \cdot \frac{1}{x}$$

$$2x + x = 6$$

$$3x = 6$$

$$x = 2$$

The number to be checked is 2. Its reciprocal is $\frac{1}{2}$. The sum of $\frac{1}{3} + \frac{1}{6}$ is $\frac{2}{6} + \frac{1}{6}$, or $\frac{3}{6}$ which is $\frac{1}{2}$, so the value checks. The number is 2.

5. The job takes Wilma 5 hours working alone and Willy 9 hours working alone. Then in 1 hour, Wilma does $\frac{1}{5}$ of the job and Willy does $\frac{1}{9}$ of the job. Working together, they can do $\frac{1}{5} + \frac{1}{9}$ of the job in 1 hour. We are supposing it takes them t hours working together, so they should do $\frac{1}{t}$ of the job in 1 hour.

This gives us an equation.

$$\frac{1}{5} + \frac{1}{9} = \frac{1}{t} , \quad LCM = 45t$$

We solve the equation.

$$45t(\frac{1}{5} + \frac{1}{9}) = 45t \cdot \frac{1}{t}$$

$$9t + 5t = 45$$

$$14t = 45$$

$$t = \frac{45}{14}$$

The possible solution is $\frac{45}{14}$ hours. If Wilma works $\frac{45}{14}$ hours, she will do $\frac{1}{5} \cdot \frac{45}{14}$, or $\frac{9}{14}$ of the job. If Willy works $\frac{45}{14}$ hours, he will do $\frac{1}{9} \cdot \frac{45}{14}$, or $\frac{5}{14}$ of the job. Altogether, they will do $\frac{9}{14} + \frac{5}{14}$ of the job, or all of it. The value checks.

Working together it will take them $\frac{45}{14}$, or $3\frac{3}{14}$ hours.

7. The pool can be filled in 12 hours with only the pipe and in 30 hours with only the hose. Then in 1 hour, the pipe fills $\frac{1}{12}$ of the pool, and the hose fills $\frac{1}{30}$ of the pool. Using both the pipe and the hose, $\frac{1}{12} + \frac{1}{30}$ of the pool can be filled in 1 hour. We suppose that it takes t hours to fill the pool using both the pipe and hose so $\frac{1}{t}$ of the pool should be filled in 1 hour. This gives us an equation.

$$\frac{1}{12} + \frac{1}{30} = \frac{1}{t} , \quad LCM = 60t$$

We solve the equation.

$$60t(\frac{1}{12} + \frac{1}{30}) = 60t \cdot \frac{1}{t}$$

$$5t + 2t = 60$$

$$7t = 60$$

$$t = \frac{60}{7}$$

The possible solution is $\frac{60}{7}$ hours. If the pipe is used $\frac{60}{7}$ hours, it fills $\frac{1}{12} \cdot \frac{60}{7}$, or $\frac{5}{7}$ of the pool. If the hose is used $\frac{60}{7}$ hours, it fills $\frac{1}{30} \cdot \frac{60}{7}$, or $\frac{2}{7}$ of the pool. Using both, $\frac{5}{7} + \frac{2}{7}$ of the pool, or all of it, will be filled. The value checks.

Using both, it will take $\frac{60}{7}$, or $8\frac{4}{7}$ hours, to fill the pool.

9. The job takes Bill 5.5 hours working alone and his partner 7.5 hours working alone. Then in 1 hour, Bill does $\frac{1}{5.5}$ of the job and his partner does $\frac{1}{7.5}$ of the job. Working together, they can do $\frac{1}{5.5} + \frac{1}{7.5}$ of the job in 1 hour. We suppose it takes them t hours working together, so they should do $\frac{1}{t}$ of the job in 1 hour. This gives us an equation.

$$\frac{1}{5.5} + \frac{1}{7.5} = \frac{1}{t} , \quad CM = (5.5)(7.5)t$$

We solve the equation.

$$(5.5)(7.5)t(\frac{1}{5.5} + \frac{1}{7.5}) = (5.5)(7.5)t \cdot \frac{1}{t}$$

$$7.5t + 5.5t = (5.5)(7.5)$$

$$13t = 41.25$$

$$t = \frac{41.25}{13}$$

$$t = 3\frac{9}{52}$$

9. (continued)

The possible solution is $3\frac{9}{52}$ hours. If Bill works $3\frac{9}{52}$ hours, he will do $\frac{2}{11} \cdot \frac{165}{52}$, or $\frac{15}{26}$ of the job. If his partner works $3\frac{9}{52}$ hours, he will do $\frac{2}{15} \cdot \frac{165}{52}$, or $\frac{11}{26}$ of the job. Together they will do $\frac{15}{26} + \frac{11}{26}$ of the job, or all of it. The value checks.

Working together, it will take them $3\frac{9}{52}$ hours.

11. Let t represent the time it takes A to paint the house alone. B takes 4 times as long as A, or 4t. Thus in 1 day A does $\frac{1}{t}$ of the job and B does $\frac{1}{4t}$ of the job. Together in 1 day they do $\frac{1}{t} + \frac{1}{4t}$, or $\frac{1}{8}$ of the job. We now have an equation.

$$\frac{1}{t} + \frac{1}{4t} = \frac{1}{8}$$

We solve the equation. The LCM = 8t.

$$8t\left(\frac{1}{t} + \frac{1}{4t}\right) = 8t \cdot \frac{1}{8}$$
$$8 + 2 = t$$
$$10 = t$$

The solution of the equation is 10, the time in days for A to paint the house alone. If B takes four times as long, then B's time is 4·10 or 40 days to paint the house alone.

$$\frac{1}{10} + \frac{1}{40} = \frac{4}{40} + \frac{1}{40} = \frac{5}{40} = \frac{1}{8}$$

It takes A 10 days working alone and B 40 days working alone.

13. We first make a drawing.

We let r represent the speed of the boat in still water. Then r - 3 is the speed upstream and r + 3 is the speed downstream. The time is the same both upstream and downstream so we just use t for each time. We organize the information in a table.

	Distance	Speed	Time
Upstream	4	r - 3	t
Downstream	10	r + 3	t

13. (continued)

Using $t = \frac{d}{r}$ we get two different equations from the rows of the table.

$t = \frac{4}{r - 3}$ and $t = \frac{10}{r + 3}$.

Since the times are the same, we get

$$\frac{4}{r - 3} = \frac{10}{r + 3}$$

We solve the equation. The LCM is $(r - 3)(r + 3)$.

$$(r - 3)(r + 3) \cdot \frac{4}{r - 3} = (r - 3)(r + 3) \cdot \frac{10}{r + 3}$$
$$4(r + 3) = 10(r - 3)$$
$$4r + 12 = 10r - 30$$
$$42 = 6r$$
$$7 = r$$

If r = 7 mph, then r - 3 is 4 mph and r + 3 is 10 mph. The time upstream is $\frac{4}{4}$, or 1 hour. The time downstream is $\frac{10}{10}$, or 1 hour. The times are the same. The values check.

The speed of the boat in still water is 7 mph.

15. We first make a drawing.

We let t represent the time for the first train. Then t - 2 represents the time for the second train. Since the distances are the same, we use d for each distance. We organize the information in a table.

Train	Distance	Speed	Time
First	d	75	t
Second	d	125	t - 2

From the rows of the table we get two different equations.

d = 75t and d = 125(t - 2).

Since the distances are the same, we get

75t = 125(t - 2)

We solve the equation.

75t = 125t - 250
250 = 50t
5 = t

15. (continued)

If t is 5 hours, then the time for the second train is 5 - 2, or 3 hours. The first train travels 75·5, or 375 km. The second train travels 125·3, or 375 km. The distances are the same.

The second train will overtake the first train 375 km from the station.

17. We organize the information in a table.

	Distance	Speed	Time
Train A	230	r - 12	t
Train B	290	r	t

We let r represent the speed of Train B. Then r - 12 represents the speed of Train A. The times are the same. We use t for each.

From the rows of the table using $t = \frac{d}{r}$, we get two equations.

$$t = \frac{230}{r - 12} \quad \text{and} \quad t = \frac{290}{r}$$

Since the times are the same, we get

$$\frac{230}{r - 12} = \frac{290}{r}$$

We solve the equation. The LCM is r(r - 12).

$$r(r - 12) \cdot \frac{230}{r - 12} = r(r - 12) \cdot \frac{290}{r}$$
$$230r = 290(r - 12)$$
$$230r = 290r - 3480$$
$$3480 = 60r$$
$$58 = r$$

If the speed of Train B is 58 mph, then the speed of Train A is 58 - 12, or 46 mph. The time for Train A is $\frac{230}{46}$, or 5 hours. The time for Train B is $\frac{290}{58}$, or 5 hours. The times are the same. The values check.

The speed of Train A is 46 mph; the speed of Train B is 58 mph.

19. We first make a drawing.

140 km	15 + r	t hours	Downstream

35 km	15 - r	t hours	Upstream

We let r represent the speed of the river. Then 15 + r is the speed downstream and 15 - r is the speed upstream. The times are the same. We organize the information in a table.

	Distance	Speed	Time
Downstream	140	15 + r	t
Upstream	35	15 - r	t

Using $t = \frac{d}{r}$, we get two equations from the table.

$$t = \frac{140}{15 + r} \quad \text{and} \quad t = \frac{35}{15 - r}$$

Since the times are the same, we have

$$\frac{140}{15 + r} = \frac{35}{15 - r}$$

We solve the equation. The LCM is (15 + r)(15 - r).

$$(15 + r)(15 - r) \cdot \frac{140}{15 + r} = (15 + r)(15 - r) \cdot \frac{35}{15 - r}$$
$$140(15 - r) = 35(15 + r)$$
$$2100 - 140r = 525 + 35r$$
$$1575 = 175r$$
$$9 = r$$

If r = 9, then the speed downstream is 15 + 9, or 24 km/h and the speed upstream is 15 - 9, or 6 km/h. The time for the trip downstream is $\frac{140}{24}$, or $5\frac{5}{6}$ hours. The time for the trip upstream is $\frac{35}{6}$, or $5\frac{5}{6}$ hours. The times are the same. The values check.

The speed of the river is 9 km/h.

21. Let x represent the number of gallons used for city driving and y represent the number of gallons used for highway driving. Then 18x represents the number of city-miles driven and 24y represents the number of highway-miles driven.

We translate the information to a system of equations.

$$x + y = 23$$
$$18x + 24y = 465$$

Solving this system we get x = 14.5 and y = 8.5.

The number of city-miles driven is 18 × 14.5, or 261 miles.

The number of highway-miles driven is 24 × 8.5, or 204 miles.

The values check since the total number of hours is 23 and the total number of miles driven is 465.

23. It helps to first make a drawing.

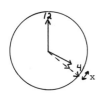

The minute hand moves 60 units per hour while the hour hand moves 5 units per hour. When the hands are in the same position the first time, the hour hand will have moved x units and the minute hand will have moved x + 20 units. The times are the same. We use t for time.

	Distance	Speed	Time
Minute	x + 20	60	t
Hour	x	5	t

Using $t = \frac{d}{r}$ we get two equations from the table.

$$t = \frac{x + 20}{60} \quad \text{and} \quad t = \frac{x}{5}$$

$$\frac{x + 20}{60} = \frac{x}{5} \qquad \text{(Using substitution)}$$

$$60 \cdot \frac{x + 20}{60} = 60 \cdot \frac{x}{5} \qquad \text{(Multiplying by the LCM)}$$

$$x + 20 = 12x$$
$$20 = 11x$$
$$\frac{20}{11} = x$$
$$\text{or} \quad x = 1\frac{9}{11}$$

If the hour hand moves $1\frac{9}{11}$ units, then the minute hand moves $1\frac{9}{11} + 20$, or $21\frac{9}{11}$ units ($21\frac{9}{11}$ minutes after 4).

23. (continued)

The time for the hour hand is $\frac{20}{11} \div 5$, or $\frac{4}{11}$ hour. The time for the minute hand is $\frac{240}{11} \div 60$, or $\frac{4}{11}$ hour. The times are the same; the values check.

At $21\frac{9}{11}$ minutes after 4:00, the hands will be in the same position.

25. We first make a drawing.

96 km	4 hr	x + r km/h	

Downstream

| 28 km | 7 hr | x - r km/hr |

Upstream

We let x represent the speed of the boat in still water and r represent the speed of the stream. Then x + r represents the speed downstream and x - r represents the speed upstream.

	Distance	Speed	Time
Downstream	96	x + r	4
Upstream	28	x - r	7

Using d = rt, we get a system of equations from the table.

$$96 = (x + r)4 \quad \text{or} \quad x + r = 24$$
$$28 = (x - r)7 \qquad x - r = 4$$

Solving the system we get (14,10).

The speed downstream is 14 + 10, or 24 km/h. The distance downstream is 24·4, or 96 km. The speed upstream is 14 - 10, or 4 km/h. The distance upstream is 4·7, or 28 km. The values check.

The speed of the boat is 14 km/h; the speed of the stream is 10 km/h.

27. We let x represent the speed of the current and 3x represent the speed of the boat. Then the speed up the river is 3x - x, or 2x, and the speed down the river is 3x + x, or 4x. The total distance is 100 km; thus the distance each way is 50 km. Using $t = \frac{d}{r}$, we can use $\frac{50}{2x}$ for the time up the river and $\frac{50}{4x}$ for the time down the river.

Since the total of the times is 10 hours, we have the following equation.

$$\frac{50}{2x} + \frac{50}{4x} = 10$$

We solve the equation. The LCM is 4x.

$$4x\left(\frac{50}{2x} + \frac{50}{4x}\right) = 4x \cdot 10$$

$$100 + 50 = 40x$$

$$150 = 40x$$

$$\frac{15}{4} = x$$

$$\text{or } x = 3\frac{3}{4}$$

If the speed of the current is $\frac{15}{4}$ km/h, then the speed of the boat is $3 \cdot \frac{15}{4}$, or $\frac{45}{4}$. The speed up the river is $\frac{45}{4} - \frac{15}{4}$, or $\frac{15}{2}$ km/h, and the time traveling up the river is $50 \div \frac{15}{2}$, or $6\frac{2}{3}$ hr. The speed down the river is $\frac{45}{4} + \frac{15}{4}$, or 15 km/h, and the time traveling down the river is $50 \div 15$, or $3\frac{1}{3}$ hr. The total time for the trip is $6\frac{2}{3} + 3\frac{1}{3}$, of 10 hr. The value checks.

The speed of the current is $3\frac{3}{4}$ km/h.

29. We make a drawing and organize the information in a table. Remember: $t = \frac{d}{r}$.

```
|<--------------200 km-------------->|
     100 km                 100 km
|----------------|------------------|
    40 km/h               60 km/h
```

	Distance	Speed	Time
1st part	100	40	$\frac{100}{40}$, or $\frac{5}{2}$
2nd part	100	60	$\frac{100}{60}$, or $\frac{5}{3}$

29. (continued)

The total distance is 200 km.

The total time is $\frac{5}{2} + \frac{5}{3}$, or $\frac{25}{6}$ hr.

$$\text{Average speed} = \frac{\text{Total distance}}{\text{Total time}}$$

$$= \frac{200 \text{ km}}{\text{hr}}$$

$$= 200 \cdot \frac{6}{25} \text{ km/h}$$

$$= 48 \text{ km/h}$$

31. Trucks A, B, and C, working together, move a load of sand in t hours. Thus, together, they do $\frac{1}{t}$ of the job in 1 hour. Truck A, alone, can move a load of sand in t + 1 hours. Thus, Truck A does $\frac{1}{t+1}$ of the job in 1 hour. Truck B, alone, can move a load of sand in t + 6 hours. Thus, Truck B does $\frac{1}{t+6}$ of the job in 1 hour. Truck C, alone, can move a load of sand in t + t, or 2t hours. Thus, Truck C does $\frac{1}{2t}$ of the job in 1 hour. Working together, they can do $\frac{1}{t+1} + \frac{1}{t+6} + \frac{1}{2t}$ of the job in 1 hour. This gives us an equation.

$$\frac{1}{t+1} + \frac{1}{t+6} + \frac{1}{2t} = \frac{1}{t}$$

The LCM is 2t(t + 1)(t + 6).

$$2t(t+1)(t+6)\left(\frac{1}{t+1} + \frac{1}{t+6} + \frac{1}{2t}\right) =$$
$$2t(t+1)(t+6) \cdot \frac{1}{t}$$

$$2t(t+6) + 2t(t+1) + (t+1)(t+6) =$$
$$2(t+1)(t+6)$$

$$2t^2 + 12t + 2t^2 + 2t + t^2 + 7t + 6 =$$
$$2(t^2 + 7t + 6)$$

$$5t^2 + 21t + 6 =$$
$$2t^2 + 14t + 12$$

$$3t^2 + 7t - 6 = 0$$

$$(3t - 2)(t + 3) = 0$$

$$3t - 2 = 0 \text{ or } t + 3 = 0$$

$$3t = 2 \text{ or } t = -3$$

$$t = \frac{2}{3} \text{ or } t = -3$$

Since the time cannot be negative, we only check $t = \frac{2}{3}$. If $t = \frac{2}{3}$, then $\frac{1}{t} = \frac{3}{2}$. If $t = \frac{2}{3}$, then working alone it takes A $\frac{2}{3} + 1$, or $\frac{5}{3}$ hr, B $\frac{2}{3} + 6$, or $\frac{20}{3}$ hr and C $2 \cdot \frac{2}{3}$, or $\frac{4}{3}$ hr. We calculate.

$$\frac{1}{\frac{5}{3}} + \frac{1}{\frac{20}{3}} + \frac{1}{\frac{4}{3}}$$

$$= \frac{3}{5} + \frac{3}{20} + \frac{3}{4} = \frac{12}{20} + \frac{3}{20} + \frac{15}{20} = \frac{30}{20} = \frac{3}{2}$$

Working together, it takes $\frac{2}{3}$ hour.

Exercise Set 6.6

1. $\dfrac{W_1}{W_2} = \dfrac{d_1}{d_2}$

$\dfrac{d_2 W_1}{W_2} = d_1$ (Multiplying by d_2)

3. $s = \dfrac{(v_1 + v_2)t}{2}$

$2s = (v_1 + v_2)t$ (Multiplying by 2)

$\dfrac{2s}{v_1 + v_2} = t$ (Multiplying by $\dfrac{1}{v_1 + v_2}$)

5. $\dfrac{1}{R} = \dfrac{1}{r_1} + \dfrac{1}{r_2}$

$Rr_1 r_2 \cdot \dfrac{1}{R} = Rr_1 r_2 \left(\dfrac{1}{r_1} + \dfrac{1}{r_2}\right)$ (Multiplying by $Rr_1 r_2$)

$r_1 r_2 = Rr_2 + Rr_1$

$r_1 r_2 - Rr_2 = Rr_1$ (Adding $-Rr_2$)

$r_2(r_1 - R) = Rr_1$ (Factoring)

$r_2 = \dfrac{Rr_1}{r_1 - R}$ (Multiplying by $\dfrac{1}{r_1 - R}$)

7. $R = \dfrac{gs}{g + s}$

$R(g + s) = gs$ (Multiplying by $g + s$)

$Rg + Rs = gs$ (Removing parentheses)

$Rg = gs - Rs$ (Adding $-Rs$)

$Rg = s(g - r)$ (Factoring)

$\dfrac{Rg}{g - R} = s$ (Multiplying by $\dfrac{1}{g - R}$)

9. $\dfrac{1}{p} + \dfrac{1}{q} = \dfrac{1}{f}$

$pqf\left(\dfrac{1}{p} + \dfrac{1}{q}\right) = pqf \cdot \dfrac{1}{f}$ (Multiplying by pqf)

$qf + pf = pq$

$qf = pq - pf$ (Adding $-pf$)

$qf = p(q - f)$ (Factoring)

$\dfrac{qf}{q - f} = p$ (Multiplying by $\dfrac{1}{q - f}$)

11. $I = \dfrac{nE}{R + nr}$

$I(R + nr) = nE$ (Multiplying by $R + nr$)

$IR + Inr = nE$ (Removing parentheses)

$Inr = nE - IR$ (Adding $-IR$)

$r = \dfrac{nE - IR}{In}$ (Multiplying by $\dfrac{1}{In}$)

13. $S = \dfrac{H}{m(t_1 - t_2)}$

$m(t_1 - t_2)S = H$ [Multiplying by $m(t_1 - t_2)$]

15. $\dfrac{E}{e} = \dfrac{R + r}{r}$

$er \cdot \dfrac{E}{e} = er \cdot \dfrac{R + r}{r}$ (Multiplying by er)

$rE = e(R + r)$

$\dfrac{rE}{R + r} = e$ (Multiplying by $\dfrac{1}{R + r}$)

17. $A = P(1 + rt)$

$A = P + Prt$ (Removing parentheses)

$A - P = Prt$ (Adding $-P$)

$\dfrac{A - P}{Pt} = r$ (Multiplying by $\dfrac{1}{Pt}$)

19. Graph: $6x - y < 6$

First graph the line $6x - y = 6$. The intercepts are $(0,-6)$ and $(1,0)$. We draw the line dashed since the inequality is $<$. Since the ordered pair $(0,0)$ is a solution of the inequality ($6 \cdot 0 - 0 < 0$ is true), we shade the upper half plane.

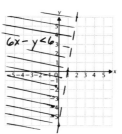

21. $t^3 + 8b^3 = t^3 + (2b)^3 = (t + 2b)(t^2 - 2bt + 4b^2)$

23. Working alone Person A can do the job in a hours. Thus, Person A can do $\dfrac{1}{a}$ of the job in 1 hour. Person B, working alone, can do the job in b hours. Thus, Person B can do $\dfrac{1}{b}$ of the job in 1 hour. Working together it takes them t hours. Thus, they do $\dfrac{1}{t}$ of the job in 1 hour. We have the following equation.

$\dfrac{1}{a} + \dfrac{1}{b} = \dfrac{1}{t}$

25. $\dfrac{1}{a} + \dfrac{1}{b} = \dfrac{1}{t}$

$abt\left(\dfrac{1}{a} + \dfrac{1}{b}\right) = abt \cdot \dfrac{1}{t}$

$bt + at = ab$

$bt = ab - at$

$bt = a(b - t)$

$\dfrac{bt}{b - t} = a$

Exercise Set 6.7

1. $y = kx$ (Direct variation)
   $24 = k \cdot 3$ (Substituting)
   $8 = k$

   The variation constant is 8.
   The equation of variation is $y = 8x$.

3. $y = kx$ (Direct variation)
   $3.6 = k \cdot 1$ (Substituting)
   $3.6 = k$

   The variation constant is 3.6.
   The equation of variation is $y = 3.6x$.

5. $y = kx$ (Direct variation)
   $0.8 = k(0.5)$ (Substituting)
   $\frac{0.8}{0.5} = k$

   $\frac{8}{5} = k$

   The variation constant is $\frac{8}{5}$.
   The equation of variation is $y = \frac{8}{5}x$.

7. $I = kV$ (Direct variation)
   $4 = k \cdot 12$ (Substituting)
   $\frac{1}{3} = k$ (Variation constant)

   $I = \frac{1}{3}V$ (Equation of variation)
   $I = \frac{1}{3} \cdot 18$ (Substituting)
   $I = 6$

   The current is 6 amperes.

9. $N = kt$ (Direct variation)
   $20,000 = k \cdot 8$ (Substituting)
   $2500 = k$ (Variation constant)
   $N = 2500t$ (Equation of variation)
   $N = 2500 \cdot 50$ (Substituting)
   $N = 125,000$

   The machine can produce 125,000 straws in 50 hours.

11. $W = kT$ (Direct variation)
    $64 = k \cdot 96$ (Substituting)
    $\frac{64}{96} = k$ (Variation constant)

    $\frac{2}{3} = k$

    $W = \frac{2}{3}T$ (Equation of variation)
    $W = \frac{2}{3} \cdot 75$ (Substituting)
    $W = 50$

    A person weighing 75 kg contains 50 kg of water.

13. $y = \frac{k}{x}$ (Inverse variation)
    $6 = \frac{k}{10}$ (Substituting)
    $60 = k$

    The variation constant is 60.
    The equation of variation is $y = \frac{60}{x}$.

15. $y = \frac{k}{x}$ (Inverse variation)
    $12 = \frac{k}{3}$ (Substituting)
    $36 = k$

    The variation constant is 36.
    The equation of variation is $y = \frac{36}{x}$.

17. $y = \frac{k}{x}$ (Inverse variation)
    $0.4 = \frac{k}{0.8}$ (Substituting)
    $0.32 = k$

    The variation constant is 0.32.
    The equation of variation is $y = \frac{0.32}{x}$.

19. $I = \frac{k}{R}$ (Inverse variation)
    $\frac{1}{2} = \frac{k}{240}$ (Substituting)
    $\frac{240}{2} = k$
    $120 = k$ (Variation constant)
    $I = \frac{120}{R}$ (Equation of variation)
    $I = \frac{120}{540}$ (Substituting)
    $I = \frac{2}{9}$

    The current is $\frac{2}{9}$ ampere.

21. $W = \dfrac{k}{L}$ (Inverse variation)

$1200 = \dfrac{k}{8}$ (Substituting)

$9600 = k$ (Variation constant)

$W = \dfrac{9600}{L}$ (Equation of variation)

$W = \dfrac{9600}{14}$ (Substituting)

$W = 685\dfrac{5}{7}$

A 14-meter beam can support $685\dfrac{5}{7}$ kg.

23. $(x + h)^3 - x^3$

$= [(x + h) - x][(x + h)^2 + (x + h)x + x^2]$

$= (x + h - x)(x^2 + 2xh + h^2 + x^2 + xh + x^2)$

$= h(3x^2 + 3xh + h^2)$

25. Graph: $2y - 5x < 10$

First graph the line $2y - 5x = 10$. The intercepts are (0,5) and (-2,0). We draw the line dashed since the inequality is <. Since the ordered pair (0,0) is a solution of the inequality ($2\cdot0 - 5\cdot0 < 10$ is true), we shade the lower half-plane.

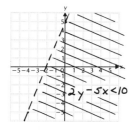

27. $I = kP$ (Direct variation

$1665 = k\cdot9000$ (Substituting)

$\dfrac{1665}{9000} = k$

$0.185 = k$ (Variation constant)

The equation of variation is $I = 0.185P$.

1. $\dfrac{\frac{1}{x} + 4}{\frac{1}{x} - 3} = \dfrac{\frac{1}{x} + \frac{4}{1}\cdot\frac{x}{x}}{\frac{1}{x} - \frac{3}{1}\cdot\frac{x}{x}}$

$= \dfrac{\frac{1 + 4x}{x}}{\frac{1 - 3x}{x}}$

$= \dfrac{1 + 4x}{x} \cdot \dfrac{x}{1 - 3x}$

$= \dfrac{x}{x} \cdot \dfrac{1 + 4x}{1 - 3x}$

$= \dfrac{1 + 4x}{1 - 3x}$

3. $\dfrac{x - \frac{1}{x}}{x + \frac{1}{x}} = \dfrac{\frac{x}{1}\cdot\frac{x}{x} - \frac{1}{x}}{\frac{x}{1}\cdot\frac{x}{x} + \frac{1}{x}}$

$= \dfrac{\frac{x^2 - 1}{x}}{\frac{x^2 + 1}{x}}$

$= \dfrac{x^2 - 1}{x} \cdot \dfrac{x}{x^2 + 1}$

$= \dfrac{x^2 - 1}{x^2 + 1} \cdot \dfrac{x}{x}$

$= \dfrac{x^2 - 1}{x^2 + 1}$

5. $\dfrac{\frac{3}{x} + \frac{4}{y}}{\frac{4}{x} - \frac{3}{y}} = \dfrac{\frac{3}{x}\cdot\frac{y}{y} + \frac{4}{y}\cdot\frac{x}{x}}{\frac{4}{x}\cdot\frac{y}{y} - \frac{3}{y}\cdot\frac{x}{x}}$

$= \dfrac{\frac{3y + 4x}{xy}}{\frac{4y - 3x}{xy}}$

$= \dfrac{3y + 4x}{xy} \cdot \dfrac{xy}{4y - 3x}$

$= \dfrac{xy}{xy} \cdot \dfrac{3y + 4x}{4y - 3x}$

$= \dfrac{3y + 4x}{4y - 3x}$

7. $\dfrac{\frac{x^2 - y^2}{xy}}{\frac{x - y}{y}}$

$= \dfrac{x^2 - y^2}{xy} \cdot \dfrac{y}{x - y}$

$= \dfrac{(x + y)(x - y)y}{xy(x - y)}$

$= \dfrac{y(x - y)}{y(x - y)} \cdot \dfrac{x + y}{x}$

$= \dfrac{x + y}{x}$

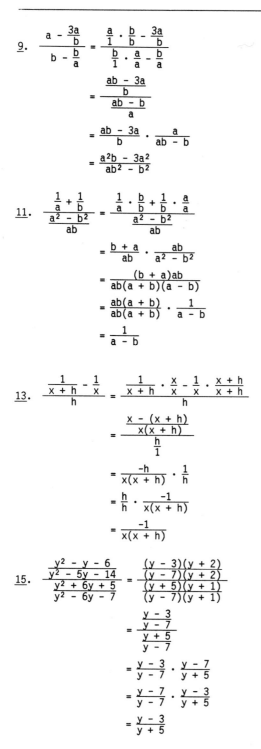

9. $\dfrac{a - \dfrac{3a}{b}}{b - \dfrac{b}{a}} = \dfrac{\dfrac{a}{1} \cdot \dfrac{b}{b} - \dfrac{3a}{b}}{\dfrac{b}{1} \cdot \dfrac{a}{a} - \dfrac{b}{a}}$

$= \dfrac{\dfrac{ab - 3a}{b}}{\dfrac{ab - b}{a}}$

$= \dfrac{ab - 3a}{b} \cdot \dfrac{a}{ab - b}$

$= \dfrac{a^2 b - 3a^2}{ab^2 - b^2}$

11. $\dfrac{\dfrac{1}{a} + \dfrac{1}{b}}{\dfrac{a^2 - b^2}{ab}} = \dfrac{\dfrac{1}{a} \cdot \dfrac{b}{b} + \dfrac{1}{b} \cdot \dfrac{a}{a}}{\dfrac{a^2 - b^2}{ab}}$

$= \dfrac{b + a}{ab} \cdot \dfrac{ab}{a^2 - b^2}$

$= \dfrac{(b + a)ab}{ab(a + b)(a - b)}$

$= \dfrac{ab(a + b)}{ab(a + b)} \cdot \dfrac{1}{a - b}$

$= \dfrac{1}{a - b}$

13. $\dfrac{\dfrac{1}{x + h} - \dfrac{1}{x}}{h} = \dfrac{\dfrac{1}{x + h} \cdot \dfrac{x}{x} - \dfrac{1}{x} \cdot \dfrac{x + h}{x + h}}{h}$

$= \dfrac{\dfrac{x - (x + h)}{x(x + h)}}{\dfrac{h}{1}}$

$= \dfrac{-h}{x(x + h)} \cdot \dfrac{1}{h}$

$= \dfrac{h}{h} \cdot \dfrac{-1}{x(x + h)}$

$= \dfrac{-1}{x(x + h)}$

15. $\dfrac{\dfrac{y^2 - y - 6}{y^2 - 5y - 14}}{\dfrac{y^2 + 6y + 5}{y^2 - 6y - 7}} = \dfrac{\dfrac{(y - 3)(y + 2)}{(y - 7)(y + 2)}}{\dfrac{(y + 5)(y + 1)}{(y - 7)(y + 1)}}$

$= \dfrac{\dfrac{y - 3}{y - 7}}{\dfrac{y + 5}{y - 7}}$

$= \dfrac{y - 3}{y - 7} \cdot \dfrac{y - 7}{y + 5}$

$= \dfrac{y - 7}{y - 7} \cdot \dfrac{y - 3}{y + 5}$

$= \dfrac{y - 3}{y + 5}$

17. $\dfrac{5x^{-1} - 5y^{-1} + 10x^{-1}y^{-1}}{6x^{-1} - 6y^{-1} + 12x^{-1}y^{-1}}$

$= \dfrac{\dfrac{5}{x} \cdot \dfrac{y}{y} - \dfrac{5}{y} \cdot \dfrac{x}{x} + \dfrac{10}{xy}}{\dfrac{6}{x} \cdot \dfrac{y}{y} - \dfrac{6}{y} \cdot \dfrac{x}{x} + \dfrac{12}{xy}}$

$= \dfrac{\dfrac{5y - 5x + 10}{xy}}{\dfrac{6y - 6x + 12}{xy}}$

$= \dfrac{5y - 5x + 10}{xy} \cdot \dfrac{xy}{6y - 6x + 12}$

$= \dfrac{5y - 5x + 10}{6y - 6x + 12} = \dfrac{5(y - x + 2)}{6(y - x + 2)} = \dfrac{5}{6}$

19. $2 + \dfrac{2}{2 + \dfrac{2}{2 + \dfrac{2}{2 + \dfrac{2}{x}}}}$

$= 2 + \dfrac{2}{2 + \dfrac{2}{2 + \dfrac{2}{\dfrac{2x + 2}{x}}}}$

$= 2 + \dfrac{2}{2 + \dfrac{2}{2 + \dfrac{2x}{2x + 2}}} = 2 + \dfrac{2}{2 + \dfrac{2}{\dfrac{6x + 4}{2x + 2}}}$

$= 2 + \dfrac{2}{2 + \dfrac{4x + 4}{6x + 4}} = 2 + \dfrac{2}{\dfrac{16x + 12}{6x + 4}}$

$= 2 + \dfrac{12x + 8}{16x + 12} = \dfrac{44x + 32}{16x + 12}$

$= \dfrac{4(11x + 8)}{4(4x + 3)} = \dfrac{11x + 8}{4x + 3}$

21. $\dfrac{(a^2 b^{-1} + b^2 a^{-1})(a^{-2} - b^{-2})}{(a^2 - ab + b^2)(a^{-2} + 2a^{-1}b^{-1} + b^{-2})}$

$= \dfrac{\left(\dfrac{a^2}{b} + \dfrac{b^2}{a}\right)\left(\dfrac{1}{a^2} - \dfrac{1}{b^2}\right)}{(a^2 - ab + b^2)\left(\dfrac{1}{a^2} + \dfrac{2}{ab} + \dfrac{1}{b^2}\right)}$

$= \dfrac{\left(\dfrac{a^3 + b^3}{ab}\right)\left(\dfrac{b^2 - a^2}{a^2 b^2}\right)}{(a^2 - ab + b^2)\left(\dfrac{b^2 + 2ab + a^2}{a^2 b^2}\right)}$

$= \dfrac{(a+b)(a^2-ab+b^2)(b+a)(b-a)}{a^3 b^3} \cdot \dfrac{a^2 b^2}{(a^2-ab+b^2)(b+a)^2}$

$= \dfrac{b - a}{ab}$

23. $\dfrac{1 - \dfrac{1}{a}}{a - 1} = \dfrac{\dfrac{a - 1}{a}}{\dfrac{a - 1}{1}} = \dfrac{a - 1}{a} \cdot \dfrac{1}{a - 1} = \dfrac{1}{a}$

The reciprocal of $\dfrac{1}{a}$ is a.

Exercise Set 6.9

$\underline{1.}$ $\dfrac{30x^8 - 15x^6 + 40x^4}{5x^4}$

$= \dfrac{30x^8}{5x^4} - \dfrac{15x^6}{5x^4} + \dfrac{40x^4}{5x^4}$

$= 6x^4 - 3x^2 + 8$

$\underline{3.}$ $(9y^4 - 18y^3 + 27y^2) \div 9y$

$= \dfrac{9y^4}{9y} - \dfrac{18y^3}{9y} + \dfrac{27y^2}{9y}$

$= y^3 - 2y^2 + 3y$

$\underline{5.}$
$$\begin{array}{r} x + 7 \\ x + 3 \overline{\smash{\big)}\ x^2 + 10x + 21} \\ \underline{x^2 + 3x} \\ 7x + 21 \qquad (10x - 3x = 7x) \\ \underline{7x + 21} \\ 0 \end{array}$$

The answer is $x + 7$.

$\underline{7.}$
$$\begin{array}{r} a - 12 \\ a + 4 \overline{\smash{\big)}\ a^2 - 8a - 16} \\ \underline{a^2 + 4a} \\ -12a - 16 \qquad (-8a - 4a = -12a) \\ \underline{-12a - 48} \\ 32 \end{array}$$

The answer is $a - 12$ with R = 32, or

or $a - 12 + \dfrac{32}{a + 4}$.

$\underline{9.}$
$$\begin{array}{r} x + 2 \\ x + 5 \overline{\smash{\big)}\ x^2 + 7x + 14} \\ \underline{x^2 + 5x} \\ 2x + 14 \\ \underline{2x + 10} \\ 4 \end{array}$$

The answer is $x + 2$ with R = 4, or $x + 2 + \dfrac{4}{x + 5}$.

$\underline{11.}$
$$\begin{array}{r} 2y^2 - y + 2 \\ 2y + 4 \overline{\smash{\big)}\ 4y^3 + 6y^2 + 0y + 14} \\ \underline{4y^3 + 8y^2} \\ -2y^2 + 0y \qquad (6y^2 - 8y^2 = -2y^2) \\ \underline{-2y^2 - 4y} \\ 4y + 14 \qquad [0y - (-4y) = 4y] \\ \underline{4y + 8} \\ 6 \end{array}$$

The answer is $2y^2 - y + 2$ with R = 6,

or $2y^2 - y + 2 + \dfrac{6}{2y + 4}$.

$\underline{13.}$
$$\begin{array}{r} 2y^2 + 2y - 1 \\ 5y - 2 \overline{\smash{\big)}\ 10y^3 + 6y^2 - 9y + 10} \\ \underline{10y^3 - 4y^2} \\ 10y^2 - 9y \\ \underline{10y^2 - 4y} \\ -5y + 10 \\ \underline{-5y + 2} \\ 8 \end{array}$$

The answer is $2y^2 + 2y - 1$ with R = 8,

or $2y^2 + 2y - 1 + \dfrac{8}{5y - 2}$.

$\underline{15.}$
$$\begin{array}{r} 2x^2 - x - 9 \\ x^2 + 2 \overline{\smash{\big)}\ 2x^4 - x^3 - 5x^2 + x - 6} \\ \underline{2x^4 \qquad + 4x^2} \\ -x^3 - 9x^2 + x \\ \underline{-x^3 \qquad - 2x} \\ -9x^2 + 3x - 6 \\ \underline{-9x^2 \qquad - 18} \\ 3x + 12 \end{array}$$

The answer is $2x^2 - x - 9$ with R = 3x + 12,

or $2x^2 - x - 9 + \dfrac{3x + 12}{x^2 + 2}$.

$\underline{17.}$ $x^2 - 5x = 0$

$x(x - 5) = 0$ (Factoring)

$x = 0$ or $x - 5 = 0$ (Principle of zero products)

$x = 0$ or $x = 5$

The solutions are 0 and 5.

$\underline{19.}$ $35t^2 + 18t = 8$

      $35t^2 + 18t - 8 = 0$

    $(5t + 4)(7t - 2) = 0$

$5t + 4 = 0$ or $7t - 2 = 0$

   $5t = -4$ or $7t = 2$

    $t = -\dfrac{4}{5}$ or $t = \dfrac{2}{7}$

The solutions are $-\dfrac{4}{5}$ and $\dfrac{2}{7}$.

$\underline{21.}$
$$\begin{array}{r} 2x^4 - 2x^3 + 5x^2 - 4x - 1 \\ x^2 + x + 1 \overline{\smash{\big)}\ 2x^6 + 0x^5 + 5x^4 - x^3 + 0x^2 + 0x + 1} \\ \underline{2x^6 + 2x^5 + 2x^4} \\ -2x^5 + 3x^4 - x^3 \\ \underline{-2x^5 - 2x^4 - 2x^3} \\ 5x^4 + x^3 + 0x^2 \\ \underline{5x^4 + 5x^3 + 5x^2} \\ -4x^3 - 5x^2 + 0x \\ \underline{-4x^3 - 4x^2 - 4x} \\ -x^2 + 4x + 1 \\ \underline{-x^2 - x - 1} \\ 5x + 2 \end{array}$$

The answer is $2x^4 - 2x^3 + 5x^2 - 4x - 1$
with R = 5x + 2.

23.
$$
\begin{array}{r}
x^2 + 2y \\
x^2 - xy + y^2\,\overline{\smash{\big)}\,x^4 - x^3y + x^2y^2 + 2x^2y - 2xy^2 + 2y^3} \\
\underline{x^4 - x^3y + x^2y^2} \\
0 + 2x^2y - 2xy^2 + 2y^3 \\
\underline{2x^2y - 2xy^2 + 2y^3} \\
0
\end{array}
$$

The answer is $x^2 + 2y$.

25.
$$
\begin{array}{r}
x^3 + x^2y + xy^2 + y^3 \\
x - y\,\overline{\smash{\big)}\,x^4 \qquad\qquad\qquad - y^4} \\
\underline{x^4 - x^3y} \\
x^3y \\
\underline{x^3y - x^2y^2} \\
x^2y^2 \\
\underline{x^2y^2 - xy^3} \\
xy^3 - y^4 \\
\underline{xy^3 - y^4} \\
0
\end{array}
$$

The answer is $x^3 + x^2y + xy^2 + y^3$.

27.
$$
\begin{array}{r}
x^2 + (-k - 2)x + (2k + 7) \\
x + 2\,\overline{\smash{\big)}\,x^3 - \quad kx^2 + \qquad 3x + \qquad 7k} \\
\underline{x^3 + \qquad 2x^2} \\
(-k - 2)x^2 + \qquad 3x \\
\underline{(-k - 2)x^2 + (-2k - 4)x} \\
(2k + 7)x + \qquad 7k \\
\underline{(2k + 7)x + (4k + 14)}
\end{array}
$$

The remainder must be 0. ⌐

Thus, we solve the following equation for k.

$7k - (4k + 14) = 0$

$7k - 4k - 14 = 0$

$3k = 14$

$k = \dfrac{14}{3}$

Exercise Set 6.10

1. $(x^3 - 2x^2 + 2x - 5) \div (x - 1)$

$$
\begin{array}{r|rrrr}
1 & 1 & -2 & 2 & -5 \\
& & 1 & -1 & 1 \\
\hline
& 1 & -1 & 1 & \!\!\!\!\big|\ -4
\end{array}
$$

The quotient is $x^2 - x + 1$. The remainder is -4.

3. $(a^2 + 11a - 19) \div (a + 4) =$
$(a^2 + 11a - 19) \div [a - (-4)]$

$$
\begin{array}{r|rrr}
-4 & 1 & 11 & -19 \\
& & -4 & -28 \\
\hline
& 1 & 7 & \!\!\!\big|\ -47
\end{array}
$$

The quotient is $a + 7$. The remainder is -47.

5. $(x^3 - 7x^2 - 13x + 3) \div (x - 2)$

$$
\begin{array}{r|rrrr}
2 & 1 & -7 & -13 & 3 \\
& & 2 & -10 & -46 \\
\hline
& 1 & -5 & -23 & \!\!\!\big|\ -43
\end{array}
$$

The quotient is $x^2 - 5x - 23$. The remainder is -43.

7. $(3x^3 + 7x^2 - 4x + 3) \div (x + 3) =$
$(3x^3 + 7x^2 - 4x + 3) \div [x - (-3)]$

$$
\begin{array}{r|rrrr}
-3 & 3 & 7 & -4 & 3 \\
& & -9 & 6 & -6 \\
\hline
& 3 & -2 & 2 & \!\!\!\big|\ -3
\end{array}
$$

The quotient is $3x^2 - 2x + 2$. The remainder is -3.

9. $(y^3 - 3y + 10) \div (y - 2) =$
$(y^3 + 0y^2 - 3y + 10) \div (y - 2)$

$$
\begin{array}{r|rrrr}
2 & 1 & 0 & -3 & 10 \\
& & 2 & 4 & 2 \\
\hline
& 1 & 2 & 1 & \!\!\!\big|\ 12
\end{array}
$$

The quotient is $y^2 + 2y + 1$. The remainder is 12.

11. $(3x^4 - 25x^2 - 18) \div (x - 3) =$
$(3x^4 + 0x^3 - 25x^2 + 0x - 18) \div (x - 3)$

$$
\begin{array}{r|rrrrr}
3 & 3 & 0 & -25 & 0 & -18 \\
& & 9 & 27 & 6 & 18 \\
\hline
& 3 & 9 & 2 & 6 & \!\!\!\big|\ 0
\end{array}
$$

The quotient is $3x^3 + 9x^2 + 2x + 6$. The remainder is 0.

13. $(x^3 - 27) \div (x - 3) =$
$(x^3 + 0x^2 + 0x - 27) \div (x - 3)$

$$
\begin{array}{r|rrrr}
3 & 1 & 0 & 0 & -27 \\
& & 3 & 9 & 27 \\
\hline
& 1 & 3 & 9 & \!\!\!\big|\ 0
\end{array}
$$

The quotient is $x^2 + 3x + 9$. The remainder is 0.

15. $(y^4 - 16) \div (y - 2) =$
$(y^4 + 0y^3 + 0y^2 + 0y - 16) \div (y - 2)$

$$
\begin{array}{r|rrrrr}
2 & 1 & 0 & 0 & 0 & -16 \\
& & 2 & 4 & 8 & 16 \\
\hline
& 1 & 2 & 4 & 8 & \!\!\!\big|\ 0
\end{array}
$$

The quotient is $y^3 + 2y^2 + 4y + 8$. The remainder is 0.

17. Graph: 2x - 3y > 6

First graph the line 2x - 3y = 6. The intercepts are (0,-2) and (3,0). We draw the line dashed since the inequality is >. Since the ordered pair (0,0) is <u>not</u> a solution of the inequality (2·0 - 3·$\overline{0}$ > 6 is false), we shade the lower half-plane.

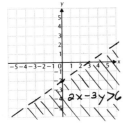

19. Graph: y > 4

First graph the line y = 4. The line is parallel to the x-axis with y-intercept (0,4). We draw the line dashed since the inequality is >.

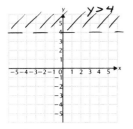

21. (3.41x⁴ - 24.25x² - 13.47) ÷ (x - 2.41)

   (3.41x⁴ + 0x³ - 24.25x² + 0x - 13.47) ÷ (x - 2.41)

   2.41|3.41 0   -24.25   0   -13.47

              8.2181 19.805621 -10.7109533 -25.813397

         3.41 8.2181 -4.444379 -10.7109533 |-39.283397

The answer is

3.41x³ + 8.2181x² - 4.444379x - 10.7109533;
R -39.283397

Exercise Set 7.1

1. $(-4m^2n^3)^0 = 1$, assuming neither m nor n is 0.

$$[a^0 = 1 \text{ if } a \neq 0]$$

3. $(x^2 + y)^1 = x^2 + y$ $[a^1 = a]$

5. $(-3r^2s^{-3})(5r^{-6}s^5)$

$= -3 \cdot 5 \cdot r^{2+(-6)} \cdot s^{-3+5}$

$= -15r^{-4}s^2$, or $-\dfrac{15s^2}{r^4}$

7. $(-2m^{-2}n^3)^3$

$= (-2)^3 \cdot (m^{-2})^3 \cdot (n^3)^3$

$= -8m^{-6}n^9$, or $-\dfrac{8n^9}{m^6}$

9. $\dfrac{5x^{-4}}{25x^{-10}} = \dfrac{5}{25} \cdot x^{-4-(-10)} = \dfrac{1}{5} x^6$, or $\dfrac{x^6}{5}$

11. $(-2a^2b^3)(6a^{-4}b^{-1})$

$= -2 \cdot 6 \cdot a^{2+(-4)} \cdot b^{3+(-1)}$

$= -12a^{-2}b^2$, or $-\dfrac{12b^2}{a^2}$

13. $\dfrac{125a^2b^{-3}}{5a^4b^{-2}} = \dfrac{125}{5} \cdot a^{2-4} \cdot b^{-3-(-2)} = 25a^{-2}b^{-1}$, or $\dfrac{25}{a^2b}$

15. $\dfrac{-6^5y^4z^{-5}}{2^{-2}y^{-2}z^3}$

$= -6^5 \cdot 2^2 \cdot y^{4-(-2)} \cdot z^{-5-3}$

$= -7776 \cdot 4 \cdot y^6 \cdot z^{-8}$

$= -31,104y^6z^{-8}$, or $-\dfrac{31,104y^6}{z^8}$

17. $(-2x^{-4}y^{-2})^{-3}$

$= (-2)^{-3} \cdot (x^{-4})^{-3} \cdot (y^{-2})^{-3}$

$= -\dfrac{1}{8} x^{12}y^6$, or $-\dfrac{x^{12}y^6}{8}$

$$\left[(-2)^{-3} = \dfrac{1}{(-2)^3} = \dfrac{1}{-8} = -\dfrac{1}{8}\right]$$

19. $\left[\dfrac{3a^{-2}b}{5a^{-7}b^5}\right]^3 = \left[\dfrac{3}{5} a^{-2-(-7)}b^{1-5}\right]^3$

$= \left[\dfrac{3}{5} a^5b^{-4}\right]^3$

$= (\dfrac{3}{5})^3 \cdot (a^5)^3 \cdot (b^{-4})^3$

$= \dfrac{27}{125} a^{15}b^{-12}$, or $\dfrac{27a^{15}}{125b^{12}}$

21. 47,000,000,000

$= 47,000,000,000 \times (10^{-10} \times 10^{10})$

$= (47,000,000,000 \times 10^{-10}) \times 10^{10}$

$= 4.7 \times 10^{10}$

23. \$932,000,000,000

$= 932,000,000,000 \times (10^{-11} \times 10^{11})$

$= (932,000,000,000 \times 10^{-11}) \times 10^{11}$

$= \$9.32 \times 10^{11}$

25. 0.000000016

$= 0.000000016 \times (10^8 \times 10^{-8})$

$= (0.000000016 \times 10^8) \times 10^{-8}$

$= 1.6 \times 10^{-8}$

27. 0.00000000007

$= 0.00000000007 \times (10^{11} \times 10^{-11})$

$= (0.00000000007 \times 10^{11}) \times 10^{-11}$

$= 7 \times 10^{-11}$

29. 6.73×10^8

$= 673,000,000$ (Moving decimal point 8 places to the right)

31. 6.6×10^{-5}

$= 0.000066$ (Moving decimal point 5 places to the left)

33. 4.8×10^{-11}

$= 0.000000000048$ (Moving decimal point 11 places to the left)

35. 8.923×10^{-10}

$= 0.0000000008923$ (Moving decimal point 10 places to the left)

37. $(2.3 \times 10^6)(4.2 \times 10^{-11})$

$= (2.3 \times 4.2)(10^6 \times 10^{-11})$

$= 9.66 \times 10^{-5}$

39. $(2.34 \times 10^{-8})(5.7 \times 10^{-4})$

$= (2.34 \times 5.7)(10^{-8} \times 10^{-4})$

$= 13.338 \times 10^{-12}$

$= (1.3338 \times 10^1) \times 10^{-12}$

$= 1.3338 \times (10^1 \times 10^{-12})$

$= 1.3338 \times 10^{-11}$

41. $\dfrac{8.5 \times 10^8}{3.4 \times 10^5}$

$= \dfrac{8.5}{3.4} \times \dfrac{10^8}{10^5}$

$= 2.5 \times 10^3$

43. $\dfrac{4.0 \times 10^{-6}}{8.0 \times 10^{-3}}$

$= \dfrac{4.0}{8.0} \times \dfrac{10^{-6}}{10^{-3}}$

$= 0.5 \times 10^{-3}$

$= (5 \times 10^{-1}) \times 10^{-3}$

$= 5 \times (10^{-1} \times 10^{-3})$

$= 5 \times 10^{-4}$

45. Each day we purchase 25,000 new automobiles. There are 365 days in a year, so the total number of cars purchased in one year is $365 \times 25{,}000$, or $9{,}125{,}000$.

$(365 \text{ days})(25{,}000)$

$= (3.65 \times 10^2)(2.5 \times 10^4)$

$= (3.65 \times 2.5)(10^2 \times 10^4)$

$= 9.125 \times 10^6$, or $9{,}125{,}000$

Automobiles per person can be expressed as a ratio.

$$\frac{9{,}125{,}000}{234{,}000{,}000} = \frac{9.125 \times 10^6}{2.34 \times 10^8}$$

$$= \frac{9.125}{2.34} \times \frac{10^6}{10^8}$$

$$\approx 3.9 \times 10^{-2}$$

47. 5.87×10^{14} miles in 100 years

$$\frac{5.87 \times 10^{14}}{100} = \frac{5.87 \times 10^{14}}{10^2} = 5.87 \times 10^{12} \text{ miles in 1 year}$$

13 weeks $= \frac{13}{52}$, or $\frac{1}{4}$ of a year

Thus in 13 weeks light travels

$\frac{1}{5} \times 5.87 \times 10^{12}$, or 1.4675×10^{12} miles.

49. $8^{3x} = 27$

$(8^x)^3 = 3^3$

$8^x = 3$

$\frac{1}{8^x} = \frac{1}{3}$

$8^{-x} = \frac{1}{3}$

51. The unit's digit in $(513)^1$ is 3.
    The unit's digit in $(513)^2$ is 9.
    The unit's digit in $(513)^3$ is 7.
    The unit's digit in $(513)^4$ is 1.
    The unit's digit in $(513)^5$ is 3.
    The unit's digit in $(513)^6$ is 9.
    The unit's digit in $(513)^7$ is 7.
    The unit's digit in $(513)^8$ is 1.

Observe the pattern 3, 9, 7, 1.

$(513)^{127} = (513)^{4 \cdot 31 + 3}$

Thus the unit's digit in $(513)^{127}$ is 7.

53. $[7y(7 - 8)^{-2} - 8y(8 - 7)^{-2}]^{-(-2)^2}$

$= [7y(-1)^{-2} - 8y(1)^{-2}]^{-4}$

$= \left[\frac{7y}{(-1)^2} - \frac{8y}{1^2}\right]^{-4}$

$= [7y - 8y]^{-4}$

$= y^{-4}$, or $\frac{1}{y^4}$

55. $[3^{-(3s+1)} - 3^{-(3s-1)} + 3^{-3s}]^{-2^2}$

$= \left[\frac{1}{3^{3s+1}} - \frac{1}{3^{3s-1}} + \frac{1}{3^{3s}}\right]^{-4}$

$= \left[\frac{1}{3^{3s}3} - \frac{1}{3^{3s}3^{-1}} + \frac{1}{3^{3s}}\right]^{-4}$

LCM $= 3^{3s} \cdot 3 \cdot 3^{-1}$, or 3^{3s}

$= \left[\frac{3^{-1} - 3 + 3 \cdot 3^{-1}}{3^{3s} \cdot 3 \cdot 3^{-1}}\right]^{-4} = \left[\frac{\frac{1}{3} - 3 + 1}{3^{3s}}\right]^{-4}$

$= \left[\frac{-\frac{5}{3}}{3^{3s}}\right]^{-4} = \left[-\frac{5}{3} \cdot \frac{1}{3^{3s}}\right]^{-4} = \left[-\frac{5}{3^{3s+1}}\right]^{-4}$

$= \frac{(-5)^{-4}}{(3^{3s+1})^{-4}} = \frac{(3^{3s+1})^4}{(-5)^4} = \frac{3^{12s+4}}{625}$

Exercise Set 7.2

1. The square roots of 16 are 4 and -4 because $4^2 = 16$ and $(-4)^2 = 16$.

3. The square roots of 144 are 12 and -12 because $12^2 = 144$ and $(-12)^2 = 144$.

5. The square roots of 400 are 20 and -20 because $20^2 = 400$ and $(-20)^2 = 400$.

7. $-\sqrt{\frac{49}{36}} = -\frac{7}{6}$ $\quad \left[\frac{7}{6} \cdot \frac{7}{6} = \frac{49}{36}\right]$

9. $\sqrt{196} = 14$ $\quad [14 \cdot 14 = 196]$

11. $-\sqrt{\frac{16}{81}} = -\frac{4}{9}$ $\quad \left[\frac{4}{9} \cdot \frac{4}{9} = \frac{16}{81}\right]$

13. $\sqrt{0.09} = 0.3$ $\quad [0.3 \times 0.3 = 0.09]$

15. $-\sqrt{0.0049} = -0.07$ $\quad [0.07 \times 0.07 = 0.0049]$

17. $5\sqrt{p^2 + 4}$
    The radicand is $p^2 + 4$.

19. $x^2 y^2 \sqrt{\frac{x}{y + 4}}$
    The radicand is $\frac{x}{y + 4}$.

21. $\sqrt{16x^2} = \sqrt{(4x)^2} = |4x| = 4|x|$

23. $\sqrt{(-7c)^2} = |-7c| = 7|c|$

25. $\sqrt{(a + 1)^2} = |a + 1|$

27. $\sqrt{x^2 - 4x + 4} = \sqrt{(x - 2)^2} = |x - 2|$

29. $\sqrt{4x^2 + 28x + 49} = \sqrt{(2x + 7)^2} = |2x + 7|$

31. $\sqrt[3]{27} = 3$ $[3^3 = 27]$

33. $\sqrt[3]{-64x^3} = -4x$ $[(-4x)^3 = -64x^3]$

35. $\sqrt[3]{-216} = -6$ $[(-6)^3 = -216]$

37. $\sqrt[3]{0.343(x + 1)^3} = 0.7(x + 1)$, or $0.7x + 0.7$
    $[(0.7(x + 1))^3 = 0.343(x + 1)^3]$

39. $\sqrt[4]{625} = 5$ $[5^4 = 625]$

41. $\sqrt[5]{-1} = -1$ $[(-1)^5 = -1]$

43. $\sqrt[5]{-\dfrac{32}{243}} = -\dfrac{2}{3}$ $\left[(-\dfrac{2}{3})^5 = -\dfrac{32}{243}\right]$

45. $\sqrt[6]{x^6} = |x|$
    Since k is even, we use absolute value.

47. $\sqrt[4]{(5a)^4} = |5a| = 5|a|$
    Since k is even, we use absolute value.

49. $\sqrt[10]{(-6)^{10}} = |-6| = 6$

51. $\sqrt[414]{(a + b)^{414}} = |a + b|$
    Since k is even, we use absolute value.

53. $\sqrt[7]{y^7} = y$
    Since k is odd, we do not use absolute value.

55. $\sqrt[5]{(x - 2)^5} = x - 2$
    Since k is odd, we do not use absolute value.

57. $|-8| = 8$

59. $4x^2 - 49 = (2x)^2 - 7^2 = (2x + 7)(2x - 7)$

61. $N = 2.5\sqrt{A}$

    a) $N = 2.5\sqrt{25}$ b) $N = 2.5\sqrt{36}$
           $= 2.5(5)$ $= 2.5(6)$
           $= 12.5$ $= 15$
           ≈ 13

    c) $N = 2.5\sqrt{49}$ d) $N = 2.5\sqrt{64}$
           $= 2.5(7)$ $= 2.5(8)$
           $= 17.5$ $= 20$
           ≈ 18

1. $\sqrt{3} \sqrt{2} = \sqrt{3 \cdot 2} = \sqrt{6}$

3. $\sqrt[3]{2} \sqrt[3]{5} = \sqrt[3]{2 \cdot 5} = \sqrt[3]{10}$

5. $\sqrt[4]{8} \sqrt[4]{9} = \sqrt[4]{8 \cdot 9} = \sqrt[4]{72}$

7. $\sqrt{3a} \sqrt{10b} = \sqrt{3a \cdot 10b} = \sqrt{30ab}$

9. $\sqrt[5]{9t^2} \sqrt[5]{2t} = \sqrt[5]{9t^2 \cdot 2t} = \sqrt[5]{18t^3}$

11. $\sqrt{x - a} \sqrt{x + a} = \sqrt{(x - a)(x + a)} = \sqrt{x^2 - a^2}$

13. $\sqrt{8} = \sqrt{4 \cdot 2} = \sqrt{4} \sqrt{2} = 2\sqrt{2}$

15. $\sqrt{24} = \sqrt{4 \cdot 6} = \sqrt{4} \sqrt{6} = 2\sqrt{6}$

17. $\sqrt{40} = \sqrt{4 \cdot 10} = \sqrt{4} \sqrt{10} = 2\sqrt{10}$

19. $\sqrt{180x^4} = \sqrt{36 \cdot 5 \cdot x^4} = \sqrt{36x^4} \sqrt{5} = 6x^2 \sqrt{5}$

21. $\sqrt[3]{54x^8} = \sqrt[3]{27 \cdot 2 \cdot x^6 \cdot x^2} = \sqrt[3]{27x^6} \sqrt[3]{2x^2} = 3x^2 \sqrt[3]{2x^2}$

23. $\sqrt{15} \sqrt{6} = \sqrt{15 \cdot 6} = \sqrt{90}$
    $= \sqrt{9 \cdot 10} = \sqrt{9} \sqrt{10} = 3\sqrt{10}$

25. $\sqrt[3]{3} \sqrt[3]{18} = \sqrt[3]{3 \cdot 18} = \sqrt[3]{54}$
    $= \sqrt[3]{27 \cdot 2} = \sqrt[3]{27} \sqrt[3]{2} = 3\sqrt[3]{2}$

27. $\sqrt{45} \sqrt{60} = \sqrt{45 \cdot 60} = \sqrt{2700}$
    $= \sqrt{900 \cdot 3} = \sqrt{900} \sqrt{3} = 30\sqrt{3}$

29. $\sqrt{5b^3} \sqrt{10c^4}$
    $= \sqrt{5b^3 \cdot 10c^4}$
    $= \sqrt{50b^3c^4}$
    $= \sqrt{25 \cdot 2 \cdot b^2 \cdot b \cdot c^4}$
    $= \sqrt{25b^2c^4} \sqrt{2b}$
    $= 5bc^2 \sqrt{2b}$

31. $\sqrt[3]{y^4} \sqrt[3]{16y^5}$
    $= \sqrt[3]{y^4 \cdot 16y^5}$
    $= \sqrt[3]{16y^9}$
    $= \sqrt[3]{8 \cdot 2 \cdot y^9}$
    $= \sqrt[3]{8y^9} \sqrt[3]{2}$
    $= 2y^3 \sqrt[3]{2}$

33. $\sqrt[3]{(b+3)^4}\ \sqrt[3]{(b+3)^2}$

$= \sqrt[3]{(b+3)^4(b+3)^2}$

$= \sqrt[3]{(b+3)^6}$

$= (b+3)^2$

35. $\sqrt{12a^3b}\ \sqrt{8a^4b^2}$

$= \sqrt{12a^3b\cdot 8a^4b^2}$

$= \sqrt{96a^7b^3}$

$= \sqrt{16\cdot 6\cdot a^6\cdot a\cdot b^2\cdot b}$

$= \sqrt{16a^6b^2}\ \sqrt{6ab}$

$= 4a^3b\sqrt{6ab}$

37. $-\frac{5}{6}$ is <u>rational</u>. $\left(-\frac{5}{6} = \frac{-5}{6}\right)$

39. $8.23\overline{23}$ is <u>rational</u>.   (Repeating decimal)

41. $\sqrt{36}$ is <u>rational</u>.   (36 is a perfect square.)

43. $2.101001...$ is <u>irrational</u>.   (Numeral does not repeat.)

45. $\pi = 3.1415926535...$
    π is <u>irrational</u>.   (Numeral does not repeat.)

47. 3.14 is <u>rational</u>. (Terminating decimal)

49. $\sqrt{48}$ is <u>irrational</u>.   (48 is <u>not</u> a perfect square.)

51. $\sqrt{0.4}$ is <u>irrational</u>.   (0.4 is <u>not</u> a perfect square.)

53. Using a calculator,
    $\sqrt{180} \approx 13.416$

    Using Table 1,
    $\sqrt{180} = \sqrt{36\cdot 5} = \sqrt{36}\ \sqrt{5} = 6\sqrt{5} \approx 6(2.236)$
    $\phantom{\sqrt{180} = \sqrt{36\cdot 5} = \sqrt{36}\ \sqrt{5} = 6\sqrt{5}} \approx 13.416.$

55. Using a calculator,
    $\frac{8 + \sqrt{480}}{4} \approx \frac{8 + 21.908902}{4} \approx \frac{29.908902}{4} \approx 7.477.$

    Using Table 1,
    $\frac{8 + \sqrt{480}}{4} = \frac{8 + \sqrt{16\cdot 30}}{4} = \frac{8 + 4\sqrt{30}}{4}$
    $\phantom{\frac{8 + \sqrt{480}}{4}} = \frac{4(2 + \sqrt{30})}{4}$
    $\phantom{\frac{8 + \sqrt{480}}{4}} = 2 + \sqrt{30}$
    $\phantom{\frac{8 + \sqrt{480}}{4}} \approx 2 + 5.477$
    $\phantom{\frac{8 + \sqrt{480}}{4}} \approx 7.477.$

57. $9x^2 - 15x = 0$
    $3x(3x - 5) = 0$
    $3x = 0 \text{ or } 3x - 5 = 0$
    $x = 0 \text{ or } \quad 3x = 5$
    $x = 0 \text{ or } \quad\quad x = \frac{5}{3}$

    The solutions are 0 and $\frac{5}{3}$.

59. $\frac{x^3 - y^3}{x + y} \cdot \frac{x^2 - y^2}{x^2 + xy + y^2}$

$= \frac{(x - y)(x^2 + xy + y^2)(x + y)(x - y)}{(x + y)(x^2 + xy + y^2)}$

$= \frac{(x + y)(x^2 + xy + y^2)}{(x + y)(x^2 + xy + y^2)} \cdot \frac{(x - y)(x - y)}{1}$

$= (x - y)^2$

61. $\sqrt{1.6 \times 10^3}\ \sqrt{36 \times 10^{-8}}$

$= \sqrt{1.6 \times 36 \times 10^3 \times 10^{-8}}$

$= \sqrt{57.6 \times 10^{-5}}$

$= \sqrt{5.76 \times 10^{-4}}$

$= \sqrt{5.76} \times \sqrt{10^{-4}}$

$= 2.4 \times 10^{-2}$

63. $\sqrt[3]{48}\ \sqrt[3]{63}\ \sqrt[3]{196}$

$= \sqrt[3]{48 \times 63 \times 196}$

$= \sqrt[3]{2\cdot 2\cdot 2\cdot 2\cdot 3 \times 7\cdot 3\cdot 3 \times 2\cdot 2\cdot 7\cdot 7}$

$= \sqrt[3]{2^6\cdot 3^3\cdot 7^3}$

$= 2^2\cdot 3\cdot 7$

$= 84$

Exercise Set 7.4

1. $\sqrt{\frac{16}{25}} = \frac{\sqrt{16}}{\sqrt{25}} = \frac{4}{5}$

3. $\sqrt[3]{\frac{64}{27}} = \frac{\sqrt[3]{64}}{\sqrt[3]{27}} = \frac{4}{3}$

5. $\sqrt{\frac{49}{y^2}} = \frac{\sqrt{49}}{\sqrt{y^2}} = \frac{7}{y}$

7. $\sqrt{\frac{25y^3}{x^4}} = \frac{\sqrt{25y^3}}{\sqrt{x^4}} = \frac{\sqrt{25y^2\cdot y}}{\sqrt{x^4}} = \frac{5y\sqrt{y}}{x^2}$

9. $\sqrt[3]{\frac{8x^5}{27y^3}} = \frac{\sqrt[3]{8x^5}}{\sqrt[3]{27y^3}} = \frac{\sqrt[3]{8x^3\cdot x^2}}{\sqrt[3]{27y^3}} = \frac{2x\sqrt[3]{x^2}}{3y}$

11. $\frac{\sqrt{21a}}{\sqrt{3a}} = \sqrt{\frac{21a}{3a}} = \sqrt{7}$

13. $\dfrac{\sqrt[3]{54}}{\sqrt[3]{2}} = \sqrt[3]{\dfrac{54}{2}} = \sqrt[3]{27} = 3$

15. $\dfrac{\sqrt{40xy^3}}{\sqrt{8x}} = \sqrt{\dfrac{40xy^3}{8x}} = \sqrt{5y^3} = \sqrt{5y \cdot y^2} = y\sqrt{5y}$

17. $\dfrac{\sqrt[3]{96a^4b^2}}{\sqrt[3]{12a^2b}} = \sqrt[3]{\dfrac{96a^4b^2}{12a^2b}} = \sqrt[3]{8a^2b} = 2\sqrt[3]{a^2b}$

19. $\dfrac{\sqrt{72xy}}{2\sqrt{2}} = \dfrac{1}{2}\sqrt{\dfrac{72xy}{2}} = \dfrac{1}{2}\sqrt{36xy} = \dfrac{1}{2} \cdot 6\sqrt{xy} = 3\sqrt{xy}$

21. $\dfrac{\sqrt{x^3 - y^3}}{\sqrt{x - y}} = \sqrt{\dfrac{x^3 - y^3}{x - y}} = \sqrt{\dfrac{(x - y)(x^2 + xy + y^2)}{x - y}}$

   $= \sqrt{x^2 + xy + y^2}$

23. $\sqrt{(6a)^3} = \sqrt{(6a)^2 \cdot 6a} = 6a\sqrt{6a}$
   or
   $(\sqrt{6a})^3 = \sqrt{6a}\,\sqrt{6a}\,\sqrt{6a} = 6a\sqrt{6a}$

25. $(\sqrt[3]{16b^2})^2$

   $= \sqrt[3]{16b^2}\,\sqrt[3]{16b^2}$

   $= \sqrt[3]{256b^4}$

   $= \sqrt[3]{64b^3 \cdot 4b}$

   $= 4b\sqrt[3]{4b}$

27. $\sqrt{(18a^2b)^3}$

   $= (\sqrt{18a^2b})^3$ (Rule C)

   $= \sqrt{18a^2b}\,\sqrt{18a^2b}\,\sqrt{18a^2b}$

   $= 18a^2b\sqrt{18a^2b}$

   $= 18a^2b\sqrt{9a^2 \cdot 2b}$

   $= 18a^2b \cdot 3a\sqrt{2b}$

   $= 54a^3b\sqrt{2b}$

29. $(\sqrt[3]{12c^2d})^2$

   $= \sqrt[3]{(12c^2d)^2}$

   $= \sqrt[3]{144c^4d^2}$

   $= \sqrt[3]{8c^3 \cdot 18cd^2}$

   $= 2c\sqrt[3]{18cd^2}$

31. $\dfrac{12x}{x - 4} - \dfrac{3x^2}{x + 4} = \dfrac{384}{x^2 - 16}$,   LCM = $(x+4)(x-4)$

   $(x+4)(x-4)\left(\dfrac{12x}{x - 4} - \dfrac{3x^2}{x + 4}\right) = (x+4)(x-4) \cdot \dfrac{384}{(x+4)(x-4)}$

   $12x(x + 4) - 3x^2(x - 4) = 384$

   $12x^2 + 48x - 3x^3 + 12x^2 = 384$

   $24x^2 + 48x - 3x^3 - 384 = 0$

   $8x^2 + 16x - x^3 - 128 = 0$

   $(8x^2 - 128) - (x^3 - 16x) = 0$

   $8(x^2 - 16) - x(x^2 - 16) = 0$

   $(8 - x)(x^2 - 16) = 0$

   $(8 - x)(x + 4)(x - 4) = 0$

   $8 - x = 0$ or $x + 4 = 0$ or $x - 4 = 0$
   $x = 8$ or $x = -4$ or $x = 4$

   Only 8 checks. It is the solution.

33. We let ℓ represent the length and w the width.

   The width is one-fourth the length.
   $w = \dfrac{1}{4}\ell$

   The area is twice the perimeter.
   $\ell w = 2(2\ell + 2w)$, or $\ell w = 4\ell + 4w$

   We now have a system of equations.

   $w = \dfrac{1}{4}\ell$

   $\ell w = 4\ell + 4w$

   We solve the system using substitution.

   $\ell w = 4\ell + 4w$

   $\ell(\dfrac{1}{4}\ell) = 4\ell + 4(\dfrac{1}{4}\ell)$ (Substituting)

   $\dfrac{1}{4}\ell^2 = 4\ell + \ell$

   $\dfrac{1}{4}\ell^2 = 5\ell$

   $\ell^2 = 20\ell$

   $\ell^2 - 20\ell = 0$

   $\ell(\ell - 20) = 0$

   $\ell = 0$ or $\ell - 20 = 0$
   $\ell = 0$ or $\ell = 20$

   We only consider $\ell = 20$ since the length must be positive. We now substitute 20 for ℓ and solve for w.

   $w = \dfrac{1}{4}\ell$

   $w = \dfrac{1}{4} \cdot 20$

   $w = 5$

33. (continued)

If ℓ = 20 and w = 5, the width is one-fourth the length and the area, 20·5 or 100, is twice the perimeter, 2(20 + 20 + 5 + 5), or 100.

If ℓ = 20 and w = 5, the width is one-fourth the length and the area is twice the perimeter.

$5 = \frac{1}{4} \cdot 20$ and $20 \cdot 5 = 2(2 \cdot 20 + 2 \cdot 5)$

5 = 5   100 = 100

The values check. The length is 20, and the width is 5.

35.

$$\frac{7\sqrt{a^2b}\ \sqrt{25xy}}{5\sqrt{a^{-4}b^{-1}}\ \sqrt{49x^{-1}y^{-3}}}$$

$$= \frac{7}{5}\sqrt{\frac{a^2b}{a^{-4}b^{-1}}}\ \sqrt{\frac{25xy}{49x^{-1}y^{-3}}}$$

$$= \frac{7}{5}\ \sqrt{a^6b^2}\ \sqrt{\frac{25}{49}x^2y^4}$$

$$= \frac{7}{5} \cdot a^3b \cdot \frac{5}{7}xy^2$$

$$= a^3bxy^2$$

37.

$$\frac{\sqrt{44x^2y^9z}\ \sqrt{22y^9z^6}}{(\sqrt{11xy^8z^2})^2}$$

$$= \frac{\sqrt{44 \cdot 22 \cdot x^2 \cdot y^9 \cdot y^9 \cdot z \cdot z^6}}{11xy^8z^2}$$

$$= \frac{\sqrt{22^2x^2y^{18}z^6}\ \sqrt{2z}}{11xy^8z^2}$$

$$= \frac{22xy^9z^3}{11xy^8z^2}\ \sqrt{2z}$$

$$= 2yz\ \sqrt{2z}$$

Exercise Set 7.5

1. $6\sqrt{3} + 2\sqrt{3} = (6 + 2)\sqrt{3} = 8\sqrt{3}$

3. $9\sqrt[3]{5} - 6\sqrt[3]{5} = (9 - 6)\sqrt[3]{5} = 3\sqrt[3]{5}$

5. $4\sqrt[3]{y} + 9\sqrt[3]{y} = (4 + 9)\sqrt[3]{y} = 13\sqrt[3]{y}$

7. $8\sqrt{2} - 6\sqrt{2} + 5\sqrt{2} = (8 - 6 + 5)\sqrt{2} = 7\sqrt{2}$

9. $4\sqrt[3]{3} - \sqrt{5} + 2\sqrt[3]{3} + \sqrt{5} = (4 + 2)\sqrt[3]{3} = 6\sqrt[3]{3}$

11. $8\sqrt{27} - 3\sqrt{3}$

$= 8\sqrt{9 \cdot 3} - 3\sqrt{3}$

$= 8 \cdot 3\sqrt{3} - 3\sqrt{3}$

$= 24\sqrt{3} - 3\sqrt{3}$

$= 21\sqrt{3}$

13. $8\sqrt{45} + 7\sqrt{20}$

$= 8\sqrt{9 \cdot 5} + 7\sqrt{4 \cdot 5}$

$= 8 \cdot 3\sqrt{5} + 7 \cdot 2\sqrt{5}$

$= 24\sqrt{5} + 14\sqrt{5}$

$= 38\sqrt{5}$

15. $18\sqrt{72} + 2\sqrt{98}$

$= 18\sqrt{36 \cdot 2} + 2\sqrt{49 \cdot 2}$

$= 18 \cdot 6\sqrt{2} + 2 \cdot 7\sqrt{2}$

$= 108\sqrt{2} + 14\sqrt{2}$

$= 122\sqrt{2}$

17. $3\sqrt[3]{16} + \sqrt[3]{54}$

$= 3\sqrt[3]{8 \cdot 2} + \sqrt[3]{27 \cdot 2}$

$= 3 \cdot 2\sqrt[3]{2} + 3\sqrt[3]{2}$

$= 6\sqrt[3]{2} + 3\sqrt[3]{2}$

$= 9\sqrt[3]{2}$

19. $2\sqrt{128} - \sqrt{18} + 4\sqrt{32}$

$= 2\sqrt{64 \cdot 2} - \sqrt{9 \cdot 2} + 4\sqrt{16 \cdot 2}$

$= 2 \cdot 8\sqrt{2} - 3\sqrt{2} + 4 \cdot 4\sqrt{2}$

$= 16\sqrt{2} - 3\sqrt{2} + 16\sqrt{2}$

$= 29\sqrt{2}$

21. $\sqrt{5a} + 2\sqrt{45a^3}$

$= \sqrt{5a} + 2\sqrt{9a^2 \cdot 5a}$

$= \sqrt{5a} + 2 \cdot 3a\sqrt{5a}$

$= (1 + 6a)\sqrt{5a}$

23. $\sqrt[3]{24x} - \sqrt[3]{3x^4}$

$= \sqrt[3]{8 \cdot 3x} - \sqrt[3]{x^3 \cdot 3x}$

$= 2\sqrt[3]{3x} - x\sqrt[3]{3x}$

$= (2 - x)\sqrt[3]{3x}$

25. $\sqrt{8y - 8} + \sqrt{2y - 2}$

$= \sqrt{4(2y - 2)} + \sqrt{2y - 2}$

$= 2\sqrt{2y - 2} + 1\sqrt{2y - 2}$

$= 3\sqrt{2y - 2}$

27. $\sqrt{x^3 - x^2} + \sqrt{9x - 9}$

$= \sqrt{x^2(x - 1)} + \sqrt{9(x - 1)}$

$= x\sqrt{x - 1} + 3\sqrt{x - 1}$

$= (x + 3)\sqrt{x - 1}$

29. $x^2 - 2.6x + 0.69$

$= x^2 - 2.6x + (1.69 - 1.69) + 0.69$

$[\frac{2.6}{2} = 1.3, (1.3)^2 = 1.69]$

$= (x^2 - 2.6x + 1.69) + (-1.69 + 0.69)$

$= (x - 1.3)^2 - 1$

$= [(x - 1.3) + 1][(x - 1.3) - 1]$

$= (x - 0.3)(x - 2.3)$

31. $\sqrt{432} - \sqrt{6125} + \sqrt{845} - \sqrt{4800}$

$= \sqrt{144 \cdot 3} - \sqrt{1225 \cdot 5} + \sqrt{169 \cdot 5} - \sqrt{1600 \cdot 3}$

$= 12\sqrt{3} - 35\sqrt{5} + 13\sqrt{5} - 40\sqrt{3}$

$= (12 - 40)\sqrt{3} + (-35 + 13)\sqrt{5}$

$= -28\sqrt{3} - 22\sqrt{5}$

33. $\frac{1}{2}\sqrt{36a^5bc^4} - \frac{1}{2}\sqrt[3]{64a^4bc^6} + \frac{1}{6}\sqrt{144a^3bc^2}$

$= \frac{1}{2}\sqrt{36a^4c^4 \cdot ab} - \frac{1}{2}\sqrt[3]{64a^3c^6 \cdot ab} + \frac{1}{6}\sqrt{144a^2c^2 \cdot ab}$

$= \frac{1}{2} \cdot 6a^2c^2\sqrt{ab} - \frac{1}{2} \cdot 4ac^2\sqrt[3]{ab} + \frac{1}{6} \cdot 12ac\sqrt{ab}$

$= (3a^2c^2 + 2ac)\sqrt{ab} - 2ac^2\sqrt[3]{ab}$

35. $\sqrt{a} + \sqrt{b} = \sqrt{a + b}$

a) The equation is true when a = 0 and b ≥ 0
    or a ≥ 0 and b = 0.

b) Any pair of numbers that does not satisfy the
    conditions stated in a) will make the equation
    false.

Exercise Set 7.6

1. $\sqrt{6}(2 - 3\sqrt{6})$

$= \sqrt{6} \cdot 2 - \sqrt{6} \cdot 3\sqrt{6}$

$= 2\sqrt{6} - 3 \cdot 6$

$= 2\sqrt{6} - 18$

3. $\sqrt{2}(\sqrt{3} - \sqrt{5})$

$= \sqrt{2}\sqrt{3} - \sqrt{2}\sqrt{5}$

$= \sqrt{6} - \sqrt{10}$

5. $\sqrt{3}(2\sqrt{5} - 3\sqrt{4})$

$= \sqrt{3}(2\sqrt{5} - 3 \cdot 2)$

$= \sqrt{3} \cdot 2\sqrt{5} - \sqrt{3} \cdot 6$

$= 2\sqrt{15} - 6\sqrt{3}$

7. $\sqrt[3]{2}(\sqrt[3]{4} - 2\sqrt[3]{32})$

$= \sqrt[3]{2}\sqrt[3]{4} - \sqrt[3]{2} \cdot 2\sqrt[3]{32}$

$= \sqrt[3]{8} - 2\sqrt[3]{64}$

$= 2 - 2 \cdot 4$

$= 2 - 8$

$= -6$

9. $\sqrt[3]{a}(\sqrt[3]{2a^2} + \sqrt[3]{16a^2})$

$= \sqrt[3]{a}\sqrt[3]{2a^2} + \sqrt[3]{a}\sqrt[3]{16a^2}$

$= \sqrt[3]{2a^3} + \sqrt[3]{16a^3}$

$= \sqrt[3]{2a^3} + \sqrt[3]{8a^3 \cdot 2}$

$= a\sqrt[3]{2} + 2a\sqrt[3]{2}$

$= 3a\sqrt[3]{2}$

11. $(\sqrt{3} - \sqrt{2})(\sqrt{3} + \sqrt{2})$

$= (\sqrt{3})^2 - (\sqrt{2})^2$

$= 3 - 2$

$= 1$

13. $(\sqrt{8} + 2\sqrt{5})(\sqrt{8} - 2\sqrt{5})$

$= (\sqrt{8})^2 - (2\sqrt{5})^2$

$= 8 - 4 \cdot 5$

$= 8 - 20$

$= -12$

15. $(\sqrt{a} + \sqrt{b})(\sqrt{a} - \sqrt{b})$

$= (\sqrt{a})^2 - (\sqrt{b})^2$

$= a - b$

17. $(3 - \sqrt{5})(2 + \sqrt{5})$

$= 3 \cdot 2 + 3\sqrt{5} - 2\sqrt{5} - (\sqrt{5})^2$

$= 6 + 3\sqrt{5} - 2\sqrt{5} - 5$

$= 1 + \sqrt{5}$

19. $(\sqrt{3} + 1)(2\sqrt{3} + 1)$

$= \sqrt{3} \cdot 2\sqrt{3} + \sqrt{3} \cdot 1 + 1 \cdot 2\sqrt{3} + 1^2$

$= 2 \cdot 3 + \sqrt{3} + 2\sqrt{3} + 1$

$= 7 + 3\sqrt{3}$

21. $(2\sqrt{7} - 4\sqrt{2})(3\sqrt{7} + 6\sqrt{2})$

$= 2\sqrt{7}\cdot3\sqrt{7} + 2\sqrt{7}\cdot6\sqrt{2} - 4\sqrt{2}\cdot3\sqrt{7} - 4\sqrt{2}\cdot6\sqrt{2}$

$= 6\cdot7 + 12\sqrt{14} - 12\sqrt{14} - 24\cdot2$

$= 42 + 12\sqrt{14} - 12\sqrt{14} - 48$

$= -6$

23. $(\sqrt{a} + \sqrt{2})(\sqrt{a} + \sqrt{3})$

$= (\sqrt{a})^2 + \sqrt{a}\sqrt{3} + \sqrt{2}\sqrt{a} + \sqrt{2}\sqrt{3}$

$= a + \sqrt{3a} + \sqrt{2a} + \sqrt{6}$

25. $(2\sqrt[3]{3} + \sqrt[3]{2})(\sqrt[3]{3} - 2\sqrt[3]{2})$

$= 2\sqrt[3]{3} \cdot \sqrt[3]{3} - 2\sqrt[3]{3}\cdot2\sqrt[3]{2} + \sqrt[3]{2}\sqrt[3]{3} - \sqrt[3]{2}\cdot2\sqrt[3]{2}$

$= 2\sqrt[3]{9} - 4\sqrt[3]{6} + \sqrt[3]{6} - 2\sqrt[3]{4}$

$= 2\sqrt[3]{9} - 3\sqrt[3]{6} - 2\sqrt[3]{4}$

27. $(2 + \sqrt{3})^2$

$= 2^2 + 2\cdot2\sqrt{3} + (\sqrt{3})^2$

$= 4 + 4\sqrt{3} + 3$

$= 7 + 4\sqrt{3}$

29. $\dfrac{5}{x - 1} + \dfrac{9}{x^2 + x + 1} = \dfrac{15}{x^3 - 1}$

Note: $x^3 - 1 = (x - 1)(x^2 + x + 1)$

LCM $= (x - 1)(x^2 + x + 1)$

$(x-1)(x^2+x+1)\left(\dfrac{5}{x - 1} + \dfrac{9}{x^2 + x + 1}\right) =$

$\qquad\qquad\qquad (x-1)(x^2+x+1) \cdot \dfrac{15}{x^3 - 1}$

$5(x^2 + x + 1) + 9(x - 1) = 15$

$5x^2 + 5x + 5 + 9x - 9 = 15$

$5x^2 + 14x - 4 = 15$

$5x^2 + 14x - 19 = 0$

$(5x + 19)(x - 1) = 0$

$5x + 19 = 0 \quad$ or $x - 1 = 0$

$5x = -19 \quad$ or $\quad x = 1$

$x = -\dfrac{19}{5} \quad$ or $\quad x = 1$

Only $-\dfrac{19}{5}$ checks. The value 1 results in division by 0. The solution is $-\dfrac{19}{5}$.

31. $\sqrt{9 + 3\sqrt{5}} \; \sqrt{9 - 3\sqrt{5}}$

$= \sqrt{(9 + 3\sqrt{5})(9 - 3\sqrt{5})}$

$= \sqrt{81 - 45}$

$= \sqrt{36}$

$= 6$

33. $(\sqrt{3} + \sqrt{5} - \sqrt{6})^2$

$= (\sqrt{3} + \sqrt{5})^2 - 2(\sqrt{3} + \sqrt{5})\sqrt{6} + (\sqrt{6})^2$

$= (3 + 2\sqrt{15} + 5) - (2\sqrt{18} + 2\sqrt{30}) + 6$

$= (8 + 2\sqrt{15}) - (6\sqrt{2} + 2\sqrt{30}) + 6$

$= 14 + 2\sqrt{15} - 6\sqrt{2} - 2\sqrt{30}$

35. $(\sqrt[3]{9} - 2)(\sqrt[3]{9} + 4)$

$= \sqrt[3]{81} + 2\sqrt[3]{9} - 8$

$= \sqrt[3]{27\cdot3} + 2 \cdot \sqrt[3]{9} - 8$

$= 3\sqrt[3]{3} + 2\sqrt[3]{9} - 8$

37. $(\sqrt{y + 10} - \sqrt{10})(\sqrt{y + 10} + \sqrt{10})$

$= (\sqrt{y + 10})^2 - (\sqrt{10})^2$

$= (y + 10) - 10$

$= y$

39. $(8\sqrt{3} + 5\sqrt{2})(6\sqrt{7} - 2\sqrt{5})$

$= 8\sqrt{3}\cdot6\sqrt{7} - 8\sqrt{3}\cdot2\sqrt{5} + 5\sqrt{2}\cdot6\sqrt{7} - 5\sqrt{2}\cdot2\sqrt{5}$

$= 48\sqrt{21} - 16\sqrt{15} + 30\sqrt{14} - 10\sqrt{10}$

41. Let $x = \sqrt{7 + 4\sqrt{3}} - \sqrt{7 - 4\sqrt{3}}$

Then square both sides.

$x^2 = (\sqrt{7 + 4\sqrt{3}})^2 - 2\sqrt{7 + 4\sqrt{3}}\sqrt{7 - 4\sqrt{3}}$
$\qquad\qquad\qquad\qquad\qquad + (\sqrt{7 - 4\sqrt{3}})^2$

$x^2 = 7 + 4\sqrt{3} - 2 + 7 - 4\sqrt{3}$

$x^2 = 12$

$x = \pm 2\sqrt{3}$

Since $\sqrt{7 + 4\sqrt{3}} > \sqrt{7 + 4\sqrt{3}}$, $x > 0$. Thus, the only solution is $2\sqrt{3}$.

Exercise Set 7.7

1. $\sqrt{\dfrac{6}{5}} = \sqrt{\dfrac{6}{5} \cdot \dfrac{5}{5}} = \sqrt{\dfrac{30}{25}} = \dfrac{\sqrt{30}}{\sqrt{25}} = \dfrac{\sqrt{30}}{5}$

3. $\sqrt{\dfrac{10}{3}} = \sqrt{\dfrac{10}{3} \cdot \dfrac{3}{3}} = \sqrt{\dfrac{30}{9}} = \dfrac{\sqrt{30}}{\sqrt{9}} = \dfrac{\sqrt{30}}{3}$

5. $\dfrac{6\sqrt{5}}{5\sqrt{3}} = \dfrac{6\sqrt{5}}{5\sqrt{3}} \cdot \dfrac{\sqrt{3}}{\sqrt{3}} = \dfrac{6\sqrt{15}}{5\cdot3} = \dfrac{2\sqrt{15}}{5}$

7. $\sqrt[3]{\dfrac{16}{9}} = \sqrt[3]{\dfrac{16}{9} \cdot \dfrac{3}{3}} = \sqrt[3]{\dfrac{48}{27}} = \dfrac{\sqrt[3]{8\cdot6}}{\sqrt[3]{27}} = \dfrac{2\sqrt[3]{6}}{3}$

9. $\dfrac{\sqrt[3]{3a}}{\sqrt[3]{5c}} = \dfrac{\sqrt[3]{3a}}{\sqrt[3]{5c}} \cdot \dfrac{\sqrt[3]{5^2c^2}}{\sqrt[3]{5^2c^2}} = \dfrac{\sqrt[3]{75ac^2}}{\sqrt[3]{5^3c^3}} = \dfrac{\sqrt[3]{75ac^2}}{5c}$

11. $\dfrac{\sqrt[3]{2y^4}}{\sqrt[3]{6x^4}} = \dfrac{\sqrt[3]{2y^4}}{\sqrt[3]{6x^4}} \cdot \dfrac{\sqrt[3]{6^2x^2}}{\sqrt[3]{6^2x^2}} = \dfrac{\sqrt[3]{72x^2y^4}}{\sqrt[3]{6^3x^6}}$

$= \dfrac{\sqrt[3]{8y^3 \cdot 9x^2y}}{6x^2} = \dfrac{2y\sqrt[3]{9x^2y}}{6x^2} = \dfrac{y\sqrt[3]{9x^2y}}{3x^2}$

13. $\dfrac{1}{\sqrt[3]{xy}} = \dfrac{1}{\sqrt[3]{xy}} \cdot \dfrac{\sqrt[3]{x^2y^2}}{\sqrt[3]{x^2y^2}} = \dfrac{\sqrt[3]{x^2y^2}}{\sqrt[3]{x^3y^3}} = \dfrac{\sqrt[3]{x^2y^2}}{xy}$

15. $\dfrac{\sqrt{7}}{\sqrt{3x}} = \dfrac{\sqrt{7}}{\sqrt{3x}} \cdot \dfrac{\sqrt{7}}{\sqrt{7}} = \dfrac{7}{\sqrt{21x}}$

17. $\sqrt{\dfrac{14}{21}} = \sqrt{\dfrac{2}{3} \cdot \dfrac{2}{2}} = \sqrt{\dfrac{4}{6}} = \dfrac{\sqrt{4}}{\sqrt{6}} = \dfrac{2}{\sqrt{6}}$

19. $\dfrac{4\sqrt{13}}{3\sqrt{7}} = \dfrac{4\sqrt{13}}{3\sqrt{7}} \cdot \dfrac{\sqrt{13}}{\sqrt{13}} = \dfrac{4 \cdot 13}{3\sqrt{91}} = \dfrac{52}{3\sqrt{91}}$

21. $\dfrac{\sqrt[3]{7}}{\sqrt[3]{2}} = \dfrac{\sqrt[3]{7}}{\sqrt[3]{2}} \cdot \dfrac{\sqrt[3]{7^2}}{\sqrt[3]{7^2}} = \dfrac{\sqrt[3]{7^3}}{\sqrt[3]{98}} = \dfrac{7}{\sqrt[3]{98}}$

23. $\sqrt{\dfrac{7x}{3y}} = \sqrt{\dfrac{7x}{3y} \cdot \dfrac{7x}{7x}} = \dfrac{\sqrt{(7x)^2}}{\sqrt{21xy}} = \dfrac{7x}{\sqrt{21xy}}$

25. $\dfrac{\sqrt[3]{5y^4}}{\sqrt[3]{6x^5}} = \dfrac{\sqrt[3]{5y^4}}{\sqrt[3]{6x^5}} \cdot \dfrac{\sqrt[3]{5^2y^2}}{\sqrt[3]{5^2y^2}} = \dfrac{\sqrt[3]{5^3y^6}}{\sqrt[3]{150x^5y^2}} = \dfrac{5y^2}{x\sqrt[3]{150x^2y^2}}$

27. $\dfrac{\sqrt{ab}}{3} = \dfrac{\sqrt{ab}}{3} \cdot \dfrac{\sqrt{ab}}{\sqrt{ab}} = \dfrac{ab}{3\sqrt{ab}}$

29. $\dfrac{5}{8 - \sqrt{6}} = \dfrac{5}{8 - \sqrt{6}} \cdot \dfrac{8 + \sqrt{6}}{8 + \sqrt{6}}$

$= \dfrac{5(8 + \sqrt{6})}{64 - 6}$

$= \dfrac{5(8 + \sqrt{6})}{58}$

31. $\dfrac{-4\sqrt{7}}{\sqrt{5} - \sqrt{3}} = \dfrac{-4\sqrt{7}}{\sqrt{5} - \sqrt{3}} \cdot \dfrac{\sqrt{5} + \sqrt{3}}{\sqrt{5} + \sqrt{3}}$

$= \dfrac{-4\sqrt{7}\,(\sqrt{5} + \sqrt{3})}{5 - 3}$

$= \dfrac{-4\sqrt{7}\,(\sqrt{5} + \sqrt{3})}{2}$

$= -2\sqrt{7}\,(\sqrt{5} + \sqrt{3})$

33. $\dfrac{\sqrt{5} - 2\sqrt{6}}{\sqrt{3} - 4\sqrt{5}} = \dfrac{\sqrt{5} - 2\sqrt{6}}{\sqrt{3} - 4\sqrt{5}} \quad \dfrac{\sqrt{3} + 4\sqrt{5}}{\sqrt{3} + 4\sqrt{5}}$

$= \dfrac{\sqrt{5}\,\sqrt{3} + \sqrt{5} \cdot 4\sqrt{5} - 2\sqrt{6}\,\sqrt{3} - 2\sqrt{6} \cdot 4\sqrt{5}}{(\sqrt{3})^2 - (4\sqrt{5})^2}$

$= \dfrac{\sqrt{15} + 20 - 6\sqrt{2} - 8\sqrt{30}}{3 - 80}$

$= \dfrac{\sqrt{15} + 20 - 6\sqrt{2} - 8\sqrt{30}}{-77}$

or $= \dfrac{-\sqrt{15} - 20 + 6\sqrt{2} + 8\sqrt{30}}{77}$

35. $\dfrac{\sqrt{x} - \sqrt{y}}{\sqrt{x} + \sqrt{y}} = \dfrac{\sqrt{x} - \sqrt{y}}{\sqrt{x} + \sqrt{y}} \cdot \dfrac{\sqrt{x} - \sqrt{y}}{\sqrt{x} - \sqrt{y}}$

$= \dfrac{(\sqrt{x})^2 - 2\sqrt{x}\,\sqrt{y} + (\sqrt{y})^2}{(\sqrt{x})^2 - (\sqrt{y})^2}$

$= \dfrac{x - 2\sqrt{xy} + y}{x - y}$

37. $\dfrac{5\sqrt{3} - 3\sqrt{2}}{3\sqrt{2} - 2\sqrt{3}} = \dfrac{5\sqrt{3} - 3\sqrt{2}}{3\sqrt{2} - 2\sqrt{3}} \cdot \dfrac{3\sqrt{2} + 2\sqrt{3}}{3\sqrt{2} + 2\sqrt{3}}$

$= \dfrac{15\sqrt{6} + 10 \cdot 3 - 9 \cdot 2 - 6\sqrt{6}}{9 \cdot 2 - 4 \cdot 3}$

$= \dfrac{12 + 9\sqrt{6}}{6}$

$= \dfrac{3(4 + 3\sqrt{6})}{3 \cdot 2}$

$= \dfrac{4 + 3\sqrt{6}}{2}$

39. $\dfrac{\sqrt{3} + 5}{8} = \dfrac{\sqrt{3} + 5}{8} \cdot \dfrac{\sqrt{3} - 5}{\sqrt{3} - 5}$

$= \dfrac{3 - 25}{8(\sqrt{3} - 5)}$

$= \dfrac{-22}{8(\sqrt{3} - 5)}$

$= \dfrac{-11}{4(\sqrt{3} - 5)}$

41. $\dfrac{\sqrt{3} - 5}{\sqrt{2} + 5} = \dfrac{\sqrt{3} - 5}{\sqrt{2} + 5} \cdot \dfrac{\sqrt{3} + 5}{\sqrt{3} + 5}$

$= \dfrac{3 - 25}{\sqrt{6} + 5\sqrt{2} + 5\sqrt{3} + 25}$

$= \dfrac{-22}{\sqrt{6} + 5\sqrt{2} + 5\sqrt{3} + 25}$

43. $\dfrac{\sqrt{x} - \sqrt{y}}{\sqrt{x} + \sqrt{y}} = \dfrac{\sqrt{x} - \sqrt{y}}{\sqrt{x} + \sqrt{y}} \cdot \dfrac{\sqrt{x} + \sqrt{y}}{\sqrt{x} + \sqrt{y}}$

$= \dfrac{(\sqrt{x})^2 - (\sqrt{y})^2}{(\sqrt{x})^2 + 2\sqrt{x}\,\sqrt{y} + (\sqrt{y})^2}$

$= \dfrac{x - y}{x + 2\sqrt{xy} + y}$

45. $\dfrac{4\sqrt{6} - 5\sqrt{3}}{2\sqrt{3} + 7\sqrt{6}} = \dfrac{4\sqrt{6} - 5\sqrt{3}}{2\sqrt{3} + 7\sqrt{6}} \cdot \dfrac{4\sqrt{6} + 5\sqrt{3}}{4\sqrt{6} + 5\sqrt{3}}$

$= \dfrac{16 \cdot 6 - 25 \cdot 3}{8\sqrt{18} + 10 \cdot 3 + 28 \cdot 6 + 35\sqrt{18}}$

$= \dfrac{96 - 75}{24\sqrt{2} + 30 + 168 + 105\sqrt{2}}$

$= \dfrac{21}{129\sqrt{2} + 198}$

$= \dfrac{3 \cdot 7}{3(43\sqrt{2} + 66)}$

$= \dfrac{7}{43\sqrt{2} + 66}$

47. $\frac{1}{2} - \frac{1}{3} = \frac{1}{t}$,   LCM = 6t

$6t(\frac{1}{2} - \frac{1}{3}) = 6t \cdot \frac{1}{t}$

$3t - 2t = 6$

$t = 6$

The number 6 checks and is the solution.

49. $\frac{\sqrt{5} + \sqrt{10} - \sqrt{6}}{\sqrt{50}} = \frac{\sqrt{5} + \sqrt{10} - \sqrt{6}}{\sqrt{50}} \cdot \frac{\sqrt{2}}{\sqrt{2}}$

$= \frac{\sqrt{10} + \sqrt{20} - \sqrt{12}}{\sqrt{100}}$

$= \frac{\sqrt{10} + 2\sqrt{5} - 2\sqrt{3}}{10}$

51. $\frac{b + \sqrt{b}}{1 + b + \sqrt{b}} = \frac{b + \sqrt{b}}{(1 + b) + \sqrt{b}} \cdot \frac{(1 + b) - \sqrt{b}}{(1 + b) - \sqrt{b}}$

$= \frac{(b + \sqrt{b})(1 + b - \sqrt{b})}{(1 + b)^2 - (\sqrt{b})^2}$

$= \frac{b + b^2 - b\sqrt{b} + \sqrt{b} + b\sqrt{b} - b}{1 + 2b + b^2 - b}$

$= \frac{b^2 + \sqrt{b}}{b^2 + b + 1}$

53. $\frac{36a^2b}{\sqrt[3]{6a^2b}} = \frac{36a^2b}{\sqrt[3]{6a^2b}} \cdot \frac{\sqrt[3]{6^2ab^2}}{\sqrt[3]{6^2ab^2}}$

$= \frac{36a^2b \sqrt[3]{6^2ab^2}}{\sqrt[3]{6^3a^3b^3}}$

$= \frac{36a^2b \sqrt[3]{6^2ab^2}}{6ab}$

$= 6a \sqrt[3]{36ab^2}$

55. $\frac{\sqrt{x+6} - 5}{\sqrt{x+6} + 5} = \frac{\sqrt{x+6} - 5}{\sqrt{x+6} + 5} \cdot \frac{\sqrt{x+6} + 5}{\sqrt{x+6} + 5}$

$= \frac{(x+6) - 25}{(x+6) + 10\sqrt{x+6} + 25}$

$= \frac{x - 19}{x + 10\sqrt{x+6} + 31}$

57. $5\sqrt{\frac{x}{y}} + 4\sqrt{\frac{y}{x}} - \frac{3}{\sqrt{xy}}$

$= 5\sqrt{\frac{x}{y} \cdot \frac{y}{y}} + 4\sqrt{\frac{y}{x} \cdot \frac{x}{x}} - \frac{3}{\sqrt{xy}} \cdot \frac{\sqrt{xy}}{\sqrt{xy}}$

$= \frac{5}{y}\sqrt{xy} + \frac{4}{x}\sqrt{xy} - \frac{3}{xy}\sqrt{xy}$

$= (\frac{5}{y} + \frac{4}{x} - \frac{3}{xy})\sqrt{xy}$

$= (\frac{5x + 4y - 3}{xy})\sqrt{xy}$

59. $\frac{1}{4 + \sqrt{3}} + \frac{1}{\sqrt{3}} + \frac{1}{\sqrt{3} - 4}$

$= \frac{1}{4 + \sqrt{3}} + \frac{1}{\sqrt{3}} + \frac{-1}{4 - \sqrt{3}}$

LCM $= \sqrt{3}(4 + \sqrt{3})(4 - \sqrt{3})$

$= \frac{\sqrt{3}(4 - \sqrt{3}) + (4 + \sqrt{3})(4 - \sqrt{3}) - \sqrt{3}(4 + \sqrt{3})}{\sqrt{3}(4 + \sqrt{3})(4 - \sqrt{3})}$

$= \frac{4\sqrt{3} - 3 + 16 - 3 - 4\sqrt{3} - 3}{13\sqrt{3}}$

$= \frac{7}{13\sqrt{3}}$

$= \frac{7}{13\sqrt{3}} \cdot \frac{\sqrt{3}}{\sqrt{3}}$

$= \frac{7\sqrt{3}}{39}$

Exercise Set 7.8

1. $x^{1/4} = \sqrt[4]{x}$

3. $(8)^{1/3} = \sqrt[3]{8} = 2$

5. $(a^2b^2)^{1/5} = \sqrt[5]{a^2b^2}$

7. $16^{3/4} = \sqrt[4]{16^3} = (\sqrt[4]{16})^3 = 2^3 = 8$

9. $\sqrt[3]{20} = 20^{1/3}$

11. $\sqrt[5]{xy^2z} = (xy^2z)^{1/5}$

13. $(\sqrt{3mn})^3 = (3mn)^{3/2}$

15. $(\sqrt[7]{8x^2y})^5 = (8x^2y)^{5/7}$

17. $x^{-1/3} = \frac{1}{x^{1/3}}$

19. $\frac{1}{x^{-2/3}} = x^{2/3}$

21. $5^{3/4} \cdot 5^{1/8} = 5^{3/4+1/8} = 5^{6/8+1/8} = 5^{7/8}$

23. $\frac{7^{5/8}}{7^{3/8}} = 7^{5/8-3/8} = 7^{2/8} = 7^{1/4}$

25. $\frac{8.3^{3/4}}{8.3^{2/5}} = 8.3^{3/4-2/5} = 8.3^{15/20-8/20} = 8.3^{7/20}$

27. $(10^{3/8})^{2/5} = 10^{(3/8)(2/5)} = 10^{6/40} = 10^{3/20}$

29. $\sqrt[6]{a^4} = a^{4/6} = a^{2/3} = \sqrt[3]{a^2}$

31. $\sqrt[3]{8y^6} = (2^3y^6)^{1/3} = 2^{3/3}y^{6/3} = 2y^2$

33. $\sqrt[4]{32} = \sqrt[4]{2^5} = 2^{5/4} = 2^{4/4} \cdot 2^{1/4} = 2\sqrt[4]{2}$

35. $\sqrt[6]{4x^2} = (2^2x^2)^{1/6} = 2^{2/6}x^{2/6}$

$\qquad = 2^{1/3}x^{1/3} = (2x)^{1/3} = \sqrt[3]{2x}$

37. $\sqrt[5]{32c^{10}d^{15}} = (2^5c^{10}d^{15})^{1/5} = 2^{5/5}c^{10/5}d^{15/5}$

$\qquad\qquad = 2c^2d^3$

39. $\sqrt[6]{\dfrac{m^{12}n^{24}}{64}} = \left[\dfrac{m^{12}n^{24}}{2^6}\right]^{1/6} = \dfrac{m^{12/6}n^{24/6}}{2^{6/6}} = \dfrac{m^2n^4}{2}$

41. $\sqrt[8]{r^4s^2} = (r^4s^2)^{1/8} = r^{4/8}s^{2/8} = r^{2/4}s^{1/4}$

$\qquad\qquad = (r^2s)^{1/4} = \sqrt[4]{r^2s}$

43. $\sqrt[3]{27a^3b^9} = (3^3a^3b^9)^{1/3} = 3^{3/3}a^{3/3}b^{9/3} = 3ab^3$

45. $\sqrt[3]{5} \cdot \sqrt{2} = 5^{1/3} \cdot 2^{1/2} = 5^{2/6} \cdot 2^{3/6}$

$\qquad = (5^2 \cdot 2^3)^{1/6}$

$\qquad = (25 \cdot 8)^{1/6}$

$\qquad = 200^{1/6}$

$\qquad = \sqrt[6]{200}$

47. $\sqrt{x}\,\sqrt[3]{2x} = x^{1/2} \cdot (2x)^{1/3} = x^{3/6} \cdot (2x)^{2/6}$

$\qquad = [x^3(2x)^2]^{1/6}$

$\qquad = (x^3 \cdot 4x^2)^{1/6}$

$\qquad = (4x^5)^{1/6}$

$\qquad = \sqrt[6]{4x^5}$

49. $\sqrt{x}\,\sqrt[3]{x-2} = x^{1/2} \cdot (x-2)^{1/3}$

$\qquad = x^{3/6} \cdot (x-2)^{2/6}$

$\qquad = [x^3(x-2)^2]^{1/6}$

$\qquad = [x^3(x^2 - 4x + 4)]^{1/6}$

$\qquad = (x^5 - 4x^4 + 4x^3)^{1/6}$

$\qquad = \sqrt[6]{x^5 - 4x^4 + 4x^3}$

51. $\dfrac{\sqrt[3]{(a+b)^2}}{\sqrt{(a+b)}} = \dfrac{(a+b)^{2/3}}{(a+b)^{1/2}} = \dfrac{(a+b)^{4/6}}{(a+b)^{3/6}}$

$\qquad\qquad = (a+b)^{4/6-3/6}$

$\qquad\qquad = (a+b)^{1/6}$

$\qquad\qquad = \sqrt[6]{a+b}$

53. $a^{2/3} \cdot b^{3/4} = a^{8/12} \cdot b^{9/12}$

$\qquad = (a^8b^9)^{1/12}$

$\qquad = \sqrt[12]{a^8b^9}$

55. $\dfrac{s^{7/12} \cdot t^{7/6}}{s^{1/3} \cdot t^{-1/6}} = \dfrac{s^{7/12} \cdot t^{7/6}}{s^{4/12} \cdot t^{-1/6}} = s^{7/12-4/12} \cdot t^{7/6-(-1/6)}$

$\qquad = s^{3/12} \cdot t^{8/6}$

$\qquad = s^{3/12} \cdot t^{16/12}$

$\qquad = s^{3/12} \cdot t^{12/12} \cdot t^{4/12}$

$\qquad = t(s^3t^4)^{1/12}$

$\qquad = t\,\sqrt[12]{s^3t^4}$

57. $\sqrt[5]{yx^2}\,\sqrt{xy} = (yx^2)^{1/5}(xy)^{1/2} = (yx^2)^{2/10}(xy)^{5/10}$

$\qquad = [(yx^2)^2(xy)^5]^{1/10}$

$\qquad = (y^2x^4 \cdot x^5y^5)^{1/10}$

$\qquad = (x^9y^7)^{1/10}$

$\qquad = \sqrt[10]{x^9y^7}$

59. $\dfrac{\sqrt{(a+b)^3}\,\sqrt[3]{(a+b)^2}}{\sqrt[4]{a+b}} = \dfrac{(a+b)^{3/2}(a+b)^{2/3}}{(a+b)^{1/4}}$

$\qquad = \dfrac{(a+b)^{18/12}(a+b)^{8/12}}{(a+b)^{3/12}}$

$\qquad = (a+b)^{18/12+8/12-3/12}$

$\qquad = (a+b)^{23/12}$

$\qquad = (a+b)^{12/12}(a+b)^{11/12}$

$\qquad = (a+b)\,\sqrt[12]{(a+b)^{11}}$

61. $(-\sqrt[4]{7}\,\sqrt[3]{w})^{12} = (-1 \cdot 7^{1/4} \cdot w^{1/3})^{12}$

$\qquad = (-1)^{12} \cdot 7^{12/4} \cdot w^{12/3}$

$\qquad = 1 \cdot 7^3 \cdot w^4$

$\qquad = 343w^4$

63. $\dfrac{1}{\sqrt[3]{3} - \sqrt[3]{2}} = \dfrac{1}{\sqrt[3]{3} - \sqrt[3]{2}} \cdot \dfrac{\sqrt[3]{9} + \sqrt[3]{6} + \sqrt[3]{4}}{\sqrt[3]{9} + \sqrt[3]{6} + \sqrt[3]{4}}$

$\qquad = \dfrac{\sqrt[3]{9} + \sqrt[3]{6} + \sqrt[3]{4}}{(\sqrt[3]{3})^3 - (\sqrt[3]{2})^3}$

$\qquad = \dfrac{\sqrt[3]{9} + \sqrt[3]{6} + \sqrt[3]{4}}{3 - 2}$

$\qquad = \sqrt[3]{9} + \sqrt[3]{6} + \sqrt[3]{4}$

65. $\sqrt[p]{x^{5p}y^{7p+1}z^{p+3}} = (x^{5p}y^{7p}y^1z^pz^3)^{1/p}$

$\qquad = x^5y^7y^{1/p}z^{3/p}$

$\qquad = x^5y^7z(y^1z^3)^{1/p}$

$\qquad = x^5y^7z\,\sqrt[p]{yz^3}$

Exercise Set 7.9

1. $\sqrt{y + 1} - 5 = 8$ Check:

   $\sqrt{y + 1} = 13$

   $(\sqrt{y + 1})^2 = 13^2$ $\dfrac{\sqrt{y + 1} - 5 = 8}{\sqrt{168 + 1} - 5 \quad \bigg| \quad 8}$

   $y + 1 = 169$ $\sqrt{169} - 5$

   $y = 168$ $13 - 5$

                                  8

   The solution is 168.

3. $\sqrt{3y + 1} = 9$ Check:

   $(\sqrt{3y + 1})^2 = 9^2$ $\dfrac{\sqrt{3y + 1} = 9}{\sqrt{3 \cdot \frac{80}{3} + 1} \quad \bigg| \quad 9}$

   $3y + 1 = 81$

   $3y = 80$ $\sqrt{80 + 1}$

   $y = \dfrac{80}{3}$ $\sqrt{81}$

                                  9

   The solution is $\dfrac{80}{3}$.

5. $\sqrt[3]{x} = -3$ Check:

   $(\sqrt[3]{x})^3 = (-3)^3$ $\dfrac{\sqrt[3]{x} = -3}{\sqrt[3]{-27} \quad \bigg| \quad -3}$

   $x = -27$ -3

   The solution is -27.

7. $\sqrt{x + 2} = -4$ Check:

   $(\sqrt{x + 2})^2 = (-4)^2$ $\dfrac{\sqrt{x + 2} = -4}{\sqrt{14 + 2} \quad \bigg| \quad -4}$

   $x + 2 = 16$ $\sqrt{16}$

   $x = 14$ 4

   The number 14 does not check. The equation has no solution.

9. $\sqrt[3]{6x + 9} + 8 = 5$ Check:

   $\sqrt[3]{6x + 9} = -3$ $\dfrac{\sqrt[3]{6x + 9} + 8 = 5}{\sqrt[3]{6(-6) + 9} + 8 \quad \bigg| \quad 5}$

   $(\sqrt[3]{6x + 9})^3 = (-3)^3$

   $6x + 9 = -27$ $\sqrt[3]{-27} + 8$

   $6x = -36$ $-3 + 8$

   $x = -6$ 5

   The solution is -6.

11. $\sqrt{3y + 1} = \sqrt{2y + 6}$ Check:

   $(\sqrt{3y + 1})^2 = (\sqrt{2y + 6})^2$ $\dfrac{\sqrt{3y + 1} = \sqrt{2y + 6}}{\sqrt{3 \cdot 5 + 1} \quad \bigg| \quad \sqrt{2 \cdot 5 + 6}}$

   $3y + 1 = 2y + 6$

   $y = 5$ $\sqrt{16} \quad \bigg| \quad \sqrt{16}$

   The solution is 5.

13. $\sqrt{y - 5} + \sqrt{y} = 5$

   $\sqrt{y - 5} = 5 - \sqrt{y}$

   $(\sqrt{y - 5})^2 = (5 - \sqrt{y})^2$

   $y - 5 = 25 - 10\sqrt{y} + y$

   $10\sqrt{y} = 30$

   $\sqrt{y} = 3$

   $(\sqrt{y})^2 = 3^2$

   $y = 9$

   The number 9 checks, so it is the solution.

15. $3 + \sqrt{z - 6} = \sqrt{z + 9}$

   $(3 + \sqrt{z - 6})^2 = (\sqrt{z + 9})^2$

   $9 + 6\sqrt{z - 6} + z - 6 = z + 9$

   $6\sqrt{z - 6} = 6$

   $\sqrt{z - 6} = 1$

   $(\sqrt{z - 6})^2 = 1^2$

   $z - 6 = 1$

   $z = 7$

   The number 7 checks, so it is the solution.

17. $\sqrt{20 - x} + 8 = \sqrt{9 - x} + 11$

   $\sqrt{20 - x} = \sqrt{9 - x} + 3$

   $(\sqrt{20 - x})^2 = (\sqrt{9 - x} + 3)^2$

   $20 - x = 9 - x + 6\sqrt{9 - x} + 9$

   $2 = 6\sqrt{9 - x}$

   $1 = 3\sqrt{9 - x}$

   $1^2 = (3\sqrt{9 - x})^2$

   $1 = 9(9 - x)$

   $1 = 81 - 9x$

   $9x = 80$

   $x = \dfrac{80}{9}$

   The number $\dfrac{80}{9}$ checks, so it is the solution.

19. $\sqrt{4y + 1} - \sqrt{y - 2} = 3$

$$\sqrt{4y + 1} = 3 + \sqrt{y - 2}$$

$$(\sqrt{4y + 1})^2 = (3 + \sqrt{y - 2})^2$$

$$4y + 1 = 9 + 6\sqrt{y - 2} + y - 2$$

$$3y - 6 = 6\sqrt{y - 2}$$

$$y - 2 = 2\sqrt{y - 2}$$

$$(y - 2)^2 = (2\sqrt{y - 2})^2$$

$$y^2 - 4y + 4 = 4(y - 2)$$

$$y^2 - 4y + 4 = 4y - 8$$

$$y^2 - 8y + 12 = 0$$

$$(y - 6)(y - 2) = 0$$

$$y - 6 = 0 \text{ or } y - 2 = 0$$

$$y = 6 \text{ or } \qquad y = 2$$

The numbers 6 and 2 check, so they are the solutions.

21. $x^2 + 2.8x$

$$\left(\frac{2.8}{2}\right)^2 = (1.4)^2 = 1.96$$

$$x^2 + 2.8x + 1.96 = (x + 1.4)^2$$

23. $\sqrt[3]{\frac{z}{4}} - 10 = 2$

$$\sqrt[3]{\frac{z}{4}} = 12$$

$$\left[\sqrt[3]{\frac{z}{4}}\right]^3 = 12^3$$

$$\frac{z}{4} = 1728$$

$$z = 6912$$

The number 6912 checks, so it is the solution.

25. $\sqrt{\sqrt{y + 49} - \sqrt{y}} = \sqrt{7}$

$$(\sqrt{\sqrt{y + 49} - \sqrt{y}})^2 = (\sqrt{7})^2$$

$$\sqrt{y + 49} - \sqrt{y} = 7$$

$$\sqrt{y + 49} = 7 + \sqrt{y}$$

$$(\sqrt{y + 49})^2 = (7 + \sqrt{y})^2$$

$$y + 49 = 49 + 14\sqrt{y} + y$$

$$0 = 14\sqrt{y}$$

$$0 = \sqrt{y}$$

$$0 = y$$

The number 0 checks and is the solution.

27. $\sqrt{\sqrt{x^2 + 9x + 34}} = 2$

$$(\sqrt{\sqrt{x^2 + 9x + 34}})^2 = 2^2$$

$$\sqrt{x^2 + 9x + 34} = 4$$

$$(\sqrt{x^2 + 9x + 34})^2 = 4^2$$

$$x^2 + 9x + 34 = 16$$

$$x^2 + 9x + 18 = 0$$

$$(x + 6)(x + 3) = 0$$

$$x + 6 = 0 \text{ or } x + 3 = 0$$

$$x = -6 \text{ or } \qquad x = -3$$

Both values check. The solutions are -6 and -3.

29. $\sqrt{x - 2} - \sqrt{x + 2} + 2 = 0$

$$\sqrt{x - 2} + 2 = \sqrt{x + 2}$$

$$(\sqrt{x - 2} + 2)^2 = (\sqrt{x + 2})^2$$

$$(x - 2) + 4\sqrt{x - 2} + 4 = x + 2$$

$$4\sqrt{x - 2} = 0$$

$$\sqrt{x - 2} = 0$$

$$(\sqrt{x - 2})^2 = 0^2$$

$$x - 2 = 0$$

$$x = 2$$

The number 2 checks, so it is the solution.

31. $\sqrt{a^2 + 30a} = a + \sqrt{5a}$

$$(\sqrt{a^2 + 30a})^2 = (a + \sqrt{5a})^2$$

$$a^2 + 30a = a^2 + 2a\sqrt{5a} + 5a$$

$$25a = 2a\sqrt{5a}$$

$$(25a)^2 = (2a\sqrt{5a})^2$$

$$625a^2 = 4a^2 \cdot 5a$$

$$625a^2 = 20a^3$$

$$0 = 20a^3 - 625a^2$$

$$0 = a^2(20a - 625)$$

$$a^2 = 0 \text{ or } 20a - 625 = 0$$

$$a = 0 \text{ or } \qquad 20a = 625$$

$$a = 0 \text{ or } \qquad a = 31.25$$

Both values check. The solutions are 0 and 31.25.

33. $\dfrac{x - 1}{\sqrt{x^2 + 3x + 6}} = \dfrac{1}{4}$,   LCM = $4\sqrt{x^2 + 3x + 6}$

$4x - 4 = \sqrt{x^2 + 3x + 6}$

$16x^2 - 32x + 16 = x^2 + 3x + 6$

$15x^2 - 35x + 10 = 0$

$3x^2 - 7x + 2 = 0$

$(3x - 1)(x - 2) = 0$

$3x - 1 = 0$ or $x - 2 = 0$

$3x = 1$ or $\quad x = 2$

$x = \dfrac{1}{3}$ or $\quad x = 2$

The number 2 does check but $\dfrac{1}{3}$ does not. The solution is 2.

Exercise Set 7.10

---

1. a = 3,   b = 5

Find c.

$c^2 = a^2 + b^2$

$c^2 = 3^2 + 5^2$

$c^2 = 9 + 25$

$c^2 = 34$

$c = \sqrt{34}$

$c \approx 5.831$

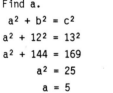

3. a = 12,   b = 12

Find c.

$c^2 = a^2 + b^2$

$c^2 = 12^2 + 12^2$

$c^2 = 144 + 144$

$c^2 = 288$

$c = \sqrt{288}$, or $12\sqrt{2}$

$c \approx 16.971$

5. b = 12,   c = 13

Find a.

$a^2 + b^2 = c^2$

$a^2 + 12^2 = 13^2$

$a^2 + 144 = 169$

$a^2 = 25$

$a = 5$

7. c = 6,   a = $\sqrt{5}$

Find b.

$a^2 + b^2 = c^2$

$(\sqrt{5})^2 + b^2 = 6^2$

$5 + b^2 = 36$

$b^2 = 31$

$b = \sqrt{31}$

$b \approx 5.568$

9. b = 1,   c = $\sqrt{13}$

Find a.

$a^2 + b^2 = c^2$

$a^2 + 1^2 = (\sqrt{13})^2$

$a^2 + 1 = 13$

$a^2 = 12$

$a = \sqrt{12}$, or $2\sqrt{3}$

$a \approx 3.464$

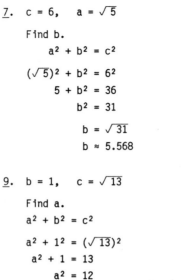

11. a = 1,   c = $\sqrt{n}$

Find b.

$a^2 + b^2 = c^2$

$1^2 + b^2 = (\sqrt{n})^2$

$1 + b^2 = n$

$b^2 = n - 1$

$b = \sqrt{n - 1}$

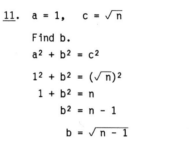

13. $d^2 = 10^2 + 15^2$

$d^2 = 100 + 225$

$d^2 = 325$

$d = \sqrt{325}$, or $5\sqrt{13}$

$d \approx 18.028$

The wire is 18.028 ft long.

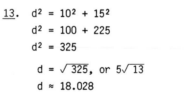

15.

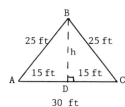

△ ABC is an isosceles triangle. The height from B to $\overline{AC}$ bisects $\overline{AC}$. Thus, $\overline{DC}$ measures 15 ft.

$h^2 + 15^2 = 25^2$

$h^2 + 225 = 625$

$h^2 = 400$

$h = \sqrt{400}$

$h = 20$

If the height of △ ABC is 20 ft and the base is 30 ft, the area is $\frac{1}{2} \cdot 30 \cdot 20$, or 300 ft².

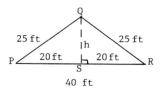

△ PQR is an isosceles triangle. The height from Q to $\overline{PR}$ bisects $\overline{PR}$. Thus, $\overline{SR}$ measrues 20 ft.

$h^2 + 20^2 = 25^2$

$h^2 + 400 = 625$

$h^2 = 225$

$h = \sqrt{225}$

$h = 15$

If the height of △ PQR is 15 ft and the base is 40 ft, the area is $\frac{1}{2} \cdot 40 \cdot 15$, or 300 ft².

The areas of the two triangles are the same.

17.

$h^2 = s^2 + s^2$

$h^2 = 2s^2$

$h = s\sqrt{2}$

19. $L = \dfrac{0.000169d^{2.27}}{h}$

$L = \dfrac{0.000169(200)^{2.27}}{4}$

≈ 7.1

The length of the letters should be 7.1 ft.

21.

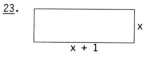

$s^2 + s^2 = (8\sqrt{2})^2$

$2s^2 = 128$

$s^2 = 64$

$s = 8$

The length of a side of the square is 8 ft.

23.

Let x represent the width. Then x + 1 represents the length.

The area of the rectantle is 90 cm².

$(x + 1)x = 90$

$x^2 + x = 90$

$x^2 + x - 90 = 0$

$(x - 9)(x + 10) = 0$

$x - 9 = 0$ or $x + 10 = 0$

$x = 9$ or $x = -10$

We only consider x = 9 since the width cannot be negative. The width is 9 cm and the length is 9 + 1, or 10 cm.

$d^2 = 10^2 + 9^2$

$d^2 = 100 + 81$

$d^2 = 181$

$d = \sqrt{181}$

$d \approx 13.454$

The length of the diagonal is 13.454 cm.

25. $y^2 - \dfrac{c}{d} y$

$\left[\dfrac{\frac{c}{d}}{2} \right]^2 = \left(\dfrac{c}{2d} \right)^2 = \dfrac{c^2}{4d^2}$

$y^2 - \dfrac{c}{d} y + \dfrac{c^2}{4d^2} = (y - \dfrac{c}{2d})^2$

Exercise Set 7.11

1. $\sqrt{-15} = \sqrt{-1 \cdot 15} = \sqrt{-1} \cdot \sqrt{15} = \sqrt{15}i$

3. $\sqrt{-16} = \sqrt{-1 \cdot 16} = \sqrt{-1} \cdot \sqrt{16} = 4i$

5. $-\sqrt{-12} = -\sqrt{-1 \cdot 12} = -\sqrt{-1} \cdot \sqrt{12} = -2\sqrt{3}i$

7. $(3 + 2i) + (5 - i)$
$= (3 + 5) + [2 + (-1)]i$
$= 8 + i$

9. $(4 - 3i) + (5 - 2i)$
$= (4 + 5) + [-3 + (-2)]i$
$= 9 - 5i$

11. $(9 - i) + (-2 + 5i)$
$= [9 + (-2)] + (-1 + 5)i$
$= 7 + 4i$

13. $(3 - i) - (5 + 2i)$
$= (3 - 5) + (-1 - 2)i$
$= -2 - 3i$

15. $(4 - 2i) - (5 - 3i)$
$= (4 - 5) + [-2 - (-3)]i$
$= -1 + i$

17. $(9 + 5i) - (-2 - i)$
$= [9 - (-2)] + [5 - (-1)]i$
$= 11 + 6i$

19. $(3 + 2i)(1 + i)$
$= 3 + 3i + 2i + 2i^2$
$= 3 + 3i + 2i - 2$
$= 1 + 5i$

21. $(2 + 3i)(6 - 2i)$
$= 12 - 4i + 18i - 6i^2$
$= 12 - 4i + 18i + 6$
$= 18 + 14i$

23. $(6 - 5i)(3 + 4i)$
$= 18 + 24i - 15i - 20i^2$
$= 18 + 24i - 15i + 20$
$= 38 + 9i$

25. $(7 - 2i)(2 - 6i)$
$= 14 - 42i - 4i + 12i^2$
$= 14 - 42i - 4i - 12$
$= 2 - 46i$

27. $i^6 = i^2 \cdot i^2 \cdot i^2 = (-1)(-1)(-1) = -1$

29. $(5i)^3 = 5^3 \cdot i^3 = 125i^2 \cdot i = -125i$

31. $(3 - 2i)^2$
$= 9 - 12i + 4i^2$
$= 9 - 12i - 4$
$= 5 - 12i$

33. $(2 + 3i)^2$
$= 4 + 12i + 9i^2$
$= 4 + 12i - 9$
$= -5 + 12i$

35. $(-2 + 3i)^2$
$= 4 - 12i + 9i^2$
$= 4 - 12i - 9$
$= -5 - 12i$

37. $\dfrac{3 + 2i}{2 + i} = \dfrac{3 + 2i}{2 + i} \cdot \dfrac{2 - i}{2 - i}$

$= \dfrac{6 - 3i + 4i - 2i^2}{4 - i^2}$

$= \dfrac{6 - 3i + 4i + 2}{4 + 1}$

$= \dfrac{8 + i}{5}$

$= \dfrac{8}{5} + \dfrac{1}{5}i$

39. $\dfrac{5 - 2i}{2 + 5i} = \dfrac{5 - 2i}{2 + 5i} \cdot \dfrac{2 - 5i}{2 - 5i}$

$= \dfrac{10 - 25i - 4i + 10i^2}{4 - 25i^2}$

$= \dfrac{10 - 25i - 4i - 10}{4 + 25}$

$= \dfrac{-29i}{29}$

$= -i$

41. $\dfrac{8 - 3i}{7i} = \dfrac{8 - 3i}{7i} \cdot \dfrac{-7i}{-7i}$

$= \dfrac{-56i + 21i^2}{-49i^2}$

$= \dfrac{-21 - 56i}{49}$

$= -\dfrac{3}{7} - \dfrac{8}{7}i$

43. Substitute $1 + 2i$ for x in the equation.

$x^2 - 2x + 5 = 0$	
$(1 + 2i)^2 - 2(1 + 2i) + 5$	0
$1 + 4i + 4i^2 - 2 - 4i + 5$	
$1 - 4 - 2 + 5$	
0	

Thus, $1 + 2i$ is a solution.

45. Substitute 1 - i for x in the equation.

$$\begin{array}{r|l} x^2 + 2x + 2 = 0 & \\ \hline (1 - i)^2 + 2(1 - i) + 2 & 0 \\ 1 - 2i + i^2 + 2 - 2i + 2 & \\ 4 - 4i & \end{array}$$

Thus, 1 - i is not a solution.

47. $\dfrac{196}{x^2 - 7x + 49} - \dfrac{2x}{x + 7} = \dfrac{2058}{x^3 + 343}$

Note: $x^3 + 343 = (x + 7)(x^2 - 7x + 49)$

The LCM = $(x + 7)(x^2 - 7x + 49)$.

$(x + 7)(x^2 - 7x + 49)\left(\dfrac{196}{x^2 - 7x + 49} - \dfrac{2x}{x + 7}\right) =$

$\qquad\qquad (x + 7)(x^2 - 7x + 49) \cdot \dfrac{2058}{x^3 + 343}$

$196(x + 7) - 2x(x^2 - 7x + 49) = 2058$

$196x + 1372 - 2x^3 + 14x^2 = 2058$

$98x - 686 - 2x^3 + 14x^2 = 0$

$49x - 343 - x^3 + 7x^2 = 0$

$49(x - 7) - x^2(x - 7) = 0$

$(49 - x^2)(x - 7) = 0$

$(7 - x)(7 + x)(x - 7) = 0$

$7 - x = 0$ or $7 + x = 0$ or $x - 7 = 0$

$\quad x = 7$ or $\qquad x = -7$ or $\qquad x = 7$

Only 7 checks. It is the solution.

49. $x^2 - 3.2x + 1.56$

$= x^2 - 3.2x + (2.56 - 2.56) + 1.56$

$\qquad \left(\dfrac{3.2}{2} = 1.6,\ 1.6^2 = 2.56\right)$

$= (x^2 - 3.2x + 2.56) + (-2.56 + 1.56)$

$= (x - 1.6)^2 - 1$

$= [(x - 1.6 + 1)(x - 1.6 - 1)]$

$= (x - 0.6)(x - 2.6)$

51. $\dfrac{1}{w - w^2}$

$= \dfrac{1}{\dfrac{1 - i}{10} - \left(\dfrac{1 - i}{10}\right)^2}$ (Substituting $\dfrac{1 - i}{10}$ for w)

$= \dfrac{1}{\dfrac{1 - i}{10} - \left(\dfrac{1 - 2i + i^2}{100}\right)}$

$= \dfrac{1}{\dfrac{10 - 10i}{100} - \dfrac{-2i}{100}}$ $\qquad \left(\dfrac{1 - i}{10} \cdot \dfrac{10}{10} = \dfrac{10 - 10i}{100}\right)$

$= \dfrac{1}{\dfrac{10 - 10i + 2i}{100}}$

$= \dfrac{100}{10 - 8i}$

$= \dfrac{50}{5 - 4i}$

$= \dfrac{50}{5 - 4i} \cdot \dfrac{5 + 4i}{5 + 4i}$

$= \dfrac{250 + 200i}{25 - 16i^2}$

$= \dfrac{250 + 200i}{41}$

$= \dfrac{250}{41} + \dfrac{200}{41} i$

53. $12 \sqrt{-\dfrac{1}{32}}$

$= 12 \sqrt{-\dfrac{1}{32} \cdot \dfrac{2}{2}}$

$= 12 \sqrt{-\dfrac{2}{64}}$

$= 12 \cdot \dfrac{i}{8} \sqrt{2}$

$= \dfrac{3\sqrt{2}}{2} i$

55. $\dfrac{i^5 + i^6 + i^7 + i^8}{(1 - i)^4}$

$= \dfrac{i - 1 - i + 1}{(1 - i)^4}$

$= \dfrac{0}{(1 - i)^4}$

$= 0$

Note:

$i = i$
$i^2 = -1$
$i^3 = -i$
$i^4 = 1$
$i^5 = i$
$i^6 = -1$
$i^7 = -i$
$i^8 = 1$

57. $\dfrac{5 - \sqrt{5}i}{\sqrt{5}i}$

$= \dfrac{5 - \sqrt{5}i}{\sqrt{5}i} \cdot \dfrac{\sqrt{5}i}{\sqrt{5}i}$

$= \dfrac{5\sqrt{5}i + 5}{-5}$

$= -\sqrt{5}i - 1$

$= -1 - \sqrt{5} i$

59. $(\frac{1}{2} - \frac{1}{3} i)^2 - (\frac{1}{2} + \frac{1}{3} i)^2$

= $(\frac{1}{4} - \frac{1}{3} i - \frac{1}{9}) - (\frac{1}{4} + \frac{1}{3} i - \frac{1}{9})$

= $\frac{1}{4} - \frac{1}{3} i - \frac{1}{9} - \frac{1}{4} - \frac{1}{3} i + \frac{1}{9}$

= $- \frac{2}{3} i$

Exercise Set 8.1

1. $4x^2 = 20$ Check: $4x^2 = 20$

$x^2 = 5$

$x = \sqrt{5}$ or $x = -\sqrt{5}$ $\dfrac{4(\pm\sqrt{5})^2 \mid 20}{}$

$4 \cdot 5$

20

The solutions are $\sqrt{5}$ and $-\sqrt{5}$, or $\pm\sqrt{5}$.

3. $25x^2 + 4 = 0$

$25x^2 = -4$

$x^2 = -\dfrac{4}{25}$

$x = \sqrt{-\dfrac{4}{25}}$ or $x = -\sqrt{-\dfrac{4}{25}}$

$x = \dfrac{2}{5}i$ or $x = -\dfrac{2}{5}i$

The solutions are $\dfrac{2}{5}i$ and $-\dfrac{2}{5}i$, or $\pm\dfrac{2}{5}i$.

5. $2x^2 - 3 = 0$

$2x^2 = 3$

$x^2 = \dfrac{3}{2}$

$x = \sqrt{\dfrac{3}{2}}$ or $x = -\sqrt{\dfrac{3}{2}}$

$x = \sqrt{\dfrac{3}{2} \cdot \dfrac{2}{2}}$ or $x = -\sqrt{\dfrac{3}{2} \cdot \dfrac{2}{2}}$

$x = \dfrac{\sqrt{6}}{2}$ or $x = -\dfrac{\sqrt{6}}{2}$

The solutions are $\dfrac{\sqrt{6}}{2}$ and $-\dfrac{\sqrt{6}}{2}$, or $\pm\dfrac{\sqrt{6}}{2}$.

7. $14x^2 + 9x = 0$

$x(14x + 9) = 0$

$x = 0$ or $14x + 9 = 0$

$x = 0$ or $x = -\dfrac{9}{14}$

Check: For 0   For $-\dfrac{9}{14}$

$\dfrac{14x^2 + 9x = 0}{14 \cdot 0^2 + 9 \cdot 0 \mid 0}$ $\dfrac{14x^2 + 9x = 0}{14(-\frac{9}{14})^2 + 9(-\frac{9}{14}) \mid 0}$

$0 + 0$ $\dfrac{81}{14} - \dfrac{81}{14}$

0 0

9. $5x^2 + 10x = 0$

$x^2 + 2x = 0$

$x(x + 2) = 0$

$x = 0$ or $x + 2 = 0$

$x = 0$ or $x = -2$

The solutions are 0 and -2.

11. $x^2 - 6x + 5 = 0$

$(x - 1)(x - 5) = 0$

$x - 1 = 0$ or $x - 5 = 0$

$x = 1$ or $x = 5$

Check: For 1   For 5

$\dfrac{x^2 - 6x + 5 = 0}{1^2 - 6 \cdot 1 + 5 \mid 0}$ $\dfrac{x^2 - 6x + 5 = 0}{5^2 - 6 \cdot 5 + 5 \mid 0}$

$1 - 6 + 5$ $25 - 30 + 5$

0 0

The solutions are 1 and 5.

13. $6x^2 - x - 2 = 0$

$(2x + 1)(3x - 2) = 0$

$2x + 1 = 0$ or $3x - 2 = 0$

$2x = -1$ or $3x = 2$

$x = -\dfrac{1}{2}$ or $x = \dfrac{2}{3}$

The solutions are $-\dfrac{1}{2}$ and $\dfrac{2}{3}$.

15. $x^2 + 8x + 15 = 0$

$(x + 5)(x + 3) = 0$

$x + 5 = 0$ or $x + 3 = 0$

$x = -5$ or $x = -3$

The solutions are -5 and -3.

17. $4x(x - 2) - 5x(x - 1) = 2$

$4x^2 - 8x - 5x^2 + 5x = 2$

$-x^2 - 3x = 2$

$0 = x^2 + 3x + 2$

$0 = (x + 2)(x + 1)$

$x + 2 = 0$ or $x + 1 = 0$

$x = -2$ or $x = -1$

The solutions are -2 and -1.

19. $14(x - 4) - (x + 2) = (x + 2)(x - 4)$

$14x - 56 - x - 2 = x^2 - 2x - 8$

$13x - 58 = x^2 - 2x - 8$

$0 = x^2 - 15x + 50$

$0 = (x - 10)(x - 5)$

$x - 10 = 0$ or $x - 5 = 0$

$x = 10$ or $x = 5$

The solutions are 10 and 5.

21. We make a drawing and label it with both known and unknown information. We let x represent the width of the frame.

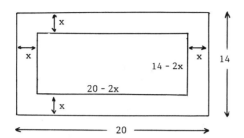

The length and width of the picture that shows are represented by 20 - 2x and 14 - 2x. The area of the picture that shows is 160 cm².

Using the formula for the area of a rectangle, A = ℓ·w, we have

160 = (20 - 2x)(14 - 2x)

We solve the equation.

160 = (20 - 2x)(14 - 2x)

160 = 280 - 68x + 4x²

  0 = 120 - 68x + 4x²

  0 = 4x² - 68x + 120

  0 = x² - 17x + 30

  0 = (x - 15)(x - 2)

x - 15 = 0 or x - 2 = 0

    x = 15 or   x = 2

We see that 15 is not a solution because when x = 15, 20 - 2x = -10 and 14 - 2x = -16, and the length and width of the frame cannot be negative. Let's check 2. When x = 2, 20 - 2x = 16, 14 - 2x = 10 and 16·10 = 160. The area is 160. The value checks.

The width of the frame is 2 in.

23. We make a drawing and label it.

We let x represent the length of the rectangle. Then x - 4 represents the width.

   A = ℓ·w

 12 = x(x - 4)   (Substituting)

We solve the equation.

 12 = x² - 4x

  0 = x² - 4x - 12

  0 = (x - 6)(x + 2)

x - 6 = 0 or x + 2 = 0

    x = 6 or   x = -2

23. (continued)

We only check 6 since the length of a rectangle cannot be negative. If x = 6, then x - 4 = 2 and the area is 6·2, or 12. The value checks.

The length is 6 ft, and the width is 2 ft.

25. We first make a drawing and label it.

We let x represent the width of the rectangle. Then 2x represents the length.

   A = ℓ·w

288 = 2x·x   (Substituting)

We solve the equation.

288 = 2x²

144 = x²

x = 12 or x = -12

We only check 12 since the width of a rectangle cannot be negative. If x = 12, then 2x = 24 and the area is 24·12, or 288. The value checks.

The length is 24 yd, and the width is 12 yd.

27. We first make a drawing.

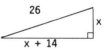

We let x represent the shorter leg. Then x + 14 represents the longer leg. We use the Pythagorean property.

      a² + b² = c²

(x + 14)² + x² = 26²   (Substituting)

We solve the equation.

x² + 28x + 196 + x² = 676

   2x² + 28x - 480 = 0

    x² + 14x - 240 = 0

  (x - 10)(x + 24) = 0

x - 10 = 0 or x + 24 = 0

    x = 10 or   x = -24

We only check 10 since the length of a leg cannot be negative. If x = 10, then x + 14 = 24.

a² + b² =	c²
24² + 10²	26²
576 + 100	676
676	

The lengths check. The lengths of the legs are 24 ft and 10 ft.

29. We first make a drawing.

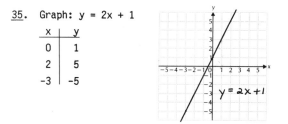

We let x represent the longer leg. Then x - 1 represents the shorter leg. We use the Pythagorean property.

$$a^2 + b^2 = c^2$$
$$x^2 + (x - 1)^2 = 5^2 \qquad \text{(Substituting)}$$

We solve the equation.

$$x^2 + x^2 - 2x + 1 = 25$$
$$2x^2 - 2x - 24 = 0$$
$$x^2 - x - 12 = 0$$
$$(x - 4)(x + 3) = 0$$

$$x - 4 = 0 \text{ or } x + 3 = 0$$
$$x = 4 \text{ or } \qquad x = -3$$

We only check 4 since the length of a leg cannot be negative. If x = 4, then x - 1 = 3.

$a^2 + b^2 = c^2$	
$4^2 + 3^2$	5^2
$16 + 9$	25
25	

The lengths check. The lengths of the legs are 4 ft and 3 ft.

31. $s = 16t^2$

$s = 16(2)^2 \qquad$ (Substituting 2)

$s = 16 \cdot 4$

$s = 64$

The object will fall 64 ft in 2 seconds.

33. $\quad s = 16t^2$

$1377 = 16t^2 \qquad$ (Substituting 1377)

$\dfrac{1377}{16} = t^2$

$\sqrt{\dfrac{1377}{16}} = t$

$\dfrac{\sqrt{1377}}{4} = t$

$9.3 \approx t$

It will take 9.3 seconds for an object to fall from the top.

35. Graph: y = 2x + 1

x	y
0	1
2	5
-3	-5

37. $14 - \sqrt{88} \approx 14 - 9.3808 \approx 4.6$

39. $25.55x^2 - 1635.2 = 0$

$\quad 25.55x^2 = 1635.2$

$\quad x^2 = \dfrac{1635.2}{25.55}$

$\quad x^2 = 64$

$\quad x = \pm 8$

41. $x(2x^2 + 9x - 56)(3x + 10) = 0$

$x(2x - 7)(x + 8)(3x + 10) = 0$

$x = 0 \text{ or } 2x - 7 = 0 \text{ or } x + 8 = 0 \text{ or } 3x + 10 = 0$

$x = 0 \text{ or } \quad x = \dfrac{7}{2} \text{ or } \quad x = -8 \text{ or } \quad x = -\dfrac{10}{3}$

The solutions are -8, $-\dfrac{10}{3}$, 0, and $\dfrac{7}{2}$.

43. It is helpful to list information in a chart and make a drawing.

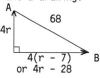

Boat	r	t	d
A	r	4	4r
B	r - 7	4	4(r - 7)

We use the Pythagorean property: $a^2 + b^2 = c^2$

$$(4r - 28)^2 + (4r)^2 = 68^2$$
$$16r^2 - 224r + 784 + 16r^2 = 4624$$
$$32r^2 - 224r - 3840 = 0$$
$$r^2 - 7r - 120 = 0$$
$$(r + 8)(r - 15) = 0$$

$r + 8 = 0 \text{ or } r - 15 = 0$

$r = -8 \text{ or } \qquad r = 15$

We only check r = 15 since the speeds of the boats cannot be negative. If the speed of Boat A is 15 km/h, then the speed of Boat B is 15 - 7, or 8 km/h, and the distances they travel are 4·15 (or 60) and 4·8 (or 32).

$$60^2 + 32^2 = 68^2$$
$$3600 + 1024 = 4624$$
$$4624 = 4624$$

The values check. The speed of Boat A is 15 km/h, and the speed of Boat B is 8 km/h.

Exercise Set 8.2

1. $x^2 + 6x + 4 = 0$

$a = 1, \quad b = 6, \quad c = 4$

$x = \dfrac{-b \pm \sqrt{b^2 - 4ac}}{2a}$

$x = \dfrac{-6 \pm \sqrt{6^2 - 4 \cdot 1 \cdot 4}}{2 \cdot 1} = \dfrac{-6 \pm \sqrt{36 - 16}}{2}$

$= \dfrac{-6 \pm \sqrt{20}}{2} = \dfrac{-6 \pm 2\sqrt{5}}{2}$

$= \dfrac{2(-3 \pm \sqrt{5})}{2} = -3 \pm \sqrt{5}$

3. $\qquad 3p^2 = -8p - 5$

$\qquad 3p^2 + 8p + 5 = 0$

$\qquad (3p + 5)(p + 1) = 0$

$3p + 5 = 0 \quad$ or $p + 1 = 0$

$p = -\dfrac{5}{3}$ or $\qquad p = -1$

The solutions are $-\dfrac{5}{3}$ and -1.

5. $x^2 - x + 1 = 0$

$a = 1, \quad b = -1, \quad c = 1$

$x = \dfrac{-(-1) \pm \sqrt{(-1)^2 - 4 \cdot 1 \cdot 1}}{2 \cdot 1} = \dfrac{1 \pm \sqrt{1 - 4}}{2}$

$= \dfrac{1 \pm \sqrt{-3}}{2} = \dfrac{1 \pm i\sqrt{3}}{2}$

7. $\qquad x^2 + 13 = 4x$

$x^2 - 4x + 13 = 0$

$a = 1, \quad b = -4, \quad c = 13$

$x = \dfrac{-(-4) \pm \sqrt{(-4)^2 - 4 \cdot 1 \cdot 13}}{2 \cdot 1} = \dfrac{4 \pm \sqrt{16 - 52}}{2}$

$= \dfrac{4 \pm \sqrt{-36}}{2} = \dfrac{4 \pm 6i}{2} = 2 \pm 3i$

9. $\qquad r^2 + 3r = 8$

$r^2 + 3r - 8 = 0$

$a = 1, \quad b = 3, \quad c = -8$

$r = \dfrac{-3 \pm \sqrt{3^2 - 4 \cdot 1 \cdot (-8)}}{2 \cdot 1} = \dfrac{-3 \pm \sqrt{9 + 32}}{2}$

$= \dfrac{-3 \pm \sqrt{41}}{2}$

11. $1 + \dfrac{2}{x} + \dfrac{5}{x^2} = 0$

$x^2 + 2x + 5 = 0$

$\qquad$ (Multiplying by the LCM, x^2)

$a = 1, \quad b = 2, \quad c = 5$

$x = \dfrac{-2 \pm \sqrt{2^2 - 4 \cdot 1 \cdot 5}}{2 \cdot 1} = \dfrac{-2 \pm \sqrt{4 - 20}}{2}$

$= \dfrac{-2 \pm \sqrt{-16}}{2} = \dfrac{-2 \pm 4i}{2} = -1 \pm 2i$

13. $\qquad 3x + x(x - 2) = 0$

$\qquad 3x + x^2 - 2x = 0$

$\qquad x^2 + x = 0$

$\qquad x(x + 1) = 0$

$x = 0$ or $x + 1 = 0$

$x = 0$ or $\qquad x = -1$

The solutions are 0 and -1.

15. $\qquad (2t - 3)^2 + 17t = 15$

$4t^2 - 12t + 9 + 17t = 15$

$\qquad 4t^2 + 5t - 6 = 0$

$\qquad (4t - 3)(t + 2) = 0$

$4t - 3 = 0$ or $t + 2 = 0$

$t = \dfrac{3}{4}$ or $\qquad t = -2$

The solutions are $\dfrac{3}{4}$ and -2.

17. $\qquad (x - 2)^2 + (x + 1)^2 = 0$

$x^2 - 4x + 4 + x^2 + 2x + 1 = 0$

$\qquad 2x^2 - 2x + 5 = 0$

$a = 2, \quad b = -2, \quad c = 5$

$x = \dfrac{-(-2) \pm \sqrt{(-2)^2 - 4 \cdot 2 \cdot 5}}{2 \cdot 2} = \dfrac{2 \pm \sqrt{4 - 40}}{4}$

$= \dfrac{2 \pm \sqrt{-36}}{4} = \dfrac{2 \pm 6i}{4}$

$= \dfrac{2(1 \pm 3i)}{2 \cdot 2} = \dfrac{1 \pm 3i}{2}$

19. $\qquad x^3 - 8 = 0$

$\qquad x^3 - 2^3 = 0$

$(x - 2)(x^2 + 2x + 4) = 0$

$x - 2 = 0$ or $x^2 + 2x + 4 = 0$

$x = 2$ or $x = \dfrac{-2 \pm \sqrt{2^2 - 4 \cdot 1 \cdot 4}}{2 \cdot 1}$

$= \dfrac{-2 \pm \sqrt{-12}}{2} = \dfrac{-2 \pm 2i\sqrt{3}}{2}$

$= \dfrac{-2 \pm 2i\sqrt{3}}{2}$

$= -1 \pm i\sqrt{3}$

The solutions are 2, and $-1 \pm i\sqrt{3}$.

21. $x^2 + 4x - 7 = 0$

a = 1,   b = 4,   c = -7

$$x = \frac{-4 \pm \sqrt{4^2 - 4 \cdot 1 \cdot (-7)}}{2 \cdot 1} = \frac{-4 \pm \sqrt{16 + 28}}{2}$$

$$= \frac{-4 \pm \sqrt{44}}{2} = \frac{-4 \pm 2\sqrt{11}}{2} = -2 \pm \sqrt{11}$$

Using a calculator we find that $\sqrt{11} \approx 3.317$.

$-2 + \sqrt{11} \approx -2 + 3.317 \approx 1.317 \approx 1.3$

$-2 - \sqrt{11} \approx -2 - 3.317 \approx -5.317 \approx -5.3$

The solutions are approximately 1.3 and -5.3.

23. $2x^2 - 3x - 7 = 0$

a = 2,   b = -3,   c = -7

$$x = \frac{-(-3) \pm \sqrt{(-3)^2 - 4 \cdot 2 \cdot (-7)}}{2 \cdot 2} = \frac{3 \pm \sqrt{9 + 56}}{4}$$

$$= \frac{3 \pm \sqrt{65}}{4}$$

Using a calculator we find that $\sqrt{65} \approx 8.062$.

$$\frac{3 + \sqrt{65}}{4} \approx \frac{3 + 8.062}{4} \approx \frac{11.062}{4} \approx 2.7655 \approx 2.8$$

$$\frac{3 - \sqrt{65}}{4} \approx \frac{3 - 8.062}{4} \approx \frac{-5.062}{4} \approx -1.2655 \approx -1.3$$

The solutions are approximately 2.8 and -1.3.

25. We let x represent the number of pounds of the $1.50 per pound kind and y represent the number of pounds of the $2.50 per pound kind. We organize the information in a table.

Coffee	Price per pound	Number of pounds	Total cost
A	$1.50	x	$1.50x
B	$2.50	y	$2.50y
Blend	$1.90	50	1.90 × 50, or $95

From the table we get the following system of equations.

x + y = 50   and   1.50x + 2.50y = 95

or

15x + 25y = 950

or

3x + 5y = 190

25. (continued)

We solve the system.

-3x - 3y = -150   (Multiplying the first equation by -3)

$\underline{3x + 5y = 190}$

2y = 40   (Adding)

y = 20

We substitute 20 for y in one of the original equations and solve for x.

x + y = 50

x + 20 = 50

x = 30

The total number of pounds in the blend is 30 + 20, or 50. The total cost of the blend is 1.50(30) + 2.50(20), or 45 + 50, or $95. The values check.

The blend consists of 30 pounds of Coffee A and 20 pounds of Coffee B.

27. $5.33x^2 - 8.23x - 3.24 = 0$

$533x^2 - 823x - 324 = 0$

(Multiplying by 100)

a = 533,   b = -823,   c = -324

$$x = \frac{-(-823) \pm \sqrt{(-823)^2 - 4(533)(-324)}}{2 \cdot 533}$$

$$= \frac{823 \pm \sqrt{677,329 + 690,768}}{1066}$$

$$= \frac{823 \pm \sqrt{1,368,097}}{1066}$$

$$\approx \frac{823 \pm 1169.657}{1066}$$

$$x \approx \frac{823 + 1169.657}{1066} \text{ or } x \approx \frac{823 - 1169.657}{1066}$$

$$x \approx 1.869 \qquad \text{or } x \approx -0.325$$

29. $2x^2 - x - \sqrt{5} = 0$

a = 2,   b = -1,   c = $-\sqrt{5}$

$$x = \frac{-(-1) \pm \sqrt{(-1)^2 - 4(2)(-\sqrt{5})}}{2 \cdot 2}$$

$$= \frac{1 \pm \sqrt{1 + 8\sqrt{5}}}{4}$$

31. $ix^2 - x - 1 = 0$

$a = i$, $b = -1$, $c = -1$

$x = \dfrac{-(-1) \pm \sqrt{(-1)^2 - 4(i)(-1)}}{2i}$

$= \dfrac{1 \pm \sqrt{1 + 4i}}{2i}$

$= \dfrac{1 \pm \sqrt{1 + 4i}}{2i} \cdot \dfrac{i}{i}$

$= \dfrac{i \pm i\sqrt{1 + 4i}}{2i^2}$

$= \dfrac{-i \pm i\sqrt{1 + 4i}}{2}$ $(2i^2 = -2)$

Exercise Set 8.3

1. $\dfrac{1}{x} = \dfrac{x - 2}{24}$,   LCM = 24x

$24x \cdot \dfrac{1}{x} = 24x \cdot \dfrac{x - 2}{24}$

$24 = x(x - 2)$

$0 = x^2 - 2x - 24$

$0 = (x - 6)(x + 4)$

$x - 6 = 0$ or $x + 4 = 0$

$x = 6$ or $x = -4$

Check:

$\dfrac{1}{x} = \dfrac{x-2}{24}$	
$\dfrac{1}{6}$	$\dfrac{6 - 2}{24}$
	$\dfrac{4}{24}$
	$\dfrac{1}{6}$

$\dfrac{1}{x} = \dfrac{x-2}{24}$	
$\dfrac{1}{-4}$	$\dfrac{-4 - 2}{24}$
$-\dfrac{1}{4}$	$-\dfrac{6}{24}$
	$-\dfrac{1}{4}$

The solutions are 6 and -4.

3. $\dfrac{1}{2x - 1} - \dfrac{1}{2x + 1} = \dfrac{1}{4}$

LCM = $4(2x - 1)(2x + 1)$

$4(2x-1)(2x+1)\left(\dfrac{1}{2x - 1} - \dfrac{1}{2x + 1}\right) = 4(2x-1)(2x+1) \cdot \dfrac{1}{4}$

$4(2x + 1) - 4(2x - 1) = (2x - 1)(2x + 1)$

$8x + 4 - 8x + 4 = 4x^2 - 1$

$8 = 4x^2 - 1$

$9 = 4x^2$

$\dfrac{9}{4} = x^2$

$x = \dfrac{3}{2}$ or $x = -\dfrac{3}{2}$

Both numbers check. The solutions are $\dfrac{3}{2}$ and $-\dfrac{3}{2}$.

5. $\dfrac{50}{x} - \dfrac{50}{x - 5} = -\dfrac{1}{2}$,   LCM = 2x(x - 5)

$2x(x - 5)\left(\dfrac{50}{x} - \dfrac{50}{x - 5}\right) = 2x(x - 5)\left(-\dfrac{1}{2}\right)$

$100(x - 5) - 100x = -x(x - 5)$

$100x - 500 - 100x = -x^2 + 5x$

$x^2 - 5x - 500 = 0$

$(x - 25)(x + 20) = 0$

$x - 25 = 0$ or $x + 20 = 0$

$x = 25$ or $x = -20$

Both numbers check. The solutions are 25 and -20.

7. $\dfrac{x + 2}{x} = \dfrac{x - 1}{2}$,   LCM = 2x

$2x \cdot \dfrac{x + 2}{x} = 2x \cdot \dfrac{x - 1}{2}$

$2(x + 2) = x(x - 1)$

$2x + 4 = x^2 - x$

$0 = x^2 - 3x - 4$

$0 = (x - 4)(x + 1)$

$x - 4 = 0$ or $x + 1 = 0$

$x = 4$ or $x = -1$

Both numbers check. The solutions are 4 and -1.

9. $x - 6 = \dfrac{1}{x + 6}$,   LCM = x + 6

$(x + 6)(x - 6) = (x + 6) \cdot \dfrac{1}{x + 6}$

$x^2 - 36 = 1$

$x^2 = 37$

$x = \sqrt{37}$ or $x = -\sqrt{37}$

Both numbers check. The solutions are $\pm\sqrt{37}$.

11. We first make a drawing.

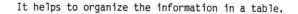

r mph t hours	r - 5 mph 3 - t hours
80 mi	35 mi
First part	Second part

It helps to organize the information in a table.

Canoe trip	Distance	Speed	Time
1st part	80	r	t
2nd part	35	r - 5	3 - t

11. (continued)

We let r represent the speed of the first part. Then r - 5 represents the speed of the second part. We let t represent the time for the first part. Then 3 - t represents the time for the second part.

Using $r = \frac{d}{t}$, we get two equations from the table.

$$r = \frac{80}{t} \quad \text{and} \quad r - 5 = \frac{35}{3 - t}$$

We substitute $\frac{80}{t}$ for r in the second equation and solve for t.

$$\frac{80}{t} - 5 = \frac{35}{3 - t} , \quad \text{LCM} = t(3 - t)$$

$$t(3 - t)(\frac{80}{t} - 5) = t(3 - t) \cdot \frac{35}{3 - t}$$

$$80(3 - t) - 5t(3 - t) = 35t$$

$$240 - 80t - 15t + 5t^2 = 35t$$

$$240 - 95t + 5t^2 = 35t$$

$$5t^2 - 130t + 240 = 0$$

$$t^2 - 26t + 48 = 0$$

$$(t - 24)(t - 2) = 0$$

$$t - 24 = 0 \text{ or } t - 2 = 0$$

$$t = 24 \text{ or } \qquad t = 2$$

Since the time cannot be negative (If t = 24, 3 - t = -21.), we only check 2 hr. If t = 2, then 3 - t = 1. The speed of the first part is $\frac{80}{2}$, or 40 mph. The speed of the second part is $\frac{35}{1}$, or 35 mph. The speed of the second part is 5 mph slower than the first part. The value checks.

The speed of the first part was 40 mph, and the speed of the second part was 35 mph.

13. We first make a drawing.

280 mi   r mph   t hours

280 mi   r + 5 mph   t - 1 hours

We organize the information in a table.

Trip	Distance	Speed	Time
Slow	280	r	t
Fast	280	r + 5	t - 1

13. (continued)

We let r represent the speed of the slower trip. Then r + 5 represents the speed of the faster trip. We let t represent the time for the slower trip. Then t - 1 represents the time for the faster trip.

Using $r = \frac{d}{t}$, we get two equations from the table.

$$t = \frac{280}{r} \quad \text{and} \quad t - 1 = \frac{280}{r + 5}$$

We substitute $\frac{280}{r}$ for t in the second equation and solve for r.

$$\frac{280}{r} - 1 = \frac{280}{r + 5} , \quad \text{LCM} = r(r + 5)$$

$$r(r + 5)(\frac{280}{r} - 1) = r(r + 5) \cdot \frac{280}{r + 5}$$

$$280(r + 5) - r(r + 5) = 280r$$

$$280r + 1400 - r^2 - 5r = 280r$$

$$275r + 1400 - r^2 = 280r$$

$$0 = r^2 + 5r - 1400$$

$$0 = (r - 35)(r + 40)$$

$$r - 35 = 0 \text{ or } r + 40 = 0$$

$$r = 35 \text{ or } \qquad r = -40$$

Since negative speed has no meaning in this problem, we only check 35. If r = 35, then the time for the slow trip is $\frac{280}{35}$, or 8 hours. If r = 35, then r + 5 = 40 and the time for the fast trip is $\frac{280}{40}$, or 7 hours. This is 1 hour less time than the slow trip took, so we have an answer to the problem.

The speed is 35 mph.

15. We make a drawing and then organize the information in a table.

A   2800 km   r km/h   t hours

B   2000 km   r + 50 km/h   t - 3 hours

Plane	Distance	Rate	Time
A	2800	r	t
B	2000	r + 50	t - 3

15. (continued)

We let r represent the speed of Plane A. Then r + 50 represents the speed of Plane B. We let t represent the time of Plane A. Then t - 3 represents the time of Plane B.

Using $r = \frac{d}{t}$, we get two equations from the table.

$$r = \frac{2800}{t} \quad \text{and} \quad r + 50 = \frac{2000}{t - 3}$$

We substitute $\frac{2800}{t}$ for r in the second equation and solve for t.

$$\frac{2800}{t} + 50 = \frac{2000}{t - 3}, \text{ LCM} = t(t - 3)$$

$$t(t - 3)(\frac{2800}{t} + 50) = t(t - 3) \cdot \frac{2000}{t - 3}$$

$$2800(t - 3) + 50t(t - 3) = 2000t$$

$$2800t - 8400 + 50t^2 - 150t = 2000t$$

$$2650t - 8400 + 50t^2 = 2000t$$

$$50t^2 + 650t - 8400 = 0$$

$$t^2 + 13t - 168 = 0$$

$$(t + 21)(t - 8) = 0$$

$$t + 21 = 0 \quad \text{or} \quad t - 8 = 0$$
$$t = -21 \quad \text{or} \quad t = 8$$

Since negative time has no meaning in this problem, we only check 8 hours. If t = 8, then t - 3 = 5. The speed of Plane A is $\frac{2800}{8}$, or 350 km/h. The speed of Plane B is $\frac{2000}{5}$, or 400 km/h. Since the speed of Plane B is 50 km/h faster then the speed of Plane A, the value checks.

The speed of Plane A is 350 km/h; the speed of Plane B is 400 km/h.

17. Let x represent the time it takes the smaller pipe to fill the tank. Then x - 3 represents the time it takes the larger pipe to fill the tank. It takes them 2 hr to fill the tank when both pipes are working together, so they can fill $\frac{1}{2}$ of the tank in 1 hr. The smaller pipe will fill $\frac{1}{x}$ of the tank in 1 hr, and the larger pipe will fill $\frac{1}{x - 3}$ of the tank in 1 hr.

We have an equation.

$$\frac{1}{x} + \frac{1}{x - 3} = \frac{1}{2}$$

17. (continued)

We solve the equation.
We multiply by the LCM which is 2x(x - 3).

$$2x(x - 3)(\frac{1}{x} + \frac{1}{x - 3}) = 2x(x - 3) \cdot \frac{1}{2}$$

$$2(x - 3) + 2x = x(x - 3)$$

$$2x - 6 + 2x = x^2 - 3x$$

$$0 = x^2 - 7x + 6$$

$$0 = (x - 6)(x - 1)$$

$$x - 6 = 0 \text{ or } x - 1 = 0$$
$$x = 6 \text{ or } \quad x = 1$$

Since negative time has no meaning in this problem, 1 is not a solution (1 - 3 = -2). We only check 6 hr. This is the time it would take the smaller pipe working alone. Then the larger pipe would take 6 - 3, or 3 hr working alone. The larger pipe would fill $2(\frac{1}{6})$, or $\frac{1}{3}$, of the tank in 2 hr, and the smaller pipe would fill $2(\frac{1}{3})$, or $\frac{2}{3}$, of the tank in 2 hr. Thus in 2 hr they would fill $\frac{1}{3} + \frac{2}{3}$ of the tank. This is all of it, so the numbers check.

It takes the smaller pipe, working alone, 6 hours to fill the tank.

19. We first make a drawing.

Upstream

    1 km   r - 2 km/h
●————————————————————————————>

                        Downstream
    r + 2 km/h   1 km
<————————————————————————————●

We organize the information in a table.

Trip	Distance	Speed	Time
Upstream	1	r - 2	$\frac{1}{r - 2}$
Downstream	1	r + 2	$\frac{1}{r + 2}$

19. (continued)

We let r represent the speed of the boat in still water. Then r - 2 is the speed upstream and r + 2 is the speed downstream. Using $t = \frac{d}{r}$, we let $\frac{1}{r-2}$ represent the time upstream and $\frac{1}{r+2}$ represent the time downstream.

The time for the round trip is 1 hour. We now have an equation.

$$\frac{1}{r-2} + \frac{1}{r+2} = 1$$

We solve the equation.
We multiply by the LCM, (r - 2)(r + 2).

$$(r-2)(r+2)\left(\frac{1}{r-2} + \frac{1}{r+2}\right) = (r-2)(r+2) \cdot 1$$
$$(r+2) + (r-2) = (r-2)(r+2)$$
$$2r = r^2 - 4$$
$$0 = r^2 - 2r - 4$$

a = 1,   b = -2,   c = -4

$$r = \frac{-(-2) \pm \sqrt{(-2)^2 - 4 \cdot 1 \cdot (-4)}}{2 \cdot 1}$$

$$= \frac{2 \pm \sqrt{4 + 16}}{2} = \frac{2 \pm \sqrt{20}}{2}$$

$$= \frac{2 \pm 2\sqrt{5}}{2} = 1 \pm \sqrt{5}$$

$$1 + \sqrt{5} \approx 1 + 2.236 \approx 3.24$$

$$1 - \sqrt{5} \approx 1 - 2.236 \approx -1.24$$

Since negative speed has no meaning in this problem, we only check 3.24 km/h. If r = 3.24, then r - 2 = 1.24 and r + 2 = 5.24. The time it takes to travel upstream is $\frac{1}{1.24}$, or 0.806 hr, and the time it takes to travel downstream is $\frac{1}{5.24}$, or 0.191 hr. The total time is 0.997 which is approximately 1 hour. The value checks.

The speed of the boat in still water is approximately 3.24 km/h.

21.
$$\sqrt{3x + 1} = \sqrt{2x - 1} + 1$$
$$(\sqrt{3x + 1})^2 = (\sqrt{2x - 1} + 1)^2$$
$$3x + 1 = 2x - 1 + 2\sqrt{2x - 1} + 1$$
$$x + 1 = 2\sqrt{2x - 1}$$
$$(x + 1)^2 = (2\sqrt{2x - 1})^2$$
$$x^2 + 2x + 1 = 4(2x - 1)$$
$$x^2 + 2x + 1 = 8x - 4$$
$$x^2 - 6x + 5 = 0$$
$$(x - 5)(x - 1) = 0$$
$$x - 5 = 0 \text{ or } x - 1 = 0$$
$$x = 5 \text{ or } \quad x = 1$$

The solutions are 5 and 1.

23. $\sqrt[3]{18y^3} \; \sqrt[3]{4x^2}$

$$= \sqrt[3]{72y^3x^2}$$

$$= \sqrt[3]{8 \cdot 9 \cdot y^3 \cdot x^2}$$

$$= 2y \sqrt[3]{9x^2}$$

25. Let x represent the time it takes for Chester to do the job alone. Then x - 1.2 represents the time it takes for Ron to do the job alone. Together it takes them 1.8 hours to complete the job. We now have two expressions for the amount of the job they get done in one hour,

$$\frac{1}{x} + \frac{1}{x - 1.2} \quad \text{and} \quad \frac{1}{1.8}.$$

We solve the following equation.

$$\frac{1}{x} + \frac{1}{x - 1.2} = \frac{1}{1.8}$$
$$1.8(x - 1.2) + 1.8x = x(x - 1.2)$$

[Multiplying by 1.8x(x - 1.2)]

$$1.8x - 2.16 + 1.8x = x^2 - 1.2x$$
$$3.6x - 2.16 = x^2 - 1.2x$$
$$0 = x^2 - 4.8x + 2.16$$
$$0 = 100x^2 - 480x + 216$$
$$0 = 25x^2 - 120x + 54$$

a = 25,   b = -20,   c = 54

$$x = \frac{-(-120) \pm \sqrt{(-120)^2 - 4(25)(54)}}{2 \cdot 25}$$

$$= \frac{120 \pm \sqrt{14,400 - 5400}}{50}$$

$$= \frac{120 \pm \sqrt{9000}}{50} = \frac{120 \pm 30\sqrt{10}}{50}$$

$$= \frac{10(12 \pm 3\sqrt{10})}{10 \cdot 5} = \frac{12 \pm 3\sqrt{10}}{5}$$

$$\approx \frac{12 \pm 3(3.16)}{5} \approx \frac{12 \pm 9.48}{5}$$

$$x \approx \frac{12 + 9.48}{5} \text{ or } x \approx \frac{12 - 9.48}{5}$$

$$x \approx 4.3 \qquad \text{or } x \approx 0.5$$

We only check 4.3 since 0.5 results in negative time for Ron (0.5 - 1.2 = -0.7). If x = 4.3, then x - 1.2 = 3.1. These values do check. Thus, it takes Chester 4.3 hours to complete the job alone, and it takes Ron 3.1 hours.

27. $\dfrac{x^2}{x-2} - \dfrac{x+4}{2} + \dfrac{2-4x}{x-2} + 1 = 0$

We multiply by $2(x-2)$ the LCM of the denominators.

$2(x^2) - (x-2)(x+4) + 2(2-4x) + 2(x-2) = 0$

$2x^2 - (x^2 + 2x - 8) + (4 - 8x) + (2x - 4) = 0$

$2x^2 - x^2 - 2x + 8 + 4 - 8x + 2x - 4 = 0$

$x^2 - 8x + 8 = 0$

$a = 1, \quad b = -8, \quad c = 8$

$x = \dfrac{-(-8) \pm \sqrt{(-8)^2 - 4\cdot 1\cdot 8}}{2\cdot 1} = \dfrac{8 \pm \sqrt{64 - 32}}{2}$

$= \dfrac{8 \pm \sqrt{32}}{2} = \dfrac{8 \pm 4\sqrt{2}}{2}$

$= \dfrac{2(4 \pm 2\sqrt{2})}{2} = 4 \pm 2\sqrt{2}$

29. The reicprocal of $a - 1$ is $a + 1$.

$\dfrac{1}{a-1} = a + 1$

$\dfrac{1}{a-1} = a + 1, \quad$ LCM $= a - 1$

$1 = (a-1)(a+1)$

$1 = a^2 - 1$

$2 = a^2$

$\pm\sqrt{2} = a$

Exercise Set 8.4

1. $x^2 - 6x + 9 = 0$

   $a = 1, \quad b = -6, \quad c = 9$

   We compute the discriminant.

   $b^2 - 4ac = (-6)^2 - 4\cdot 1\cdot 9$

   $= 36 - 36$

   $= 0$

   Since $b^2 - 4ac = 0$, there is just one solution, and it is a real number.

3. $x^2 + 7 = 0$

   $a = 1, \quad b = 0, \quad c = 7$

   We compute the discriminant.

   $b^2 - 4ac = 0^2 - 4\cdot 1\cdot 7$

   $= -28$

   Since $b^2 - 4ac < 0$, there are two nonreal solutions.

5. $x^2 - 2 = 0$

   $a = 1, \quad b = 0, \quad c = -2$

   We compute the discriminant.

   $b^2 - 4ac = 0^2 - 4\cdot 1\cdot (-2)$

   $= 8$

   Since $b^2 - 4ac > 0$, there are two real solutions.

7. $4x^2 - 12x + 9 = 0$

   $a = 4, \quad b = -12, \quad c = 9$

   We compute the discriminant.

   $b^2 - 4ac = (-12)^2 - 4\cdot 4\cdot 9$

   $= 144 - 144$

   $= 0$

   Since $b^2 - 4ac = 0$, there is just one solution, and it is a real number.

9. $x^2 - 2x + 4 = 0$

   $a = 1, \quad b = -2, \quad c = 4$

   We compute the discriminant.

   $b^2 - 4ac = (-2)^2 - 4\cdot 1\cdot 4$

   $= 4 - 16$

   $= -12$

   Since $b^2 - 4ac < 0$, there are two nonreal solutions.

11. $9t^2 - 3t = 0$

    $a = 9, \quad b = -3, \quad c = 0$

    We compute the discriminant.

    $b^2 - 4ac = (-3)^2 - 4\cdot 9\cdot 0$

    $= 9 - 0$

    $= 9$

    Since $b^2 - 4ac > 0$, there are two real solutions.

13. $y^2 = \dfrac{1}{2}y + \dfrac{3}{5}$

    $y^2 - \dfrac{1}{2}y - \dfrac{3}{5} = 0 \qquad$ (Standard form)

    $a = 1, \quad b = -\dfrac{1}{2}, \quad c = -\dfrac{3}{5}$

    We compute the discriminant.

    $b^2 - 4ac = (-\dfrac{1}{2})^2 - 4\cdot 1\cdot (-\dfrac{3}{5})$

    $= \dfrac{1}{4} + \dfrac{12}{5}$

    $= \dfrac{53}{20}$

    Since $b^2 - 4ac > 0$, there are two real solutions.

15. $4x^2 - 4\sqrt{3}x + 3 = 0$

$a = 4, \quad b = -4\sqrt{3}, \quad c = 3$

We compute the discriminant.

$b^2 - 4ac = (-4\sqrt{3})^2 - 4\cdot4\cdot3$

$\qquad\qquad = 48 - 48$

$\qquad\qquad = 0$

Since $b^2 - 4ac = 0$, there is just one solution, and it is a real number.

17. The solutions are -11 and 9.

$\qquad x = -11 \text{ or } \qquad x = 9$

$x + 11 = 0 \quad \text{or } x - 9 = 0$

$\qquad (x + 11)(x - 9) = 0 \qquad$ (Principle of zero products)

$\qquad\qquad x^2 + 2x - 99 = 0 \qquad$ (FOIL)

19. The only solution is 7. It must be a double solution.

$\qquad x = 7 \text{ or } \qquad x = 7$

$x - 7 = 0 \text{ or } x - 7 = 0$

$\qquad (x - 7)(x - 7) = 0 \qquad$ (Principle of zero products)

$\qquad\qquad x^2 - 14x + 49 = 0 \qquad$ (FOIL)

21. The solutions are $-\frac{2}{5}$ and $\frac{6}{5}$.

$\qquad x = -\frac{2}{5} \text{ or } \qquad x = \frac{6}{5}$

$x + \frac{2}{5} = 0 \quad \text{or } x - \frac{6}{5} = 0$

$\qquad (x + \frac{2}{5})(x - \frac{6}{5}) = 0 \qquad$ (Principle of zero products)

$\qquad x^2 - \frac{4}{5}x - \frac{12}{25} = 0 \qquad$ (FOIL)

$\qquad 25x^2 - 20x - 12 = 0 \qquad$ (Multiplying by 25)

23. The solutions are $\frac{c}{2}$ and $\frac{d}{2}$.

$\qquad x = \frac{c}{2} \text{ or } \qquad x = \frac{d}{2}$

$\qquad x - \frac{c}{2} = 0 \text{ or } x - \frac{d}{2} = 0$

$\qquad (x - \frac{c}{2})(x - \frac{d}{2}) = 0$

$\qquad x^2 - \frac{d}{2}x - \frac{c}{2}x + \frac{cd}{4} = 0$

or $\qquad x^2 - \frac{d + c}{2}x + \frac{cd}{4} = 0$

or $4x^2 - 2(c + d)x + cd = 0$

25. The solutions are $\sqrt{2}$ and $3\sqrt{2}$.

$\qquad x = \sqrt{2} \text{ or } \qquad x = 3\sqrt{2}$

$x - \sqrt{2} = 0 \quad \text{or } x - 3\sqrt{2} = 0$

$\qquad (x - \sqrt{2})(x - 3\sqrt{2}) = 0$

$\qquad\qquad x^2 - 4\sqrt{2}x + 6 = 0$

27. Let x represent the number of 30-second commercials and y represent the number of 60-second commercials. We organize the information in a chart.

Commercial	Number	Amt. of time
30-second	x	30x seconds
60-second	y	60y seconds

The total number of commercials is 12.

$x + y = 12$

The amount of time for the 30-second commercials (30x seconds) is 6 minutes (or 360 seconds) less than the total amount of time for all 12 commercials (30x + 60y seconds).

$30x = (30x + 60y) - 360$

$360 = 60y$

$\quad 6 = y$

The resulting system is

$x + y = 12$

$y = 6$

Substituting 6 for y, we get $x = 6$.

The values check. The TV show contained six 30-second commercials and six 60-second commercials.

29. $ax^2 + bx + c = 0$

The solutions are $x = \dfrac{-b \pm \sqrt{b^2 - 4ac}}{2a}$.

The product of the solutions is

$\left(\dfrac{-b + \sqrt{b^2 - 4ac}}{2a}\right)\left(\dfrac{-b - \sqrt{b^2 - 4ac}}{2a}\right)$

$= \dfrac{(-b)^2 - (\sqrt{b^2 - 4ac})^2}{(2a)^2}$

$= \dfrac{b^2 - (b^2 - 4ac)}{4a^2}$

$= \dfrac{4ac}{4a^2}$

$= \dfrac{c}{a}$

31. a) $kx^2 - 2x + k = 0$; one solution is -3

We first find k by substituting -3 for x.

$k(-3)^2 - 2(-3) + k = 0$

$9k + 6 + k = 0$

$10k = -6$

$k = -\dfrac{6}{10}$

$k = -\dfrac{3}{5}$

b) $-\dfrac{3}{5} x^2 - 2x + (-\dfrac{3}{5}) = 0$

$3x^2 + 10x + 3 = 0$

$(3x + 1)(x + 3) = 0$

$3x + 1 = 0$ or $x + 3 = 0$

$3x = -1$ or $x = -3$

$x = -\dfrac{1}{3}$ or $x = -3$

The other solution is $-\dfrac{1}{3}$.

33. For $ax^2 + bx + c = 0$, or $x^2 + \dfrac{b}{a} x + \dfrac{c}{a} = 0$, $-\dfrac{b}{a}$ is the sum of the solutions

and

$\dfrac{c}{a}$ is the product of the solutions.

Thus

$-\dfrac{b}{a} = \sqrt{3}$ and $\dfrac{c}{a} = 8$

$ax^2 + bx + c = 0$

$x^2 + \dfrac{b}{a} x + \dfrac{c}{a} = 0$ (Multiplying by $\dfrac{1}{a}$)

$x^2 - (-\dfrac{b}{a})x + \dfrac{c}{a} = 0$

$x^2 - \sqrt{3}x + 8 = 0$ (Substituting $\sqrt{3}$ for $-\dfrac{b}{a}$ and 8 for $\dfrac{c}{a}$)

Exercie Set 8.5

1. $A = 6s^2$

$\dfrac{A}{6} = s^2$

$\sqrt{\dfrac{A}{6}} = s$

3. $F = \dfrac{Gm_1 m_2}{r^2}$

$Fr^2 = Gm_1 m_2$

$r^2 = \dfrac{Gm_1 m_2}{F}$

$r = \sqrt{\dfrac{Gm_1 m_2}{F}}$

5. $E = mc^2$

$\dfrac{E}{m} = c^2$

$\sqrt{\dfrac{E}{m}} = c$

7. $a^2 + b^2 = c^2$

$b^2 = c^2 - a^2$

$b = \sqrt{c^2 - a^2}$

9. $N = \dfrac{k^2 - 3k}{2}$

$2N = k^2 - 3k$

$0 = k^2 - 3k - 2N$

$a = 1,$ $b = -3,$ $c = -2N$

$k = \dfrac{-(-3) \pm \sqrt{(-3)^2 - 4 \cdot 1 \cdot (-2N)}}{2 \cdot 1}$

$= \dfrac{3 \pm \sqrt{9 + 8N}}{2}$

Since taking the negative square root would result in a negative answer, we take the positive one.

$k = \dfrac{3 + \sqrt{9 + 8N}}{2}$

11. $A = 2\pi r^2 + 2\pi rh$

$0 = 2\pi r^2 + 2\pi rh - A$

$a = 2\pi,$ $b = 2\pi h,$ $c = -A$

$r = \dfrac{-2\pi h \pm \sqrt{(2\pi h)^2 - 4 \cdot 2\pi \cdot (-A)}}{2 \cdot 2\pi}$

$= \dfrac{-2\pi h \pm \sqrt{4\pi^2 h^2 + 8\pi A}}{4\pi}$

$= \dfrac{-2\pi h \pm 2\sqrt{\pi^2 h^2 + 2\pi A}}{4\pi}$

$= \dfrac{-\pi h \pm \sqrt{\pi^2 h^2 + 2\pi A}}{2\pi}$

Since taking the negative square root would result in a negative answer, we take the positive one.

$r = \dfrac{-\pi h + \sqrt{\pi^2 h^2 + 2\pi A}}{2\pi}$

13. $T = 2\pi \sqrt{\dfrac{\ell}{g}}$

$\dfrac{T}{2\pi} = \sqrt{\dfrac{\ell}{g}}$ (Multiplying by $\dfrac{1}{2\pi}$)

$\dfrac{T^2}{4\pi^2} = \dfrac{\ell}{g}$ (Squaring)

$gT^2 = 4\pi^2 \ell$ (Multiplying by $4\pi^2 g$)

$g = \dfrac{4\pi^2 \ell}{T^2}$ (Multiplying by $\dfrac{1}{T^2}$)

15.
$$P_1 - P_2 = \frac{32LV}{gD^2}$$
$$gD^2(P_1 - P_2) = 32LV$$
$$D^2 = \frac{32LV}{g(P_1 - P_2)}$$
$$D = \sqrt{\frac{32LV}{g(P_1 - P_2)}}$$

17.
$$m = \frac{m_0}{\sqrt{1 - \frac{v^2}{c^2}}}$$
$$m^2 = \frac{m_0^2}{1 - \frac{v^2}{c^2}}$$
$$m^2\left(1 - \frac{v^2}{c^2}\right) = m_0^2$$
$$m^2 - \frac{m^2v^2}{c^2} = m_0^2$$
$$m^2 - m_0^2 = \frac{m^2v^2}{c^2}$$
$$c^2(m^2 - m_0^2) = m^2v^2$$
$$\frac{c^2(m^2 - m_0^2)}{m^2} = v^2$$
$$\sqrt{\frac{c^2(m^2 - m_0^2)}{m^2}} = v$$
$$\frac{c}{m}\sqrt{m^2 - m_0^2} = v$$

19. $\sqrt{-20} = \sqrt{-1 \cdot 4 \cdot 5} = 2\sqrt{5}i$

21. Solve: $\sqrt{x^2} = -20$

There is no solution since $\sqrt{x^2}$ is always nonnegative.

Exercise Set 8.6

1. $x - 10\sqrt{x} + 9 = 0$

Let $u = \sqrt{x}$ and think of x as $(\sqrt{x})^2$.
  $u^2 - 10u + 9 = 0$ (Substituting u for $\sqrt{x}$)
  $(u - 9)(u - 1) = 0$

$u - 9 = 0$ or $u - 1 = 0$
  $u = 9$ or $u = 1$

Now we substitute $\sqrt{x}$ for u and solve these equations:

$\sqrt{x} = 9$ or $\sqrt{x} = 1$
  $x = 81$ or $x = 1$

The numbers 81 and 1 both check. They are the solutions.

3. $x^4 - 10x^2 + 25 = 0$

Let $u = x^2$ and think of x^4 as $(x^2)^2$.
  $u^2 - 10u + 25 = 0$ (Substituting u for x^2)
  $(u - 5)(u - 5) = 0$

$u - 5 = 0$ or $u - 5 = 0$
  $u = 5$ or $u = 5$

Now we substitute x^2 for u and solve the equation.
$x^2 = 5$

$x = \pm\sqrt{5}$

Both $\sqrt{5}$ and $-\sqrt{5}$ check. They are the solutions.

5. $(x^2 - 6x)^2 - 2(x^2 - 6x) - 35 = 0$

Let $u = x^2 - 6x$.
  $u^2 - 2u - 35 = 0$ (Substituting u for $x^2 - 6x$)
  $(u - 7)(u + 5) = 0$

$u - 7 = 0$ or $u + 5 = 0$
  $u = 7$ or $u = -5$

Now we substitute $x^2 - 6x$ for u and solve these equations.

$x^2 - 6x = 7$	or	$x^2 - 6x = -5$
$x^2 - 6x - 7 = 0$		$x^2 - 6x + 5 = 0$
$(x - 7)(x + 1) = 0$		$(x - 5)(x - 1) = 0$
$x - 7 = 0$ or $x + 1 = 0$		$x - 5 = 0$ or $x - 1 = 0$
$x = 7$ or $x = -1$		$x = 5$ or $x = 1$

The numbers -1, 1, 5, and 7 check. They are the solutions.

7. $(y^2 - 5y)^2 - 2(y^2 - 5y) - 24 = 0$

Let $u = y^2 - 5y$.
  $u^2 - 2u - 24 = 0$ (Substituting u for $y^2 - 5y$)
  $(u - 6)(u + 4) = 0$

$u - 6 = 0$ or $u + 4 = 0$
  $u = 6$ or $u = -4$

Now we substitute $y^2 - 5y$ for u and solve these equations.

$y^2 - 5y = 6$	or	$y^2 - 5y = -4$
$y^2 - 5y - 6 = 0$		$y^2 - 5y + 4 = 0$
$(y - 6)(y + 1) = 0$		$(y - 4)(y - 1) = 0$
$y - 6 = 0$ or $y + 1 = 0$		$y - 4 = 0$ or $y - 1 = 0$
$y = 6$ or $y = -1$		$y = 4$ or $y = 1$

The numbers -1, 1, 4, and 6 check. They are the solutions.

9. $w^4 - 4w^2 - 2 = 0$

Let $u = w^2$ and think of w^4 as $(w^2)^2$.

$u^2 - 4u - 2 = 0$ (Substituting u for w^2)

$$u = \frac{-(-4) \pm \sqrt{(-4)^2 - 4 \cdot 1 \cdot (-2)}}{2 \cdot 1}$$

$$= \frac{4 \pm \sqrt{16 + 8}}{2}$$

$$= \frac{4 \pm \sqrt{24}}{2}$$

$$= \frac{4 \pm 2\sqrt{6}}{2}$$

$$= 2 \pm \sqrt{6}$$

Now we substitute w^2 for u and solve these equations.

$w^2 = 2 + \sqrt{6}$ or $w^2 = 2 - \sqrt{6}$

$w = \pm\sqrt{2 + \sqrt{6}}$ or $w = \pm\sqrt{2 - \sqrt{6}}$

The numbers $\sqrt{2 + \sqrt{6}}$, $-\sqrt{2 + \sqrt{6}}$, $\sqrt{2 - \sqrt{6}}$, and $-\sqrt{2 - \sqrt{6}}$ check. They are the solutions. Note that $\sqrt{2 - \sqrt{6}}$ is nonreal.

11. $x^{-2} - x^{-1} - 6 = 0$

Let $u = x^{-1}$ and think of x^{-2} as $(x^{-1})^2$.

$u^2 - u - 6 = 0$ (Substituting u for x^{-1})

$(u - 3)(u + 2) = 0$

$u - 3 = 0$ or $u + 2 = 0$

$u = 3$ or $u = -2$

Now we substitute x^{-1} for u and solve these equations.

$x^{-1} = 3$ or $x^{-1} = -2$

$\frac{1}{x} = 3$ or $\frac{1}{x} = -2$

$x = \frac{1}{3}$ or $x = -\frac{1}{2}$

Both $\frac{1}{3}$ and $-\frac{1}{2}$ check. They are the solutions.

13. $2x^{-2} + x^{-1} - 1 = 0$

Let $u = x^{-1}$ and think of x^{-2} as $(x^{-1})^2$.

$2u^2 + u - 1 = 0$ (Substituting u for x^{-1})

$(2u - 1)(u + 1) = 0$

$2u - 1 = 0$ or $u + 1 = 0$

$2u = 1$ or $u = -1$

$u = \frac{1}{2}$ or $u = -1$

13. (continued)

Now we substitute x^{-1} for u and solve these equations.

$x^{-1} = \frac{1}{2}$ or $x^{-1} = -1$

$\frac{1}{x} = \frac{1}{2}$ or $\frac{1}{x} = -1$

$x = 2$ or $x = -1$

Both 2 and -1 check. They are the solutions.

15. $\sqrt{3x^2}\sqrt{3x^3} = \sqrt{9x^5} = \sqrt{9x^4 \cdot x} = 3x^2\sqrt{x}$

17. $\dfrac{x + 1}{x - 1} - \dfrac{x + 1}{x^2 + x + 1}$

LCM $= (x - 1)(x^2 + x + 1)$

$= \dfrac{x + 1}{x - 1} \cdot \dfrac{x^2 + x + 1}{x^2 + x + 1} - \dfrac{x + 1}{x^2 + x + 1} \cdot \dfrac{x - 1}{x - 1}$

$= \dfrac{(x^3 + 2x^2 + 2x + 1) - (x^2 - 1)}{(x - 1)(x^2 + x + 1)}$

$= \dfrac{x^3 + x^2 + 2x + 2}{x^3 - 1}$

19. $\pi x^4 - \pi^2 x^2 - \sqrt{99.3} = 0$

$a = \pi$, $b = -\pi^2$, $c = -\sqrt{99.3}$

$x^2 = \dfrac{-(-\pi^2) \pm \sqrt{(-\pi^2)^2 - 4\pi(-\sqrt{99.3})}}{2\pi}$

$x^2 = \dfrac{\pi^2 \pm \sqrt{\pi^4 + 4\pi\sqrt{99.3}}}{2\pi}$

$x^2 \approx \dfrac{9.8596 \pm \sqrt{97.2117 + 12.56(9.9649)}}{6.28}$

$x^2 \approx \dfrac{9.8596 \pm \sqrt{222.3708}}{6.28}$

$x^2 \approx \dfrac{9.8596 + 14.9121}{6.28}$ $(x^2 \geqslant 0)$

$x^2 \approx 3.9445$

$x \approx \pm 1.986$

21. $\left[\sqrt{\dfrac{x}{x - 3}}\right]^2 - 24 = 10\sqrt{\dfrac{x}{x - 3}}$

Let $u = \sqrt{\dfrac{x}{x - 3}}$ and substitute.

$u^2 - 24 = 10u$

$u^2 - 10u - 24 = 0$

$(u - 12)(u + 2) = 0$

$u - 12 = 0$ or $u + 2 = 0$

$u = 12$ or $u = -2$

<u>21.</u> (continued)

Now we substitute $\sqrt{\dfrac{x}{x-3}}$ for u and solve for x.

$$\sqrt{\dfrac{x}{x-3}} = 12 \qquad \text{or} \qquad \sqrt{\dfrac{x}{x-3}} = -2$$

$$\dfrac{x}{x-3} = 144$$

There is no real solution since principal square roots are never negative.

$$x = 144x - 432$$
$$432 = 143x$$
$$\dfrac{432}{143} = x$$

The number $\dfrac{432}{143}$ checks. It is the solution.

<u>23.</u>
$$a^3 - 26a^{3/2} - 27 = 0$$
$$(a^{3/2})^2 - 26a^{3/2} - 27 = 0$$

Let $u = a^{3/2}$ and substitute.

$$u^2 - 26u - 27 = 0$$
$$(u - 27)(u + 1) = 0$$
$$u - 27 = 0 \quad \text{or} \quad u + 1 = 0$$
$$u = 27 \quad \text{or} \qquad u = -1$$

Now substitute $a^{3/2}$ for u and solve for a.

$$a^{3/2} = 27 \qquad \text{or} \qquad a^{3/2} = -1$$
$$a^3 = 729 \qquad \text{or} \qquad a^3 = 1$$
$$a = 9 \qquad \text{or} \qquad a = 1$$

Only the number 9 checks. The solution is 9.

Exercise Set 8.7

<u>1.</u> $y = kx^2$

We first find k.

$$0.15 = k(0.1)^2 \qquad \text{(Substituting 0.15 for y and 0.1 for x)}$$
$$0.15 = 0.01k$$
$$\dfrac{0.15}{0.01} = k$$
$$15 = k$$

The equation of variation is $y = 15x^2$.

<u>3.</u> $y = \dfrac{k}{x^2}$

We first find k.

$$0.15 = \dfrac{k}{(0.1)^2} \qquad \text{(Substituting 0.15 for y and 0.1 for x)}$$
$$0.15 = \dfrac{k}{0.01}$$
$$0.15(0.01) = k$$
$$0.0015 = k$$

The equation of variation is $y = \dfrac{0.0015}{x^2}$.

<u>5.</u> $y = kxz$

We first find k.

$$56 = k \cdot 7 \cdot 8 \qquad \text{(Substituting 56 for y, 7 for x, and 8 for z)}$$
$$56 = 56k$$
$$1 = k$$

The equation of variation is $y = xz$.

<u>7.</u> $y = kxz^2$

We first find k.

$$105 = k \cdot 14 \cdot 5^2 \qquad \text{(Substituting 105 for y, 14 for x, and 5 for z)}$$
$$105 = 350k$$
$$\dfrac{105}{350} = k$$
$$0.3 = k$$

The equation of variation is $y = 0.3xz^2$.

<u>9.</u> $y = k\dfrac{xz}{wp}$

We first find k.

$$\dfrac{3}{28} = k\,\dfrac{3 \cdot 10}{7 \cdot 8} \qquad \text{(Substituting } \tfrac{3}{28} \text{ for y, 3 for x, 10 for z, 7 for w, and 8 for p)}$$
$$\dfrac{3}{28} = k \cdot \dfrac{30}{56}$$
$$\dfrac{3}{28} \cdot \dfrac{56}{30} = k$$
$$\dfrac{1}{5} = k$$

The equation of variation is $y = \dfrac{xz}{5wp}$.

<u>11.</u> $d = kr^2$

We first find k.

$$200 = k \cdot 60^2 \qquad \text{(Substituting 200 for d and 60 for r)}$$
$$200 = 3600k$$
$$\dfrac{200}{3600} = k$$
$$\dfrac{1}{18} = k$$

The equation of variation is $d = \dfrac{1}{18}r^2$.

Substitute 80 for r and solve for d.

$$d = \dfrac{1}{18} \cdot 80^2 = \dfrac{6400}{18} = 355\dfrac{5}{9}$$

It will take $355\dfrac{5}{9}$ ft to stop when traveling 80 mph.

13. $W = \dfrac{k}{d^2}$

We first find k.

$$100 = \dfrac{k}{(6400)^2} \qquad \text{(Substituting 100 for W and 6400 for d)}$$

$$100 = \dfrac{k}{40,960,000}$$

$$4,096,000,000 = k$$

The equation of variation is $W = \dfrac{4,096,000,000}{d^2}$.

Substitute 6600(6400 + 200) for d and solve for W.

$$W = \dfrac{4,096,000,000}{(6600)^2} = \dfrac{4,096,000,000}{43,560,000} = 94\,\dfrac{34}{1089}$$

When the astronaut is 200 km above the surface of the earth, his weight is $94\,\dfrac{34}{1089}$ kg.

15. $A = k\,\dfrac{R}{I}$

We first find k.

$$2.92 = k \cdot \dfrac{85}{262} \qquad \text{(Substituting 2.92 for A, 85 for R, and 262 for I)}$$

$$2.92\left(\dfrac{262}{85}\right) = k$$

$$9 \approx k$$

The equation of variation is $A = \dfrac{9R}{I}$.

Substitute 2.92 for A and 300 for I and solve for R.

$$2.92 = \dfrac{9R}{300}$$

$$876 = 9R$$

$$\dfrac{876}{9} = R$$

$$97 \approx R$$

For an earned run average of 2.92 in 300 innings, the pitcher would have to give up 97 earned runs.

17. $A = kd^2$

$\dfrac{A}{d^2} = k$

19. $A = kd^2$ (Direct variation)

$\pi r^2 = k(2r)^2$ (Substituting πr^2 for A and 2r for d)

$\pi r^2 = 4r^2 k$

$\dfrac{\pi r^2}{4r^2} = k$

$\dfrac{\pi}{4} = k$

1. Graph: $f(x) = 5x^2$

We choose some values of x and compute $f(x)$. Then we plot these ordered pairs and connect them with a smooth curve.

x	f(x)
0	0
1	5
-1	5
2	20
-2	20

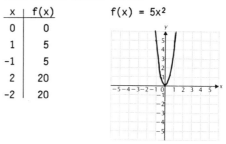

3. Graph: $f(x) = \dfrac{1}{4} x^2$

We choose some values of x and compute $f(x)$. Then we plot these ordered pairs and connect them with a smooth curve.

x	f(x)
0	0
2	1
-2	1
4	4
-4	4

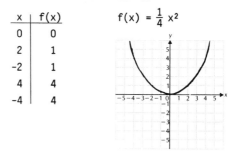

5. Graph: $f(x) = -\dfrac{1}{2} x^2$

We choose some values of x and compute $f(x)$. Then we plot these ordered pairs and connect them with a smooth curve.

x	f(x)
0	0
2	-2
-2	-2
3	$-\dfrac{9}{2}$
-3	$-\dfrac{9}{2}$

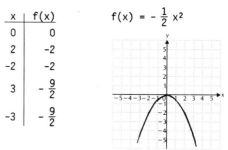

7. Graph: f(x) = -4x²

We choose some values of x and compute f(x).
Then we plot these ordered pairs and connect
them with a smooth curve.

x	f(x)
0	0
1	-4
-1	-4
2	-16
-2	-16

f(x) = -4x²

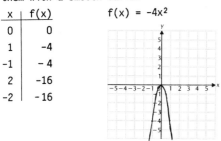

9. Graph: f(x) = (x - 3)²

We choose some values of x and compute f(x).
Then we plot these ordered pairs and connect
them with a smooth curve.

x	f(x)
3	0
4	1
2	1
5	4
1	4

f(x) = (x - 3)²

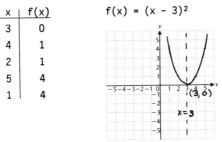

Vertex: (3,0)
Line of symmetry: x = 3

The graph of f(x) = (x - 3)² looks like the graph
of f(x) = x² except that it is moved three units
to the right.

11. Graph: y = 2(x - 4)²

We choose some values of x and compute y. Then
we plot these ordered pairs and connect them
with a smooth curve.

x	y
4	0
5	2
3	2
6	8
2	8

y = 2(x - 4)²

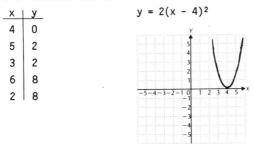

The graph of y = 2(x - 4)² looks like the graph
of y = 2x² except that it is moved four units to
the right.

13. Graph: f(x) = -2(x + 6)²
            = -2[x - (-6)]²

We choose some values of x and compute f(x).
Then we plot these ordered pairs and connect
them with a smooth curve.

x	f(x)
-6	0
-5	-2
-7	-2
-4	-8
-8	-8

f(x) = -2(x + 6)²

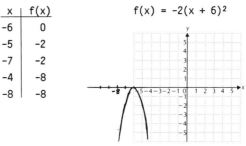

The graph of f(x) = -2(x + 6)² looks like the
graph of f(x) = 2x² except that it is moved six
units to the left and opens downward.

15. Graph: f(x) = 3(x - 1)²

We choose some values of x and compute f(x).
Then we plot these ordered pairs and connect
them with a smooth curve.

x	f(x)
1	0
2	3
0	3
3	12
-1	12

f(x) = 3(x - 1)²

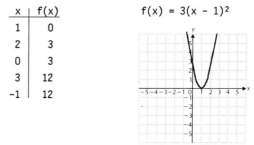

The graph of f(x) = 3(x - 1)² looks like the
graph of f(x) = 3x² except that it is moved one
unit to the right.

17. Graph: f(x) = (x - 3)² + 1

We choose some values of x and compute f(x).
Then we plot these ordered pairs and connect
them with a smooth curve.

x	f(x)
3	1
4	2
2	2
5	5
1	5

f(x) = (x - 3)² + 1

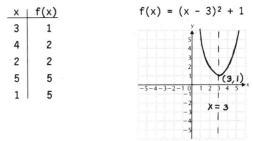

Vertex: (3,1)
Line of symmetry: x = 3

The graph of f(x) = (x - 3)² + 1 looks like the
graph of f(x) = x² except that it is moved three
units right and one unit up.

19. Graph: $y = \frac{1}{2}(x - 1)^2 - 3$

$= \frac{1}{2}(x - 1)^2 + (-3)$

We choose some values of x and compute y. Then we plot these ordered pairs and connect them with a smooth curve.

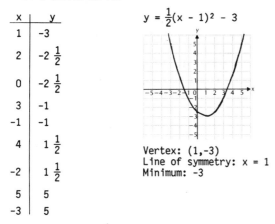

$y = \frac{1}{2}(x - 1)^2 - 3$

x	y
1	-3
2	$-2\frac{1}{2}$
0	$-2\frac{1}{2}$
3	-1
-1	-1
4	$1\frac{1}{2}$
-2	$1\frac{1}{2}$
5	5
-3	5

Vertex: (1,-3)
Line of symmetry: x = 1
Minimum: -3

The graph of $y = \frac{1}{2}(x - 1)^2 - 3$ looks like the graph of $y = \frac{1}{2} x^2$ except that it is moved one unit right and three units down.

21. Graph: $f(x) = -3(x + 4)^2 + 1$

$= -3[x - (-4)]^2 + 1$

We choose some values of x and compute f(x). Then we plot these ordered pairs and connect them with a smooth curve.

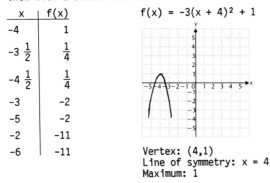

$f(x) = -3(x + 4)^2 + 1$

x	f(x)
-4	1
$-3\frac{1}{2}$	$\frac{1}{4}$
$-4\frac{1}{2}$	$\frac{1}{4}$
-3	-2
-5	-2
-2	-11
-6	-11

Vertex: (4,1)
Line of symmetry: x = 4
Maximum: 1

The graph of $f(x) = -3(x + 4)^2 + 1$ looks like the graph of $f(x) = 3x^2$ except that it is moved four units left and one unit up and opens downward.

23. Graph: $y = -2(x + 2)^2 - 3$

$= -2[x - (-2)]^2 + (-3)$

We choose some values of x and compute y. Then we plot these ordered pairs and connect them with a smooth curve.

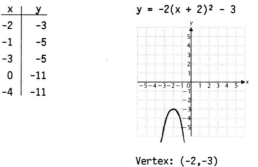

$y = -2(x + 2)^2 - 3$

x	y
-2	-3
-1	-5
-3	-5
0	-11
-4	-11

Vertex: (-2,-3)
Line of symmetry: x = -2
Maximum: -3

The graph of $y = -2(x + 2)^2 - 3$ looks like the graph of $y = 2x^2$ except that it is moved two units left and three units down and opens downward.

25. Graph: $f(x) = -(x + 1)^2 - 2$

$= -[x - (-1)]^2 + (-2)$

We choose some values of x and compute f(x). Then we plot these ordered pairs and connect them with a smooth curve.

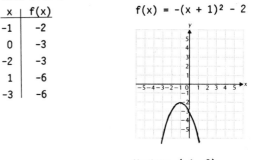

$f(x) = -(x + 1)^2 - 2$

x	f(x)
-1	-2
0	-3
-2	-3
1	-6
-3	-6

Vertex: (-1,-2)
Line of symmetry: x = -1
Maximum: -2

The graph of $f(x) = -(x + 1)^2 - 2$ looks like the graph of $f(x) = x^2$ except that it is moved one unit left and two units down and opens downward.

27. 500 = 4a + 2b + c
     300 = a + b + c
       0 = c

Substitute 0 for c in the first two equations and solve the resulting system for a and b.

500 = 4a + 2b

300 = a + b

We use the addition method.

 500 = 4a + 2b

-600 = -2a - 2b   (Multiplying by -2)

-100 = 2a

 -50 =   a

Next substitute -50 for a and solve for b.

300 = a + b

300 = -50 + b

350 = b

The values check. The solution is (-50,350,0).

Exercise Set 8.9

---

1. $f(x) = x^2 - 2x - 3$

       $= (x^2 - 2x) - 3$

We complete the square inside parentheses.
We take half the x-coefficient and square it.

$\frac{1}{2} \cdot (-2) = -1 \longrightarrow (-1)^2 = 1$

Then we add 1 - 1 inside the parentheses.

$f(x) = (x^2 - 2x + 1 - 1) - 3$

       $= (x^2 - 2x + 1) - 1 - 3$

       $= (x - 1)^2 - 4$

       $= (x - 1)^2 + (-4)$

Vertex: (1,-4)
Line of symmetry: x = 1

We plot a few points and draw the curve.

x	f(x)
1	-4
2	-3
0	-3
3	0
-1	0
4	5
-2	5

$f(x) = x^2 - 2x - 3$

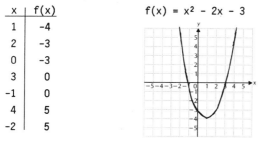

3. $f(x) = -x^2 + 4x + 1$

       $= -(x^2 - 4x) + 1$

We complete the square inside parentheses.
We take half the x-coefficient and square it.

$\frac{1}{2} \cdot (-4) = -2 \longrightarrow (-2)^2 = 4$

Then we add 4 - 4 inside parentheses.

$f(x) = -(x^2 - 4x + 4 - 4) + 1$

       $= -(x^2 - 4x + 4) + 4 + 1$

       $= -(x - 2)^2 + 5$

Vertex: (2,5)
Line of symmetry: x = 2

We plot a few points and draw the curve.

x	f(x)
2	5
3	4
1	4
4	1
0	1
5	-4
-1	-4

$f(x) = -x^2 + 4x + 1$

5. $f(x) = 3x^2 - 24x + 50$

       $= 3(x^2 - 8x) + 50$

We complete the square inside parentheses.
We take half the x-coefficient and square it.

$\frac{1}{2} \cdot (-8) = -4 \longrightarrow (-4)^2 = 16$

Then we add 16 - 16 inside parentheses.

$f(x) = 3(x^2 - 8x + 16 - 16) + 50$

       $= 3(x^2 - 8x + 16) - 48 + 50$

       $= 3(x - 4)^2 + 2$

Vertex: (4,2)
Line of symmetry: x = 4

We plot a few points and draw the curve.

x	f(x)
4	2
5	5
3	5
6	14
2	14

$f(x) = 3x^2 - 24x + 50$

7. $f(x) = -2x^2 + 2x + 1$

$\quad\quad = -2(x^2 - x) + 1$

We complete the square inside parentheses.
We take half the x-coefficient and square it.

$\frac{1}{2} \cdot (-1) = -\frac{1}{2} \longrightarrow (-\frac{1}{2})^2 = \frac{1}{4}$

Then we add $\frac{1}{4} - \frac{1}{4}$ inside parentheses.

$f(x) = -2(x^2 - x + \frac{1}{4} - \frac{1}{4}) + 1$

$\quad\quad = -2(x^2 - x + \frac{1}{4}) + \frac{1}{2} + 1$

$\quad\quad = -2(x - \frac{1}{2})^2 + \frac{3}{2}$

Vertex: $(\frac{1}{2}, \frac{3}{2})$
Line of symmetry: $x = \frac{1}{2}$

We plot a few points and draw the curve.

x	f(x)
$\frac{1}{2}$	$\frac{3}{2}$
1	1
0	1
2	-3
-1	-3

$f(x) = -2x^2 + 2x + 1$

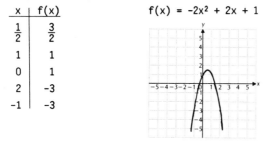

9. $f(x) = 5 - x^2$

$\quad\quad = -x^2 + 5$

$\quad\quad = -(x - 0)^2 + 5$

Vertex: (0,5)
Line of symmetry: $x = 0$

We plot a few points and draw the curve.

x	f(x)
0	5
1	4
-1	4
2	1
-2	1
3	-4
-3	-4

$f(x) = 5 - x^2$

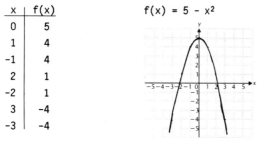

11. $f(x) = x^2 + 6x + 10$

We solve the equation $0 = x^2 + 6x + 10$ using the quadratic formula.

$x = \dfrac{-6 \pm \sqrt{6^2 - 4\cdot1\cdot10}}{2\cdot1}$

$\quad = \dfrac{-6 \pm \sqrt{36 - 40}}{2}$

$\quad = \dfrac{-6 \pm \sqrt{-4}}{2}$

$\quad = \dfrac{-6 \pm 2i}{2}$

$\quad = -3 \pm i$

The solutions are not real. Thus, there are no x-intercepts.

13. $f(x) = -x^2 + 3x + 4$

We solve the following equation.

$0 = -x^2 + 3x + 4$

$0 = x^2 - 3x - 4$

$0 = (x - 4)(x + 1)$

$x - 4 = 0$ or $x + 1 = 0$

$\quad x = 4$ or $\quad\quad x = -1$

The x-intercepts are (4,0) and (-1,0).

15. $f(x) = 2x^2 + 4x - 1$

We solve the equation $0 = 2x^2 + 4x - 1$ using the quadratic formula.

$x = \dfrac{-4 \pm \sqrt{4^2 - 4\cdot2\cdot(-1)}}{2\cdot2}$

$\quad = \dfrac{-4 \pm \sqrt{16 + 8}}{4}$

$\quad = \dfrac{-4 \pm 2\sqrt{6}}{4}$

$\quad = \dfrac{-2 \pm \sqrt{6}}{2}$

The x-intercepts are $(\dfrac{-2 + \sqrt{6}}{2}, 0)$ and $(\dfrac{-2 - \sqrt{6}}{2}, 0)$.

17. $f(x) = 3x^2 - 6x + 1$

We solve the equation $0 = 3x^2 - 6x + 1$ using the quadratic formula.

$$x = \frac{-(-6) \pm \sqrt{(-6)^2 - 4\cdot3\cdot1}}{2\cdot3}$$

$$= \frac{6 \pm \sqrt{36 - 12}}{6}$$

$$= \frac{6 \pm \sqrt{24}}{6}$$

$$= \frac{6 \pm 2\sqrt{6}}{6}$$

$$= \frac{2(3 \pm \sqrt{6})}{2\cdot3}$$

$$= \frac{3 \pm \sqrt{6}}{3}$$

The x-intercepts are $(\frac{3 + \sqrt{6}}{3}, 0)$ and $(\frac{3 - \sqrt{6}}{3}, 0)$.

19. $\sqrt{5x - 4} + \sqrt{13 - x} = 7$

$$\sqrt{5x - 4} = 7 - \sqrt{13 - x}$$

$$(\sqrt{5x - 4})^2 = (7 - \sqrt{13 - x})^2$$

$$5x - 4 = 49 - 14\sqrt{13 - x} + 13 - x$$

$$5x - 4 = 62 - 14\sqrt{13 - x} - x$$

$$6x - 66 = -14\sqrt{13 - x}$$

$$3x - 33 = -7\sqrt{13 - x}$$

$$(3x - 33)^2 = (-7\sqrt{13 - x})^2$$

$$9x^2 - 198x + 1089 = 49(13 - x)$$

$$9x^2 - 198x + 1089 = 637 - 49x$$

$$9x^2 - 149x + 452 = 0$$

$$(9x - 113)(x - 4) = 0$$

$$9x - 113 = 0 \quad \text{or} \quad x - 4 = 0$$

$$9x = 113 \text{ or} \qquad x = 4$$

$$x = \frac{113}{9} \text{ or} \qquad x = 4$$

The number $\frac{113}{9}$ does not check. Only 4 checks and is the solution.

21. $f(x) = 2.899x^2 - 5.901x + 0.969$

We solve the equation $0 = 2.899x^2 - 5.901x + 0.969$ using the quadratic formula.

$$x = \frac{-(-5.901) \pm \sqrt{(-5.901)^2 - 4(2.899)(0.969)}}{2(2.899)}$$

$$\approx \frac{5.901 \pm \sqrt{34.822 - 11.237}}{5.798}$$

$$\approx \frac{5.901 \pm \sqrt{23.585}}{5.798}$$

$$\approx \frac{5.901 \pm 4.856}{5.798}$$

$$x \approx \frac{5.901 + 4.856}{5.798} \text{ or } x \approx \frac{5.901 - 4.856}{5.798}$$

$$x \approx 1.855 \qquad \text{or } x \approx 0.180$$

The x-intercepts are $(1.855, 0)$ and $(0.180, 0)$.

23. Graph: $y \leqslant -x^2 - 2x + 3$

We first graph the parabola $y = -x^2 - 2x + 3$. We draw the curve solid since the inequality symbol is $\leqslant$.

x	y
-1	4
0	3
-2	3
1	0
-3	0
2	-5
-4	-5

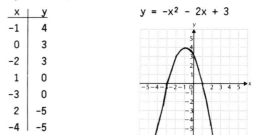

$y = -x^2 - 2x + 3$

We determine whether to shade above or below the parabola by trying some point off the parabola. The point $(0,0)$ is easy to check.

$0 \leqslant -0^2 - 2\cdot0 + 3$ (Substituting 0 for x and 0 for y)

$0 \leqslant 3$

Since $0 \leqslant 3$ is true, the point is in the graph. Thus, we shade below the parabola. The graph consists of the region below the parabola and the solid parabola as well.

$y \leqslant -x^2 - 2x + 3$

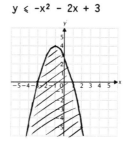

Exercise Set 8.10

1. We make a drawing and label it.

Perimeter = $2\ell + 2w$
Area = $\ell \cdot w$

We have a system of equations.

$2\ell + 2w = 76$

$A = \ell w$

We first solve $2\ell + 2w = 76$ for ℓ.

$2\ell + 2w = 76$

$\ell + w = 38$

$\ell = 38 - w$

Next we substitute $38 - w$ for ℓ in the second equation.

$A = \ell w$

$A = (38 - w)w$

$= -w^2 + 38w$

Completing the square, we get

$A = -(w^2 - 38w)$

$= -(w^2 - 38w + 361 - 361)$

$= -(w^2 - 38w + 361) + 361$

$= -(w - 19)^2 + 361$

The maximum function value is 361 when w is 19. When w = 19, $\ell = 38 - 19$, or 19.

We check a function value for w less than 19 and for w greater than 19.

$A(18) = -(18)^2 + 38 \cdot 18 = 360$

$A(20) = -(20)^2 + 38 \cdot 20 = 360$

Since 361 is greater than these numbers, it looks as though we have a maximum. The maximum area is 361 ft² when the dimensions are 19 ft by 19 ft.

3. We let x and y represent the numbers.

We have two equations.

$x + y = 22$

$P = xy$

We first solve $x + y = 22$ for y.

$x + y = 22$

$y = 22 - x$

Next we substitute $22 - x$ for y in the second equation.

$P = xy$

$P = x(22 - x)$

$= -x^2 + 22x$

3. (continued)

Completing the square, we get

$P = -(x^2 - 22x)$

$= -(x^2 - 22x + 121 - 121)$

$= -(x^2 - 22x + 121) + 121$

$= -(x - 11)^2 + 121$

The maximum function value is 121 when x is 11. When x = 11, y = 22 - 11, or 11.

We check a function value for x less than 11 and for x greater than 11.

$P(10) = -(10)^2 + 22 \cdot 10 = 120$

$P(12) = -(12)^2 + 22 \cdot 12 = 120$

Since 121 is greater than these numbers, it looks as though we have a maximum. The maximum product is 121 when the numbers are 11 and 11.

5. We let x and y represent the numbers.

We have two equations.

$x - y = 4$

$P = xy$

We first solve $x - y = 4$ for y.

$x - y = 4$

$x - 4 = y$

Next we substitute $x - 4$ for y in the second equation.

$P = xy$

$P = x(x - 4)$

$= x^2 - 4x$

Completing the square, we get

$P = x^2 - 4x + 4 - 4$

$= (x^2 - 4x + 4) - 4$

$= (x - 2)^2 - 4$

The minimum function value is -4 when x is 2. When x = 2, y = 2 - 4, or -2.

We check a function value for x less than 2 and for x greater than 2.

$P(1) = 1^2 - 4 \cdot 1 = -3$

$P(3) = 3^2 - 4 \cdot 3 = -3$

Since -4 is less than these numbers, it looks as though we have a minimum. The minimum product is -4 when the numbers are 2 and -2.

7. We let x and y represent the numbers.

We have two equations.

x − y = 5

P = xy

We first solve x − y = 5 for y.

x − y = 5

x − 5 = y

Next we substitute x − 5 for y in the second equation.

P = xy

P = x(x − 5)

  = x² − 5x

Completing the square, we get

$P = x^2 - 5x + \frac{25}{4} - \frac{25}{4}$

$\quad = (x - \frac{5}{2})^2 - \frac{25}{4}$

The minimum function value is $-\frac{25}{4}$ when x is $\frac{5}{2}$.
When $x = \frac{5}{2}$, $y = \frac{5}{2} - 5$, or $-\frac{5}{2}$.

We check a function value for x less than $\frac{5}{2}$ and for x greater than $\frac{5}{2}$.

P(2) = 2² − 5·2 = −6

P(3) = 3² − 5·3 = −6

Since $-\frac{25}{4}$ is less than these numbers, it looks as though we have a minimum. The minimum product is $-\frac{25}{4}$ when the numbers are $\frac{5}{2}$ and $-\frac{5}{2}$.

9. We look for a function f(x) = ax² + bx + c. We substitute some values of x and f(x).

  4 = a(1)² + b(1) + c

 −2 = a(−1)² + b(−1) + c

 13 = a(2)² + b(2) + c

or

 a + b + c = 4

 a − b + c = −2

4a + 2b + c = 13

Solving this system we get

a = 2   b = 3   and   c = −1.

Therefore the function we are looking for is
f(x) = 2x² + 3x − 1.

11. We look for a function f(x) = ax² + bx + c.
We substitute some values for x and f(x).

5 = a(1)² + b(1) + c

9 = a(2)² + b(2) + c

7 = a(3)² + b(3) + c

or

 a + b + c = 5

4a + 2b + c = 9

9a + 3b + c = 7

Solving this system we get

a = −3   b = 13   and   c = −5

Therefore the function we are looking for is
f(x) = −3x² + 13x − 5.

13. a) f(x) = ax² + bx + c

We substitute some values for x and f(x).

38 = a(1)² + b(1) + c

66 = a(2)² + b(2) + c

86 = a(3)² + b(3) + c

or

 a + b + c = 38

4a + 2b + c = 66

9a + 3b + c = 86

Solving this system, we get

a = −4   b = 40   and   c = 2.

Therefore the function we are looking for is
f(x) = −4x² + 40x + 2.

b) f(x) = −4x² + 40x + 2

f(4) = −4(4)² + 40(4) + 2

   = −64 + 160 + 2

   = 98

The earnings for the fourth week will probably be $98.

15. a) $f(x) = ax^2 + bx + c$

We substitute some values for x and f(x).
$200 = a(60)^2 + b(60) + c$
$130 = a(80)^2 + b(80) + c$
$100 = a(100)^2 + b(100) + c$
or
$3600a + 60b + c = 200$
$6400a + 80b + c = 130$
$10,000a + 100b + c = 100$

Solving this system we get
$a = 0.05$ $b = -10.5$ and $c = 650$

Therefore the function we are looking for is
$f(x) = 0.05x^2 - 10.5x + 650$.

b) $f(x) = 0.05x^2 - 10.5x + 650$

$f(50) = 0.05(50)^2 - 10.5(50) + 650$
$\qquad = 125 - 525 + 650$
$\qquad = 250$

The number of daytime accidents that will occur at 50 km/h will probably be 250.

17. a) $f(x) = ax^2 + bx + c$

We substitute some values for x and f(x).
$3 = a(8)^2 + b(8) + c$
$4.25 = a(12)^2 + b(12) + c$
$5.75 = a(16)^2 + b(16) + c$
or
$64a + 8b + c = 3$
$144a + 12b + c = 4.25$
$256a + 16b + c = 5.75$

Solving this system, we get
$a = 0.0078125$ $b = 0.15625$ and $c = 1.25$

Therefore the function we are looking for is
$f(x) = 0.0078125x^2 + 0.15625x + 1.25$.

b) $f(x) = 0.0078125x^2 + 0.15625x + 1.25$

$f(14) = 0.0078125(14)^2 + 0.15625(14) + 1.25$
$\qquad = 1.53125 + 2.1875 + 1.25$
$\qquad = 4.96875$

The price of a 14-in. pizza is approximately $4.97.

19. $R(x) = 200x - x^2$
$C(x) = 5000 + 8x$

$P(x) = R(x) - C(x)$
$\qquad = (200x - x^2) - (5000 + 8x)$
$\qquad = 200x - x^2 - 5000 - 8x$
$\qquad = -x^2 + 192x - 5000$

$P(x) = -(x^2 - 192x) - 5000$
$\qquad = -(x^2 - 192x + 9216 - 9216) - 5000$
$\qquad = -(x^2 - 192x + 9216) + 9216 - 5000$
$\qquad = -(x - 96)^2 + 4216$

The maximum value of the profit function is $4216 when 96 units are produced and sold.

21. $\sqrt{9a^3}\ \sqrt{16ab^4}$

$= \sqrt{144a^4b^4}$
$= 12a^2b^2$

23.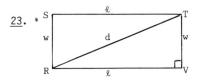

$2\ell + 2w = 44$, or $\ell + w = 22$, or $w = \ell - 22$

$d^2 = \ell^2 + w^2$ (Pythagorean property)
$d^2 = \ell^2 + (\ell - 22)^2$ (Substituting $\ell - 22$ for w)
$\quad = \ell^2 + \ell^2 - 44\ell + 484$
$\quad = 2\ell^2 - 44\ell + 484$
$\quad = 2(\ell^2 - 22\ell) + 484$
$\quad = 2(\ell^2 - 22\ell + 121 - 121) + 484$
$\quad = 2(\ell^2 - 22\ell + 121) - 242 + 484$
$\quad = 2(\ell - 11)^2 + 242$

The minimum value of d^2 is 242. Thus, the minimum value of d is $\sqrt{242}$, or $11\sqrt{2}$ ft.

Exercise Set 9.1

1. $d = \sqrt{(x_1 - x_2)^2 + (y_1 - y_2)^2}$

Let $(x_1,y_1) = (9,5)$ and $(x_2,y_2) = (6,1)$.

$d = \sqrt{(9 - 6)^2 + (5 - 1)^2}$ (Substituting)

$= \sqrt{(3)^2 + (4)^2}$

$= \sqrt{9 + 16}$

$= \sqrt{25}$

$= 5$

3. $d = \sqrt{(x_1 - x_2)^2 + (y_1 - y_2)^2}$

Let $(x_1,y_1) = (0,-7)$ and $(x_2,y_2) = (3,-4)$.

$d = \sqrt{(0 - 3)^2 + [-7 - (-4)]^2}$ (Substituting)

$= \sqrt{(-3)^2 + (-3)^2}$

$= \sqrt{9 + 9}$

$= \sqrt{18}$

≈ 4.243

5. $d = \sqrt{(x_1 - x_2)^2 + (y_1 - y_2)^2}$

Let $(x_1,y_1) = (2,2)$ and $(x_2,y_2) = (-2,-2)$.

$d = \sqrt{[2 - (-2)]^2 + [2 - (-2)]^2}$ (Substituting)

$= \sqrt{4^2 + 4^2}$

$= \sqrt{16 + 16}$

$= \sqrt{32}$

≈ 5.657

7. $d = \sqrt{(x_1 - x_2)^2 + (y_1 - y_2)^2}$

Let $(x_1,y_1) = (8.6,-3.4)$ and $(x_2,y_2) = (-9.2,-3.4)$.

$d = \sqrt{[8.6 - (9.2)]^2 + [-3.4 - (-3.4)]^2}$

(Substituting)

$= \sqrt{17.8^2 + 0^2}$

$= \sqrt{17.8^2}$

$= 17.8$

9. $d = \sqrt{(x_1 - x_2)^2 + (y_1 - y_2)^2}$

Let $(x_1,y_1) = (\frac{5}{7},\frac{1}{14})$ and $(x_2,y_2) = (\frac{1}{7},\frac{11}{14})$.

$d = \sqrt{(\frac{5}{7} - \frac{1}{7})^2 + (\frac{1}{14} - \frac{11}{14})^2}$ (Substituting)

$= \sqrt{(\frac{4}{7})^2 + (-\frac{5}{7})^2}$

$= \sqrt{\frac{16}{49} + \frac{25}{49}}$

$= \sqrt{\frac{41}{49}}$

$= \frac{\sqrt{41}}{7}$

≈ 0.915

11. $\left[\frac{x_1 + x_2}{2},\frac{y_1 + y_2}{2} \right]$ (Midpoint formula)

Let $(x_1,y_1) = (-3,6)$ and $(x_2,y_2) = (2,-8)$.

The midpoint is $\left[\frac{-3 + 2}{2},\frac{6 + (-8)}{2} \right]$, or $(-\frac{1}{2},-1)$.

13. $\left[\frac{x_1 + x_2}{2},\frac{y_1 + y_2}{2} \right]$ (Midpoint formula)

Let $(x_1,y_1) = (8,5)$ and $(x_2,y_2) = (-1,2)$.

The midpoint is $\left[\frac{8 + (-1)}{2},\frac{5 + 2}{2} \right]$, or $(\frac{7}{2},\frac{7}{2})$.

15. $\left[\frac{x_1 + x_2}{2},\frac{y_1 + y_2}{2} \right]$ (Midpoint formula)

Let $(x_1,y_1) = (-8,-5)$ and $(x_2,y_2) = (6,-1)$.

The midpoint is $\left[\frac{-8 + 6}{2},\frac{-5 + (-1)}{2} \right]$, or $(-1,-3)$.

17. $\left[\frac{x_1 + x_2}{2},\frac{y_1 + y_2}{2} \right]$ (Midpoint formula)

Let $(x_1,y_1) = (-3.4,8.1)$ and $(x_2,y_2) = (2.9,-8.7)$.

The midpoint is

$\left[\frac{-3.4 + 2.9}{2},\frac{8.1 + (-8.7)}{2} \right]$

$= (\frac{-0.5}{2},\frac{-0.6}{2})$

$= (-0.25,-0.3)$

19. $\left[\dfrac{x_1 + x_2}{2}, \dfrac{y_1 + y_2}{2}\right]$ (Midpoint formula)

Let $(x_1, y_1) = (\frac{1}{6}, -\frac{3}{4})$ and $(x_2, y_2) = (-\frac{1}{3}, \frac{5}{6})$.

The midpoint is

$$\left[\dfrac{\frac{1}{6} + (-\frac{1}{3})}{2}, \dfrac{-\frac{3}{4} + \frac{5}{6}}{2}\right]$$

$$= \left[\dfrac{-\frac{1}{6}}{2}, \dfrac{\frac{1}{12}}{2}\right]$$

$$= (-\tfrac{1}{12}, \tfrac{1}{24})$$

21. $\left[\dfrac{x_1 + x_2}{2}, \dfrac{y_1 + y_2}{2}\right]$ (Midpoint formula)

Let $(x_1, y_1) = (\sqrt{2}, -1)$ and $(x_2, y_2) = (\sqrt{3}, 4)$.

The midpoint is $\left[\dfrac{\sqrt{2} + \sqrt{3}}{2}, \dfrac{-1 + 4}{2}\right]$, or

$\left[\dfrac{\sqrt{2} + \sqrt{3}}{2}, \dfrac{3}{2}\right]$.

23. $2x + 3y = 8$
$x - 2y = -3$

We use the addition method.
$$2x + 3y = 8$$
$$\underline{-2x + 4y = 6}\qquad \text{(Multiplying by -2)}$$
$$7y = 14 \qquad \text{(Adding)}$$
$$y = 2$$

Substitute 2 for y in either of the original equations and solve for x.
$$x - 2y = -3$$
$$x - 2\cdot 2 = -3 \qquad \text{(Substituting)}$$
$$x - 4 = -3$$
$$x = 1$$

The solution is (1,2).

25. $y = x^2 - 4x + 8$
$= (x^2 - 4x) + 8$
$= (x^2 - 4x + 4 - 4) + 8$
$= (x^2 - 4x + 4) - 4 + 8$
$= (x - 2)^2 + 4$

Vertex: (2,4)
Line of symmetry: x = 2

25. (continued)

We plot a few points and draw the curve.

x	y
2	4
3	5
1	5
4	8
0	8

$y = x^2 - 4x + 8$

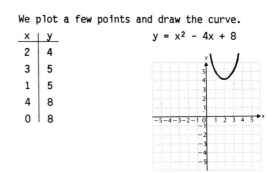

27. $d = \sqrt{(x_1 - x_2)^2 + (y_1 - y_2)^2}$

Let $(x_1, y_1) = (-1, 3k)$ and $(x_2, y_2) = (6, 2k)$.

$d = \sqrt{(-1 - 6)^2 + (3k - 2k)^2}$ (Substituting)

$= \sqrt{(-7)^2 + (k)^2}$

$= \sqrt{49 + k^2}$

29. $d = \sqrt{(x_1 - x_2)^2 + (y_1 - y_2)^2}$

Let $(x_1, y_1) = (6m, -7n)$ and $(x_2, y_2) = (-2m, n)$.

$d = \sqrt{[6m - (-2m)]^2 + (-7n - n)^2}$ (Substituting)

$= \sqrt{(8m)^2 + (-8n)^2}$

$= \sqrt{64m^2 + 64n^2}$

$= \sqrt{64(m^2 + n^2)}$

$= 8\sqrt{m^2 + n^2}$

31. $d = \sqrt{(x_1 - x_2)^2 + (y_1 - y_2)^2}$

Let $(x_1, y_1) = (-3\sqrt{3}, 1 - \sqrt{6})$ and $(x_2, y_2) = (\sqrt{3}, 1 + \sqrt{6})$.

$d = \sqrt{(-3\sqrt{3} - \sqrt{3})^2 + (-\sqrt{6} - \sqrt{6})^2}$

(Substituting)

$= \sqrt{(-4\sqrt{3})^2 + (-2\sqrt{6})^2}$

$= \sqrt{48 + 24}$

$= \sqrt{72}$

$= \sqrt{36\cdot 2}$

$= 6\sqrt{2}$

33. The distance between $(-8,-5)$ and $(6,1)$ is

$$\sqrt{(-8 - 6)^2 + (-5 - 1)^2} = \sqrt{196 + 36} = \sqrt{232}.$$

The distance between $(6,1)$ and $(-4,5)$ is

$$\sqrt{[6 - (-4)]^2 + (1 - 5)^2} = \sqrt{100 + 16} = \sqrt{116}.$$

The distance between $(-4,5)$ and $(-8,-5)$ is

$$\sqrt{[-4 - (-8)]^2 + [5 - (-5)]^2} = \sqrt{16 + 100} = \sqrt{116}$$

Since $(\sqrt{116})^2 + (\sqrt{116})^2 = (\sqrt{232})^2$, the points are vertices of a right triangle.

35. $\left[\dfrac{x_1 + x_2}{2}, \dfrac{y_1 + y_2}{2} \right]$ (Midpoint formula)

Let $(x_1,y_1) = (2 - \sqrt{3}, 5\sqrt{2})$ and $(x_2,y_2) = (2 + \sqrt{3}, 3\sqrt{2})$.

The midpoint is

$$\left[\frac{(2 - \sqrt{3}) + (2 + \sqrt{3})}{2}, \frac{5\sqrt{2} + 3\sqrt{2}}{2} \right]$$

$$= (\frac{4}{2}, \frac{8\sqrt{2}}{2})$$

$$= (2, 4\sqrt{2})$$

Exercise Set 9.2

1. $(x + 1)^2 + (y + 3)^2 = 4$
$[x - (-1)]^2 + [y - (-3)]^2 = 2^2$ (Standard form)

The center is $(-1,-3)$, and the radius is 2.

$(x + 1)^2 + (y + 3)^2 = 4$

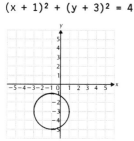

3. $(x - 3)^2 + y^2 = 2$
$(x - 3)^2 + (y - 0)^2 = (\sqrt{2})^2$ (Standard form)

The center is $(3,0)$, and the radius is $\sqrt{2}$.

$(x - 3)^2 + y^2 = 2$

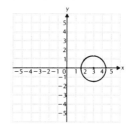

5. $x^2 + y^2 = 25$
$(x - 0)^2 + (y - 0)^2 = 5^2$ (Standard form)

The center is $(0,0)$, and the radius is 5.

$x^2 + y^2 = 25$

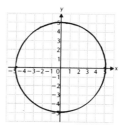

7. $(x - a)^2 + (y - b)^2 = r^2$ (Standard form)
$(x - 0)^2 + (y - 0)^2 = 7^2$ (Substituting)
$x^2 + y^2 = 49$

9. $(x - a)^2 + (y - b)^2 = r^2$ (Standard form)
$[x - (-2)]^2 + (y - 7)^2 = (\sqrt{5})^2$ (Substituting)
$(x + 2)^2 + (y - 7)^2 = 5$

11. $x^2 + y^2 + 8x - 6y - 15 = 0$
$x^2 + 8x + y^2 - 6y = 15$
$(x^2 + 8x + 16) + (y^2 - 6y + 9) = 15 + 16 + 9$
$(x + 4)^2 + (y - 3)^2 = 40$
$[x - (-4)]^2 + (y - 3)^2 = (2\sqrt{10})^2$
(Standard form)
The center is $(-4,3)$, and the radius is $2\sqrt{10}$.

13. $x^2 + y^2 - 8x + 2y + 13 = 0$
$x^2 - 8x + y^2 + 2y = -13$
$(x^2 - 8x + 16) + (y^2 + 2y + 1) = -13 + 16 + 1$
$(x - 4)^2 + (y + 1)^2 = 4$
$(x - 4)^2 + [y - (-1)]^2 = 2^2$ (Standard form)

The center is $(4,-1)$, and the radius is 2.

15.
$$x^2 + y^2 - 4x = 0$$
$$x^2 - 4x + y^2 = 0$$
$$(x^2 - 4x + 4) + y^2 = 4$$
$$(x - 2)^2 + (y - 0)^2 = 2^2 \qquad \text{(Standard form)}$$

The center is (2,0), and the radius is 2.

17. $\frac{x^2}{4} + \frac{y^2}{1} = 1$

$\frac{x^2}{2^2} + \frac{y^2}{1^2} = 1$

The x-intercepts are (2,0) and (-2,0).
The y-intercepts are (0,1) and (0,-1).

We plot these points and fill in an oval-shaped curve.

$\frac{x^2}{4} + \frac{y^2}{1} = 1$

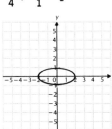

19. $\frac{x^2}{9} + \frac{y^2}{16} = 1$

$\frac{x^2}{3^2} + \frac{y^2}{4^2} = 1$

The x-intercpets are (3,0) and (-3,0).
The y-intercepts are (0,4) and (0,-4).

We plot these points and fill in an oval-shaped curve.

$\frac{x^2}{9} + \frac{y^2}{16} = 1$

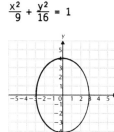

21. We first find the length of the radius which is the distance between (0,0) and $(\frac{1}{4}, \frac{\sqrt{31}}{4})$.

$$r = \sqrt{(\frac{1}{4} - 0)^2 + (\frac{\sqrt{31}}{4} - 0)^2}$$

$$= \sqrt{(\frac{1}{4})^2 + (\frac{\sqrt{31}}{4})^2}$$

$$= \sqrt{\frac{1}{16} + \frac{31}{16}}$$

$$= \sqrt{\frac{32}{16}}$$

$$= \sqrt{2}$$

$(x - a)^2 + (y - b)^2 = r^2 \qquad \text{(Standard form)}$
$(x - 0)^2 + (y - 0)^2 = (\sqrt{2})^2$

[Substituting (0,0) for the center and $\sqrt{2}$ for the radius]

$x^2 + y^2 = 2$

23.

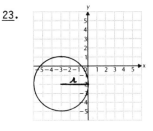

The center is (-3,-2) and the radius is 3.

$(x - a)^2 + (y - b)^2 = r^2 \qquad \text{(Standard form)}$
$[x - (-3)]^2 + [y - (-2)]^2 = 3^2 \qquad \text{(Substituting)}$
$(x + 3)^2 + (y + 2)^2 = 9$

25.
$$16x^2 + y^2 + 96x - 8y + 144 = 0$$
$$(16x^2 + 96x) + (y^2 - 8y) + 144 = 0$$
$$16(x^2 + 6x) + (y^2 - 8y) + 144 = 0$$
$$16(x^2+6x+9-9) + (y^2-8y+16-16) + 144 = 0$$
$$16(x^2+6x+9) + (y^2-8y+16) - 144 - 16 + 144 = 0$$
$$16(x + 3)^2 + (y - 4)^2 = 16$$
$$\frac{(x + 3)^2}{1} + \frac{(y - 4)^2}{16} = 1$$
$$\frac{[x - (-3)]^2}{1^2} + \frac{(y - 4)^2}{4^2} = 1$$

Center: (-3,4)
Vertices: [1 + (-3),4], [-1 + (-3),4], (-3,4 + 4), (-3,-4 + 4)

or

(-2,4), (-4,4), (-3,8), (-3,0)

25. (continued)

$$(x + 3)^2 + \frac{(y - 4)^2}{16} = 1$$

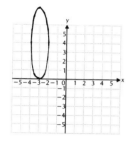

Exercise Set 9.3

1. Graph: $y = x^2$

The graph is a parabola. The vertex is $(0,0)$; the line of symmetry is $x = 0$. The curve opens upward.

x	y
0	0
1	1
-1	1
2	4
-2	4

$y = x^2$

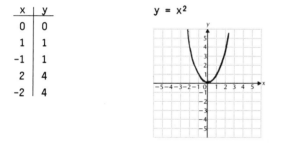

3. Graph: $x = y^2 + 4y + 1$

We complete the square on y.

$x = (y^2 + 4y + 4 - 4) + 1$

  $= (y^2 + 4y + 4) - 4 + 1$

  $= (y + 2)^2 - 3$, or

  $= [y - (-2)]^2 + (-3)$

The graph is a parabola. The vertex is $(-3,-2)$; the line of symmetry is $y = -2$. The curve opens to the right.

x	y
-3	-2
-2	-3
-2	-1
1	-4
1	0

$x = y^2 + 4y + 1$

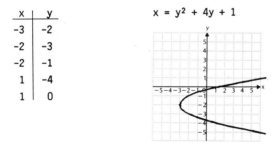

5. Graph: $y = -x^2 + 4x - 5$

We complete the square on x.

$y = -(x^2 - 4x) - 5$

  $= -(x^2 - 4x + 4 - 4) - 5$

  $= -(x^2 - 4x + 4) + 4 - 5$

  $= -(x - 2)^2 - 1$

  $= -(x - 2)^2 + (-1)$

The graph is a parabola. The vertex is $(2,-1)$; The line of symmetry is $x = 2$. The curve opens downward.

x	y
2	-1
1	-2
3	-2
0	-5
4	-5

$y = -x^2 + 4x - 5$

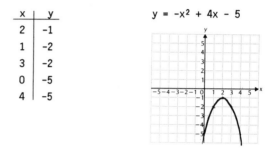

7. Graph: $x = -3y^2 - 6y - 1$

We complete the square on y.

$x = -3(y^2 + 2y) - 1$

  $= -3(y^2 + 2y + 1 - 1) - 1$

  $= -3(y^2 + 2y + 1) + 3 - 1$

  $= -3(y + 1)^2 + 2$

  $= -3[y - (-1)]^2 + 2$

The graph is a parabola. The vertex is $(2,-1)$; the line of symmetry is $y = -1$. The curve opens to the left.

x	y
2	-1
-1	-2
-1	0
-10	-3
-10	1

$x = -3y^2 - 6y - 1$

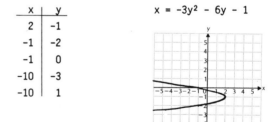

9. Graph: $\frac{x^2}{16} - \frac{y^2}{16} = 1$

$\frac{x^2}{4^2} - \frac{y^2}{4^2} = 1$ (a = 4, b = 4)

The intercepts are (4,0) and (-4,0).

The asymptotes are $y = \frac{4}{4}x$ and $y = -\frac{4}{4}x$, or $y = x$ and $y = -x$.

We sketch the asymptotes and plot the intercepts. Through each intercept we draw a smooth curve that approaches the asymptotes closely.

$\frac{x^2}{16} - \frac{y^2}{16} = 1$

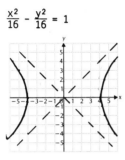

11. Graph: $\frac{y^2}{16} - \frac{x^2}{9} = 1$

$\frac{y^2}{4^2} - \frac{x^2}{3^2} = 1$ (a = 3, b = 4)

The intercpets are (0,4) and (0,-4).

The asymptotes are $y = \frac{4}{3}x$ and $y = -\frac{4}{3}x$.

We sketch the asymptotes and plot the intercepts. Through each intercept we draw a smooth curve that approaches the asymptotes closely.

$\frac{y^2}{16} - \frac{x^2}{9} = 1$

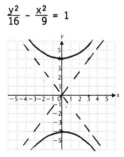

13. Graph: $\frac{x^2}{25} - \frac{y^2}{36} = 1$

$\frac{x^2}{5^2} - \frac{y^2}{6^2} = 1$ (a = 5, b = 6)

The intercpets are (5,0) and (-5,0).

The asymptotes are $y = \frac{6}{5}x$ and $y = -\frac{6}{5}x$.

We sketch the asymptotes and plot the intercepts. Through each intercept we draw a smooth curve that approaches the asymptotes closely.

13. (continued)

$\frac{x^2}{25} - \frac{y^2}{36} = 1$

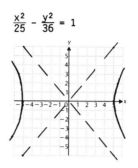

15. Graph: $xy = 6$

$y = \frac{6}{x}$ (Solving for y)

x	y		x	y
1	6		-1	-6
2	3		-2	-3
3	2		-3	-2
6	1		-6	-1
$\frac{1}{2}$	12		$-\frac{1}{2}$	-12
$\frac{1}{3}$	18		$-\frac{1}{3}$	-18

Note that we cannot use 0 for x. The x-axis and the y-axis are the asymptotes.

$xy = 6$

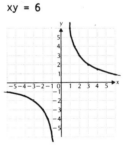

17. Graph: $xy = -1$

$y = -\frac{1}{x}$ (Solving for y)

x	y		x	y
1	-1		-1	1
2	$-\frac{1}{2}$		-2	$\frac{1}{2}$
3	$-\frac{1}{3}$		-3	$\frac{1}{3}$
4	$-\frac{1}{4}$		-4	$\frac{1}{4}$
$\frac{1}{2}$	-2		$-\frac{1}{2}$	2
$\frac{1}{3}$	-3		$-\frac{1}{3}$	3
$\frac{1}{4}$	-4		$-\frac{1}{4}$	4

17. (continued)

Note that we cannot use 0 for x. The x-axis and the y-axis are the asymptotes.

$xy = -1$

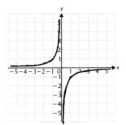

19. $\sqrt[3]{125t^{15}} = \sqrt[3]{5^3 t^{15}} = 5t^5$

21. $\dfrac{4\sqrt{2} - 5\sqrt{3}}{6\sqrt{3} - 8\sqrt{2}}$

$= \dfrac{4\sqrt{2} - 5\sqrt{3}}{6\sqrt{3} - 8\sqrt{2}} \cdot \dfrac{6\sqrt{3} + 8\sqrt{2}}{6\sqrt{3} + 8\sqrt{2}}$

$= \dfrac{24\sqrt{6} + 64 - 90 - 40\sqrt{6}}{108 - 128}$

$= \dfrac{-26 - 16\sqrt{6}}{-20}$

$= \dfrac{13 + 8\sqrt{6}}{10}$

23.
$$x^2 + y^2 - 10x + 8y - 40 = 0$$
$$x^2 - 10x + y^2 + 8y = 40$$
$$(x^2 - 10x + 25) + (y^2 + 8y + 16) = 40 + 25 + 16$$
$$(x - 5)^2 + (y + 4)^2 = 81$$

The graph is a <u>circle</u>.

25.
$$1 - 3y = 2y^2 - x$$
$$x = 2y^2 + 3y - 1$$

The graph is a <u>parabola</u>.

27.
$$4x^2 + 25y^2 - 8x - 100y + 4 = 0$$
$$4x^2 - 8x + 25y^2 - 100y = -4$$
$$4(x^2 - 2x + 1) + 25(y^2 - 4y + 4) = -4 + 4 + 100$$
$$4(x - 1)^2 + 25(y - 2)^2 = 100$$
$$\frac{(x - 1)^2}{25} + \frac{(y - 2)^2}{4} = 1$$

The graph is an <u>ellipse</u>.

29. $y = ax^2 + bx + c$ (Standard form of parabola with line of symmetry parallel to the y-axis.)

We substitute values for x and y.

$3 = a(0)^2 + b(0) + c$ (Substituting 0 for x and 3 for y)

$6 = a(-1)^2 + b(-1) + c$ (Substituting -1 for x and 6 for y)

$9 = a(2)^2 + b(2) + c$ (Substituting 2 for x and 9 for y)

or

$3 = c$

$6 = a - b + c$

$9 = 4a + 2b + c$

Next we substitute 3 for c in the second and third equations and solve the resulting system for a and b.

$6 = a - b + 3$ or $a - b = 3$

$9 = 4a + 2b + 3$ $4a + 2b = 6$

Solving this system we get a = 2 and b = -1. Thus the equation of the parabola whose line of symmetry is parallel to the y-axis and passes through (0,3), (-1,6), and (2,9) is

$y = 2x^2 - x + 3$

Exercise Set 9.4

1. $x^2 + y^2 = 25$ (1)

$y - x = 1$ (2)

First solve equation (2) for y.

$y - x = 1$

$y = x + 1$ (3)

Then substitute x + 1 for y in equation (1) and solve for x.

$$x^2 + y^2 = 25 \qquad (1)$$
$$x^2 + (x + 1)^2 = 25$$
$$x^2 + x^2 + 2x + 1 = 25$$
$$2x^2 + 2x - 24 = 0$$
$$x^2 + x - 12 = 0$$
$$(x + 4)(x - 3) = 0$$

$x + 4 = 0$ or $x - 3 = 0$

$x = -4$ or $x = 3$

Now substitute these numbers into equation (3) and solve for y.

$y = x + 1$ (3)

When x = -4, y = -4 + 1, or -3.

When x = 3, y = 3 + 1, or 4.

The pairs (-4,-3) and (3,4) check, so they are the solutions.

3. $4x^2 + 9y^2 = 36$ (1)

   $3y + 2x = 6$ (2)

First solve equation (2) for y.

$3y + 2x = 6$

   $3y = -2x + 6$

    $y = -\frac{2}{3}x + 2$ (3)

Then substitute $-\frac{2}{3}x + 2$ for y in equation (1) and solve for x.

$$4x^2 + 9y^2 = 36 \quad (1)$$

$$4x^2 + 9(-\frac{2}{3}x + 2)^2 = 36$$

$$4x^2 + 9(\frac{4}{9}x^2 - \frac{8}{3}x + 4) = 36$$

$$4x^2 + 4x^2 - 24x + 36 = 36$$

$$8x^2 - 24x = 0$$

$$x^2 - 3x = 0$$

$$x(x - 3) = 0$$

$x = 0$ or $x = 3$

Now substitute these numbers in equation (3) and solve for y.

$y = -\frac{2}{3}x + 2$ (3)

When $x = 0$, $y = -\frac{2}{3} \cdot 0 + 2$, or 2.

When $x = 3$, $y = -\frac{2}{3} \cdot 3 + 2$, or 0.

The pairs (0,2) and (3,0) check, so they are the solutions.

5. $y^2 = x + 3$ (1)

   $2y = x + 4$ (2)

First solve equation (2) for x.

   $2y = x + 4$

$2y - 4 = x$ (3)

Then substitute $2y - 4$ for x in equation (1) and solve for y.

$$y^2 = x + 3 \quad (1)$$

$$y^2 = (2y - 4) + 3$$

$$y^2 = 2y - 1$$

$$y^2 - 2y + 1 = 0$$

$$(y - 1)(y - 1) = 0$$

$y - 1 = 0$ or $y - 1 = 0$

   $y = 1$ or $y = 1$

Now substitute 1 for y in equation (3) and solve for x.

   $2y - 4 = x$ (3)

$2 \cdot 1 - 4 = x$

     $-2 = x$

The ordered pair (-2,1) checks. It is the solution.

7. $x^2 - xy + 3y^2 = 27$ (1)

   $x - y = 2$ (2)

First solve equation (2) for y.

$x - y = 2$

$x - 2 = y$ (3)

Then substitute $x - 2$ for y in equation (1) and solve for x.

$$x^2 - xy + 3y^2 = 27 \quad (1)$$

$$x^2 - x(x - 2) + 3(x - 2)^2 = 27$$

$$x^2 - x^2 + 2x + 3x^2 - 12x + 12 = 27$$

$$3x^2 - 10x - 15 = 0$$

$$x = \frac{-(-10) \pm \sqrt{(-10)^2 - 4(3)(-15)}}{2 \cdot 3}$$

$$= \frac{10 \pm \sqrt{100 + 180}}{6}$$

$$= \frac{10 \pm \sqrt{280}}{6}$$

$$= \frac{10 \pm 2\sqrt{70}}{6}$$

$$= \frac{5 \pm \sqrt{70}}{3}$$

Now substitute these numbers in equation (3) and solve for y.

$y = x - 2$ (3)

When $x = \frac{5 + \sqrt{70}}{3}$, $y = \frac{5 + \sqrt{70}}{3} - 2 = \frac{-1 + \sqrt{70}}{3}$.

When $x = \frac{5 - \sqrt{70}}{3}$, $y = \frac{5 - \sqrt{70}}{3} - 2 = \frac{-1 - \sqrt{70}}{3}$.

The ordered pairs $\left[\frac{5 + \sqrt{70}}{3}, \frac{-1 + \sqrt{70}}{3} \right]$ and $\left[\frac{5 - \sqrt{70}}{3}, \frac{-1 - \sqrt{70}}{3} \right]$ check, so they are the solutions.

9. $2a + b = 1$ (1)

   $b = 4 - a^2$ (2)

Substitute $4 - a^2$ for b in equation (1) and solve for a.

   $2a + b = 1$ (1)

$2a + 4 - a^2 = 1$

      $0 = a^2 - 2a - 3$

      $0 = (a - 3)(a + 1)$

$a - 3 = 0$ or $a + 1 = 0$

   $a = 3$ or $a = -1$

Now substitute these numbers for a in equation (2) and solve for b.

$b = 4 - a^2$

When $a = 3$, $b = 4 - 3^2 = 4 - 9$, or -5.

When $a = -1$, $b = 4 - (-1)^2 = 4 - 1$, or 3.

The ordered pairs (3,-5) and (-1,3) check, so they are the solutions.

11. $m^2 + 3n^2 = 10$ (1)

$m - n = 2$ (2)

First solve equation (2) for m.

$m - n = 2$

$m = n + 2$ (3)

Then substitute n + 2 for m in equation (1) and solve for n.

$m^2 + 3n^2 = 10$ (1)

$(n + 2)^2 + 3n^2 = 10$

$n^2 + 4n + 4 + 3n^2 = 10$

$4n^2 + 4n + 4 = 10$

$4n^2 + 4n - 6 = 0$

$2n^2 + 2n - 3 = 0$

Using the quadratic formula we get

$n = \dfrac{-2 \pm \sqrt{2^2 - 4(2)(-3)}}{2 \cdot 2}$

$= \dfrac{-2 \pm \sqrt{28}}{4}$

$= \dfrac{-2 \pm 2\sqrt{7}}{4}$

$= \dfrac{-1 \pm \sqrt{7}}{2}$

Now substitute these numbers in equation (3) and solve for m.

$m = n + 2$

When $n = \dfrac{-1 + \sqrt{7}}{2}$, $m = \dfrac{-1 + \sqrt{7}}{2} + 2$

$= \dfrac{-1 + \sqrt{7}}{2} + \dfrac{4}{2}$

$= \dfrac{3 + \sqrt{7}}{2}$

When $n = \dfrac{-1 - \sqrt{7}}{2}$, $m = \dfrac{-1 - \sqrt{7}}{2} + 2$

$= \dfrac{-1 - \sqrt{7}}{2} + \dfrac{4}{2}$

$= \dfrac{3 - \sqrt{7}}{2}$

The ordered pairs $\left(\dfrac{3 + \sqrt{7}}{2}, \dfrac{-1 + \sqrt{7}}{2} \right)$ and $\left(\dfrac{3 - \sqrt{7}}{2}, \dfrac{-1 - \sqrt{7}}{2} \right)$ check, so they are the solutions.

13. Let x and y represent the numbers.

The sum of two numbers is 13.

$x + y = 13$

The sum of their squares is 109.

$x^2 + y^2 = 109$

We solve the following system:

$x + y = 13$ (1)

$x^2 + y^2 = 109$ (2)

First solve equation (1) for y.

$x + y = 13$

$y = 13 - x$ (3)

Then substitute 13 - x for y in equation (2) and solve for x.

$x^2 + y^2 = 109$

$x^2 + (13 - x)^2 = 109$

$x^2 + 169 - 26x + x^2 = 109$

$2x^2 - 26x + 60 = 0$

$x^2 - 13x + 30 = 0$

$(x - 10)(x - 3) = 0$

$x - 10 = 0$ or $x - 3 = 0$

$x = 10$ or $x = 3$

Now substitute these numbers in equation (3) and solve for y.

$y = 13 - x$ (3)

When x = 10, y = 13 - 10, or 3.

When x = 3, y = 13 - 3, or 10.

The sum of the numbers is 10 + 3, or 13. The sum of their squares is 100 + 9, or 109. The numbers check. The numbers are 10 and 3.

15. We first make a drawing.

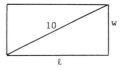

We let ℓ and w represent the length and width.

The perimeter is 28 ft.

$2\ell + 2w = 28$, or $\ell + w = 14$

15. (continued)

Using the Pythagorean property we have another equation.

$\ell^2 + w^2 = 10^2$, or $\ell^2 + w^2 = 100$

We solve the following system:

$\ell + w = 14$ (1)
$\ell^2 + w^2 = 100$ (2)

First solve equation (1) for w.

$\ell + w = 14$
$w = 14 - \ell$ (3)

Then substitute $14 - \ell$ for w in equation (2) and solve for ℓ.

$$\ell^2 + w^2 = 100 \qquad (2)$$
$$\ell^2 + (14 - \ell)^2 = 100$$
$$\ell^2 + 196 - 28\ell + \ell^2 = 100$$
$$2\ell^2 - 28\ell + 96 = 0$$
$$\ell^2 - 14\ell + 48 = 0$$
$$(\ell - 8)(\ell - 6) = 0$$

$\ell - 8 = 0$ or $\ell - 6 = 0$
$\ell = 8$ or $\ell = 6$

We substitute these numbers in equation (3) and solve for w.

$w = 14 - \ell$ (3)

When $\ell = 8$, $w = 14 - 8$, or 6.
When $\ell = 6$, $w = 14 - 6$, or 8.

When the dimensions are 8 ft and 6 ft, the perimeter is $2 \cdot 8 + 2 \cdot 6$, or 28 ft, and the diagonal is $\sqrt{8^2 + 6^2}$, or $\sqrt{100}$, or 10. The dimensions check.

The dimensions are 8 ft by 6 ft.

17. We first make a drawing.

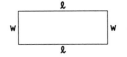

The perimeter of the field is 210 yd.
$2\ell + 2w = 210$, or $\ell + w = 105$

The area of the field is 2250 yd².
$\ell w = 2250$

We solve the following system:
$\ell + w = 105$ (1)
$\ell w = 2250$ (2)

First solve equation (1) for w.
$\ell + w = 105$
$w = 105 - \ell$ (3)

17. (continued)

Then substitute $150 - \ell$ for w in equation (2) and solve for ℓ.

$$\ell w = 2250$$
$$\ell(150 - \ell) = 2250$$
$$150\ell - \ell^2 = 2250$$
$$0 = \ell^2 - 150\ell + 2250$$
$$0 = (\ell - 75)(\ell - 30)$$

$\ell - 75 = 0$ or $\ell - 30 = 0$
$\ell = 75$ or $\ell = 30$

We substitute these numbers in equation (3) and solve for w.

$w = 105 - \ell$

When $\ell = 75$, $w = 105 - 75$, or 30.
When $\ell = 30$, $w = 105 - 30$, or 75.

When the dimensions are 75 yd and 30 yd, the perimeter is $2 \cdot 75 + 2 \cdot 30$, or 210 yd and the area is $75 \cdot 30$, or 2250 yd². The dimensions check. The dimensions are 75 yd by 30 yd.

19.
$$3x^2 + 6 = 5x$$
$$3x^2 - 5x + 6 = 0$$
$$x = \frac{-(-5) \pm \sqrt{(-5)^2 - 4 \cdot 3 \cdot 6}}{2 \cdot 3}$$
$$= \frac{5 \pm \sqrt{25 - 72}}{6}$$
$$= \frac{5 \pm \sqrt{-47}}{6}$$
$$= \frac{5 \pm i\sqrt{47}}{6}$$

21. $\sqrt{48} = \sqrt{16 \cdot 3} = 4\sqrt{3}$

23. Let x and y represent the numbers.
Then $\frac{1}{x}$ and $\frac{1}{y}$ represent their reciprocals.

We translate to a system of equations.
The product of two numbers is 2.

$xy = 2$ (1)

The sum of the reciprocals is $\frac{33}{8}$.

$\frac{1}{x} + \frac{1}{y} = \frac{33}{8}$ (2)

First solve equation (1) for y.

$xy = 2$ (1)

$y = \frac{2}{x}$

Next substitute $\frac{2}{x}$ for y in equation (2) and
solve for x.

$$\frac{1}{x} + \frac{1}{y} = \frac{33}{8}$$

$$\frac{1}{x} + \frac{1}{2/x} = \frac{33}{8}$$ (Substituting)

$$\frac{1}{x} + \frac{x}{2} = \frac{33}{8}$$ (LCM = 8x)

$$8x(\frac{1}{x} + \frac{x}{2}) = 8x(\frac{33}{8})$$

$$8 + 4x^2 = 33x$$

$$4x^2 - 33x + 8 = 0$$

$$(4x - 1)(x - 8) = 0$$

$4x - 1 = 0$ or $x - 8 = 0$

$x = \frac{1}{4}$ or $x = 8$

Both values check. The solutions are $\frac{1}{4}$ and 8.

25. It is helpful to draw a picture.

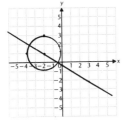

Let (h,k) represent the point on the line
5x + 8y = -2 which is the center of a circle that
passes through the points (-2,3) and (-4,1). The
distance between (h,k) and (-2,3) is the same as
the distance between (h,k) and (-4,1). This gives
us one equation:

$$\sqrt{[h - (-2)]^2 + (k - 3)^2} = \sqrt{[h - (-4)]^2 + (k - 1)^2}$$

$$(h + 2)^2 + (k - 3)^2 = (h + 4)^2 + (k - 1)^2$$

$$h^2 + 4h + 4 + k^2 - 6k + 9 =$$
$$h^2 + 8h + 16 + k^2 - 2k + 1$$

$$4h - 6k + 13 = 8h - 2k + 17$$

$$-4h - 4k = 4$$

$$h + k = -1$$

25. (continued)

We get a second equation by substituting (h,k) in
5x + 8y = -2.

$5h + 8k = -2$

We now solve the following system:

$h + k = -1$
$5h + 8k = -2$

The solution, which is the center of the circle,
is (-2,1).

Next we find the length of the radius. We can
use either (-2,3) and (-4,1) with the center
(-2,1). Here we use (-2,3).

$$r = \sqrt{[-2 - (-2)]^2 + (1 - 3)^2}$$

$$= \sqrt{0^2 + (-2)^2}$$

$$= \sqrt{4}$$

$$= 2$$

We now have an equation knowing that the center
is (-2,1) and the radius is 2.

$$(x - a)^2 + (y - b)^2 = r^2$$ (Standard form)

$$[x - (-2)]^2 + (y - 1)^2 = 2^2$$

$$(x + 2)^2 + (y - 1)^2 = 4$$

Exercise Set 9.5

1. $x^2 + y^2 = 25$ (1)
   $y^2 = x + 5$ (2)

We substitute x + 5 for y^2 in equation (1) and
solve for x.

$$x^2 + y^2 = 25$$ (1)

$$x^2 + (x + 5) = 25$$ (Substituting)

$$x^2 + x - 20 = 0$$

$$(x + 5)(x - 4) = 0$$

$x + 5 = 0$ or $x - 4 = 0$
   $x = -5$ or $x = 4$

Next we substitute these numbers for x in either
equation (1) or equation (2) and solve for y. Here
we use equation (2).

$y^2 = x + 5$ (2)

When x = -5, $y^2 = -5 + 5 = 0$ and y = 0.

When x = 4, $y^2 = 4 + 5 = 9$ and y = ±3.

The possible solutions are (-5,0), (4,3), and
(4,-3).

1. (continued)

Check:

For (-5,0):

$$\frac{x^2 + y^2 = 25}{(-5)^2 + 0^2 \;\big|\; 25}$$
$$25 + 0$$
$$25$$

$$\frac{y^2 = x + 5}{0^2 \;\big|\; -5 + 5}$$
$$0 \;\big|\; 0$$

For (4,3):

$$\frac{x^2 + y^2 = 25}{4^2 + 3^2 \;\big|\; 25}$$
$$16 + 9$$
$$25$$

$$\frac{y^2 = x + 5}{3^2 \;\big|\; 4 + 5}$$
$$9 \;\big|\; 9$$

For (4,-3):

$$\frac{x^2 + y^2 = 25}{4^2 + (-3)^2 \;\big|\; 25}$$
$$16 + 9$$
$$25$$

$$\frac{y^2 = x + 5}{(-3)^2 \;\big|\; 4 + 5}$$
$$9 \;\big|\; 9$$

The solutions are (-5,0), (4,3), and (4,-3).

3. $x^2 + y^2 = 9$ (1)

   $x^2 - y^2 = 9$ (2)

Here we use the addition method.

$$x^2 + y^2 = 9$$
$$\underline{x^2 - y^2 = 9}$$
$$2x^2 \quad\;\; = 18 \quad \text{(Adding)}$$
$$x^2 = 9$$
$$x = \pm 3$$

We substitute these numbers for x in either equation (1) or equation (2) and solve for y. Here we use equation (1).

$x^2 + y^2 = 9$ (1)

When x = 3,
$$3^2 + y^2 = 9$$
$$9 + y^2 = 9$$
$$y^2 = 0$$
$$y = 0$$

When x = -3,
$$(-3)^2 + y^2 = 9$$
$$9 + y^2 = 9$$
$$y^2 = 0$$
$$y = 0$$

The possible solutions are (3,0) and (-3,0).

Check:

$$\frac{x^2 + y^2 = 9}{(\pm 3)^2 + (0)^2 \;\big|\; 9}$$
$$9 + 0$$
$$9$$

$$\frac{x^2 - y^2 = 9}{(\pm 3)^2 - (0)^2 \;\big|\; 9}$$
$$9 - 0$$
$$9$$

The solutions are (3,0) and (-3,0).

5. $x^2 + y^2 = 5$ (1)

  $xy = 2$ (2)

First we solve equation (2) for y.

$$xy = 2$$
$$y = \frac{2}{x}$$

Then we substitute $\frac{2}{x}$ for y in equation (1) and solve for x.

$$x^2 + y^2 = 5 \quad\quad (1)$$
$$x^2 + \left(\frac{2}{x}\right)^2 = 5 \quad \text{(Substituting)}$$
$$x^2 + \frac{4}{x^2} = 5$$
$$x^4 + 4 = 5x^2 \quad \text{(Multiplying by } x^2)$$
$$x^4 - 5x^2 + 4 = 0$$
$$u^2 - 5u + 4 = 0 \quad \text{(Letting } u = x^2)$$
$$(u - 4)(u - 1) = 0$$
$$u - 4 = 0 \text{ or } u - 1 = 0$$
$$u = 4 \text{ or } \quad u = 1$$

We now substitute x^2 for u and solve for x.
$$x^2 = 4 \quad \text{ or } \quad x^2 = 1$$
$$x = \pm 2 \quad\quad\quad x = \pm 1$$

We substitute these numbers for x in either equation (1) or equation (2) and solve for y. Here we use equation (2).

$$xy = 2, \text{ or } y = \frac{2}{x} \quad (2)$$

When x = 2, $y = \frac{2}{2}$, or 1.

When x = -2, $y = \frac{2}{-2}$, or -1.

When x = 1, $y = \frac{2}{1}$, or 2.

When x = -1, $y = \frac{2}{-1}$, or -2.

The ordered pairs (2,1), (-2,-1), (1,2), and (-1,-2) all check. They are the solutions.

7. $xy - y^2 = 2$ (1)

$2xy - 3y^2 = 0$ (2)

First we multiply equation (1) by -2 and then add.

$-2xy + 2y^2 = -4$ (Multiplying by -2)

$\underline{2xy - 3y^2 = 0}$

$-y^2 = -4$ (Adding)

$y^2 = 4$

$y = \pm 2$

Then substitute these numbers for y in either of the original equations and solve for x.

$xy - y^2 = 2$, or $x = \dfrac{y^2 + 2}{y}$

When $y = 2$, $x = \dfrac{2^2 + 2}{2}$, or 3.

When $y = -2$, $x = \dfrac{(-2)^2 + 2}{-2}$, or -3.

The ordered pairs (3,2) and (-3,-2) both check. They are the solutions.

9. $4a^2 - 25b^2 = 0$ (1)

$2a^2 - 10b^2 = 3b + 4$ (2)

First we multiply equation (2) by -2 and then add.

$4a^2 - 25b^2 = 0$

$\underline{-4a^2 + 20b^2 = -6b - 8}$ (Multiplying by -2)

$-5b^2 = -6b - 8$ (Adding)

$5b^2 = 6b + 8$

$5b^2 - 6b - 8 = 0$

$(5b + 4)(b - 2) = 0$

$5b + 4 = 0$ or $b - 2 = 0$

$b = -\dfrac{4}{5}$ or $b = 2$

Then substitute these numbers for b in either of the original equations and solve for a.

$4a^2 - 25b^2 = 0$ (1)

When $b = -\dfrac{4}{5}$, $4a^2 - 25(-\dfrac{4}{5})^2 = 0$

$4a^2 - 25(\dfrac{16}{25}) = 0$

$4a^2 - 16 = 0$

$a^2 - 4 = 0$

$a^2 = 4$

$a = \pm 2$

When $b = 2$, $4a^2 - 25(2)^2 = 0$

$4a^2 - 100 = 0$

$a^2 - 25 = 0$

$a^2 = 25$

$a = \pm 5$

The ordered pairs $(2,-\dfrac{4}{5})$, $(-2,-\dfrac{4}{5})$, (5,2), and (-5,2) all check. They are the solutions.

11. $ab - b^2 = -4$ (1)

$ab - 2b^2 = -6$ (2)

Multiply equation (2) by -1 and then add.

$ab - b^2 = -4$

$\underline{-ab + 2b^2 = 6}$ (Multiplying by -1)

$b^2 = 2$ (Adding)

$b = \pm\sqrt{2}$

Substitute these numbers for b in either of the original equations and solve for a.

$ab - b^2 = -4$ (1)

When $b = \sqrt{2}$, $a(\sqrt{2}) - (\sqrt{2})^2 = -4$

$\sqrt{2}a - 2 = -4$

$\sqrt{2}a = -2$

$a = -\dfrac{2}{\sqrt{2}}$

$a = -\dfrac{2}{\sqrt{2}} \cdot \dfrac{\sqrt{2}}{\sqrt{2}}$

$a = -\sqrt{2}$

When $b = -\sqrt{2}$, $a(-\sqrt{2}) - (-\sqrt{2})^2 = -4$

$-\sqrt{2}a - 2 = -4$

$-\sqrt{2}a = -2$

$a = \dfrac{2}{\sqrt{2}}$

$a = \dfrac{2}{\sqrt{2}} \cdot \dfrac{\sqrt{2}}{\sqrt{2}}$

$a = \sqrt{2}$

The ordered pairs $(-\sqrt{2},\sqrt{2})$ and $(\sqrt{2},-\sqrt{2})$ both check. They are the solutions.

13. Let x and y represent the numbers.

The product of the two numbers is 156.
$xy = 156$

The sum of their squares is 313.
$x^2 + y^2 = 313.$

We solve the following system:
$xy = 156$ (1)
$x^2 + y^2 = 313$ (2)

First solve equation (1) for y.
$xy = 156$

$y = \dfrac{156}{x}$

Then we substitute $\dfrac{156}{x}$ for y in equation (2) and solve for x.

$$x^2 + y^2 = 313 \quad (2)$$

$$x^2 + \left(\frac{156}{x}\right)^2 = 313 \quad \text{(Substituting)}$$

$$x^2 + \frac{24,336}{x^2} = 313$$

$$x^4 + 24,336 = 313x^2$$

$$x^4 - 313x^2 + 24,336 = 0$$

$$u^2 - 313u + 24,336 = 0 \quad \text{(Letting } u = x^2)$$

$$(u - 169)(u - 144) = 0$$

$u - 169 = 0$ or $u - 144 = 0$
     $u = 169$ or $u = 144$

We now substitute x^2 for u and solve for x.
$x^2 = 169$ or $x^2 = 144$
$x = \pm 13$ $x = \pm 12$

We substitute these numbers for x in either equation (1) or equation (2) and solve for y. Here we use equation (1).

$xy = 156$ or $y = \dfrac{156}{x}$ (1)

When $x = 13$, $y = \dfrac{156}{13}$, or 12.

When $x = -13$, $y = \dfrac{156}{-13}$, or -12.

When $x = 12$, $y = \dfrac{156}{12}$, or 13.

When $x = -12$, $y = \dfrac{156}{-12}$, or -13.

The possible solutions are 13, 12 and -13, -12. The product of 13 and 12 is 156. The product of -13 and -12 is 156. The sum of their squares is $(\pm 13)^2 + (\pm 12)^2 = 169 + 144 = 313$. The numbers are 13, 12 and -13, -12.

15. We first make a drawing.

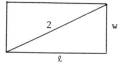

We let ℓ and w represent the length and width.

The area is $\sqrt{3}$ m².
$\ell \cdot w = \sqrt{3}$

Using the Pythagorean property we get a second equation.
$\ell^2 + w^2 = 2^2$

We solve the following system:
$\ell w = \sqrt{3}$ (1)
$\ell^2 + w^2 = 4$ (2)

We first solve equation (1) for w.
$\ell w = \sqrt{3}$

$w = \dfrac{\sqrt{3}}{\ell}$

Then we substitute $\dfrac{\sqrt{3}}{\ell}$ for w in equation (2) and solve for ℓ.

$$\ell^2 + w^2 = 4 \quad (2)$$

$$\ell^2 + \left(\frac{\sqrt{3}}{\ell}\right)^2 = 4 \quad \text{(Substituting)}$$

$$\ell^2 + \frac{3}{\ell^2} = 4$$

$$\ell^4 + 3 = 4\ell^2$$

$$\ell^4 - 4\ell^2 + 3 = 0$$

$$u^2 - 4u + 3 = 0 \quad \text{(Letting } u = \ell^2)$$

$$(u - 3)(u - 1) = 0$$

$u - 3 = 0$ or $u - 1 = 0$
     $u = 3$ or $u = 1$

We now substitute ℓ^2 for u and solve for ℓ.
$\ell^2 = 3$ or $\ell^2 = 1$
$\ell = \pm\sqrt{3}$ $\ell = \pm 1$

Since length cannot be negative, we only consider $\sqrt{3}$ and 1. We substitute these numbers for ℓ in either equation (1) or equation (2) and solve for w.

$w = \dfrac{\sqrt{3}}{\ell}$ (1)

When $\ell = \sqrt{3}$, $w = \dfrac{\sqrt{3}}{\sqrt{3}}$, or 1.

When $\ell = 1$, $w = \dfrac{\sqrt{3}}{1}$, or $\sqrt{3}$.

The possible dimensions are $\sqrt{3}$ m by 1 m. The area is $\sqrt{3} \cdot 1$, or $\sqrt{3}$ m². The length of the diagonal is $\sqrt{(\sqrt{3})^2 + 1^2}$, or $\sqrt{4}$, or 2. The dimensions check. The dimensions are $\sqrt{3}$ m by 1 m.

17. We first make a drawing.

Area: x^2 Area: y^2

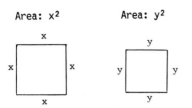

We let x be the length of a side of one peanut bed and y the length of a side of the other. Their areas are represented by x^2 and y^2.

The sum of their areas is 832 ft².

$x^2 + y^2 = 832$

The difference of their areas is 320 ft².

$x^2 - y^2 = 320$

We solve the system using the addition method.

$$
\begin{array}{ll}
x^2 + y^2 = 832 & (1) \\
\underline{x^2 - y^2 = 320} & (2) \\
2x^2 = 1152 & \\
x^2 = 576 & \\
x = \pm 24 &
\end{array}
$$

We substitute 24 and −24 for x in either equation (1) or equation (2) and solve for y. Here we use equation (1).

$$
\begin{array}{ll}
x^2 + y^2 = 832 & (1) \\
(\pm 24)^2 + y^2 = 832 & \text{(Substituting)} \\
576 + y^2 = 832 & \\
y^2 = 256 & \\
y = \pm 16 &
\end{array}
$$

Since the length of a side cannot be negative, we only consider x = 24 and y = 16. The areas of the peanut beds are 24², or 576, and 16², or 256. The sum of the areas is 576 + 256, or 832. The difference of their areas is 576 − 256, or 320. The values check. The lengths of the squares are 24 ft and 16 ft.

19. $\dfrac{\sqrt{x} - \sqrt{h}}{\sqrt{x} + \sqrt{h}}$

$= \dfrac{\sqrt{x} - \sqrt{h}}{\sqrt{x} + \sqrt{h}} \cdot \dfrac{\sqrt{x} + \sqrt{h}}{\sqrt{x} + \sqrt{h}}$

$= \dfrac{x - h}{x + 2\sqrt{xh} + h}$

21. We organize the information in a chart.

	r	t	d
Upstream	r − 2	$\dfrac{4}{r-2}$	4
Downstream	r + 2	$\dfrac{4}{r+2}$	4

We let r represent the speed of the boat in still water. Then r − 2 represents the speed upstream and r + 2 represents the speed downstream. Using d = rt, or $t = \dfrac{d}{r}$, we get $\dfrac{4}{r-2}$ for the time upstream and $\dfrac{4}{r+2}$ for the time downstream. The total time is 3 hours. We solve the following equation.

$$\frac{4}{r-2} + \frac{4}{r+2} = 3, \quad \begin{array}{l} \text{LCM} = \\ (r-2)(r+2) \end{array}$$

$$(r-2)(r+2)\left(\frac{4}{r-2} + \frac{4}{r+2}\right) = (r-2)(r+2)3$$

$$4(r+2) + 4(r-2) = 3(r^2 - 4)$$

$$4r + 8 + 4r - 8 = 3r^2 - 12$$

$$8r = 3r^2 - 12$$

$$0 = 3r^2 - 8r - 12$$

$$r = \frac{-(-8) \pm \sqrt{(-8)^2 - 4(3)(-12)}}{2 \cdot 3}$$

$$= \frac{8 \pm \sqrt{64 + 144}}{6} = \frac{8 \pm \sqrt{208}}{6}$$

$$= \frac{8 \pm 4\sqrt{13}}{6} = \frac{4 \pm 2\sqrt{13}}{3}$$

$$\approx \frac{4 \pm 2(3.606)}{3} \approx \frac{4 \pm 7.212}{3}$$

$$x \approx \frac{4 + 7.212}{3} \quad \text{or} \quad x \approx \frac{4 - 7.212}{3}$$

$$\approx 3.7 \qquad \text{or} \qquad \approx -1.4$$

Since the speed of the boat cannot be negative, we only check 3.7. The value does check. The speed of the boat in still water is 3.7 mph.

23. $(x - h)^2 + (y - k)^2 = r^2$ (Standard form)

We substitute values for x and y.

$(4 - h)^2 + (6 - k)^2 = r^2$ (1)

[Substituting (4,6)]

$(-6 - h)^2 + (2 - k)^2 = r^2$ (2)

[Substituting (-6,2)]

$(1 - h)^2 + (-3 - k)^2 = r^2$ (3)

[Substituting (1,-3)]

Using substitution with equations (1) and (2) we get

$(4 - h)^2 + (6 - k)^2 = (-6 - h)^2 + (2 - k)^2$

Using substitution with equations (2) and (3) we get

$(-6 - h)^2 + (2 - k)^2 = (1 - h)^2 + (-3 - k)^2$

Simplifying we get the resulting system:

$5h + 2k = 3$

$7h - 5k = -15$

We solve using the addition method. The solution is $h = -\frac{5}{13}$ and $k = \frac{32}{13}$. Thus the center of the circle is $(-\frac{5}{13}, \frac{32}{13})$. To find the radius, we calculate the distance between the center and any one of the given points. Here we use (4,6).

$$r = \sqrt{(-\frac{5}{13} - 4)^2 + (\frac{32}{13} - 6)^2}$$

$$= \sqrt{(-\frac{5}{13} - \frac{52}{13})^2 + (\frac{32}{13} - \frac{78}{13})^2}$$

$$= \sqrt{(-\frac{57}{13})^2 + (-\frac{46}{13})^2}$$

$$= \sqrt{\frac{3249}{169} + \frac{2116}{169}}$$

$$= \sqrt{\frac{5365}{169}}$$

Thus $r^2 = \frac{5365}{169}$ and the equation of the circle is

$$[x - (-\frac{5}{13})]^2 + (y - \frac{32}{13})^2 = \frac{5365}{169}$$

$$(x + \frac{5}{13})^2 + (y - \frac{32}{13})^2 = \frac{5365}{169}$$

1. $(x - 5)(x + 3) > 0$

The solutions of $(x - 5)(x + 3) = 0$ are 5 and -3. They are not solutions of the inequality, but they divide the real-number line in a natural way. The product $(x - 5)(x + 3)$ is positive or negative, for values other than 5 and -3, depending on the signs of the factors $x - 5$ and $x + 3$.

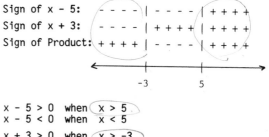

Sign of x - 5:   - - - - | - - - - | + + + +
Sign of x + 3:   - - - - | + + + + | + + + +
Sign of Product: + + + + | - - - - | + + + +

                    -3   5

$x - 5 > 0$ when $x > 5$
$x - 5 < 0$ when $x < 5$
$x + 3 > 0$ when $x > -3$
$x + 3 < 0$ when $x < -3$

For the product $(x - 5)(x + 3)$ to be positive, both factors must be positive or both factors must be negative. We see from the diagram that numbers satisfying $x < -3$ or $x > 5$ are solutions. The solution set of the inequality is

$\{x | x < -3$ or $x > 5\}$.

3. $(x + 1)(x - 2) \leq 0$

The solutions of $(x + 1)(x - 2) = 0$ are -1 and 2. They divide the real-number line in a natural way. The product $(x + 1)(x - 2)$ is positive or negative, for values other than -1 and 2, depending on the signs of the factors $x + 1$ and $x - 2$.

Sign of x + 1:   - - - - | + + + + | + + + +
Sign of x - 2:   - - - - | - - - - | + + + +
Sign of Product: + + + + | - - - - | + + + +

                    -1   2

$x + 1 > 0$ when $x > -1$
$x + 1 < 0$ when $x < -1$
$x - 2 > 0$ when $x > 2$
$x - 2 < 0$ when $x < 2$

For the product $(x + 1)(x - 2)$ to be negative one factor must be positive and the other negative. The only situation in the table for which this happens is when $-1 < x < 2$. The intercepts are also solutions. The solution set of the inequality is

$\{x | -1 \leq x \leq 2\}$.

5. $x^2 - x - 2 < 0$

$(x + 1)(x - 2) < 0$

See Exercise 3 above. In Exercise 3 the intercepts were also solutions. In Exercise 5 they are not included. The solution set is

$\{x | -1 < x < 2\}$.

7. $9 - x^2 \leqslant 0$

$(3 - x)(3 + x) \leqslant 0$

The solutions of $(3 - x)(3 + x) = 0$ are 3 and -3. They divide the real-number line in a natural way. The product $(3 - x)(3 + x)$ is positive or negative, for values other than 3 and -3, depending on the signs of the factors $3 - x$ and $3 + x$.

Sign of 3 - x: + + + + | + + + + | - - - -
Sign of 3 + x: - - - - | + + + + | + + + +
Sign of Product: - - - - | + + + + | - - - -

```
      <--------+--------+-------->
              -3        3
```

3 - x > 0 when x < 3
3 - x < 0 when x > 3
3 + x > 0 when x > -3
3 + x < 0 when x < -3

For the product $(3 - x)(3 + x)$ to be negative, one factor must be positive and the other negative. We see from the diagram that numbers satisfying $x < -3$ or $x > 3$ are solutions. The intercepts are also solutions. The solution set of the inequality is

$\{x | x \leqslant -3 \text{ or } x \geqslant 3\}$.

9. $x^2 - 2x + 1 \geqslant 0$

$(x - 1)(x - 1) \geqslant 0$

$(x - 1)^2 \geqslant 0$

The solution of $(x - 1)(x - 1) = 0$ is 1. For all values of x except 1, $(x - 1)^2$ will be positive. The solution set of $(x - 1)^2 \geqslant 0$ consists of all real numbers.

11. $x^2 + 8 < 6x$

$x^2 - 6x + 8 < 0$

$(x - 4)(x - 2) < 0$

The solutions of $(x - 4)(x - 2) = 0$ are 4 and 2. They are not solutions of the inequality, but they divide the real-number line in a natural way. The product $(x - 4)(x - 2)$ is positive or negative, for values other than 4 and 2, depending on the signs of the factors $x - 4$ and $x - 2$.

Sign of x - 4:   - - - | - - - - | + + + +
Sign of x - 2:   - - - | + + + + | + + + +
Sign of Product: + + + + | - - - - | + + + +

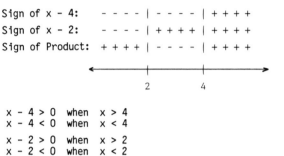

```
      <--------+--------+-------->
              2        4
```

x - 4 > 0 when x > 4
x - 4 < 0 when x < 4

x - 2 > 0 when x > 2
x - 2 < 0 when x < 2

For the product $(x - 4)(x - 2)$ to be negative one factor must be positive and the other negative. The only situation in the table for which this happens is when $2 < x < 4$. The solution set of the inequality is

$\{x | 2 < x < 4\}$.

13. $3x(x + 2)(x - 2) < 0$

The solutions of $3x(x + 2)(x - 2) = 0$ are 0, -2, and 2. They are not solutions of the inequality, but they divide the real-number line in a natural way. The product $3x(x + 2)(x - 2)$ is positive or negative, for values other than 0, -2, and 2, depending on the signs of the factors x, $x + 2$, and $x - 2$.

Sign of x: - - - -|- - - -|+ + + +|+ + + +
Sign of x + 2:   - - - -|+ + + +|+ + + +|+ + + +
Sign of x - 2:   - - - -|- - - -|- - - -|+ + + +
Sign of Product: - - - -|+ + + +|- - - -|+ + + +

```
      <--------+--------+--------+-------->
              -2        0        2
```

x + 2 > 0 when x > -2
x + 2 < 0 when x < -2

x - 2 > 0 when x > 2
x - 2 < 0 when x < 2

The product of these numbers is negative when all three are negative or two are positive and one is negative. We see from the diagram that numbers satisfying $x < -2$ or $0 < x < 2$ are solutions. The solution set of the inequality is

$\{x | x < -2 \text{ or } 0 < x < 2\}$.

183

15. $(x + 3)(x - 2)(x + 1) > 0$

The solutions of $(x + 3)(x - 2)(x + 1) = 0$ are
-3, 2, and -1. They are not solutions of the
inequality, but they divide the real-number line
in a natural way. The product
$(x + 3)(x - 2)(x + 1)$ is positive or negative,
for values other than -3, 2, and -1, depending
on the signs of the factors $x + 3$, $x - 2$, and
$x + 1$.

```
Sign of x + 3:   - - - -|+ + + +|+ + + +|+ + + +
Sign of x - 2:   - - - -|- - - -|- - - -|+ + + +
Sign of x + 1:   - - - -|- - - -|+ + + +|+ + + +
Sign of Product: - - - -|+ + + +|- - - -|+ + + +
```

```
        ←——+————————+————————+——→
          -3       -1        2
```

$x + 3 > 0$ when $x > -3$
$x + 3 < 0$ when $x < -3$

$x - 2 > 0$ when $x > 2$
$x - 2 < 0$ when $x < 2$

$x + 1 > 0$ when $x > -1$
$x + 1 < 0$ when $x < -1$

The product of three numbers is positive when all
three are positive or two are negative and one is
positive. We see from the diagram that numbers
satisfying $-3 < x < -1$ or $x > 2$ are solutions.
The solution set of the inequality is

$\{x | -3 < x < -1$ or $x > 2\}$.

17. $(x + 3)(x + 2)(x - 1) < 0$

The solutions of $(x + 3)(x + 2)(x - 1) = 0$ are
-3, -2, and 1. They are not solutions of the
inequality, but they divide the real-number line
in a natural way. The product
$(x + 3)(x + 2)(x - 1)$ is positive or negative,
for values other than -3, -2, and 1, depending
on the signs of the factors $x + 3$, $x + 2$, and
$x - 1$.

```
Sign of x + 3:   - - - -|+ + + +|+ + + +|+ + + +
Sign of x + 2:   - - - -|- - - -|+ + + +|+ + + +
Sign of x - 1:   - - - -|- - - -|- - - -|+ + + +
Sign of Product: - - - -|+ + + +|- - - -|+ + + +
```

```
        ←——+————————+————————+——→
          -3       -2        1
```

$x + 3 > 0$ when $x > -3$
$x + 3 < 0$ when $x < -3$

$x + 2 > 0$ when $x > -2$
$x + 2 < 0$ when $x < -2$

$x - 1 > 0$ when $x > 1$
$x - 1 < 0$ when $x < 1$

The product of three numbers is negative when all
three are negative or two are positive and one is
negative. We see from the diagram that numbers
satisfying $x < -3$ or $-2 < x < 1$ are solutions.
The solution set of the inequality is

$\{x | x < -3$ or $-2 < x < 1\}$.

19. $\dfrac{1}{x - 4} < 0$

There are no solutions of the equality $\dfrac{1}{x - 4} = 0$.
We now consider the inequality $\dfrac{1}{x - 4} < 0$. The
solution of $x - 4 = 0$ is 4. This cannot be a
solution of the inequality because it makes the
denominator 0, but 4 divides the real-number line
in a natural way. The quotient is positive or
negative depending on the sign of $x - 4$.

```
Sign of 1:        + + + +|+ + + +
Sign of x - 4:    - - - -|+ + + +
Sign of Quotient: - - - -|+ + + +
```

```
        ←—————————+—————————→
                  4
```

$x - 4 > 0$ when $x > 4$
$x - 4 < 0$ when $x < 4$

We see from the diagram that the solution set of
the inequality $\dfrac{1}{x - 4} < 0$ is

$\{x | x < 4\}$.

21. $\dfrac{x + 1}{x - 3} > 0$

We first consider the equality $\dfrac{x + 1}{x - 3} = 0$. Note
that -1 is the solution of the equality, but -1 is
not a solution of the inequality. Next, consider
the inequality $\dfrac{x + 1}{x - 3} > 0$. The solution of
$x - 3 = 0$ is 3. This cannot be a solution of the
inequality because it makes the denominator 0, but
3 and -1 divide the number line in a natural way.
The quotient is positive or negative depending on
the signs of $x + 1$ and $x - 3$.

```
Sign of x + 1:    - - - -|+ + + +|+ + + +
Sign of x - 3:    - - - -|- - - -|+ + + +
Sign of Quotient: + + + +|- - - -|+ + + +
```

```
        ←——+————————+——→
          -1        3
```

$x + 1 > 0$ when $x > -1$
$x + 1 < 0$ when $x < -1$

$x - 3 > 0$ when $x > 3$
$x - 3 < 0$ when $x < 3$

We see from the diagram that the solution set of
the inequality $\dfrac{x + 1}{x - 3} > 0$ is

$\{x | x < -1$ or $x > 3\}$.

23. $\frac{3x + 2}{x - 3} \leq 0$

We first consider the equality $\frac{3x + 2}{x - 3} = 0$. This has the solution $-\frac{2}{3}$. Thus, $-\frac{2}{3}$ is in the solution set. Next, consider the inequality $\frac{3x + 2}{x - 3} < 0$. The solution of $x - 3 = 0$ is 3. This cannot be a solution to the inequality because it makes the denominator 0, but 3 and $-\frac{2}{3}$ divide the real-number line in a natural way. The quotient is positive or negative depending on the signs of $3x + 2$ and $x - 3$.

Sign of 3x + 2:   – – – –|+ + + +|+ + + +
Sign of x – 3:   – – – –|– – – –|+ + + +
Sign of Quotient: + + + +|– – – –|+ + + +

$$\begin{array}{ccc} & | & | \\ & -\frac{2}{3} & 3 \end{array}$$

$3x + 2 > 0$ when $x > -\frac{2}{3}$
$3x + 2 < 0$ when $x < -\frac{2}{3}$

$x - 3 > 0$ when $x > 3$
$x - 3 < 0$ when $x < 3$

We see from the diagram that the solution set of the inequality $\frac{3x + 2}{x - 3} < 0$ is $\{x | -\frac{2}{3} < x < 3\}$. Thus, the solution set of the original inequality is

$\{x | -\frac{2}{3} \leq x < 3\}$.

25. $\frac{x - 1}{x - 2} > 3$

$\frac{x - 1}{x - 2} - 3 > 0$

$\frac{x - 1}{x - 2} - 3 \cdot \frac{x - 2}{x - 2} > 0$

$\frac{x - 1 - 3x + 6}{x - 2} > 0$

$\frac{-2x + 5}{x - 2} > 0$

We first consider the equality $\frac{-2x + 5}{x - 2} = 0$. Note that $\frac{5}{2}$ is the solution of the equality, but $\frac{5}{2}$ is not a solution of the inequality. Next, consider the inequality $\frac{-2x + 5}{x - 2} > 0$. The solution of $x - 2 = 0$ is 2. This cannot be a solution of the inequality because it makes the denominator 0, but 2 and $\frac{5}{2}$ divide the number line in a natural way. The quotient is positive or negative depending on the signs of $-2x + 5$ and $x - 2$.

25. (continued)

Sign of –2x + 5: + + + +|+ + + +|– – – –
Sign of x – 2: – – – –|+ + + +|+ + + +
Sign of Quotient: – – – –|+ + + +|– – – –

$$\begin{array}{ccc} & | & | \\ & 2 & \frac{5}{2} \end{array}$$

$-2x + 5 > 0$ when $x < \frac{5}{2}$
$-2x + 5 < 0$ when $x > \frac{5}{2}$

$x - 2 > 0$ when $x > 2$
$x - 2 < 0$ when $x < 2$

We can see from the diagram that the solution set of the inequality $\frac{-2x + 5}{x - 2} > 0$ is

$\{x | 2 < x < \frac{5}{2}\}$.

27. $\frac{(x - 2)(x + 1)}{x - 5} < 0$

We first consider the equality $\frac{(x - 2)(x + 1)}{x - 5} = 0$. Note that 2 and –1 are solutions of the inequality, but they are not solutions of the inequality. Next consider the inequality $\frac{(x - 2)(x + 1)}{x - 5} < 0$. The solution of $x - 5 = 0$ is 5. This cannot be a solution of the inequality because it makes the denominator 0, but 5, 2, and –1 divide the number line in a natural way. The quotient is positive or negative depending on the signs of $x - 2$, $x + 1$, and $x - 5$.

Sign of x – 2:   – – – –|– – – –|+ + + +|+ + + +
Sign of x + 1:   – – – –|+ + + +|+ + + +|+ + + +
Sign of (x–2)(x+1): + + + +|– – – –|+ + + +|+ + + +
Sign of x – 5:   – – – –|– – – –|– – – –|+ + + +
Sign of Quotient: – – – –|+ + + +|– – – –|+ + + +

$$\begin{array}{cccc} & | & | & | \\ & -1 & 2 & 5 \end{array}$$

$x - 2 > 0$ when $x > 2$
$x - 2 < 0$ when $x < 2$

$x + 1 > 0$ when $x > -1$
$x + 1 < 0$ when $x < -1$

$x - 5 > 0$ when $x > 5$
$x - 5 < 0$ when $x < 5$

We see from the diagram that the solution set of the inequality $\frac{(x - 2)(x + 1)}{x - 5} < 0$ is

$\{x | x < -1 \text{ or } 2 < x < 5\}$.

29. $\frac{x}{x - 2} \geqslant 0$

We first consider the equality $\frac{x}{x - 2} = 0$. This has the solution 0. Thus, 0 is in the solution set. Next consider the inequality $\frac{x}{x - 2} > 0$. The solution of $x - 2 = 0$ is 2. This cannot be a solution to the inequality because it makes the denominator 0, but 2 and 0 divide the real-number line in a natural way. The quotient is positive or negative depending on the signs of x and $x - 2$.

Sign of x: - - - -|+ + + +|+ + + +
Sign of x - 2:   - - - -|- - - -|+ + + +
Sign of Quotient: + + + +|- - - -|+ + + +

```
  ←────────┼────────┼────────→
           0        2
```

$x - 2 > 0$ when $\boxed{x > 2}$
$x - 2 < 0$ when $x < 2$

We see from the diagram that the solution set of the inequality $\frac{x}{x - 2} > 0$ is $\{x | x < 0$ or $x > 2\}$. Thus, the solution of the original inequality is

$\{x | x \leqslant 0$ or $x > 2\}$.

31. $\frac{x - 5}{x} < 1$

            $\frac{x - 5}{x} - 1 < 0$

        $\frac{x - 5}{x} - 1 \cdot \frac{x}{x} < 0$

                $\frac{-5}{x} < 0$

The quotient $\frac{-5}{x}$ is only negative when x is positive. Thus the solution set of the inequality $\frac{-5}{x} < 0$ is

$\{x | x > 0\}$.

33. $\frac{x - 1}{(x - 3)(x + 4)} \boxed{<} 0$

We first consider the equality $\frac{x - 1}{(x - 3)(x + 4)} = 0$. Note that 1 is the solution of the equality, but it is not a solution of the inequality. Next consider the inequality $\frac{x - 1}{(x - 3)(x + 4)} < 0$. The solutions of $(x - 3)(x + 4) = 0$ are 3 and -4. They cannot be solutions of the inequality because they make the denominator 0, but 3, -4, and 1 divide the number line in a natural way. The quotient is positive or negative depending on the signs of $x - 1$, $x - 3$, $x + 4$.

33. (continued)

Sign of x - 1:   - - - -|- - - -|+ + + +|+ + + +
Sign of x - 3:   - - - -|- - - -|- - - -|+ + + +
Sign of x + 4:   - - - -|+ + + +|+ + + +|+ + + +
Sign of (x-3)(x+4): + + + +|- - - -|- - - -|+ + + +
Sign of Quotient: - - - -|+ + + +|- - - -|+ + + +

```
  ←──────┼────────┼────────┼──────→
        -4        1        3
```

$x - 1 > 0$ when $x > 1$
$x - 1 < 0$ when $\boxed{x < 1}$
$x - 3 > 0$ when $x > 3$
$x - 3 < 0$ when $\boxed{x < 3}$
$x + 4 > 0$ when $x > -4$
$x + 4 < 0$ when $\boxed{x < -4}$

We can see from the diagram that the solution set of the inequality $\frac{x - 1}{(x - 3)(x + 4)} < 0$ is $\{x | \boxed{x < -4}$ or $1 < \boxed{x} < 3\}$.

35. $2 < \frac{1}{x}$

    $0 < \frac{1}{x} - 2$

    $0 < \frac{1}{x} - \frac{2x}{x}$

    $0 < \frac{1 - 2x}{x}$

We first consider the equality $\frac{1 - 2x}{x} = 0$. Note that $\frac{1}{2}$ is the solution of the equality, but it is not a solution of the inequality. Next consider the inequality $\frac{1 - 2x}{x} > 0$. The number 0 cannot be a solution of the inequality because it makes the denominator 0, but 0 and $\frac{1}{2}$ divide the number line in a natural way. The quotient is positive or negative depending on the signs of $1 - 2x$ and x.

Sign of 1 - 2x: + + + +|+ + + +|- - - -
Sign of x: - - - -|+ + + +|+ + + +
Sign of Quotient: - - - -|+ + + +|- - - -

```
  ←──────┼────────┼────────→
         0        ½
```

$1 - 2x > 0$ when $x < \frac{1}{2}$
$1 - 2x < 0$ when $\boxed{x > \frac{1}{2}}$

We can see from the diagram that the solution set of the inequality $\frac{1 - 2x}{x} > 0$ is

$\{x | 0 < x < \frac{1}{2}\}$.

37. $x^2 - 2x \leqslant 2$

$x^2 - 2x - 2 \leqslant 0$

The graph of the quadratic function
$f(x) = x^2 - 2x - 2$ opens upward since the leading
coefficient is positive. Function values will be
negative between the intercepts. We find the
intercepts by setting the polynomial equal to 0
and solving.

Here we use the quadratic formula.

$x^2 - 2x - 2 = 0$

$x = \dfrac{-(-2) \pm \sqrt{(-2)^2 - 4(1)(-2)}}{2 \cdot 1}$

$= \dfrac{2 \pm \sqrt{12}}{2}$

$= \dfrac{2 \pm 2\sqrt{3}}{2}$

$= 1 \pm \sqrt{3}$

The intercepts are $x = 1 - \sqrt{3}$ and $x = 1 + \sqrt{3}$.

The solution set is

$\{x | 1 - \sqrt{3} \leqslant x \leqslant 1 + \sqrt{3}\}$.

Exercise Set 10.1

1. Graph: $y = 2^x$

We compute some function values, thinking of y as f(x), and keep the results in a table.

$f(0) = 2^0 = 1$

$f(1) = 2^1 = 2$

$f(2) = 2^2 = 4$

$f(-1) = 2^{-1} = \frac{1}{2^1} = \frac{1}{2}$

$f(-2) = 2^{-2} = \frac{1}{2^2} = \frac{1}{4}$

x	f(x)
0	1
1	2
2	4
3	8
-1	$\frac{1}{2}$
-2	$\frac{1}{4}$
-3	$\frac{1}{8}$

Next we plot these points and connect them with a smooth curve.

$y = 2^x$

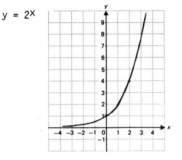

3. Graph: $y = 5^x$

We compute some function values, thinking of y as f(x), and keep the results in a table.

$f(0) = 5^0 = 1$

$f(1) = 5^1 = 5$

$f(2) = 5^2 = 25$

$f(-1) = 5^{-1} = \frac{1}{5^1} = \frac{1}{5}$

$f(-2) = 5^{-2} = \frac{1}{5^2} = \frac{1}{25}$

x	f(x)
0	1
1	5
2	25
-1	$\frac{1}{5}$
-2	$\frac{1}{25}$

Next we plot these points and connect them with a smooth curve.

$y = 5^x$

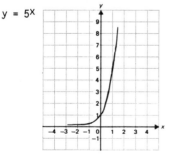

5. Graph: $y = 2^{x+1}$

We compute some function values, thinking of y as f(x), and keep the results in a table.

$f(0) = 2^{0+1} = 2^1 = 2$

$f(-1) = 2^{-1+1} = 2^0 = 1$

$f(-2) = 2^{-2+1} = 2^{-1} = \frac{1}{2^1} = \frac{1}{2}$

$f(-3) = 2^{-3+1} = 2^{-2} = \frac{1}{2^2} = \frac{1}{4}$

$f(1) = 2^{1+1} = 2^2 = 4$

$f(2) = 2^{2+1} = 2^3 = 8$

x	f(x)
0	2
-1	1
-2	$\frac{1}{2}$
-3	$\frac{1}{4}$
1	4
2	8

Next we plot these points and connect them with a smooth curve.

$y = 2^{x+1}$

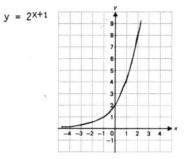

7. Graph: $y = \left(\frac{1}{2}\right)^x$

We compute some function values, thinking of y as f(x), and keep the results in a table.

$f(0) = \left(\frac{1}{2}\right)^0 = 1$

$f(1) = \left(\frac{1}{2}\right)^1 = \frac{1}{2}$

$f(2) = \left(\frac{1}{2}\right)^2 = \frac{1}{4}$

$f(3) = \left(\frac{1}{2}\right)^3 = \frac{1}{8}$

$f(-1) = \left(\frac{1}{2}\right)^{-1} = \frac{1}{\left(\frac{1}{2}\right)^1} = \frac{1}{\frac{1}{2}} = 2$

$f(-2) = \left(\frac{1}{2}\right)^{-2} = \frac{1}{\left(\frac{1}{2}\right)^2} = \frac{1}{\frac{1}{4}} = 4$

$f(-3) = \left(\frac{1}{2}\right)^{-3} = \frac{1}{\left(\frac{1}{2}\right)^3} = \frac{1}{\frac{1}{8}} = 8$

x	f(x)
0	1
1	$\frac{1}{2}$
2	$\frac{1}{4}$
3	$\frac{1}{8}$
-1	2
-2	4
-3	8

Next we plot these points and connect them with a smooth curve.

$y = \left(\frac{1}{2}\right)^x$

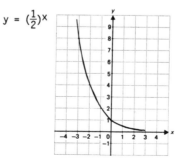

9. Graph: $y = (\frac{1}{4})^x$

We compute some function values, thinking of y as f(x), and keep the results in a table.

$f(0) = (\frac{1}{4})^0 = 1$

$f(1) = (\frac{1}{4})^1 = \frac{1}{4}$

$f(2) = (\frac{1}{4})^2 = \frac{1}{16}$

$f(-1) = (\frac{1}{4})^{-1} = \frac{1}{(\frac{1}{4})^1} = \frac{1}{\frac{1}{4}} = 4$

$f(-2) = (\frac{1}{4})^{-2} = \frac{1}{(\frac{1}{4})^2} = \frac{1}{\frac{1}{16}} = 16$

x	f(x)
0	1
1	$\frac{1}{4}$
2	$\frac{1}{16}$
-1	4
-2	16

Next we plot these points and connect them with a smooth curve.

$y = (\frac{1}{4})^x$

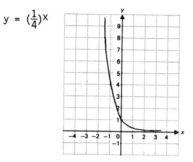

11. Graph: $x = 4^y$

We select numbers for y and find the corresponding values for x. The results are listed in the table.

If we choose 0 for y, $x = 4^0 = 1$.

If we choose 1 for y, $x = 4^1 = 4$.

If we choose 2 for y, $x = 4^2 = 16$.

If we choose -1 for y, $x = 4^{-1} = \frac{1}{4}$.

If we choose -2 for y, $x = 4^{-2} = \frac{1}{16}$.

Plot these points and connect them with a smooth curve.

x	y
1	0
4	1
16	2
$\frac{1}{4}$	-1
$\frac{1}{16}$	-2

$x = 4^y$

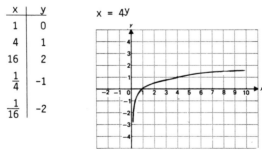

13. Graph: $x = (\frac{1}{4})^y$

We select numbers for y and find the corresponding values for x. The results are listed in the table.

If we choose 0 for y, $x = (\frac{1}{4})^0 = 1$.

If we choose 1 for y, $x = (\frac{1}{4})^1 = \frac{1}{4}$.

If we choose 2 for y, $x = (\frac{1}{4})^2 = \frac{1}{16}$.

If we choose -1 for y, $x = (\frac{1}{4})^{-1} = 4$.

If we choose -2 for y, $x = (\frac{1}{4})^{-2} = 16$.

Plot these points and connect them with a smooth curve.

x	y
1	0
$\frac{1}{4}$	1
$\frac{1}{16}$	2
4	-1
16	-2

$x = (\frac{1}{4})^y$

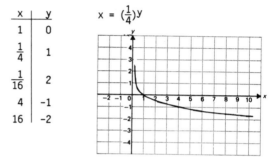

15. $(x^{-3})^4 = x^{-3 \cdot 4} = x^{-12}$

17. $5^0 = 1$ ($a^0 = 1$ if $a \neq 0$)

19. Graph: $y = (\frac{1}{2})^x - 1$

When $x = 0$, $y = (\frac{1}{2})^0 - 1 = 1 - 1 = 0$.

When $x = 1$, $y = (\frac{1}{2})^1 - 1 = \frac{1}{2} - 1 = -\frac{1}{2}$.

When $x = 2$, $y = (\frac{1}{2})^2 - 1 = \frac{1}{4} - 1 = -\frac{3}{4}$.

When $x = 3$, $y = (\frac{1}{2})^3 - 1 = \frac{1}{8} - 1 = -\frac{7}{8}$.

When $x = -1$, $y = (\frac{1}{2})^{-1} - 1 = 2 - 1 = 1$.

When $x = -2$, $y = (\frac{1}{2})^{-2} - 1 = 4 - 1 = 3$.

When $x = -3$, $y = (\frac{1}{2})^{-3} - 1 = 8 - 1 = 7$.

19. (continued)

x	y
0	0
1	$-\frac{1}{2}$
2	$-\frac{3}{4}$
3	$-\frac{7}{8}$
-1	1
-2	3
-3	7

$y = \left(\frac{1}{2}\right)^x - 1$

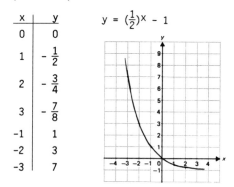

21. Graph: $y = 2^{-(x-1)^2}$

When $x = -2$, $y = 2^{-(-2-1)^2} = 2^{-9} = \frac{1}{512}$.

When $x = -1$, $y = 2^{-(-1-1)^2} = 2^{-4} = \frac{1}{16}$.

When $x = 0$, $y = 2^{-(0-1)^2} = 2^{-1} = \frac{1}{2}$.

When $x = 1$, $y = 2^{-(1-1)^2} = 2^0 = 1$.

When $x = 2$, $y = 2^{-(2-1)^2} = 2^{-1} = \frac{1}{2}$.

When $x = 3$, $y = 2^{-(3-1)^2} = 2^{-4} = \frac{1}{16}$.

x	y
-2	$\frac{1}{512}$
-1	$\frac{1}{16}$
0	$\frac{1}{2}$
1	1
2	$\frac{1}{2}$
3	$\frac{1}{16}$

$y = 2^{-(x-1)^2}$

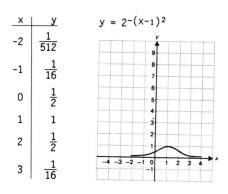

Exercise Set 10.2

1. Graph: $y = \log_2 x$

This equation is equivalent to $x = 2^y$. We select values for y and then compute the x values.

For $y = 0$, $x = 2^0 = 1$.
For $y = 1$, $x = 2^1 = 2$.
For $y = 2$, $x = 2^2 = 4$.
For $y = 3$, $x = 2^3 = 8$.
For $y = -1$, $x = 2^{-1} = \frac{1}{2}$.
For $y = -2$, $x = 2^{-2} = \frac{1}{4}$.
For $y = -3$, $x = 2^{-3} = \frac{1}{8}$.

x	y
1	0
2	1
4	2
8	3
$\frac{1}{2}$	-1
$\frac{1}{4}$	-2
$\frac{1}{8}$	-3

We plot the ordered pairs and connect them with a smooth curve.

$y = \log_2 x$

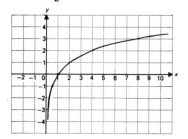

3. $10^3 = 1000$ (Exponential)

    $3 = \log_{10} 1000$ (Logarithmic)

5. $5^{-3} = \frac{1}{125}$ (Exponential)

    $-3 = \log_5 \frac{1}{125}$ (Logarithmic)

7. $8^{1/3} = 2$ (Exponential)

    $\frac{1}{3} = \log_8 2$ (Logarithmic)

9. $10^{0.3010} = 2$ (Exponential)

    $0.3010 = \log_{10} 2$ (Logarithmic)

11. $t = \log_3 8$ (Logarithmic)

    $3^t = 8$ (Exponential)

13. $\log_5 25 = 2$ (Logarithmic)

    $5^2 = 25$ (Exponential)

15. $\log_{10} 0.1 = -1$ (Logarithmic)

$10^{-1} = 0.1$ (Exponential)

17. $\log_{10} 7 = 0.845$ (Logarithmic)

$10^{0.845} = 7$ (Exponential)

19. $\log_3 x = 2$

$3^2 = x$

$9 = x$

21. $\log_x 49 = 2$

$x^2 = 49$

$x = \pm 7$

Since all logarithm bases must be positive, $\log_{-7} 49$ is not defined. Therefore, -7 is not a solution.

$\log_7 49 = 2$ because $7^2 = 49$. Thus 7 is a solution.

23. $\log_2 x = -1$

$2^{-1} = x$

$\frac{1}{2} = x$

25. $\log_8 x = \frac{1}{3}$

$8^{1/3} = x$

$\sqrt[3]{8} = x$

$2 = x$

27. Let $\log_{10} 100 = x$.

Then $10^x = 100$

$10^x = 10^2$

$x = 2$

Thus $\log_{10} 100 = 2$.

29. Let $\log_{10} 0.1 = x$.

Then $10^x = 0.1 = \frac{1}{10}$

$10^x = 10^{-1}$

$x = -1$

Thus $\log_{10} 0.1 = -1$.

31. Let $\log_{10} 1 = x$.

Then $10^x = 1$

$10^x = 10^0$ $(10^0 = 1)$

$x = 0$

Thus $\log_{10} 1 = 0$.

33. Let $\log_5 625 = x$.

Then $5^x = 625$

$5^x = 5^4$

$x = 4$

Thus $\log_5 625 = 4$.

35. Let $\log_5 \frac{1}{25} = x$.

Then $5^x = \frac{1}{25}$

$5^x = 5^{-2}$

$x = -2$

Thus $\log_5 \frac{1}{25} = -2$.

37. $\log_3 3 = 1$ $(\log_a a = 1)$

39. $5240 = 5240 \times (10^{-3} \times 10^3)$

$= (5240 \times 10^{-3}) \times 10^3$

$= 5.24 \times 10^3$

41. $8^{-4} = \frac{1}{8^4} = \frac{1}{4096}$

43. $5^1 = 5$ $(a^1 = a)$

45. Graph: $y = \log_2 (x - 1)$

This equation is equivalent to $x - 1 = 2^y$, or $x = 1 + 2^y$.

For $y = 0$, $x = 1 + 2^0 = 1 + 1 = 2$.

For $y = 1$, $x = 1 + 2^1 = 1 + 2 = 3$.

For $y = 2$, $x = 1 + 2^2 = 1 + 4 = 5$.

For $y = 3$, $x = 1 + 2^3 = 1 + 8 = 9$.

For $y = -1$, $x = 1 + 2^{-1} = 1 + \frac{1}{2} = 1\frac{1}{2}$

For $y = -2$, $x = 1 + 2^{-2} = 1 + \frac{1}{4} = 1\frac{1}{4}$

For $y = -3$, $x = 1 + 2^{-3} = 1 + \frac{1}{8} = 1\frac{1}{8}$

x	y
2	0
3	1
5	2
9	3
$1\frac{1}{2}$	-1
$1\frac{1}{4}$	-2
$1\frac{1}{8}$	-3

$y = \log_2 (x - 1)$

47. $|\log_3 x| = 3$

$\log_3 x = -3 \quad$ or $\quad \log_3 x = 3$

$3^{-3} = x \quad$ or $\quad 3^3 = x$

$\frac{1}{27} = x \quad$ or $\quad 27 = x$

The solutions are $\frac{1}{27}$ and 27.

49. $\log_4 (3x - 2) = 2$

$4^2 = 3x - 2$

$16 = 3x - 2$

$18 = 3x$

$6 = x$

51. $\log_8 (2x + 1) = -1$

$8^{-1} = 2x + 1$

$\frac{1}{8} = 2x + 1$

$-\frac{7}{8} = 2x$

$-\frac{7}{16} = x$

53. Let $\log_{1/4} \frac{1}{64} = x$.

Then $\quad (\frac{1}{4})^x = \frac{1}{64}$

$4^{-x} = 4^{-3}$

$-x = -3$

$x = 3$

Thus $\log_{1/4} \frac{1}{64} = 3$.

55. Let $\log_{1/5} 25 = x$.

Then $\quad (\frac{1}{5})^x = 25$

$(5^{-1})^x = 25$

$5^{-x} = 5^2$

$-x = 2$

$x = -2$

Thus $\log_{1/5} 25 = -2$.

57. $\log_{81} 3 = \frac{1}{4}$, $\log_3 81 = 4$

Thus $(\log_{81} 3)(\log_3 81) = \frac{1}{4} \cdot 4 = 1$.

---

1. $\log_2 (32 \cdot 8) = \log_2 32 + \log_2 8$ (Property 1)

3. $\log_4 (64 \cdot 16) = \log_4 64 + \log_4 16$ (Property 1)

5. $\log_c Bx = \log_c B + \log_c x$ (Property 1)

7. $\log_a 6 + \log_a 70 = \log_a (6 \cdot 70)$, or $\log_a 420$ (Property 1)

9. $\log_c K + \log_c y = \log_c Ky$ (Property 1)

11. $\log_a x^3 = 3 \log_a x$ (Property 2)

13. $\log_a \frac{67}{5} = \log_a 67 - \log_a 5$ (Property 3)

15. $\log_a 15 - \log_a 7 = \log_a \frac{15}{7}$ (Property 3)

17. $\log_a x^2 y^3 z$

$= \log_a x^2 + \log_a y^3 + \log_a z$ (Property 1)

$= 2 \log_a x + 3 \log_a y + \log_a z$ (Property 2)

19. $\log_b \frac{xy^2}{z^3}$

$= \log_b xy^2 - \log_b z^3$ (Property 3)

$= \log_b x + \log_b y^2 - \log_b z^3$ (Property 1)

$= \log_b x + 2 \log_b y - 3 \log_b z$ (Property 2)

21. $\log_c \sqrt{\frac{x^4}{y^3 z^2}}$

$= \log_c \left[\frac{x^4}{y^3 z^2} \right]^{1/2}$

$= \frac{1}{2} \log_c \frac{x^4}{y^3 z^2}$ (Property 2)

$= \frac{1}{2}(\log_c x^4 - \log_c y^3 z^2)$ (Property 3)

$= \frac{1}{2}\left[\log_c x^4 - (\log_c y^3 + \log_c z^2) \right]$

(Property 1)

$= \frac{1}{2}(\log_c x^4 - \log_c y^3 - \log_c z^2)$

$= \frac{1}{2}(4 \log_c x - 3 \log_c y - 2 \log_c z)$

(Property 2)

$= 2 \log_c x - \frac{3}{2} \log_c y - \log_c z$

23. $\frac{2}{3} \log_a x - \frac{1}{2} \log_a y$

$= \log_a x^{2/3} - \log_a y^{1/2}$ (Property 2)

$= \log_a \sqrt[3]{x^2} - \log_a \sqrt{y}$

$= \log_a \frac{\sqrt[3]{x^2}}{\sqrt{y}}$ or $\log_a \frac{x^{2/3}}{y^{1/2}}$ (Property 3)

25. $\log_a 2x + 3(\log_a x - \log_a y)$

$= \log_a 2x + 3 \log_a x - 3 \log_a y$

$= \log_a 2x + \log_a x^3 - \log_a y^3$ (Property 2)

$= \log_a 2x^4 - \log_a y^3$ (Property 1)

$= \log_a \frac{2x^4}{y^3}$ (Property 3)

27. $\log_a (x^2 - 4) - \log_a (x - 2)$

$= \log_a \frac{x^2 - 4}{x - 2}$ (Property 3)

$= \log_a \frac{(x + 2)(x - 2)}{x - 2}$

$= \log_a (x + 2)$

29. $i^{29} = i^{28} \cdot i = 1 \cdot i = i$

31. $\frac{2 + i}{2 - i}$

$= \frac{2 + i}{2 - i} \cdot \frac{2 + i}{2 + i}$

$= \frac{4 + 4i + i^2}{4 - i^2}$

$= \frac{4 + 4i - 1}{4 + 1}$

$= \frac{3 + 4i}{5}$

$= \frac{3}{5} + \frac{4}{5} i$

33. $\log_a (x^8 - y^8) - \log_a (x^2 + y^2)$

$= \log_a \frac{x^8 - y^8}{x^2 + y^2}$ (Property 3)

$= \log_a \frac{(x^4 + y^4)(x^2 + y^2)(x + y)(x - y)}{x^2 + y^2}$

$= \log_a [(x^4 + y^4)(x^2 - y^2)]$

$= \log_a (x^6 - x^4y^2 + x^2y^4 - y^6)$

35. $\log_a \sqrt{1 - s^2}$

$= \log_a (1 - s^2)^{1/2}$

$= \frac{1}{2} \log_a (1 - s^2)$

$= \frac{1}{2} \log_a [(1 + s)(1 - s)]$

$= \frac{1}{2} \log_a (1 + s) + \frac{1}{2} \log_a (1 - s)$

1. $\log_{10} (7 \times 2) = \log_{10} 7 + \log_{10} 2$

$\approx 0.8451 + 0.3010$

$= 1.1461$

$7 \times 2 \approx \text{antilog}_{10} 1.1461 \approx 14$

3. $\log_{10} \frac{12}{3} = \log_{10} 12 - \log_{10} 3$

$\approx 1.0792 - 0.4771$

$= 0.6021$

$\frac{12}{3} \approx \text{antilog}_{10} 0.6021 \approx 4$

5. $\log 2.46 = 0.3909$

7. $\log 5.31 = 0.7251$

9. $\log 1.07 = 0.0294$

11. $\log 347 = \log (3.47 \times 10^2)$

$= \log 3.47 + \log 10^2$

$\approx 0.5403 + 2$

≈ 2.5403

13. $\log 52.5 = \log (5.25 \times 10^1)$

$= \log 5.25 + \log 10^1$

$\approx 0.7202 + 1$

≈ 1.7202

15. $\log 3870 = \log (3.87 \times 10^3)$

$= \log 3.87 + \log 10^3$

$\approx 0.5877 + 3$

≈ 3.5877

17. $\log 0.64 = \log (6.4 \times 10^{-1})$

$= \log 6.4 + \log 10^{-1}$

$\approx 0.8062 + (-1)$

19. $\log 0.0000404 = \log (4.04 \times 10^{-5})$

$= \log 4.04 + \log 10^{-5}$

$\approx 0.6064 + (-5)$

21. $\text{antilog } 3.3674 = 10^{3.3674}$

$= 10^3 \times 10^{0.3674}$

$\approx 10^3 \times 2.33$

≈ 2330

23. $\text{antilog } 1.2553 = 10^{1.2553}$

$= 10^1 \times 10^{0.2553}$

$\approx 10^1 \times 1.80$

≈ 18

25. antilog $[0.7875 + (-1)] = 10^{0.7875+(-1)}$
$= 10^{0.7875} \times 10^{-1}$
$\approx 6.13 \times 10^{-1}$
≈ 0.613

27. antilog $[0.5391 + (-3)] = 10^{0.5391+(-3)}$
$= 10^{0.5391} \times 10^{-3}$
$\approx 3.46 \times 10^{-3}$
≈ 0.00346

29. $10^{1.4014} = 10^1 \times 10^{0.4014}$
$\approx 10^1 \times 2.52$
≈ 25.2

31. $10^{0.9881+(-3)} = 10^{0.9881} \times 10^{-3}$
$\approx 9.73 \times 10^{-3}$
≈ 0.00973

33. $10^{0.7875+(-4)} = 10^{0.7875} \times 10^{-4}$
$\approx 6.13 \times 10^{-4}$
≈ 0.000613

35. $\log 768,340 \approx 5.8856$

37. $\log 5070 \approx 3.7050$

39. $\log 487.2 \approx 2.6877$

41. $\log 0.345 \approx -0.4622$
  or
$\approx -0.4622 + (1 - 1)$
$\approx 0.5378 + (-1)$

43. $\log 0.00789 \approx -2.1029$
  or
$\approx -2.1029 + (3 - 3)$
$\approx 0.8971 + (-3)$

45. $\log 0.1123 \approx -0.9496$
  or
$\approx -0.9496 + (1 - 1)$
$\approx 0.0504 + (-1)$

47. antilog $1.256 = 10^{1.256} \approx 18.0302$

49. antilog $6.789 = 10^{6.789} \approx 6,151,768.73$

51. antilog $(-3) = 10^{-3} = 0.001$

53. antilog $(-8.7) = 10^{-8.7} \approx 0.000000002$

55. antilog $6 = 10^6 = 1,000,000$

57. antilog $(-6.324) = 10^{-6.324} \approx 0.000000474$

59. antilog $7.5 = 10^{7.5} \approx 31,622,776.6$

61. antilog $9.233 = 10^{9.233} \approx 1,710,015,315$

63. $\ln 5894 \approx 8.6817$

65. $\ln 0.0182 \approx -4.0063$

67. $\ln 1.88 \approx 0.6313$

69. $\ln 0.0299 \approx -3.5099$

71. $\ln 807 \approx 6.6933$

73. antilog $_e 2.34 = e^{2.34} \approx 10.3812$

75. antilog $_e 4.5689 = e^{4.5689} \approx 96.4380$

77. antilog $_e (-4.567) = e^{-4.567} \approx 0.0104$

79. antilog $_e (-8.7801) = e^{-8.7801} \approx 0.0002$

81. $ax^2 - b = 0$
$ax^2 = b$
$x^2 = \dfrac{b}{a}$

$x = \pm\sqrt{\dfrac{b}{a}}$

83. $x^{1/2} - 6x^{1/4} + 8 = 0$

Let $u = x^{1/4}$. Then $u^2 = x^{1/2}$.

Substitute and solve for u.
$u^2 - 6u + 8 = 0$
$(u - 4)(u - 2) = 0$

$u - 4 = 0$ or $u - 2 = 0$
$u = 4$ or $\quad u = 2$

Then substitute $x^{1/4}$ for u and solve for x.
$x^{1/4} = 4 \quad$ or $\quad x^{1/4} = 2$
$(x^{1/4})^4 = 4^4 \quad$ or $\quad (x^{1/4})^4 = 2^4$
$x = 256 \quad$ or $\quad x = 16$

Both values check. The solutions are 256 and 16.

85. $\dfrac{\log_a M}{c}$

$= \dfrac{1}{c} \log_a M$

$= \log_a M^{1/c}$ $\qquad\qquad$ (Property 3)

Thus, $\dfrac{\log_a M}{c} = \log_a M^{1/c}$ is true.

87. $8 \log_a x = \log_a x^8$ (Property 3)

$\log_a \frac{1}{8} x \neq 8 \log_a x$

Thus, $\log_a \frac{1}{8} x = 8 \log_a x$ is <u>false</u>.

Exercise Set 10.5

1. $2^x = 9$

$\log 2^x = \log 9$

$x \cdot \log 2 = \log 9$

$x = \frac{\log 9}{\log 2}$

$x \approx \frac{0.9542}{0.3010}$

$x \approx 3.1701$

3. $2^x = 10$

$\log 2^x = \log 10$

$x \cdot \log 2 = \log 10$

$x = \frac{\log 10}{\log 2}$

$x \approx \frac{1}{0.3010}$

$x \approx 3.3223$

5. $5^{4x-7} = 125$

$5^{4x-7} = 5^3$

$4x - 7 = 3$

$4x = 10$

$x = \frac{10}{4}$

$x = \frac{5}{2}$

7. $3^{x^2} \cdot 3^{4x} = \frac{1}{27}$

$3^{x^2+4x} = \frac{1}{27}$

$3^{x^2+4x} = \frac{1}{3^3}$

$3^{x^2+4x} = 3^{-3}$

$x^2 + 4x = -3$

$x^2 + 4x + 3 = 0$

$(x + 3)(x + 1) = 0$

$x + 3 = 0$ or $x + 1 = 0$

$x = -3$ or $x = -1$

The solutions are -3 and -1.

9. $4^x = 7$

$\log 4^x = \log 7$

$x \cdot \log 4 = \log 7$

$x = \frac{\log 7}{\log 4}$

$x \approx \frac{0.8451}{0.6021}$

$x \approx 1.4036$

11. $e^t = 100$

$\ln e^t = \ln 100$

$t = \ln 100$ $(\log_a a^k = k)$

$t \approx 4.6052$

13. $e^{-t} = 0.1$

$\ln e^{-t} = \ln 0.1$

$-t = \ln 0.1$ $(\log_a a^k = k)$

$t = -\ln 0.1$

$t \approx 2.3026$

15. $e^{-0.02t} = 0.06$

$\ln e^{-0.02t} = \ln 0.06$

$-0.02t = \ln 0.06$ $(\log_a a^k = k)$

$t = \frac{\ln 0.06}{-0.02}$

$t \approx \frac{-2.8134}{-0.02}$

$t \approx 140.67$

17. $\log_5 (2x - 7) = 3$

$2x - 7 = 5^3$

$2x - 7 = 125$

$2x = 132$

$x = 66$

19. $\log x + \log (x - 9) = 1$

$\log x(x - 9) = 1$

$x(x - 9) = 10^1$

$x^2 - 9x - 10 = 0$

$(x - 10)(x + 1) = 0$

$x - 10 = 0$ or $x + 1 = 0$

$x = 10$ or $x = -1$

The number -1 is not a solution because negative numbers do not have logarithms. The solution is 10.

21. $\log x - \log (x + 3) = -1$

$$\log \frac{x}{x + 3} = -1$$

$$\frac{x}{x + 3} = 10^{-1}$$

$$\frac{x}{x + 3} = \frac{1}{10}$$

$$10x = x + 3$$

$$9x = 3$$

$$x = \frac{3}{9}$$

$$x = \frac{1}{3}$$

23. $\log_2 (x + 1) + \log_2 (x - 1) = 3$

$$\log_2 (x + 1)(x - 1) = 3$$

$$\log_2 (x^2 - 1) = 3$$

$$x^2 - 1 = 2^3$$

$$x^2 - 1 = 8$$

$$x^2 = 9$$

$$x = \pm 3$$

The number -3 is not a solution because negative numbers do not have logarithms. The solution is 3.

25. $\log_4 (x + 6) - \log_4 x = 2$

$$\log_4 \frac{x + 6}{x} = 2$$

$$\frac{x + 6}{x} = 4^2$$

$$x + 6 = 16x$$

$$6 = 15x$$

$$\frac{6}{15} = x$$

$$\frac{2}{5} = x$$

27. $x^2 + y^2 = 25$ (1)

   $y - x = 1$ (2)

First solve equation (2) for y.

$y - x = 1$ (2)

  $y = x + 1$

Then substitute x + 1 for y in equation (1) and solve for x.

$$x^2 + y^2 = 25 \qquad (1)$$
$$x^2 + (x + 1)^2 = 25 \qquad \text{(Substituting)}$$
$$x^2 + x^2 + 2x + 1 = 25$$
$$2x^2 + 2x - 24 = 0$$
$$x^2 + x - 12 = 0$$
$$(x + 4)(x - 3) = 0$$

$x + 4 = 0$ or $x - 3 = 0$

   $x = -4$ or $x = 3$

27. (continued)

We now substitute these numbers for x in equation (2) and solve for y.

$y = x + 1$ (2)

When x = -4, y = -4 + 1, or -3.

When x = 3, y = 3 + 1, or 4.

The ordered pairs (-4,-3) and (3,4) check and are the solutions.

29. $2x^2 + 1 = y^2$ or $2x^2 - y^2 = -1$ (1)

  $2y^2 + x^2 = 22$ $x^2 + 2y^2 = 22$ (2)

Solve the system using the addition method.

$4x^2 - 2y^2 = -2$ (Multiplying by 2)

$\underline{x^2 + 2y^2 = 22}$

$5x^2 = 20$ (Adding)

$x^2 = 4$

$x = \pm 2$

Substitute these values for x in either of the original equations and solve for y. Here we use equation (1).

$2x^2 + 1 = y^2$ (1)

When x = 2, $y^2 = 2 \cdot 2^2 + 1$, or 9. Thus y = ± 3.

When x = -2, $y^2 = 2(-2)^2 + 1$, or 9. Thus y = ± 3.

The ordered pairs (2,3), (2,-3), (-2,3), and (-2,-3) check and are the solutions.

31. $8^x = 16^{3x+9}$

$(2^3)^x = (2^4)^{3x+9}$

$2^{3x} = 2^{12x+36}$

$3x = 12x + 36$

$-9x = 36$

$x = -4$

33. $\log_6 (\log_2 x) = 0$

$$\log_2 x = 6^0$$

$$\log_2 x = 1$$

$$x = 2^1$$

$$x = 2$$

35. $\log x^2 = (\log x)^2$

$2 \log x = (\log x)^2$

$0 = (\log x)^2 - 2 \log x$

$0 = (\log x)(\log x - 2)$

$\log x = 0$ or $\log x - 2 = 0$

    $x = 10^0$ or $\log x = 2$

    $x = 1$ or $x = 10^2$

    $x = 1$ or $x = 100$

The solutions are 1 and 100.

37. $x \log \frac{1}{8} = \log 8$

$x \log 8^{-1} = \log 8$

$-x \log 8 = \log 8$

$-x = 1$

$x = -1$

39. $(\log_a x)^{-1} = \log_a x$

$\frac{1}{\log_a x} = \log x$

$1 = (\log_a x)^2$

$0 = (\log_a x)^2 - 1$

$0 = (\log_a x - 1)(\log_a x + 1)$

$\log_a x - 1 = 0$ or $\log_a x + 1 = 0$

$\log_a x = 1$ or $\log_a x = -1$

$x = a^1$ or $x = a^{-1}$

$x = a$ or $x = \frac{1}{a}$

The solutions are a and $\frac{1}{a}$.

Exercise Set 10.6

1. $R = 0.85 \log P + 0.05$

$R = 0.85 \log 175 + 0.05$

(Substituting 175 for P)

$\approx 0.85(2.2430) + 0.05$

$\approx 1.90655 + 0.05$

≈ 1.95655

≈ 2.0

The average walking speed of people living in Lincoln, Nebraska is about 2.0 ft/sec.

3. $R = 0.85 \log P + 0.05$

$R = 0.85 \log 50.4 + 0.05$

(Substituting 50.4 for P, $50.4 \times 1000 = 50,400$)

$\approx 0.85(1.7024) + 0.05$

$\approx 1.44704 + 0.05$

≈ 1.49704

≈ 1.5

The average walking speed of people living in Rome, New York is about 1.5 ft/sec.

5. In 1996, t = 20.

$P = 4e^{0.019t}$

$P = 4e^{0.019(20)}$ (Substituting 20 for t)

$= 4e^{0.38}$

$\approx 4(1.4623)$

≈ 5.8492

≈ 5.85

The population of the world in 1996 will be about 5.85 billion.

7. In 1987, t = 20.

$P = 100e^{0.06t}$

$P = 100e^{0.06(20)}$ (Substituting 20 for t)

$= 100e^{1.2}$

$\approx 100(3.3201)$

≈ 332.01

In 1987 goods and services will cost about $332.01.

9. $P = P_0 e^{kt}$

$P = 5e^{0.097t}$ ($P_0 = 5$ and $k = 9.7\%$, or 0.97)

11. $P = P_0 e^{-0.00012t}$

If an animal bone has lost 20% of its Carbon-14 from an initial amount P_0, then $80\%(P_0)$ is the amount present.

$80\% P_0 = P_0 e^{-0.00012t}$ (Substituting 80% P_0 for P)

$0.8 = e^{-0.00012t}$

$\ln 0.8 = \ln e^{-0.00012t}$

$\ln 0.8 = -0.00012t$

$\frac{\ln 0.8}{-0.00012} = t$

$\frac{-0.2231}{-0.00012} \approx t$

$1859 \approx t$

The ivory tusk is about 1859 years old.

13. $A = P(1 + r)^t$

$2000 = 1000(1 + 0.10)^t$

(Substituting 2000 for A, 1000 for P, and 0.10 for r)

$2 = 1.1^t$

$\log 2 = \log 1.1^t$

$\log 2 = t \log 1.1$

$\frac{\log 2}{\log 1.1} = t$

$\frac{0.3010}{0.0414} \approx t$

$7.3 \approx t$

It will take about 7.3 years for the investment to double itself when the interest is compounded annually at 10%.

15. $R = \log \dfrac{I}{I_0}$

$R = \log \dfrac{(10^{8.4})I_0}{I_0}$ (Substituting $10^{8.4}$ for I_0)

$= \log 10^{8.4}$

$= 8.4$

The magnitude on the Richter scale is 8.4

17. $P = P_0 e^{kt}$

After 1 year,

$P = 1000e^{0.14 \cdot 1}$

$= 1000e^{0.14}$

$\approx 1000(1.15027)$

$\approx \$1150.27$

After 2 years,

$P = 1000e^{0.14 \cdot 2}$

$= 1000e^{0.28}$

$\approx 1000(1.32313)$

$\approx \$1323.13$

After 10 years,

$P = 1000e^{0.14 \cdot 10}$

$= 1000e^{1.4}$

$\approx 1000(4.05520)$

$\approx \$4055.20$

19. $P = P_0 e^{kt}$

$2P_0 = P_0 e^{kT}$ (Substituting $2P_0$ for P and T for t)

$2 = e^{kT}$

$\ln 2 = \ln e^{kT}$

$\ln 2 = kT$

$\dfrac{\ln 2}{k} = T$